CREATING VALUE IN FINANCIAL SERVICES

Strategies, Operations and Technologies

CREATING VALUE IN FINANCIAL SERVICES

Strategies, Operations and Technologies

Edited by

Edward L. Melnick
Praveen R. Nayyar
Michael L. Pinedo
Sridhar Seshadri

Stern School of Business
New York University

Kluwer Academic Publishers
Boston/Dordrecht/London

Distributors for North, Central and South America:
Kluwer Academic Publishers
101 Philip Drive
Assinippi Park
Norwell, Massachusetts 02061 USA
Telephone (781) 871-6600
Fax (781) 871-6528
E-Mail <kluwer@wkap.com>

Distributors for all other countries:
Kluwer Academic Publishers Group
Distribution Centre
Post Office Box 322
3300 AH Dordrecht, THE NETHERLANDS
Telephone 31 78 6392 392
Fax 31 78 6546 474
E-Mail <orderdept@wkap.nl>

Electronic Services <http://www.wkap.nl>

Library of Congress Cataloging-in-Publication

Creating value in financial services : strategies, operations and technologies / edited
by Edward L. Melnick...[et al].
    p. cm.
    Includes bibliographical references.
    ISBN 0-7923-8572-1
    1. Financial services industry--Management. I. Melnick, Edward L.

  HG173.C74 1999
  332.1'068--dc21

                                                 99-047411

This book is the result of a joint effort by

- Center for Information Intensive Organizations
- The New York University Salomon Center
- Department of Operations Management
- Department of Statistics and Operations Research

at the Stern School of Business, New York University.

CONTENTS

Contributors

John Alouisa
Prudential Securities Inc.
One New York Plaza
New York, NY 10292

William Anderson
Prudential Securities Inc.
One New York Plaza
New York, NY 10292

Ernest Battifarano
Salomon Analytics
388 Greenwich Street, 10th Floor
New York, NY 10013

Akshaya Bhargava
Citibank a.s.
178 Evropska
Prague 166 40
Czech Republic

Richard Castro
Prudential Securities Inc.
One New York Plaza
New York, NY 10292

Richard B. Chase
Marshall School of Business
University of Southern California
Los Angeles, CA 90089-1421

Wayne I. Cutler
First Manhattan Consulting Group
90 Park Ave
New York, NY 10016

Sanjeev Dewan
Business School
University of Washington
Seattle, WA 98195

Roger L.M. Dunbar
Stern School of Business
New York University
40 West 4th Street
New York, NY 10012-1118

Raymond Ennis
Prudential Securities Inc.
One New York Plaza
New York, NY 10292

Ming Fan
Graduate School of Business
The University of Texas at Austin
Austin, TX 78712

Frances X. Frei
Harvard Business School
Soldiers Field
Boston, MA 02163

Raghu Garud
Stern School of Business
New York University
40 West 4th Street
New York, NY 10012-1118

Jeffrey Gevarter
Prudential Securities Inc.
One New York Plaza
New York, NY 10292

Patrick T. Harker
The Wharton School
University of Pennsylvania
Philadelphia, PA 19104-6366

Andrew Hosking
Andersen Consulting
1345 Avenue of the Americas
New York, NY 10105

Ajit Kambil
Andersen Consulting
100 Williams Street
Wellesley, MA 02181

Uday Karmarkar
Anderson Graduate School of
Management
University of California in Los Angeles
405 Hilgard Ave
Los Angeles, CA 90024

Richard C. Larson
Sloan School of Management
Massachusetts Institute of Technology
Cambridge, MA 02139

Amanda Lister
Andersen Consulting
1345 Avenue of the Americas
New York, NY 10105

John O. Matthews
Economics Department
Villanova University
Villanova, PA 19085

Kevin McGilloway
Lehman Brothers
3 World Financial Center
New York, NY 10285

Edward L. Melnick
Stern School of Business
New York University
40 West 4th Street
New York, NY 10012-1118

Haim Mendelson
Graduate School of Business
Stanford University
Stanford, CA 94305-5015

Thomas L. Monahan III
Corporate Executive Board Company
2000 Pennsylvania Avenue
Washington, DC 20006

Praveen R. Nayyar
Stern School of Business
New York University
40 West 4th Street
New York, NY 10012-1118

Russell Pandolfo
Prudential Securities Inc.
One New York Plaza
New York, NY 10292

Paresh D. Patel
Corporate Executive Board Company
2000 Pennsylvania Avenue
Washington, DC 20006

Michael L. Pinedo
Stern School of Business
New York University
40 West 4th Street
New York, NY 10012-1118

Edieal J. Pinker
William E. Simon
Graduate School of Business
University of Rochester
Rochester, NY 14627

Alexander H.G. Rinnooy Kan
ING Group
P.O. Box 810
1000 AV Amsterdam
The Netherlands

David Rogers
Stern School of Business
New York University
40 West 4th Street
New York, NY 10012-1118

Aleda V. Roth
Kenan Flagler Business School
University of North Carolina
Chapel Hill, NC 27599-3490

Cathy A. Rusinko
Management Department
Villanova University
Villanova, PA 19085

Sridhar Seshadri
Stern School of Business
New York University
40 West 4th Street
New York, NY 10012-1118

J. George Shanthikumar
Haas School of Business
University of California at Berkeley
Berkeley, CA 94720

Jan Stallaert
Graduate School of Business
The University of Texas at Austin
Austin, TX 78712

Robert Solow
Department of Economics
Massachusetts Institute of Technology
Cambridge, MA 02139

Chris Voss
London Business School
Sussex Place, Regent's Park
London NW1 4SA,
United Kingdom

Ingo Walter
Stern School of Business
New York University
44 West 4th Street
New York, NY 10012-1118

Andrew B. Whinston
Department of Management Science
and Information Systems
The University of Texas at Austin
Austin, TX 78712

Larry Zicklin
Neuberger, Berman, LLC
605 Third Avenue
New York, NY 10158

FOREWORD

Remember the old aphorism about college professors being great academic achievers with no practical skills? I'm not sure it was ever true, but *Creating Value in Financial Services* disproves anything that happens to remain of this now antediluvian adage. Professors Edward L. Melnick, Praveen R. Nayyar, Michael L. Pinedo and Sridhar Seshadri, all from New York University, have created a work that will most certainly be of interest to both academic and business readers with an interest in the future of global financial services. In reading this book, it becomes apparent that our business is changing at an ever-increasing rate while the tools we use seem always to be one step behind the curve.

It may not be an over-simplification to define the new paradigm in terms of serving all clients, wherever they are in the world, in a cost efficient and effective manner. Unlike times past, nobody can be said to "own the customer." The concept of "loyalty" is largely outmoded and we might better think of the client as temporarily "rented" to the extent that we could service him/her in a satisfactory manner. The failure to meet continually escalating client demands will most certainly result in competing organizations being immediately enriched. As the twin revolutions of disintermediation and deregulation combine with rapid advances in technology, competitive forces will certainly reduce the number of providers able to meet the demands of the marketplace.

Recognizing the need for a multi-disciplinary approach to the problem, the editors of *Creating Value in Financial Services* have called upon colleagues at a number of academic and business institutions to fashion a resource for those who wish to understand and begin to address the challenges that lie ahead. Whether they write about distribution, regulation, consolidation or diversification, the authors provide a well-conceived description of the problems and an analysis of potential solutions. There are chapters that identify sources of value-added for end-users, skews in customer profitability and the increase in consumer price sensitivity that will make profitability in financial services more difficult to attain. If economics is too important to be left to economists, the editors of this book understand that the new and rapidly changing world of financial services is too important to be left to financial writers continually focusing on daily events while ignoring the much larger picture that is rapidly emerging.

As technology continues to improve, the consumer will have the ability to choose from among an assortment of specialized providers while employing only a single relationship to meet any number of financial needs. One need only be aware of Charles Schwab's new Access Account, which enables clients to write checks, make deposits, transfer money, get cash, and pay bills via the internet, to understand the implications of what may be accurately classified as a financial revolution. The ability of customers to easily search for and find new providers, combined with the minimum effort required to simply and inexpensively transfer their business, while leaving the bookkeeping with the primary supplier, will put increasing pressure on traditional relationships.

Technology is giving the buyers of financial services increasing power. Providers will have to innovate or face a competitive climate of commodity pricing. As this is written, Merrill Lynch, in what may be a watershed event, has changed its historic, and highly successful bundled approach, and is dividing its business into advice that will be fee-based and brokerage which will be available on-line and priced more like a commodity. This move will have financial and cultural implications both for Merrill, the company's 15,000 financial consultants and its competitors alike. It will likely result in greater pressures on firm profits and employee earnings, while providing increasingly favorable options for customers. It almost sounds like a textbook description of capitalism at work.

In identifying the problem of the upheaval in financial services, the editors have given the reader a great deal to contemplate. They make clear that deregulation, including the probable passage of broad new financial legislation now in the congress, is accelerating the blurring of boundaries between insurance, commercial banking, investment banking and brokerage. The implications are most certainly a level of competition even greater than previously experienced. At the same time, the worldwide demographics for the financial services industry have never been better. This convergence of competitive change and increasing opportunity make a book like this especially timely. As one who is involved in the industry, I share their emphasis on the need for specialized consumer services delivered both efficiently and with moderate cost, combined with the flexibility for uncomplicated change. The problem may have always been one of providing superior value, but in the past, it took time for the buyer to figure out who was providing it and who wasn't. Now it only takes a few moments and almost no cost to be a knowledgeable consumer. I believe that by describing the current landscape and providing some potential solutions, this book makes a significant contribution to the managerial dilemma. Ignoring it is akin to getting under the covers and hoping it will all go away; but it won't.

Larry Zicklin
Managing Principal
Neuberger, Berman, L.L.C.

PREFACE

Value. The new mantra for business. Three years ago some of us in the financial capital of the world were looking for ways to make our courses relevant to our MBA students, a vast majority of whom seeking careers in financial services. We came from disparate backgrounds – statisticians, operations researchers, strategists, services – but we shared a simple vision that our students would benefit greatly if we could teach them how to recognize and manage the antecedents of value creation in businesses, especially financial services. We also recognized that value creation was not the domain of any one discipline; all aspects of a firm could affect value creation.

As we set out to examine our courses, we spoke with several persons in the financial services sector to identify what issues were relevant to them as they sought to manage their financial services firms into the next decade. Our horizon was only a decade; we knew that anything beyond that was bound to change. We soon concluded from these conversations that four aspects of financial services firms were a major concern to practicing managers – strategies, products and services, systems, and measures of success – although not necessarily in that order. Many managers also were concerned about people issues and marketing services.

We also consulted with several academics to see what they were researching that was of relevance to financial services. We learnt that many academics were actively examining many facets of business management but they were seldom focused on financial services although a few academics had some expertise with issues of immense relevance to such services.

We did not find a readily available body of literature around which we could structure our understanding of value creation in financial services. We did not find any dominant paradigm for creating value in financial services. But, listening to the various perspectives we thought that significant gains could be obtained—a great leap forward—by encouraging and facilitating an on-going dialog between the various constituencies interested in financial services. Thus, slowly, the concept of a series of focused workshops developed under the auspices of The Leonard N. Stern School of Business at New York University.

The first workshop was held in March 1997 and was entitled Creating Value in Financial Services. Over 150 people attended. The second workshop was held in April 1998 and was entitled Operations and Productivity in Financial Services. Over 200 people attended. The third workshop was held in April 1999 and was entitled Distribution Channels in Insurance and Financial Services. Over 150 people attended. For all three workshops we invited leading scholars and practitioners from a wide cross-section of academia and industry to share their ideas.

This book contains many of the ideas presented at the three workshops. It also contains contributions from a selected few leading thinkers on financial services who could not be present at the three workshops. In every case, the chapters represent state-of-the-art approaches to dealing with contemporary issues facing financial services firms. Lest anyone be left with the impression that the ideas in this book are relevant only to financial services, we hasten to add that most service businesses and even some service components of manufacturing businesses would benefit from reading many of the chapters of this book.

To provide coherence to the wide diversity of perspectives in this book, but retain the possibility for disagreement, we coined the term CVFS Engine and developed a graphic to represent it and its main implications. In the days leading up to the first workshop, the acronym CVFS, which contained the first letter of each word in the workshop title, began to be used among us to refer to the workshop. It stuck. To be consistent with that acronym, we sought a way to use it to develop an image of the work represented here. The CVFS Engine rapidly evolved one warm summer afternoon in a windowless room in July 1999 as we struggled to get the book assembled to send to the publisher. We hope that it does justice to the wonderfully rich ideas contributed by our authors. The nice thing about the image it conveys is that it is dynamic. So, as we continue to delve into the workings of the financial services sector, it too could morph just as the ideas in the book could morph to tackle the realities of the next millennium and, perhaps, beyond. Although, that may be stretching its longevity a bit.

We have been relentless in our pursuit of our authors to contribute and then revise their chapters, sometimes several times. We thank them for indulging us our eccentricities. It is never easy to deal with an academic. Dealing with four academics demands stoicism. We are glad to report that our authors came through with flying colors. We thank them for their contributions. Many others helped us in designing and managing the workshops. At the risk of forgetting to include some important contributors, we thank Dean George Daly for supporting our endeavors, Michael Moses for always encouraging us and helping clear organizational roadblocks, Myron Uretsky, Edward Stohr, and Ingo Walter for providing all kinds of help in the organization of the workshops. As the book came together, it placed increasing demands on our time. Eitan Zemel helped us by keeping our plate from becoming overloaded. Carmen Alvarado, Jeannine Rizzi and Angie Chung helped us with editing and compiling the authors' papers into chapters we could send to publishers.

Kluwer Academic Publishers believed in this work from the start and offered to run with it. Gary Folven at Kluwer actively, yet patiently, cheered us on. We thank him.

New York

Edward L. Melnick
Praveen R. Nayyar
Michael L. Pinedo
Sridhar Seshadri

Chapter 1

Creating Value in Financial Services

Edward L. Melnick
Praveen R. Nayyar
Michael L. Pinedo
Sridhar Seshadri
New York University

1.1 Introduction

Financial services firms everywhere have undergone major changes over the last several decades. These firms include retail commercial banks, investment banks, insurance companies, mutual fund companies, securities brokers, and credit card companies. The decade of the nineties has witnessed a significant number of mergers among these firms worldwide. Some mergers were intended to achieve economies of scale from greater size and geographic diversity, e.g., the merger of Chase and Chemical. Some mergers were intended to establish a bridge between different financial services in the hope of creating synergies e.g., the merger of Travelers Group with Citicorp.

Simultaneously with consolidation in the financial services sector, many new financial services have also been introduced: cash management accounts, mortgage backed securities, and index funds. The decade has also witnessed many new technologies coming to fruition, especially in computers and communications. These new technologies, especially the Internet, have spawned new firms such as the E*Trade Group, Inc. and TeleBanc Financial Corporation, while also changing the ways of doing business at established companies, e.g., Charles Schwab and Merrill Lynch. The goal of all these new developments in strategy, services, processes, and technologies was to create value.

There is little data comparing the impact of these innovations on value creation by the financial services sector with value creation by other industries. What little evidence there is suggests that the financial services sector has not created as much value as it should have. At the outset, it is important to recognize that value creation varies across industries as well as within industries. And, value creation varies across time. To put value creation by financial services firms in perspective, consider Figure 1 below. One measure of value created by a firm is Market Value Added (MVA), defined as the difference between the market value of a firm's equity and debt and its economic book value, which is the amount that is invested in the firm. To calibrate MVA, it is useful to compare it with the Capital Employed by a firm. A ratio above 1 indicates that a firm has created value. A ratio below 1 indicates that it has destroyed value.

Using Market Value Added divided by Capital Employed as a measure of value created by firms, Figure 1 shows that some financial services firms (in this instance, banks) have performed rather poorly over the period 1992 to 1995 in comparison with other industries. In particular, during these years banks' MVA/CE hovered in the 50% range. During 1992-1995, banks were unable to even recover the capital invested in them! Only transportation destroyed more value; while manufacturing struggled to stay above water; hotels were barely breaking even and retail firms were experiencing a spectacular nosedive. In contrast, firms in industries as diverse as healthcare and consumer products created large amounts of value during the same period.

Figure 1. Value Creation and Destruction *Across* Industries

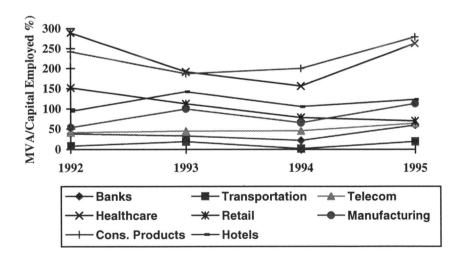

Sources: Smith Barney, Stern Stewart, *Business Week*

One implication of these data is that financial services firms may benefit from studying the value-creating practices employed by firms in industries as diverse as healthcare and consumer products. These two industries showcase two very different practices. Healthcare firms have relentlessly pursued cost control while consumer products firms have single-mindedly focused on customers and consumers to understand their wants and needs and then designed and delivered well-suited products efficiently. Could financial services firms emulate such practices?

In particular, could a bank intent on improving itself learn anything from other banks? Figure 1 suggests that this is a rhetorical question and one not even worth addressing. However, Figure 1, tells only part of the story. Consider Figure 2 that shows variations in value creation within four industries. Now we find that there is at least one bank that creates significantly more value than other banks. How? What does this bank do that creates so much value? Figure 2 also shows that there is at least one retail firm and one telecommunications firm that create more value than even the best-performing bank. How? What do this retail firm and this telecommunications firm do that creates so much value?

More recent data suggests that financial services firms, including banks, have improved their record of value creation. To see this and also to get a longer-term perspective on value creation across industries, consider the data in Table 1 below excerpted from the Stern Stewart & Company's list of the top 1000 firms based on market value added as of December 31, 1998. Table 1 lists in descending order the 5-year average return on capital divided by the 5-year

---

Figure 2. Value Creation and Destruction *Within* Industries

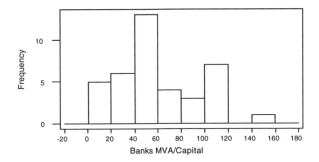

Figure 2. Value Creation and Destruction *Within* Industries

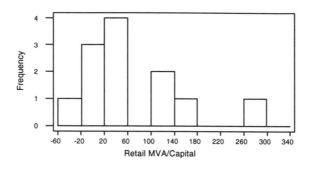

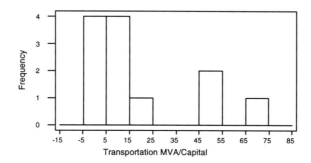

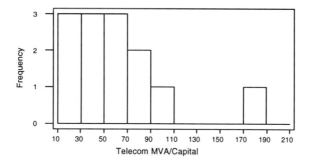

Sources: Smith Barney, Stern Stewart, *Business Week*

average cost of capital for banks, retailers, transportation firms, and telecommunications firms. A number greater than 1 indicates that a firm is creating value. Most of the financial services firms listed in Table 1 created value. Moreover, the best to worst ratio for financial services firms (in this list) is not as high as is the same ratio for retail, telecommunications, and transportation firms. It should be noted that this result might be an artifact of this list because financial services is a more fragmented sector than the other sectors. Thus, many financial services firms are not represented on this list although most of the firms in the other industries are included. Despite this limitation, the fact remains that the worst financial services firm listed in Table 1 has a long way to go before catching up with the value creation effort of the best firm on the list. A similar conclusion is reached by perusing the credit ratings of insurance firms.

1.2 How Does A Financial Services Firm Create Value?

For long it was thought that functional excellence created value. Thus, a bank that excelled at, for example, origination, distribution, servicing, bundling, inter-mediating, or making markets was considered likely to succeed in creating value for its customers and ultimately in creating shareholder value. But, customers did not really care about functional excellence. Further, functional excellence could be easily imitated. This view was replaced with the view that unique resources controlled by firms helped create value for customers. Thus, a bank that was large in scale and scope, or one that possessed vast amounts of information, or one that had the greatest reach or best-risk customers was considered most likely to succeed. However, customers did not really care about size or information or reach or risk exposure. And, banks with narrow spheres of operation were better able to serve their local markets than their larger counterparts.

More recently, strategists share the view that a focus on customers in terms of anticipating, understanding and responding to their needs rapidly and efficiently, and ultimately establishing enduring relationships between service providers and customers, creates value that is sustainable and often difficult to imitate. How does that happen? Certainly not by functionally specialized hierarchies, but rather by designing and managing customer-focused processes. For example, Merrill Lynch long held out against Internet trading. Instead, it chose to focus on leveraging existing unique resources and functional excellence embodied in its large brokerage sales force. Its customers, however, began to migrate to Internet trading. Recently, Merrill Lynch gave in and announced that it, too, will join the Internet fray to be able to better meet its customers' needs. Citigroup attributed its recent boost in second quarter earnings to greater customer focus that enabled it to complete 67 fees-based investment banking transactions made possible by the combined efforts of the former Travelers Group and Citicorp units acting in unison to meet customer needs (*New York Times*, July 20, 1999).

Table 1: Index of Value Creation and Destruction, 1992-1997			
Financial Services Firm	Index	Retail Firm	Index
MBNA Corporation	2.76	Dollar General	2.46
Merrill Lynch & Co., Inc.	2.26	Autozone	1.94
Star Banc Corporation	2.18	Home Depot	1.55
Allstate Corporation	2.17	Wal-Mart Stores	1.28
American Express Company	1.85	May Department Store	1.28
Morgan Stanley, Dean Witter	1.83	Costco Companies	1.15
National Commerce Bancorporation	1.82	Limited	1.12
First Tennessee National Corp.	1.64	Kohl's	1.07
Comerica Incorporated	1.63	Consolidated Stores	1.05
Norwest Corporation	1.58	Dillard's	1.05
SunTrust Banks, Inc.	1.56	Toys "R" Us	1.01
Synovus Financial Corp.	1.54	Dayton Hudson	1.00
Summit Bancorp	1.53	Sears Roebuck	0.89
Citicorp	1.46	Staples	0.87
Northern Trust Corporation	1.46	Nordstrom	0.87
BB&T Corporation	1.42	Kmart	0.85
BankBoston Corporation	1.38	Federated Department Stores	0.77
State Street Corporation	1.38	J.C. Penney	0.76
Firstar Corporation	1.38	Pep Boys	0.70
Union Planters Corporation	1.37	Loews Corporation	0.43
First Commerce Corporation	1.37		
Old Kent Financial Corporation	1.36		
Fifth Third Bancorp	1.35		
First American Corporation	1.34		
Mellon Bank Corporation	1.33		
SouthTrust Corporation	1.33		
AmSouth Bancorporation	1.31		
Fleet Financial Group, Inc.	1.30		
Huntington Bancshares, Inc.	1.30		
Bank of New York Company, Inc.	1.29		
First Union Corporation	1.28		
First of America Bank Corporation	1.26		
Chase Manhattan Corporation (The)	1.25		
Associates First Capital Corporation	1.25		
National City Corporation	1.25		
J.P. Morgan & Company, Inc.	1.23		
Bankers Trust New York Corp.	1.21		
NationsBank Corporation	1.20		
U.S. Bancorp	1.19		
Regions Financial Corporation	1.18		
Wachovia Corporation	1.16		
Mercantile Bancorporation, Inc.	1.13		
Republic New York Corporation	1.13		
BankAmerica Corporation	1.09		
First Chicago NBD Corporation	1.05		
CoreStates Financial Corp	1.01		
KeyCorp	0.99		
Hibernia Corporation	0.99		
PNC Bank Corp.	0.98		
Bank One Corporation	0.96		
Wells Fargo & Company	0.91		

Table 1: Index of Value Creation and Destruction, 1992-1997 (contd)			
Transportation Firm	**Index**	**Telecommunications Firm**	**Index**
Apollo Group	2.56	Tellabs	3.19
Continental Airlines	2.55	SBC Communications	1.73
Northwest Airlines	1.59	Bell Atlantic	1.39
Airborne Express	1.48	Ameritech	1.19
UAL Corp.	1.36	GTE	1.19
Delta Air Lines	1.32	Alltel Communications	1.15
CNF Transportation	1.30	BellSouth	1.14
USAir	1.29	Frontier	0.97
Trinity	1.22	US West	0.89
Budget Group	1.17	Sprint	0.82
AMR Corporation	1.13	AirTouch Communications	0.79
Rollins Truck Leasing	1.10	AT&T	0.57
Ryder System	1.07	MCI	0.42
Southwest Airlines	0.98	Nextel Communications	-1.11
Burlington Northern Sante Fe	0.86		
FDX Corp.	0.83	Qwest Communications	N/A
CSX	0.81		
Brunswick	0.80		
Atlas Air	0.80		
Norfolk Southern	0.72		
Alexander & Baldwin	0.72		
GATX	0.63		
Overseas Shipping	0.54		
Union Pacific	0.53		
AMERCO	0.49		
Newport News Shipbuilding	-0.42		

The index is defined as the 5-year average return on capital divided by the 5-year average cost of capital.
Source: Stern Stewart & Co.

Much of the recent wave of improvement in performance of financial services firms in terms of creating value could be the result of the adoption of, so called, "best practices". Together with the ever-present comparisons made across industries, across firms within industries, and across time, the adoption of best practices is often considered as a means to improve value creation. Lest the quest for identifying and adopting best practice go too far, consider Figure 3 below. Figure 3 is a speculative figure. On its horizontal axis is the extent to which an organization has adopted best practices. For example, this could be measured by the number of best practices adopted, such as Total Quality Management, Just-in-Time materials management, straight-through processing, and Benchmarking. Or, it could be an index created to measure the coverage of best practices within an organization. On its vertical axis is a measure of value created by the adoption of best practices. It would be very useful to know the relationship between the extent of adoption of best practices and value creation. Is this relationship linear? Does it have a threshold? Is it asymptotic to some limit? Does it exhibit increasing or decreasing returns? Unfortunately, to the best of our knowledge, this relationship of best practices to value created is unknown. Is it unknowable? We think not.

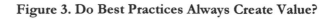

Figure 3. Do Best Practices Always Create Value?

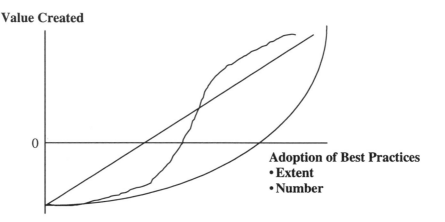

As an example, consider the data in Table 2. It shows the change in stock market value of firms that announced changes in the level and kind of customer service they provide. (For more details see Nayyar, 1995.) One would expect that increased levels of customer service would be positively valued while decreased levels would be negatively valued. In many cases this general expectation is true as indicated by the percent positive and percent negative columns respectively. Of all customer service increases 67% were positively valued while of all decreases 82% were negatively valued. Conversely, 33 percent of *increases* were *negatively* valued and 18 percent of *decreases* were *positively* valued (there were no zero-valued changes). Why did the stock market act in this seemingly perverse manner?

Nayyar (1995) speculated that there might exist optimum levels of customer service beyond which customers and the stock market do not reward firms. In effect, adopting best practices beyond a certain point destroys value. These findings also suggest many other possibilities including decreasing returns and threshold effects. This is but one example of attempts to understand the relationship between adoption of best practices and value creation. The chapters in this book rise to the challenge of connecting best practices to value creation in financial services.

Table 2. Adopting Best Practices and Creating Value: The Case of
Customer Service

Stock Market Reaction

3-Day Market-Adjusted Cumulative Abnormal Returns (%)

Actions	Customer Service			
	Increases		Decreases	
	Mean CAR	% Positive	Mean CAR	% Negative
Purchase Risk	0.62	65	-0.43	88
Purchasing Cost	0.58	67	-0.20	82
Ease, Convenience & Cost of Use	0.30	65	-0.23	92
Personalization	0.28	76	-0.09	67
All Actions	0.46	67	-0.22	82

A 1% 3-day abnormal return is equivalent to an annual return of 137%. A 1% abnormal return for an average firm on the *Business Week 1000*, with a market value of $3.8 billion on March 5, 1993, results in an increase in market value, after adjusting for overall market movements, of $38 million in 3 days. (Source: Nayyar, 1995.)

1.3 Beyond Best Practices: The CVFS Engine

What lies beyond best practices? Of course, the creation of value! How then is value created? We suggest that firms must not merely focus on customers. Instead, we advocate that firms must be Customer Value Focused. The difference lies in the explicit attention to creating value for customers. Creating value for customers, in turn, creates value for employees and shareholders.

Once a firm becomes customer value focused, it immediately realizes that it is not only best practices that help it create value. Many other factors affect value creation in financial services firms. Some factors, such as globalization, deregulation, maturing and efficiency of financial markets and changing customer needs and tastes, may be external factors outside the control of individual firms. Others, such as scale and scope of product portfolios and operations, product designs, process designs and technological choices and deployment, are internal factors within the control of individual firms. It is this latter type of factors that this book addresses. Of course, the two sets of factors are not independent. Their interactions must be considered as well.

Furthermore, beyond these two sets of factors are the multiple dimensions of organization design, risk taking, innovation, social awareness and responsibility that can be used to partly explain success and failure in value creation efforts. In fact, financial services, more so than many others, are integral to both the local and global communities within which they operate. Different clients, different regulations, different economies, different employees, might elicit a different response.

Value creation is both an outcome and a process. Value creation is the result of a smoothly running engine that we call the CVFS Engine. It has four key elements—strategies, services, systems and measures of success—that must be carefully designed and meshed to create customer focused value. We extend the notion of customer focus to one of customer value focus. This subtle distinction, we believe, provides the necessary focal point for all of a firm's efforts at understanding the needs of its customers and delivering appropriate services to them at the right time, at the right place and at the right price. Each element of the CVFS Engine and, by extension, each element of all firms, must contribute to customer value. We espouse the view that value is created through the design and operation of the CVFS Engine comprising the following four elements:

- Customer Value Focused Strategies
- Customer Value Focused Services
- Customer Value Focused Systems, and
- Customer Value Focused Measures of Success.

These four elements are neither independent of one another nor independent of the external environment. This is depicted by the intermeshing gears in Figure 4. And, if the rotation of the gears is not perfectly synchronized the whole system grinds to a halt! This book focuses on each of the four elements.

The need for perfect harmony among the four elements of the CVFS Engine may be illustrated by a few examples of what happens when the gears do not mesh properly. If a large insurance firm that primarily uses independent agents to sell products and services to affluent clients installs a web based process for selling products over the Internet, it would generate conflicts with its existing customer base and may create conflicts in the distribution system of agents. If the measure of success in a bank is defined as the efficiency with which applications are processed, to the extent that such a measure increases the exposure of the bank to the risk of loan-defaults, existing customers who enjoy a relatively low borrowing rate will eventually feel the effects of such a change and will not be quite satisfied. If a competitor introduces technology that significantly lowers costs without reducing quality, the focus may shift from cost reduction to providing additional information services. A firm in response to this move may have to change its strategy, services, systems and success measures rapidly to stay in business.

Figure 4. The CVFS Engine: Creating Value in Financial Services

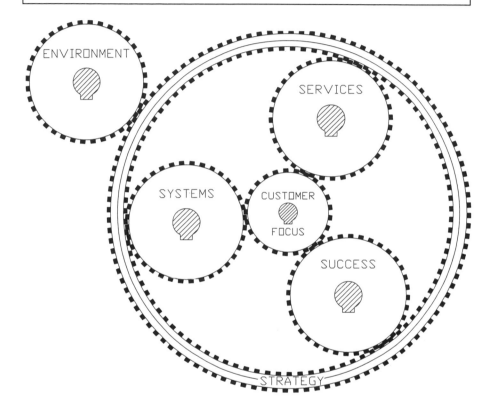

The CVFS Engine evokes an image of a precision machine, such as a finely crafted watch, in which every part is precisely designed to fulfill a specific purpose that has value only as a part of a much greater whole. By itself, each element of the CVFS Engine is important but it cannot act alone to create value.

The CVFS Engine also evokes an image of motion. An engine at rest does not create any output. Similarly, the CVFS Engine at rest does not create customer value. It must be in motion to work. Each element must also be able to shoulder its share of the load on the engine in order for the four elements acting together to develop and deliver the desired power to the central drive shaft. If the four elements do not carry the apportioned load, one or more of the elements could be strained beyond breaking point resulting in the total loss of power. If that happens, value cannot be created.

The CVFS Engine meshes smoothly with its environment. It uses inputs from the environment to regulate the rate at which it rotates. It also attempts to "push" the environment to adjust its speed, if necessary, to stay synchronized with the increasing rate of change needed to deliver customer value. Thus, the CVFS Engine both works with and works on the environment in the interest of its customers.

The chapters in this book offer a rich and varied collection of ideas to design and operate the CVFS Engine. Although we have collected the chapters into four sections—strategies, services, systems, and measures of success—this does not imply that each chapter is somehow restricted in its applicability to only one element of the CVFS Engine. On the contrary, every chapter paints a wide canvas. We invite you to see the whole picture by sampling from the book as you like. In this way, each reader will paint her own mosaic. And, each financial services firm will find a unique way to create value.

We do not attempt to offer generally applicable prescriptions for all financial services firms. Instead, this book contains a menu of options that financial services firms could consider. Many options will, if adopted, need to be adapted to suit the particular circumstances of a particular firm. It is our hope that the chapters in this book provide sufficient detail to begin the task of exploration within financial services firms as they determine how best to prepare for, create and exploit future opportunities.

The remaining chapters in the book are organized into four sections. Section 1 contains broad-perspective discussions of customer value focused strategies—both corporate and competitive—for financial services firms. Section 2 discusses customer value focused services using examples from four very specific financial service types. Section 3 highlights various customer value focused systems—technology and process design—that financial services firms need to consider going forward. Section 4 discusses customer value focused measures of success at both the macro- and micro-level to help financial services firms better calibrate the results of their efforts at improving performance.

1.4 Customer Value Focused Strategies

Value creation begins with strategy. A carefully crafted strategy that appropriately addresses customers' needs and wants is a prerequisite for success. The chapters in Section 1 consider customer value focused strategies for financial services firms. Rinnooy Kan (Chapter 2) presents a perspective on the future of global financial services. He sets a stage upon which the ideas contained in this book must play their part in helping to create value in financial services.

The financial world has changed dramatically in only a few decades. Rinnooy Kan considers three main categories of changes: in the market place, on the demand side and on the supply side of the financial services industry. The first category includes developments such as the globalization of financial markets, the changed role of governments and the revolution in the field of information technology. On the demand side, financial services companies have to satisfy more demanding and less faithful consumers who live longer and who expect higher returns on their savings. On the supply side, banks and insurers face competition not only from each other, but also from new suppliers such as supermarkets with banking outlets and providers who know their way on the Internet. Rinnooy Kan argues that although capital and know-how will continue to be crucial for financial services companies, distribution will be the main key to success.

One form of distribution is universal banking. Rogers (Chapter 3) and Walter (Chapter 4) discuss whether and how universal banks create value. Rogers discusses the characteristics of high and low performing commercial banks. Drawing on eight analytical case studies on U.S. and British banks, other case materials and industry statistics he addresses the question of what mix of strategy and organization infrastructure is particularly associated with rising and declining performance. Rogers concludes that although a strategy of growth-by-diversification has met with only equivocal success, forces such as unreflective herd instincts, behavioral contagion, and the diffusion of managerial fads drive managers to nevertheless pursue such strategies.

Since universal banks supply a collection of financial services, Walter suggests that shareholders, in essence, own a "closed-end fund" of assets intended to maximize risk-adjusted returns and hence the market value of the enterprise in relation to its book value. He traces the various sources of value-creation and value-destruction that ultimately explain market capitalization, including a survey of the main empirical findings in the literature. He then suggests alternative ways of enhancing market value of universal banks.

Across all segments of the financial services industry and across all markets, the development and sustenance of enduring multi-product relationships with consumers remains the most hallowed strategic objective. Monahan (Chapter 5) notes, however, that research conducted by The Executive Board Company identified a growing current of dissatisfaction with the payoff from "traditional" relationship strategies (defined as the cross-sales of proprietary products). Despite major investments in more detailed customer knowledge and the growing freedom to sell additional types of products, most institutions reported wide skews in customer profitability, increasing consumer price sensitivity, and greater consumer reliance on multiple providers. Increasing pressure on the traditional relationship suggests a deeper, structural change in retail financial markets caused by falling barriers to entry, decreasing search and switching costs and the rise of advice and consolidation "pure plays". He concludes that this evidence of the rise of buyer power in consumer financial services points to the emergence of a newly powerful customer that has driven pioneering institutions to rethink all the components of their relationship strategies, including deployment of staff, branding, product design, and delivery channels.

Relationships with customers often result in financial services firms offering multiple services as a part of their product-mix. Nayyar (Chapter 6) notes that most such diversifying moves are motivated by expected synergies from either reduced costs or increased revenues. However, cost-reduction is seldom achieved and revenue-enhancement is extremely difficult to accomplish because it requires substantial changes in the way businesses are organized and managed. Nayyar's examination of the performance effects of cost-reduction and revenue-enhancement driven diversification strategies in service firms revealed that revenue-enhancement strategies created value while cost-reduction strategies destroyed value. These results depended upon the type of service involved. The revenue-enhancement strategy was particularly valuable for firms offering services whose quality cannot be determined until after purchase and, even then, with some difficulty such as asset and risk management services. For services whose quality can be determined prior to purchase such as tax return processing, consumer finance, and mortgage lending, cost-reduction strategies could marginally create value.

Nayyar also discusses appropriate organization design—structures and processes—to help attain the desired benefits from diversification by service firms. Since each source of benefits is based on different underlying mechanisms, attaining each benefit relies on the adoption of appropriate organizational structures and processes. For example, attaining cost-reduction benefits requires structuring organizational units based on the particular resources shared between different services. In contrast, attaining revenue-enhancement benefits requires structuring organizational units based on the particular customers shared between services.

Contrary to the view that banks serve narrowly defined market niches, Bhargava (Chapter 7) argues that banks entering emerging markets succeed by building capabilities to serve many markets otherwise they cannot develop any sustainable competitive advantages in the face of fierce competition from well-entrenched local banks. He offers a framework to evaluate and choose business strategies for entry and competition in commercial banking in emerging markets. He argues that global commercial banks have inherent advantages in expanding their operations into emerging markets. However, in the corporate and institutional marketplace, this often does not translate into sustainable competitive advantage because of an inappropriate fit of the product delivery strategy with the overall business strategy for the bank. He illustrates this phenomenon for the transaction services business using the cash management product family as an example. He argues that the only tenable long-term proposition for a global bank is timely investment in delivery capability to serve multiple non-traditional segments in emerging markets.

Melnick (Chapter 8) develops a model that may be used to help financial services firms determine their product portfolio for emerging markets. Using multi-objective optimization, he describes a methodology for determining the location of facilities to serve a spatially dispersed population. The technique is suitable for emerging markets because it combines ideas from the design of experiments with techniques for updating that will suggest modifications as environmental factors change over time. Melnick describes an example of a financial institution considering expansion into an emerging market and at the same time attempting to maximize its customer base. The decision variables he uses are the number and location of branches and the percent of activities that will be dedicated to low-income customers. This approach can be extended to analyze the effects of other policy variables of relevance to a financial services institution.

1.5 Customer Value Focused Services

Firms must design and deliver appropriate products and services[*]. The chapters in Section II discuss customer value focused products and services for financial services firms. Financial services are becoming more complex and the rate of innovation of complex products is increasing as firms attempt to stay ahead in the commoditization race where new products are rapidly imitated. Rapid innovation of financial products creates problems for firms due to a lack of standards, a lack of clearly defined responsibilities in the management of new

---

[*] The term "products" includes goods and services. In practice, however, "products" refers to specific service offerings such as CDs, derivatives, mortgages and insurance.

financial services among end users, and a lack of definition of clearly defined responsibilities of dealers to end users.

As one example of how to develop and implement customer value focused services, Matthews and Rusinko (Chapter 9) examine two sets of solutions to these problems: standards and the use of specific risk management techniques. These solutions have improved the management of financial derivatives for U.S. financial services firms. Further, they suggest that financial services firms benefit from organizational learning to change strategic direction, organizational structure, deployable technologies, and information management systems when introducing new financial services.

Hosking, Kambil and Lister (Chapter 10) examine trends in electronic brokerage and how major brokerage firms are adapting to an online market place characterized by low transactions costs and margins. They examine strategies of incumbents and new entrants and outline the future of electronic brokerage. They also discuss the relationship between various electronic agents for brokerage and new forms of exchange.

The Internet is transforming the delivery of financial services, and the Charles Schwab Corporation is among the firms at the forefront of this revolution. Dewan and Mendelson (Chapter 11) use Schwab as a case study of the use of the Internet channel. They show how the Internet has come to occupy a place at the core of Schwab's business strategy. They draw lessons from the Schwab experience to shed light on the broader impact of on-line trading on the brokerage industry.

There is a large and growing need for sophisticated analytical software and high-powered computers to evaluate risks associated with complicated securities. Battifarano (Chapter 12) uses the experience of developing The Yield Book, a new product at Salomon Brothers, to draw some critical lessons for conceiving, designing, introducing and growing a new financial service. He argues that broker-dealers, in general, are highly qualified to develop analytical software and manage hardware to satisfy their own internal needs as well as those of the financial community at large. He also suggests that the key to good customer service is providing not only information but also tools to deliver information directly and efficiently to customer's desktops.

1.6 Customer Value Focused Systems

The chapters in Section III consider systems—technological and process design—for financial services firms. Regulatory and technical changes occurring in the financial services and information technology sectors of the economy are driving a revolutionary convergence of hitherto vertical market segments. Squeezed between these revolutions on its demand and supply sides, McGilloway (Chapter 13) argues that corporate information technology departments will also undergo a profound revolution in the way they are organized and in the services they provide. He suggests that the open nature of standards in the financial services and information technology arenas offer tremendous scope for Chief Information Officers (CIOs) to shrink (cut costs) and link with users (collaborate). Therefore, he expects that the role of the CIO will shift to Chief Integrator or Coordinator.

Karmarkar (Chapter 14) suggests that access is a key aspect of competition in financial service markets. New technologies for information collection and distribution are altering the costs and value structures associated with access to information intensive services. As a result, significant changes are occurring in the configuration of service systems and in industry structure. Karmarkar discusses the role of access in service competition and the effect of technological changes on access, location and configuration. These effects are most visible today in transaction-intensive financial services such as retail banking and brokerage. He argues that they will increasingly affect all financial services and indeed all information based industry sectors.

Dunbar and Garud (Chapter 15) examine the implementation of virtual office technologies in financial services firms. Virtual office technologies are of interest to firms in financial services because of the real estate cost savings and increased productivity that such strategies offer. They argue that it is not clear which functions in financial services are most suitable for implementing such virtual office technologies. They use case experiences to develop a conceptual framework for assessing the value likely to be added by making different functions virtual.

Fan, Stallaert and Whinston (Chapter 16) examine the emergence and growth of electronic financial services such as Schwab and E*trade. The growing popularity of Internet-based transactions is radically transforming long-established business paradigms in every sector of the economy. They focus on the market mechanisms in use in the financial system to explore the implications of a shift to open electronic networks on the traditional relationships between financial institutions and their clients, both household investors and corporate borrowers. They present a design of an Internet-based marketplace where individual investors trade financial assets directly with each other and settle transactions instantaneously. Such systems, they suggest, will render mutual funds and other pooling mechanisms obsolete.

Financial services institutions are providing a rapidly expanding variety of products and services; technology is making customers more mobile, and delay is unacceptable in financial transactions. These attributes of the financial services sector mean that firms must provide effective, efficient and reliable service or quickly lose customers to competitors. To avoid huge labor costs, financial services firms must develop innovative approaches to managing their workforces and their service delivery process. Larson and Pinker (Chapter 17) outline and provide examples of effective techniques for managing part time and flexible personnel in back room operations, bank teller scheduling and management, improving customer queuing experiences, and the design and operation of call centers to take into account cross-training, learning and cross selling.

Call centers are becoming more important in financial services. They are of importance to retail banking operations, credit card operations and mutual fund organizations. A significant part of the dynamics of call centers in financial services is similar to call centers in other industries. Analyzing both static and dynamic aspects of managing call centers, Pinedo, Seshadri and Shanthikumar (Chapter 18) discuss necessary service, security, and database requirements for call centers in financial services firms. They also analyze the differences between call centers in financial services and call centers in other industries such as airlines. These differences center around the more extensive database requirements necessary to handle each call, as well as the fact that customers of financial institutions tend to be more captive than customers of airlines.

Alouisa, Anderson, Castro, Ennis, Gevarter, and Pandolfo (Chapter 19) discuss Prudential's solution to complex call center problems. Since Prudential is a service oriented business, its success and competitive advantage lies in its ability to give customers the highest quality of service possible, "wherever and whenever" they want it. Managers at Prudential determined that without the proper tools to do the job, service quality would be diminished. PruServ™, a powerful call center application, effectively solved the business problem by providing users with a robust and exciting application that resulted in "world-class" customer service. This translated to the firm capturing an increased percentage of clients' assets and generating incremental revenues.

1.7 Customer Value Focused Measures of Success

Cost, quality, time, productivity and satisfaction are often good broad themes around which performance measures can be developed. However, when it comes down to actually defining and measuring performance there can be large gaps between what was originally meant to be measured and achieved versus what gets measured and the actions taken. Two reasons for the distortion or myopia of measures are lack of foresight and excessive internal focus. The chapters in this section consider several important antecedents and consequences of customer value focused measures of success for financial services firms.

Patel (Chapter 20) posits that the quality movement in the financial services industry stalled in the mid-1990s after tremendous momentum in the mid-1980s. Significant factors in the failure of the movement include the measures and measurement processes used to evaluate the progress of quality programs and to construct product or process enhancements. Patel calls for financial institutions to employ more sophisticated measurement tools to focus quality efforts on those areas with the greatest impact on customer behavior and tangible financial outcomes. He discusses four statistical methods for linking quality outcomes to financial returns, concluding that, to the average practitioner, the best choice is one that achieves the best blend of accuracy, ease of use and ease of interpretation. From a broader perspective, however, he argues that no matter how sophisticated the measurement processes are, institutions hoping to differentiate themselves need to focus less on incremental improvements in individual metrics and more on wholesale process change.

Chase, Roth and Voss (Chapter 21) compare service practice and service performance of financial services with that of other major service sectors in the U.S. They found that financial services lag hotels, which is the exemplar service sector in both practice and performance. Several practice drivers separated financial services from exemplar counterparts. Relative weaknesses of the financial services sector were seen primarily in the areas of service quality and customer growth, which was ascribed to financial services' improper management of "moments of truth" (the encounters) with customers. They suggest that this is a result of financial services personnel management practices emphasizing cost cutting re-engineering while not emphasizing quality leadership and employee empowerment.

Frei and Harker (Chapter 22) suggest that the development of total quality management, reengineering, and other tools have led organizations to focus on the design and management of production processes. In services, and in particular in banking, this process orientation deals directly with customer interactions with the organization. This focus raises two important questions: (a) does such a process-orientation matter to the overall efficiency of an organization? and (b) what are the characteristics of effective process management in financial services firms? They summarize a four-year research effort to understand the role of process performance in the overall efficiency of banks. They recommend effective approaches for designing and managing key service delivery processes for financial services firms.

Cutler (Chapter 23) suggests that, for at least the past decade, banks have made three promises with regard to improving productivity. First, that new technology will reduce the workforce size. Second, that closing branches and migrating customers to lower cost distribution channels will increase productivity. And third, service levels (i.e., greater convenience, zero defects, and expanded product sets) will rise leading to higher customer satisfaction. Research conducted at Booz, Allen and Hamilton, a management consulting firm, reveals some alarming insights into the true productivity trends of the major banks in the U.S. Notwithstanding this, he argues that there are some institutions that are achieving superior productivity by focusing on instilling disciplined operations management capabilities.

Presenting a macroeconomic perspective on productivity growth in services, Solow (Chapter 24) discusses important issues in productivity definition and measurement for services. Highlighting some particularly vexing problems in measuring productivity in service industries, he suggests that the financial services sector, in collaboration with business schools or other interested research agencies, could make a valuable contribution in developing ways to define and measure the real output in this and similar service industries.

1.8 Conclusion

We believe that the CVFS Engine is an effective and parsimonious framework for designing and delivering financial services in an increasingly competitive global economy. It evokes images of precision, motion and oneness with its ever-changing environment. Every chapter in this book assists financial services firms to design and operate their own CVFS Engine—one that uniquely addresses the needs of customers to create value for them.

References

Nayyar, P. 'Stock market reactions to customer service changes', *Strategic Management Journal*, 16(1), 1995, pp. 39-53.

SECTION I:

CUSTOMER VALUE FOCUSED STRATEGIES

Chapter 2

The Changing Global Environment of Financial Services

Alexander Rinnooy Kan
ING Group

2.1 Introduction

'The horse is here to stay, but the automobile is only a novelty – a fad.'

This statement made in 1903 by the president of a bank advising Horace Rackham not to invest in the Ford Motor Company proves how dangerous it is to make predictions. Nevertheless, this chapter attempts to investigate how the changes that are taking place in the financial services industry will impact the future of this sector.

If we had asked ambitious students ten years ago in which branches of industry they expected to find a challenging career, very few would opt for retail banking or insurance. This industry has not yet managed to shake off its dusty image completely. However, there is, in fact, no industry that is changing as rapidly and as drastically as the financial services sector.

In what follows we explore the changes in the financial world. In doing so, we will illustrate our view that distribution is the key to success in coping with these changes. Distribution is also the core element of International Nederlander Group's (ING) integrated financial services strategy. We will explain what this entails and what the results of the strategy are, and we will conclude with the prediction that this concept will find its way into our market in which banking and insurance are still strictly separated.

But let us first concentrate on what is turning the financial landscape upside down. We have divided the changes into a number of categories: changes in the market place, changes in demand, and changes in supply.

2.2 Changes in the Market Place

Looking at the changes in the market place, the first factor that should be examined is the globalization of financial markets.

The US, Japan and Europe are still the main economic powers, but the distribution of wealth and capital flows around the world are changing substantially. There has been a vast increase in capital flows to emerging markets as well as an increase in the overall size of the flows. The developing world already generates around 40% of the global output. The emerging markets have 85% of the world's population, they account for 77% of its land and produce 63% of its commodities. The political changes and liberalization measures, enacted since the mid-1980's, that have enfranchised four billion people around the world, are irreversible. The drive towards further capitalist development will continue.

The economic growth prospects in emerging markets remain significantly higher than in industrialized countries. In addition, emerging markets demonstrate generally improved macro-economic performance, albeit with significant divergence between the different regions.

In addition to the changes with respect to emerging markets, we would also like to mention the European monetary integration. The introduction of the Economic and Monetary Union and the single currency in Europe will have a substantial impact on capital markets. Later on, we will discuss ING's response to the creation of the Euromarket.

Not only has the distribution of money changed, but also the distribution of power in the financial world.

Changes in legislation have reshaped the financial landscape. The most important change is the lifting of legal barriers between banking and insurance in several countries. Contrary to the US, which still maintains a strict legal separation between banking and insurance, a number of European countries have liberalized their financial markets. This resulted in the creation of ING Group and in many other cooperation agreements between insurance companies and banks. This process continues.

The role of governments in demarcating the market, e.g., through their role in the provision of social security, is also changing in many countries. Forced by budget problems, many governments are scaling down state provisions and are giving more scope to private enterprise. In the Netherlands, for instance, this has resulted in substantial opportunities for private financial service companies in the fields of disability insurance, sickness benefits and benefits paid to a partner in case of premature death. In addition, the future affordability of state pensions is under pressure, which has increased the demand for private pension and life insurance plans as well for other types of investment products, such as mutual funds. When discussing ING's strategy, we will explain how we are addressing the challenges in the Dutch market.

One of the greatest driving forces of change in our industry is the distribution of information. Information technology has become one of the crucial success factors in our industry. The speed of developments in this field is incredible. Information systems have a tremendous impact on product development, marketing, administrative support and after sales service. Information systems require substantial investments. ING, for instance, has invested approximately $3 billion in the past five years to update existing and develop new information systems. Financial services providers are confronted with the tough challenge of selecting those systems which give them an edge on the competition and which do not become obsolete in one or two years. This challenge complicates the investment process in information technology.

2.3 Changes in Demand

Our present clients are different from those some decades ago. Formerly, many clients did not understand or did not bother to understand the banking and insurance products they bought. They completely relied on their insurance broker or their bank branch for advice. Today's consumers are better educated than in the past and they are more demanding. Products and prices have become more transparent, which enables consumers to compare accurately the many options that are available. As a result, clients shop around more often and are less faithful to one particular brand. Many of today's clients know exactly what they want and they might expect services tailored to their needs. Rightly so, we might add.

The higher consumer demands have also resulted in longer business hours. It may seem odd to mention this in the US, which has had a 24-hour economy for many years. However, until recently, business hours in the Netherlands were strictly from nine to six. More flexible business hours have led to the introduction of many varieties of flexi-time labor.

Demographic developments are also causing substantial changes on the demand side. People live longer through better nutrition and better medical care. This longer life expectancy, in combination with the desire to retire at an earlier age, has created the demand for new superannuation products. The reduced role of the government in social security provision, which we already mentioned, has accelerated this process.

With the low interest rate levels of the past few years, people are no longer content with the return they receive from placing their money in a traditional savings account or life insurance policy. They demand high returns and are prepared to take higher risks to achieve those returns. The result is an almost infinite number of investment-linked banking and insurance products. Investment funds are booming and the latest types of funds are offering prospects of returns that may exceed the average stock market performance by a substantial margin. This places a great strain on our investors.

The fact that people live longer creates important opportunities for financial service companies. Later in this chapter, we will explain ING's approach to the promising senior citizen market. However, besides opportunities, the longer life expectancy also poses a serious threat to the life insurance industry. Past premium levels did not allow for this longer life expectancy. At ING we have strengthened our provisions in recent years by more than $1 billion to cover the longevity risk of our life insurance portfolio. We are surprised that insurers in some countries, such as the US, still do not perceive the longevity risk as a serious problem. We feel that insurers who do not take measures to cover this risk will find it difficult to guarantee their pension benefit levels in the 21st century.

Genetic technology, a subject that has attracted much publicity in the past few days, also poses a potential threat to the insurance industry. If genetic engineering were to be applied to humans on a large scale, this would completely overthrow the underwriting principles of life and medical insurance.

Another threat to the insurance industry, which is a direct consequence of the more demanding and critical consumer attitude, are the developments in the field of liability. In this respect, we may mention that European financial services providers are dreading the prospect of further adoption of US jurisprudence in this field. American judges are awarding liability damages which, in our opinion, will ultimately lead to uninsurability of certain types of liability risks.

2.4 Changes on the Supply Side

The changes on the supply side are, of course, closely linked to the changes on the demand side.

Here again, distribution is key. In the past, banks only faced competition from other banks. The same applied to the insurance industry. Nowadays, they are not only facing competition from each other, but from other providers. Direct marketing has proved to be very successful in the retail market for financial services. In the UK, for instance, the Royal Bank of Scotland's subsidiary, Direct Line, has captured the leading position for motor insurance in a short period of time. We also have an excellent example within the ING Group. Postbank is a subsidiary that sells a wide range of financial services through direct marketing to 6.5 million accountholders in the Netherlands.

Some pessimists in our industry are even saying that bank branches and insurance intermediaries are due for extinction. We don't think so. We are convinced that as the number and complexity of products increases there will be a good future for professional intermediaries who are able to prove the added value of their advice to their clients.

The same applies to branch banking. The number of branches will decrease. The ones that remain will be larger branches that often have a regional function. They will be financial supermarkets where clients can obtain specialist advice for all their financial needs.

In order to cover the costs of their expensive networks of branches or agents, banks and insurers are developing additional distribution channels. They are also seeking strategic partnerships, not only with each other, but also with companies from other branches of industry. Banking desks in supermarkets are already a familiar phenomenon in the US. They are outlets of well-established banks. Supermarkets in the UK are taking this concept a step further. Supergrocer Tesco is setting up its own financial services company with the assistance of the Royal Bank of Scotland. They are planning to make a range of banking and insurance products available to their clients through the combination of home banking via the telephone and banking desks in Tesco supermarkets. Tesco believes it will be able to translate the confidence of its regular customers into a significant share of the financial services market.

Banks and insurers will certainly face keen competition from these new providers. However, practice has proven that not all ventures of new players in the financial services markets are successful.

The Internet should also be mentioned. Millions of people are already familiar with the worldwide web and the number of web users is growing rapidly. Many financial services providers are exploring the opportunities of the Internet. There is no doubt that they will be substantial, especially when it will be possible to make payments safely through the network. Two of our companies that market their products through direct marketing are actively using the Internet as a sales outlet. Other business units have sites that provide information about their products and services.

Interactive TV may also be a medium for distribution of financial products. Furthermore, many companies are enabling their clients to transact via a personal computer and a modem.

We have already mentioned the word distribution several times. Capital and know-how will certainly remain important success factors in the financial sector, but we firmly believe that distribution is *the* key.

The recent developments at the stock exchange here on Wall Street are a case in point. In the past, large pension funds dominated the volume of stock exchange transactions. Investment bankers like Salomon Brothers and Goldman Sachs built up solid reputations by advising these clients and developing innovative financial instruments tailored to their needs. Nowadays, the assets from individual pension saving accounts have outnumbered the assets of pension funds. The individual accounts are marketed through broker networks. Many specialists regard the merger of Morgan Stanley and Dean Witter as a sign that the financial supermarket concept will be a major force on Wall Street.

Financial services providers are choosing different solutions for the distribution of their products. Some are sticking to their present distribution channels and core activities, while others are seeking to expand their distribution facilities by adding new outlets and systems or by entering into partnerships with other providers.

2.5 The ING Core

In what follows we describe the ING solution, which is characterized by three ingredients:

1) integrated financial services;
2) multi-distribution channels;
3) a global approach with emphasis on emerging markets.

ING Group was established in 1991 through the merger of Holland's largest insurance company, Nationale-Nederlanden, and one of the country's largest banks, NMB Postbank Group, which is now operating under the name of ING Bank. The roots of these companies go back to the middle of the 19th century. The companies merged when the Dutch government lifted the legal barriers between banking and insurance. They joined forces because their distribution channels complemented each other perfectly and because their combined financial strength enabled the group to step up its international expansion.

The creation of ING was the first large-scale merger between a European bank and an insurance company on the basis of equality. It was also one of the few balanced mergers. We opted for a full merger instead of a looser form of cooperation since we felt that the synergies between our banking and our insurance operations could only be optimally realized through a complete integration of our activities. The core element of our business philosophy is our integrated financial services concept. This means that we want to offer a full range of banking, investment and insurance products and services to both personal and corporate clients through the *distribution channels of their choice.*

The foundation of this concept was laid in our home market, the Netherlands, where we are the market leader in funds transfer and life insurance, and one of the largest parties in the markets for non-life insurance, savings, deposits, mortgages, consumer and commercial loans and investment funds. In the Netherlands, ING has access to four major distribution channels for financial services: direct marketing, independent insurance intermediaries, bank branches and tied agents. Through these four channels we have a business relationship with 75% of Dutch households (See figure 1). We grouped our banking and insurance business units by distribution channel under a single, central management, which enabled us to integrate the organization and thus make optimum use of the opportunities for synergy.

The results of this approach in the past six years have been rewarding. Our direct marketing operation, Postbank, has generated insurance premium income of $254 million, making it a medium-sized insurer in the Dutch market. This is an attractive source of income, especially when you consider that we developed this channel in a prudent manner in order not to anger the independent insurance intermediaries who bring in the bulk of our insurance business. When ING was created they were very concerned about our plans to use direct marketing as an additional distribution channel for insurance. This experience has taught us that you can never rush a multi-distribution strategy.

Figure 1: Synergies in Retail Market

Synergies retail market 1996

- Insurance through direct marketing: US $ 254 million
- Insurance through bank branches: US $ 165 million
- Lending products through insurance agents: US $ 312 million
- Savings products through insurance agents: US $ 80 million

© ING Group

Our network of bank branches has also been a valuable distribution channel for our insurance products. Conversely, we are making a range of banking products available to independent and tied insurance agents. These products are an important source of income to them and enable them to broaden their role as comprehensive financial services advisors.

Our integrated financial services concept is not confined to cross selling. The cooperation of our Dutch business units results in the development of new products and services, which combine banking, insurance and investment aspects.

In this connection, our new strategy for the senior citizen market provides an interesting example.

With the graying population, the number of senior citizens will be increasing rapidly. To give you an indication, ING's business units in the Netherlands currently have 3 million clients who are over the age 55. In 2010 that number will have increased to approximately 5 million.

We have conducted detailed market research into the requirements of current and future senior citizens. One of the main conclusions was that they wish to retain their independence as long as possible. They are active, critical consumers who place greater emphasis on comfort and quality than on price, no matter whether they are purchasing finance, leisure, housing, transport or health care products. ING decided to develop a concept that would cater to the needs of this target group in three areas: finance, health care, and housing. We are designing special packages with products and services in each of these areas. Most of these products will be developed in-house. For others, such as home nursing, we will act as an intermediary. One of our business units is conducting a pilot program. Others will follow shortly.

Our integrated financial services concept is also paying off in the corporate market where we are able to support corporations for all the items on their balance sheet. We have a strong track record in corporate finance both in and outside the Netherlands. The combination of financial and human resources have enabled us to undertake large-scale and multi-discipline projects such as infrastructure works and the creation of a mobile telephone network. Our activities in the field of employee benefits are a good example of our integrated concept in the corporate market. ING is the only provider in the Netherlands that is able to supply a full range of employee benefits through one single contract. Employers can arrange pension plans, saving accounts, sickness benefits, medical and disability insurance and other benefits for their employees with maximum convenience and full automation support. (See figure 2)

Figure 2: Synergies in the Corporate Market

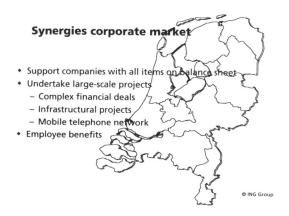

Synergies corporate market

- Support companies with all items on balance sheet
- Undertake large-scale projects
  - Complex financial deals
  - Infrastructural projects
  - Mobile telephone network
- Employee benefits

© ING Group

We are gradually exporting the expertise we have gained with integrated financial services in the Netherlands to other countries where this concept is possible and profitable.

We sell bank products through our network of insurance agents in several countries. In Poland our majority stake in the local Bank Slaski has given us a valuable additional distribution outlet for our life insurance products. In Canada, where we have a strong position in the insurance market, we are setting up a new company, which will sell bank products through direct marketing. If this project proves to be successful, we will certainly look for opportunities to carry out similar initiatives in the US.

Currently, ING has more than 60,000 employees in 58 countries. We operate under many different brand names, which have strong reputation in specific markets. This is in keeping with our policy of local autonomy. While applying the principle of shared responsibility, we give our companies our full support and considerable degree of autonomy to serve their clients.

Our international banking operations focus mainly on emerging markets. Since the early 1980s, ING Bank has built up leading worldwide positions in debt conversion and trade and commodity finance. It has gradually broadened its operations and now has developed a wide range of services in five main areas: international corporate banking, emerging markets banking, international capital markets, international private banking and asset management. The acquisition of the British merchant bank Barings, which also has a strong position in emerging markets, proved to be a perfect strategic fit for the international operations of ING Bank.

Though ING has substantial non-life insurance operations in North America, Australia and Belgium, the emphasis in our insurance activities is on life insurance. ING was the first European company to be licensed in the life insurance markets of Japan, Korea and Taiwan. We have substantial life insurance operations in South America and Central Europe.

We have found that the two core strategies of ING – our integrated financial services concept and our focus on emerging markets – complement each other very well. On the one hand, we can serve emerging markets as a bridge to the international capital markets, while on the other hand we can contribute to strengthening the domestic sector of these countries through life insurance, pensions and investment funds. Our challenge will be to create retail opportunities in emerging markets and to be client-driven in mature markets.

The introduction of the single currency and the Economic and Monetary Union in 1999 will create a large European market. The euro will become an important, hard currency, which will be an alternative to the US dollar and the Japanese yen. Our strategy for the next few years places greater emphasis on Europe. We will not launch a host of small initiatives over the full range of our activities. Instead, we will concentrate on a number of market segments in which we intend to build up strong positions through organic growth as well as through acquisitions and alliances. These segments include direct marketing, employee benefits, corporate finance, treasury, clearing and asset management.

2.6 Conclusion

We would like to conclude with a discussion on the financial services in the United States. ING has been active in the US for more than a century. The strict separation of banking and insurance was actually one of the major challenges confronting the ING merger in 1991. Both Nationale-Nederlanden and the former NMB Bank were active in the United States and US law did not allow us to continue these activities on the same basis after the merger. Since we had a much more extensive presence in the North American insurance market, we decided to change the nature and structure of our banking operations.

Figure 3 depicts a number of our principal business units in the US. As you can see they occupy significant positions in a number of segments of the US financial services market.

In total we have more than 8,000 employees in this country. Our North American operations generated more than 21% of our total income in 1995. In view of the size and the diversity of our activities, we would be very interested in implementing our integrated financial services concept in North America.

We are noticing the first signs that the strict demarcation between banking and insurance may be loosened. Supreme Court rulings have provided clarification of the authority of national banks to sell insurance and annuities.

Some banks are already entering into innovative joint venture agreements with insurance companies in the field of variable annuities.

There has been a strong anti-bank lobby by US insurance agents who are afraid that the price of insurance distribution will decline as a result of increased bank participation. However, a new breed of intermediary is emerging who is interested in extending the portfolio with other financial services such as mutual funds and consumer loans. This growing segment of the agent population is expected to diffuse the anti-bank lobby.

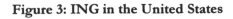

Figure 3: ING in the United States

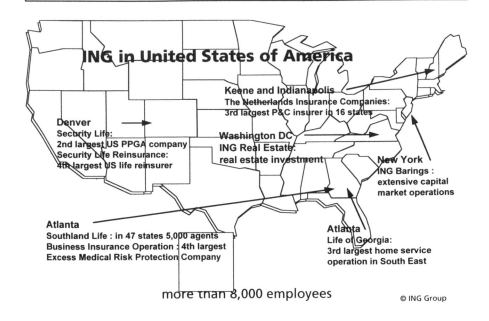

A factor which complicates closer links between US banks and insurers is that banking supervision is organized on the federal level, while the emphasis in insurance supervision is on state level. In very basic terms, the crucial question is who will regulate combination products?

The regulators in the Netherlands were confronted with the same problem. The Dutch Central Bank, which supervises ING's banking operations, and the Insurance Supervisory Board, which supervises ING's insurance operations, drew up a joint protocol, which regulates the supervision of financial conglomerates. Their joint, pragmatic supervision is working well.

We hope and trust that the laws will eventually follow the market and that there will be opportunities for integrated financial services in the United States within the next five to ten years. You can be sure that ING will be among the first to take advantages of these opportunities.

Let us return briefly to the statement we made at the beginning of this chapter. When the US banker advised Horace Rackham in 1903 not to invest in Ford because he felt the automobile was nothing but a fad, Mr. Rackham chose to ignore that advice. He bought $5,000 worth of stock in Henry Ford's company and sold it for $12.5 million several years later. Mr. Rackham was rewarded for his vision.

We believe there will be rewards for bankers, insurers, and other financial services providers who recognize now that integrated financial services will have a good future in the US market.

Editor's Note: *This chapter is based on a keynote address given by Dr. Alexander Rinnooy Kan at the Leonard N. Stern School of Business, New York University in 1997, during the first conference on "Creating Value in Financial Services." It, of course, predates the merger of Citibank with The Travelers Group. This merger combines for the first time in the United States an insurance company with a bank.*

Chapter 3

Universal Banking: Does It Work?

David Rogers
New York University

3.1 Introduction

Since the early 1970s, commercial banking worldwide has become a turbulent, hyper-competitive industry. A series of driving forces, globalization, deregulation, new technology, the rise of capital markets, and a consequent dis-intermediation, have eroded commercial banking's previously protected market position. It has become an industry in secular decline, as its traditional credit businesses, taking in deposits and providing loans, are increasingly being replaced by securities products. On the liability side, deposits have given way to money market mutual funds, while on the assets side, large corporations are increasingly turning to capital markets products – junk bonds and commercial paper rather than bank loans – for their capital needs. A major issue facing commercial banks has become how to reposition them to survive.

For the past decade, I have been conducting intensive field studies of US and British banks to assess their efforts at such adaptation (Rogers, 1993, 1999). My studies included Chase, Citicorp, Bankers Trust, JP Morgan, and super-regional banks in the US as well as the Big Four clearing banks, Lloyds, Barclays, NatWest, and Midland, in Britain. The central issue has been to ascertain the mix of strategies and organization infrastructures associated with different degrees of success. I have been particularly interested in distinguishing the high from the low performers, as measured by such indicators as return on equity (ROE), return on assets (ROA), cost/income ratios, and share price.

While such a small number of banks hardly seems an adequate base from which to generalize, I was engaged in hypothesis-generating rather than hypothesis-testing research. I followed a methodology advocated by banking scholars Pilloff and Santomero (1996), who argued that we need more longitudinal, field-based, and managerial process, case studies to understand better why there is no statistically significant gain in value or performance from bank merger activity.

Over time, I focused on the merits of the product and geographic diversification strategy; one that commercial banks worldwide had increasingly adopted to improve their performance. While other financial services firms, including investment banks, insurance companies, brokerage houses, and savings and loans institutions, had also diversified, commercial banks are now among the leaders in that strategy. As securities and insurance products were replacing traditional credit ones, commercial banks sought to diversify into those financial services. Firms in other segments had already been diversifying into commercial banking, e.g., Merrill Lynch's cash management accounts (CMAs), targeting the same customers as commercial banks, and it seemed only fair for commercial banks to be able to do likewise (the level playing field argument).

The result has been for increasing numbers of commercial banks to acquire investment banks, insurance businesses, asset management services, and retail brokerage functions. The trend had become a stampede by the late 90s, as financial writers often referred to a "feeding frenzy" to characterize the massive consolidation now taking place. It is happening within and across various segments of financial services and is increasingly cross-border, e.g., Deutsche Bank acquiring Morgan Grenfell and Bankers Trust. Much of the impetus is coming from commercial banks that are following their corporate clients to the capital markets and their individual customers to institutionalized savings products.

3.2 Universal Banking

The widely used term in Europe to characterize this strategy is "universal banking." It has also been referred to as "conglomerate banking" and, in the business press, as the "financial supermarket." Universal banking generally refers to the capacity to deliver a wide range of financial services, including "deposit-taking and lending, trading of financial instruments and foreign exchange (and their derivatives), underwriting of new debt and equity issues, brokerage, investment management, and insurance" (Saunders and Walter, 1994).   My purpose in this chapter is to evaluate this strategy as a way of commercial banks' improving their performance, since it has been such a focus of their efforts at re-positioning. Indeed, the often mentioned pattern of commercial banks imitating one another in an unreflective herd instinct fashion may well be taking place with regard to these consolidations, just as had been the case before with the strategies of global expansion, and loans to sovereign nations, commercial real estate projects and LBOs. Pilloff and Santomero (1996) even suggest that perhaps bank managers are suffering from self-delusion in pursuing such consolidations.

A key question is whether such a diversification strategy does in fact improve bank performance, addressing the issue of what happens as the strategy gets implemented. One way of addressing that question is to compare highly diversified commercial banks with much more focused ones. In the US, it was much more difficult than in Britain for commercial banks to diversify, for example, into investment banking and insurance, because of obvious regulatory barriers, e.g., Glass Steagall and the power of the insurance industry lobby in the state and the federal governments. Despite those obstacles, there has been progressive erosion of the barriers through various administrative and court decisions. In Britain, the de-regulation of the stock market and the securities industry in 1986, known as Big Bang, permitting commercial and investment banking to be combined for the first time, provided the impetus for such diversification; and all four of the British clearing banks diversified at some point into investment banking and insurance.

3.3 Arguments For and Against Diversification

Those favoring diversification for commercial banks, most of which is related-diversification into other financial services businesses, cite such potential benefits as smoothing income flows, thereby minimizing risk by protecting the firm from losses in any particular businesses; realizing economies of scope by permitting a transfer of expertise (products, technology, distribution systems) across various financial services businesses; providing one-stop shopping by cross selling a variety of financial services to particular individual or institutional clients; and gaining greater market power by having an increasingly prominent position in several financial services products. Overall, proponents argue that there are many synergies that result from a single financial services firm providing multiple products.

Equally compelling, however, are arguments citing the costs of diversification. They include: the many complexities of developing transfer pricing mechanisms to support collaborative efforts across firms; the difficulties of headquarters keeping track of costs and revenues across multiple businesses, and of establishing controls over their functioning; and, perhaps most important of all, managing the many cultural, political, and systems conflicts across the various businesses.   Those between commercial and investment banking have been especially acute, for example, over issues of compensation and degree of autonomy of investment bankers from headquarters control. One student of strategic management has coined the term "internal pollution" to characterize these inter-business relationships in commercial banks. (Campbell, 1995)

An irony of the movement toward diversification in commercial banking is that it runs counter to a long-term trend in other industries, particularly manufacturing. Many strategic management researchers have documented the clear move away from diversification in the 1980s and 90s, after a persistent and strong trend toward it from the late 1940s through the 70s (Grant, 1995; Goold, Campbell, and Alexander, 1994; Campbell & Lucks, 1992; and Markides, 1995). Rumelt's classic studies of the Fortune 500, for example, indicate a sharp decline of single-business companies from 42% in 1949 to 14.4% in 1974, an increase in related-business companies from 25.7% to 42.3% during those years and a much more dramatic one of unrelated-business companies from 4.1% to 20.7%. The 60s, 70s, and early 80s, then, were the era of the conglomerates (Rumelt, 1982).

In contrast, a study of acquisitions and divestitures by large diversified US corporations indicated that the dominant trend in the late 80s and 90s was "the divestment of unrelated businesses and a restructuring around fewer, more closely related businesses" (Williams, Paez, and Sanders, 1988). Grant (1995) concludes from this and other studies that a "back to basics" trend is strong in North America and Western Europe. This trend underlies the conclusion of Peters and Waterman in their much critiqued, but still relevant, *In Search of Excellence*: "Organizations that do branch out but stick very close to their knitting outperform the others" (Peters and Waterman, 1982).

Why has this trend away from diversification for both related and unrelated businesses been so pronounced since the early 1980s? A main reason is that very high levels of diversification appear to give rise to problems of managing complexity, particularly for firms pursuing a related-diversification strategy. The reason for the complexity is that the related businesses are structured to collaborate, thereby contributing to synergies or collective benefits from transferring competencies such as technology, products, and managerial know-how, among the group. The complexity comes from establishing incentives and structures that make that collaboration actually take place. Those complexity problems include the many costs discussed above and are reflected strongly in the marked shift that has been found in the relationship between diversification and profitability over time. Diversification has become a less profitable activity during the 1980s and 1990s than it was in previous decades (Grant, 1995). One explanation is that increasing environmental turbulence in recent years has increased the costs of managing large, diversified enterprises. Markides' (1995) findings provide further support for this thesis. He found refocusing announcements by diversified companies have been accompanied by abnormal positive stock market returns.

Turning to financial services, the concept of the financial supermarket, a manifestation of the universal bank, had been widely discredited from negative experiences in the 1980s, at least in the US. This replicated the experience of non-financial services industries. American Express is a classic example, along with Sears and Prudential (Freedman and Vohr, 1991). For a variety of reasons, these attempts at achieving synergies through so-called one-stop shopping and cross-selling multiple products to the same customers were not successful (Friedman, 1992).

Problems associated with managing the complexity and scale that such financial supermarkets represented were overwhelming and frequently prevented the synergies from occurring. Instead, these newly diversified conglomerates often experienced unmanageable conflicts. Culture clashes, territorial disputes, and consequent difficulties in team building and providing incentives for collaboration across product groups, along with a limited consumer interest in one-stop shopping, were among the main obstacles to effective implementation. An April 1998 survey of 1,011 consumers by Synergistics Research Corporation of Atlanta, for example, found that only 15% had most of their household's financial accounts with a single institution, and only one in six looked favorably on one-stop shopping (*The American Banker*, 1998). It is still not clear, however, whether the 15% that had accounts at one financial institution were satisfied, and whether such customers were more attractive than the remaining 85% who conducted their business with multiple financial institutions.

One of the few empirical studies comparing the performance of diversified financial service companies with that of specialist companies found that the ROE and ROA earned by the former was, overall, below that earned by comparable specialist companies (Grant, 1992). The diversified companies in his study included American Express, BankAmerica, Citicorp, Merrill Lynch, Prudential, and Sears Roebuck. While the poor performance was not uniform across the group, not one of the diversified companies was able to outperform specialist companies on both ROE and ROA.

Despite the trend away from diversification in many other industries and the limited success of financial supermarkets, diversification has re-appeared in financial services in the mid- and late-90s, and shows no signs of letting up. My studies of U.S. and British banks suggest that it may be ill founded and at the very least bears critical examination.

3.4 U. S. and British Banks: Focus Beats Diversification[1]

In the US, notwithstanding regulatory constraints noted above, Citicorp and Chase both pursued a strategy of diversification in the 1970s and 80s, while Bankers Trust and JP Morgan were much more focused, niche players. Citicorp and Chase were heavily committed to both wholesale and retail banking, and Citicorp, in particular, committed itself to multiple financial services businesses. Bankers Trust and JP Morgan, by contrast, concentrated on wholesale banking, with both changing over to becoming primarily investment banks. Since Citicorp set a tone for the entire industry as a leading edge bank, its experiences are worth examining in more detail.

Citicorp's CEO for much of this period (1968-1984), Walter Wriston, reportedly wanted it to become a financial supermarket, just like American Express, Prudential, Sears, and Merrill Lynch. "If those guys can do it," he is reported to have said, "why can't we?" He pushed Citicorp to become an archetype in the US of the diversified, conglomerate bank, committed to growing its way out of trouble.

The direction he followed was to pursue five business clusters: individual (retail) banking, institutional (corporate) banking, investment banking, insurance, and the information systems business. Citicorp was heavily committed to all of them, moving from being primarily a wholesale New York bank in the mid 1960s, with roughly $16 billion in assets, 20,000 employees, and a single set of businesses to a highly diversified global giant in 1990, with assets of over $230 billion, 95,000 employees, and providing financial services in 92 nations. In doing so, it followed an entrepreneurial, prospector strategy of ambitious growth, pursuing the goal of 15% annual increase in gross profits. It became a first mover world-wide in many areas of banking: developing the negotiable certificate of deposit (CD) in 1960 to generate more funds; adopting the bank holding company device in 1967 to facilitate product expansion; investing earlier and more heavily than competitors in electronic communications technology in the 1960s and 70s; in global banking; consumer banking; the information business; and back office modernization.

These initiatives were supported by its highly decentralized, fluid organization, its vast meritocracy of talented MBAs, technologists, marketers, and international

---

[1] The following discussion is taken from Rogers (1993).

relations trained staff, its advanced technologies, and most importantly, its culture of entrepreneurship, high tolerance for mistakes, and internal competition. Wriston, through Citicorp, had dramatically changed the paradigm for commercial banking from that of a risk averse public utility to a high growth and diversification oriented institution.

By late 1990, reinforced by an economic recession, this paradigm had failed both at Citicorp and among its money center followers. Comparative data from Keefe, Bruyette & Woods, a firm specializing in bank research, indicated that among the 50 largest banks in 1990, Citicorp ranked forty-first in quality of loans, forty-third in profits, and fiftieth in risk-adjusted capital. An article in *Newsday* (1991) concluded: "Overall, no other New York bank fares as poorly." In 1989, for example, it ranked 32nd in overall performance ratings among the 35 biggest US bank holding companies; its ROE was 5%, and its share price was to decline from $34 to 8 ¾ a year later, as its non-performing loans, limited reserves, and capital adequacy problems became quite severe. (Salomon Brothers, Stock Research, 1989, and Rogers, 1993)

Along the way, Citicorp was registering enormous losses in the information business, investment banking, commercial real estate, and LDC and LBO loans. Quotron, its information services business, for example, had increasing losses every year from $34 million in 1986 when Citicorp acquired it to over $200 million in 1990. Federal Reserve examiners visited Citicorp on a regular basis in 1990 and for a time thereafter to push for a restoration of its past credit culture.

In sum, Citicorp's aggressive pursuit of growth, size, and diversification had gone well beyond its capacity to manage these businesses effectively. In several instances, e.g., Quotron in the information services business, ailing S&Ls, and Scrimmegour Vickers, the British brokerage house, the underlying businesses were so poor to begin with that this alone accounted for much of their poor performance, independent of the difficulties of integrating them to create synergies.

Miller (1992) refers to this trajectory of aggressive expansion run wild, of which Citicorp was a prototype, as exemplifying what he referred to as the Icarus paradox. Icarus, in the ancient Greek fable, wearing wings his father had fabricated, flew so close to the sun that it melted the wax that held the wings in place. He then plunged to his death in the Aegean Sea. The moral is that competitive strengths and the early success they bring may lead to failure if pushed too far.

The bigger point is that Citicorp was not an isolated case. It had set a standard toward which many large money-center banks had moved. Virtually all of them, including Chase, Chemical, Manufacturers Hanover, and BankAmerica, had experienced similar losses in pursuing a growth and diversification strategy.

In contrast, Bankers Trust and JP Morgan had both become very high performers in the late 80s and early 90s while pursuing a more focused, niche strategy. Both were almost exclusively wholesale investment banks, with literally no retail banking at all – Bankers Trust had sold its entire retail banking operation in the 1970s and early 80s, and JP Morgan had never entered retail banking.

A comparison of the financial performances of Bankers Trust and Morgan with those of Citicorp and Chase indicated just how much of a difference focus seemed to make. While Citicorp was floundering in the late 1980s, Bankers Trust ranked #1 among the 35 largest US bank holding companies in 1988 (Salomon Brothers, 1990). Its ROE moved from between 8% and 9% in the late 70s to 27% in 1990.

JP Morgan had a similarly strong comparative performance. It outperformed Citicorp and Chase on ROE, ROA, problem loans, and the Q ratio, which compares a firm's stock price to its book value. While the average Q ratio for the 35 biggest US banks in the 1980s was just over 100%, Morgan's was 121%, compared with Citicorp with 89% and Chase at 64% (Rogers, 1993).

On the other hand, it is important to note that both JP Morgan and Bankers Trust have experienced big losses in the late 1990s, particularly in securities trading and in their emerging markets businesses. This indicates that focus alone will not improve performance, if there are weaknesses in the underlying business. Related to these weaknesses, Bankers Trust was bought in late 1998 by Deutsche Bank, while much speculation has ensued in the financial press about JP Morgan needing a merger to survive as a significant player in wholesale global banking.

Nevertheless, further support for the strategic focus strategy came from the performance of the US super-regional banks, such as Bank One, Nations Bank, Wells Fargo, and First Union, whose primary business was domestic retail banking. They constituted the vast majority of highest performers among the top 35, far surpassing the money center banks in the 1980s on most indicators. In fact, in 1989, the top ten in overall performance ratings, as judged by the Salomon Brothers Stock Research group, were super-regional banks.

Another suggestive trend was that the comeback of the money center banks in the 1990s was associated with their exit from many weak businesses, thereby simplifying their portfolio. Citicorp was perhaps the most dramatic exemplar of the trend, as it phased out much of its investment banking (M&A, retail brokerage) and finally sold off Quotron.

My study of the four British clearing banks was designed to extend and perhaps further refine the limits of universal banking. These banks constituted what sociologists call a "strategic research site" because, unlike the US, Britain had been engaged in universal banking at least since Big Bang in 1986.

The history of these four banks since the 70s includes one dramatic success, Lloyds, perhaps an equally dramatic fall from grace, Midland, which had been the world's largest bank up through the 1950s, and at best, uneven performance by Barclays and NatWest. The latter two were by far the biggest of the clearers that had diversified into investment banking on a significant scale, and had experienced such big losses from those businesses that they exited from most of them by the end of 1997, essentially abandoning the quest to become universal banks.

The outlier among the four was Lloyds. Its CEO from 1983-1996, Sir Brian Pitman, and now board chair, broke the traditional paradigm of his British competitors who concentrated on size, product diversification, and global expansion by emphasizing instead strategic focus, simplicity, and particularly shareholder value. He became widely known as the visionary of British banking in the 80s and 90s. Under his leadership, Lloyds cut back drastically its international business, eliminated its investment banking, slashed operating costs, and focused overwhelmingly on UK retail banking.

Lloyds was a deviant case in two related respects. First, it moved relentlessly toward a simplified portfolio and institutional style. Second, its financial performance in the 90s far surpassed that of the others. Thus, over the 1990-95 period, Lloyds averaged an ROE of 21.5% compared with an average of only 12.8% for the five largest British banks. This high performance may be short-lived, since UK retailing, Lloyds' area of core competence, has become increasingly competitive, with such new non-bank entrants as the building societies (the UK's S&Ls), mass retailers, supermarkets, and high-tech firms. But the co-existence of Lloyds' focused or niche approach with its high performance seems at least suggestive of some deeper dynamic. To the extent that this focus strategy enables Lloyds to provide superior products and drive down costs and prices, its seemingly outstanding reputation among both shareholders and customers will continue.

Despite Lloyds' increasing focus, however, it did diversify. In 1989, it bought an insurance company, Abbey Life, a building society with a strong home mortgage business, Cheltenham and Gloucester, in 1995, and a savings bank, TSB, in 1996.

These acquisitions, however, were in UK retail banking, deepening the product line and, in the case of TSB, broadening the customer base. Thus, Lloyds moved from being a predominantly UK retail bank to becoming a diversified, retail financial services business.

Midland, the lowest performer, had so many internal problems—those of leadership, culture, and organization—that it could not be seen as a test of any strategy. During 1988–1993, for example, its average ROE after taxes was 4.80%, compared with Lloyds at 19.68%, NatWest at 6.82% and Barclays at 5.8% (Bloomberg, Financial Analysis). Midland had historically been a provincial bank, serving Britain's industrial heartland north of London, in Manchester and Birmingham. Though it moved its headquarters to London in the 1890s, it retained its provincial roots. When commercial banking globalized in the 1960s and 70s, Midland was a late and reluctant player, pursuing instead a correspondent and consortium approach to international banking. Trying to recoup from its late start, Midland made the ill-conceived purchase of Crocker Bank of San Francisco in 1980, sold Crocker in 1986 at a loss of roughly $1 billion, and did not recover from that debacle until 1992 when Hong Kong & Shanghai Bank Corporation (HSBC) bought it. Since then, under the tight, cost cutting controls of HSBC, Midland has been revived. Thus, its average ROE after taxes was up to 22.9% during 1994–1997, second only to Lloyds' 31.2% among the four clearers, and compared favorably with NatWest's 12.8% and Barclays' 19.8%. (Bloomberg, op. cit.)

The bigger story for our purposes is what happened to Barclays and NatWest. Often referred to as the supertankers of British banking, both invested heavily in investment banking after Big Bang, pursuing a global universal banking strategy. Both, however, suffered enormous losses in investment banking as they experienced major problems in understanding and controlling these businesses. As a result, these two banks sold off much of their investment banking in 1997 and 1998 respectively, particularly the equities and corporate advisory parts. With ROEs from investment banking in the single digits, and with enormous costs in technology and compensation in trying to keep up with competitors, their senior managers felt they could no longer justify to shareholders the pursuit of those businesses. In that sense, they adopted a strategy similar to Lloyds', only they did so ten years later.

The problem was that Barclays and NatWest, like their European universal banking competitors, did not have the capabilities (staff, managerial, technology, products, distribution, etc.) to compete with the US so-called "bulge bracket" investment banks. They always remained second-or third-tier players. In attempts to catch up with their US competitors by buying capabilities, they were forced to pay inflated salaries and bonuses to investment bankers, (only to lose many along the way), who preferred to move on to leading US firms. Required investments in technology were also steep. Thus, in what Professor Roy Smith of New York University's Stern School of Business refers to as his "Gorilla Tables", American banks constituted eight of the top ten global wholesale banks in market share at the end of 1997, with Barclays Capital and NatWest Markets finishing 19th and 20th respectively.

The internal problems of managing such universal banks were among the main contributors to the failure of Barclays and NatWest to break into the ranks of first tier players. First, the CEOs and most other senior managers were commercial bankers, knew little about managing investment banks, and consequently failed to introduce the kinds of controls necessary in those businesses. One result was big and often unexpected losses. Barclays, for example, had gained much acclaim from bank analysts for the risk management system its CEO, Martin Taylor, had introduced. Yet, it was devastated by $300 million losses in 1997 from its positions in the Long Term Capital Management hedge fund and with the devaluation of the Russian ruble. Taylor had even said shortly before becoming CEO in 1994 that no British bank had yet discovered the full secret of managing a commercial/investment bank. "These are relatively new kinds of organizations, and there's no template for them," he noted. How right he was.

NatWest's experience was at least as difficult. In early 1997, it acknowledged an 85 million pound ($125 million) loss from the mispricing of interest-rate options. This had resulted from a chain of failures over a two-year period that had involved several traders and had gone undetected. Whatever controls NatWest had instituted to monitor its investment bank, they were not working well enough to detect this series of transactions that later contributed to NatWest's decision to exit much of investment banking.

One lesson from the British experience is that diversification strategies are not a substitute for core competencies in the primary businesses that comprise such strategies. Ultimately, firms need to compete effectively in the many product markets in which they have a presence. Thus, the absence of basic capabilities at Barclays and NatWest, resulting in their woes, cannot in itself be an indictment of diversification strategies. Conversely, even if they did have the capabilities to compete successfully in each of the businesses they entered, there could be no hope for their success, since they also suffered from many internal problems of managing universal banks.

These British banks were not alone. The financial performance of the main European universal banks, as indicated above, has also been poor. They too exist as second and third tier players, with little likelihood of much improvement over the short term. Even in a bull market, they have had ROEs in single digits and have faced rapidly rising technology and compensation costs.

Deutsche Bank is another dramatic example. Despite its merger with Morgan Grenfell in 1989 and its stated goal of becoming a top global player in wholesale and investment banking, it only emerged at the end of 1997 as 15th in that group. Also, it had an ROE that year of only 6.4%. Its record with Morgan Grenfell included: many unresolved conflicts between investment and commercial bankers and subsequent investment banker defections; a fund management fraud leading to serious questions about internal controls; and constant reorganizations in which Morgan Grenfell was first kept autonomous and later integrated, causing much confusion and dissatisfaction among the investment bankers. Also, since that acquisition, Deutsche did much poaching of teams of investment bankers from top competitors for big compensation packages, leading its board "to worry that it was creating a monster of an investment bank, based on hugely expensive egos" (*The Economist*, 1998).

This experience has been repeated elsewhere. In a piece entitled "Out of Their League?", *The Economist* reported that Dredsner Kleinwort Benson faced much internal strife and earned little more than Deutsche Bank, and that Dutch-owned ING Barings as having experienced defections on such a scale as to leave its securities arm "on its knees" (*The Economist*, 1997).

3.5 Culture Conflicts Between Investment and Commercial Bankers

Perhaps the most significant obstacles to effectiveness in diversified commercial banks are the conflicts between commercial and investment bankers. Sociologists distinguish between white-collar professionals with more "local" and those with more "cosmopolitan" career orientations. Investment bankers are an extreme example of the latter. They often have minimal commitment to the firm where they are currently employed, they do not like to be managed, preferring instead as much autonomy as possible, and, as a corollary, they resist being melded into teams of collaborative financial services providers.

There have been investment banks where such teamwork and collegiality have existed, largely through supportive cultures. Goldman Sachs and Morgan Stanley are examples in the US, but they may well be the exceptions.

Instead, investment bankers are highly mobile, measuring their success in large part by the extent to which their present employer is providing compensation that at least matches, if not surpasses, that of the highest paying competitors. In an industry where firms are constantly bidding for the services of talented specialists, investment bankers have much leverage. They want the freedom to trade, do deals, and provide financial advice, with a minimum of interference, and they want to be compensated well, regardless of their performance in a given year.

The culture conflicts between commercial and investment bankers are particularly severe. The credit culture of commercial banking tends to be risk averse, emphasizing long-term relationships with corporate clients, more standard products, and a structured way of doing things. Major loan decisions are usually made through committees and only after systematic review by senior managers. Moreover, the amount of commercial bankers' compensation has traditionally been tied to level in the hierarchy, with little variation across people at a given level, and with bonuses constituting a small share.

Investment banking involves many more non-routine tasks and much creativity, for example, in putting together deals, providing advisory services, or structuring new hedging products. This makes investment bankers' contributions very different from those of clearing bankers. Investment banking operates much like the "professional bureaucracy", where the professionals carry out the main production activities and are subject to minimal managerial controls. They like to operate in flat, decentralized organizations, with minimal constraints on what they do. And many equate management with oppressive interference, making it even more difficult to monitor and regulate their behavior (Eccles and Crain, 1988).

Putting commercial and investment bankers together in the same teams to service particular institutional clients, when their cultures and work styles are so different, is very challenging. The fact that the investment bankers might earn 5 to 10 times what commercial bankers would earn, when bonuses were factored in, has made matters worse. Managing these relationships has understandably been problematic in commercial banks. Many started out by separating the two groups, in an effort to attract and retain able investment bankers and to facilitate their operations. Later, when there was much duplication between commercial and investment banking divisions in servicing corporate clients, and when there was increasing recognition within the bank of the importance of maintaining controls over the investment bankers, the two were often consolidated. Integrating the two businesses has been problematic as well, however, as investment bankers grew restless with increasing controls and as commercial bankers became more aware of the compensation differences between the two. It is not at all clear what organization design solutions are appropriate.

3.6 Contradictions in Universal Banking[2]

Reviewing the failures of financial conglomerates in the US, Britain, and Europe, a basic organizational contradiction inherent in the concept of universal banking and in its implementation may provide an explanation. That contradiction relates to the need for simultaneously maintaining both high levels of internal diversity or differentiation and of integration. Universal banking cannot work unless it brings together a wide variety of different businesses and product groups – commercial and investment banking, asset management, and insurance. Yet, each of these businesses exists in a different competitive environment and requires different skills. In brief, each has its own differentiated culture and must maintain that to be effective.

At the same time, universal banking can only work when there are synergies across these businesses. That, however, only takes place when the businesses are tightly coupled or linked. There is a need in that sense for the high performing universal bank to be a seamless organization that reduces transactions costs for customers and provides much cross selling

The problem is that no financial services institution to date has figured out how to make these two demands compatible. There is a need for the diversity of businesses and therefore of cultures. But that diversity is only a means to provide one-stop shopping opportunities for the consumer through extensive cross-selling. The managerial challenge is one of managing such diverse cultures in an integrated way.

The conflicts across these businesses are so great that the firms end up keeping them apart. That just increases agency costs, however, with each pursuing its own goals, following its own compensation practices, and maintaining its own culture. Seamless organizations that provide one-stop shopping do not develop from such separatism.

In brief, the centrifugal forces, or those of differentiation, are so strong that they prevent managers from fostering powerful enough centripetal or integrative ones to make universal banking work. The cultural integrity of each of the many financial services businesses contained in a single firm must be maintained for it to be effective. Yet, maintaining those differences makes it hard to bring them together to provide one-stop shopping. Furthermore, the fact that each of these businesses itself exists in a highly changing, uncertain market environment makes

---

[2] I am indebted to Professor Richard Freedman for insight on these matters.

the challenge of integration even more difficult, since they must keep adapting themselves to that changing environment to be effective.

3.7 The Future?

If the performance of such conglomerate banks is so poor, relative to that of more focused banks, why has consolidation continued? I referred earlier to the unreflective herd instinct so prevalent in the banking industry, and perhaps something analogous to that is operating in this instance. The history of commercial banking is replete with examples of strategic fads that bankers blindly followed, many of them bringing in their wake tremendous losses. If commercial bankers do not reflect more deeply on the implementation complexities of diversification, they may fall into one more black hole that will damage the future prospects of the industry.

Students of mergers have noted as well the benefits to top management from mergers, serving as another explanation for their prevalence. Salaries, power, and status of senior managers all grow with organization size, providing a strong incentive over the short run for bankers to continue with their merger activity (Grant, 1995).

The spread of the diversification strategy in financial services, despite its dubious contributions to profitability and shareholder value, merits much closer scrutiny than it has had in the past. Otherwise, commercial banking may experience even more jolts than it has had in the past, and face the prospect of many negative spillovers, both for the competitiveness of individual banks and of the nations in which they are embedded.

References

1. *The American Banker*, June 8, 1998, p. 6A.
2. Campbell, A. and K. S. Luchs, (eds). Strategic Synergy. Butterworth-Heinemann, London, 1992.
3. Dugas, C. and G. Steinmetz. John Reed of Citicorp: Can He Hold On? *Newsday*, July 7, 1991.
4. Eccles, R. G. and D. B. Crane. Doing Deals. Harvard Business School Press, Boston, MA, 1988.
5. *The Economist*, July 26, 1997, p. 67.
6. *The Economist*, November 28, 1998, p. 73.
7. Freedman, R. and J. Vohr. American Express, Stern School of Business, New York University, 1991.

8. Friedman, J. House of Cards: Inside the Troubled Empire of American Express. Pitman, New York, 1992.
9. Goold, M., Campbell, A., and Alexander, M. Corporate-Level Strategy. Wiley, New York, 1994.
10. Grant, R. M. Contemporary Strategy Analysis. Blackwell Business, Cambridge, MA, 1995.
11. Grant, R. M. Diversification in the Financial Services Industry. In Campbell, A. and K. S. Luchs, (eds). Strategic Synergy. Butterworth-Heinemann, London, 1992.
12. Markides, C. C. Diversification, Refocusing, and Economic Performance. MIT Press, Cambridge, MA, 1995.
13. Miller, D. The Icarus Paradox: How Exceptional Companies Bring About Their Own Downfall. Harper Business, New York, 1990.
14. Peters, T. and Waterman, R. In Search of Excellence. Harper & Row, New York, 1982.
15. Pilloff, S. and A. Santomero. The Value Effects of Bank Mergers and Acquisitions. Presented at the Conference on Mergers of Financial Institutions, New York University Salomon Center, Stern School of Business, in association with New York University Law School, Center for the Study of Central Banks, October 11, 1996.
16. Rogers, D. The Future of American Banking. McGraw Hill, New York, 1993.
17. Rogers, D. The Big Four British Banks: Organization, Strategy and The Future. Macmillan, London, 1999.
18. Rumelt, R. Diversification Strategy and Profitability. *Strategic Management Journal*, 3, 1982, pp. 359-370.
19. Salomon Brothers. Stock Research. A Review of Bank Performance: 1990 Edition, pp. 31-32.
20. Williams, J. R., B. L. Paez, and L. Sanders. Conglomerates Revisited. *Strategic Management Journal*, 9, 1988, pp. 403-414.

Chapter 4

Universal Banking: A Shareholder Value Perspective[1]

Ingo Walter
New York University

4.1 Introduction

In their historical development, organizational structure, and strategic direction, universal banks constitute multi-product firms within the financial services sector. Certainly within their home environments, universal banks effectively target most or all client-segments, and make an effort to provide each with a full range of the appropriate financial services. Outside the home market, they usually adopt a narrower competitive profile, in the majority of cases focusing on wholesale banking and securities activities as well as international private banking—occasionally building a retail presence in foreign environments as well.

This stylized profile of universal banks presents shareholders with an amalgam of more or less distinct businesses that are linked-together in a complex network that draws on a set of centralized financial, information, human and organizational resources—a profile that tends to be extraordinarily difficult to manage in a way that achieves an optimum use of invested capital. The key issue for the investor is whether shares in a universal bank represent an attractive asset-allocation alternative from the perspective of both risk-adjusted total-return and portfolio-

---

[1]Based on Ingo Walter, "Universal Banking: A Shareholder Value Perspective," European Management Journal, August 1997.

efficiency. The answer to this question influences a universal bank's cost of capital and its performance against rivals with a narrower business focus.

This chapter considers these issues within a simple conceptual framework. We begin by adding to presumptive adjusted book value of a universal bank's equity a number of building blocks that ultimately determine the market value of its equity. We then ask whether that market value of equity is in fact the *maximum* value attainable from the perspective of the shareholder. Finally, we outline some of the strategic and tactical alternatives, inside and outside the bank, that are open to management to achieve a hypothetical maximum value of shareholder equity. Any empirical evidence available in the literature is discussed as appropriate.

4.2 Structure of the Universal Bank

Universal banking organizations may take a number of more or less distinct forms.[2] These are stylized in Exhibit 1 below.

- A fully integrated universal bank (Type-A) provides a broad range of financial services (banking, securities and insurance) under a single corporate structure supported by a single capital base. There are, at present, no good examples of this particular model.

- A partially integrated universal bank (Type-B) conducts both commercial and investment banking within the same entity, but undertakes insurance underwriting and distribution, mortgage banking, asset management, lease-financing, factoring, management consulting, and other specialized activities through separately-capitalized subsidiaries, either because such activities are separately regulated, or because they involve significant potential for exploitation of conflicts of interest, or a combination of such factors. Deutsche Bank is a good example of this type of universal banking structure.

- In a Type-C universal bank, the commercial bank, whose core business is taking deposits and making commercial loans, is the parent of subsidiaries engaged in a variety of other financial services ranging from investment banking to insurance. An example is Barclays Bank.

- A final universal banking structure (Type-D) involves creation of a holding company which controls affiliates engaged in commercial banking, investment banking, insurance, and possibly other types of financial and non-financial businesses. Examples include J.P. Morgan and CS Holding.

---

[2]For a detailed discussion, see Saunders and Walter [1994].

Exhibit 1: Universal Bank Organization Structures

Type-A: FULL INTEGRATION

UNIVERSAL BANK

Bank Activities	Securities Activities	Insurance Activities	Other

Type-B: PARTIAL INTEGRATION

UNIVERSAL BANK

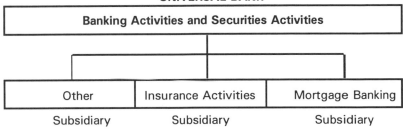

Banking Activities and Securities Activities		
Other	Insurance Activities	Mortgage Banking
Subsidiary	Subsidiary	Subsidiary

Type-C: BANK PARENT STRUCTURE

UNIVERSAL BANK

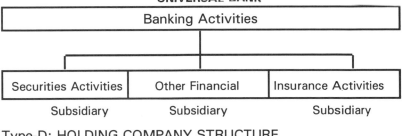

Banking Activities		
Securities Activities	Other Financial	Insurance Activities
Subsidiary	Subsidiary	Subsidiary

Type-D: HOLDING COMPANY STRUCTURE

HOLDING COMPANY

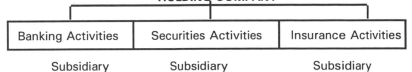

Banking Activities	Securities Activities	Insurance Activities
Subsidiary	Subsidiary	Subsidiary

The specific structures that universal banks adopt are driven by regulatory considerations, by the production-function characteristic of financial services, and by demand-side issues relating to market structure and client preferences. American regulation, for example, mandates a Type-D form of organization, with the Glass-Steagall provisions of the Banking Act of 1933 for over 60 years requiring separation of banking (taking deposits and extending commercial loans) and most types of securities activities (underwriting and dealing in corporate debt and equities and their derivatives, as well as state and local revenue bonds). Each type of business must be carried out through separately capitalized subsidiaries, and there are strict "firewalls" between them. U.S. bank holding companies have also been enjoined from most types of insurance underwriting and distribution. British universal banking follows the Type-C model, with securities and insurance activities carried out via subsidiaries of the bank itself. Most continental European countries seem to follow the Type-B model, with full integration of banking and securities activities within the bank itself (despite functional regulation), and insurance, mortgage banking and other specialized financial and non-financial activities carried out through subsidiaries. As noted, the Type-A universal banking model, with all activities carried out within a single corporate entity, seems not to exist even in environments characterized by a monopoly regulator such as, for example, the Monetary Authority of Singapore.

From a production-function perspective, the structural form of universal banking appears to depend on the ease with which operating efficiencies and scale and scope economies can be exploited—determined in large part by product and process technologies—and the comparative organizational effectiveness in optimally satisfying client requirements and bringing to bear market power.[3]

4.3 From Book Value of Equity to Market Value of Equity

Realization of shareholder value can begin by tracing the sources of value-increments in excess of book value of equity (BVE). For universal banks, the BVE is the sum of: (1) the par value of shares when originally issued; (2) the surplus paid by investors when the shares were issued; (3) retained earnings; and (4) reserves set aside for loan losses [Saunders, 1996]. Depending on the prevailing regulatory and accounting system, BVE must be increased by unrealized capital gains associated with assets such as equity holdings carried on the books of the bank at historical cost and their prevailing replacement values (hidden reserves), as well as the

---

[3] *In this context, Switzerland presents an interesting case study, with the three major universal banks operating under a single set of domestic regulatory parameters having adopted rather different structural forms in the past but with more recent signs of substantial convergence.*

replacement values of other assets and liabilities that differ materially from historical values due to credit and market risk considerations, i.e., their mark-to-market values.

We thus have the presumptive adjusted book value of equity (ABVE), which is not normally revealed in bank financial statements due to a general absence of market-value accounting across broad categories of universal banking activities—with the exception of trading-account securities, derivatives and open foreign exchange positions, for example.

As in non-financial firms such as McDonalds, Coca-Cola or any other publicly traded firm, shareholder interests in a universal bank are tied to the market value of its equity (MVE)—the number of shares outstanding times the prevailing market price. MVE normally should be significantly in excess of ABVE, reflecting as it does current and expected future net earnings, adjusted for risk. The MVE/ABVE so-called "Q" ratio can, however, be either higher or lower than 1, and is clearly susceptible to enhancement through managerial or shareholder action. If it is significantly below 1, for example, it may be that breaking-up the bank can serve the interests of shareholders—if ABVE or more can be realized as a result—in the same way as restructurings have raised shareholder value under appropriate circumstances in industrial companies.

Assuming a universal bank's MVE exceeds ABVE, what factors can explain the difference? Exhibit 2, begins with ABVE and sequentially identifies incremental-value sources, which are explained in the following sections, to arrive at MVE.

4.4 Economies of Scale

Whether economies of scale exist in financial services has been at the heart of strategic and regulatory discussions about optimum firm size in the financial services sector. Can increased size increase shareholder value? In an information-and distribution-intensive industry with high fixed costs, such as financial services, there should be ample potential for scale economies, as well as potential for diseconomies of scale attributable to administrative overhead, agency problems and other cost factors once very large firm-size is reached. If economies of scale prevail, increased size will help create shareholder value. If diseconomies prevail, shareholder value will be destroyed.

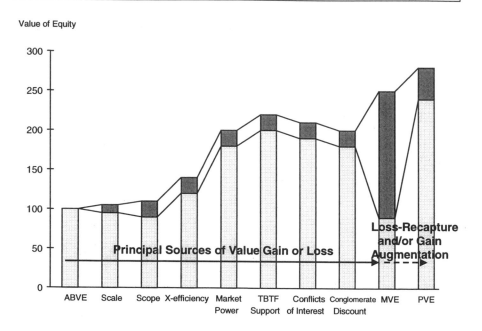

Exhibit 2: Book, Market and Potential Equity Values in Universal Banks

Large banks themselves vary greatly in asset size, ranging among the world's top-100 at year-end 1995, for example, from BancOne's $91 billion (ranked 95th) to Chase Manhattan's $121 billion (ranked 70th), J.P. Morgan's $185 billion (ranked 47th), Union Bank of Switzerland's $235 billion (ranked 16th), Deutsche Bank's $502 billion (ranked 4th) and Mitsubishi-Tokyo's $723 billion, ranked first. Bankers regularly argue that "bigger is better" from a shareholder value perspective, and usually point to economies of scale as a major reason why.

4.5 Economies of Scope

There should also be ample potential for economies and diseconomies of scope in the financial services sector from either supply- or demand-side linkages.[4] On the supply side, scope economies relate to cost-savings through sharing of overheads and improving technology through joint production of generically similar groups

---

[3]This market-profile can be depicted as covering the full state-space of the domestic arena of the C-A-P taxonomy presented in Walter [1988] and using that as a platform to target a narrower range of (usually wholesale) financial services and clients in offshore and national markets abroad.

of services. Supply-side diseconomies of scope may arise from such factors as inertia and lack of responsiveness and creativity that may come with increased firm size and bureaucratization, "turf" and profit-attribution conflicts that increase costs or erode product quality in meeting client needs, or serious cultural differences across the organization that inhibit seamless delivery of a broad range of financial services.

On the demand side, economies of scope (cross-selling) arise when the all-in cost to the buyer of multiple financial services from a single supplier—including the price of the service, plus information, search, monitoring, contracting and other transaction costs—is less than the cost of purchasing them from separate suppliers. Demand-related diseconomies of scope could arise, for example, through agency costs that may develop when the multi-product financial firm acts against the interests of the client in the sale of one service in order to facilitate the sale of another, or as a result of internal information-transfers considered inimical to the client's interests. Management of universal banks often argue that broader product and client coverage, and the increased throughput volume this makes possible, represents shareholder-value enhancement.

Network economies associated with universal banking may be considered a special type of demand-side economy of scope. [Economides, 1995] Like telecommunications, banking relationships with end-users of financial services represent a network structure wherein additional client linkages add value to existing clients by increasing the feasibility or reducing the cost of accessing them—so-called "network externalities" which tend to increase with the absolute size of the network itself. Every client link to the bank potentially "complements" every other one and thus potentially adds value through either one-way or two-way exchanges though incremental information or access to liquidity. The size of network benefits depends on technical compatibility and coordination in time and location, which the universal bank is in a position to provide. And networks tend to be self-reinforcing in that they require a minimum critical mass and tend to grow in dominance as they increase in size, thus precluding perfect competition in network-driven financial services. This characteristic is evident in activities such as securities clearance and settlement, global custody, funds transfer and international cash management, forex and securities dealing, and the like. Networks tend to lock-in users insofar as switching-costs tend to be relatively high, creating the potential for significant market power.

4.6 X-efficiency

Besides economies of scale and scope, it seems likely that universal banks of roughly the same size and providing roughly the same range of services may have very different cost levels per unit of output. There is ample evidence of such performance differences, for example, in comparative cost-to-income ratios among banks both within and between national financial-services markets. The reasons involve efficiency-differences in the use of labor and capital, effectiveness in the sourcing and application of available technology, and perhaps effectiveness in the acquisition of productive inputs, organizational design, compensation and incentive systems—and just plain better management.

X-efficiency may be related to size if, for example, large organizations are differentially capable of the massive and "lumpy" capital outlays required to install and maintain the most efficient information-technology and transactions-processing infrastructures. Exhibit 3 shows information technology spend-levels that only large banks can afford. If such spend-levels result in higher X-efficiency, then large banks will gain in competition relative to smaller ones from a shareholder-value perspective. However, smaller organizations ought to be able to pool their resources or outsource in order to capture similar efficiencies. From a shareholder-value point of view, management is (or should be) under constant pressure though their boards of directors to do better, to maximize X-efficiency in their organizations, and to transmit this pressure throughout the enterprise.

Exhibit 3: Information Technology Spending Levels

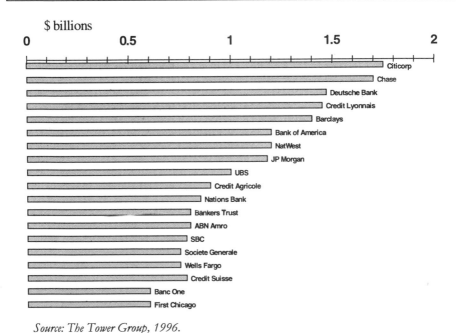

Source: The Tower Group, 1996.

4.7 Empirical Evidence of Economies of Scale, Scope and X-efficiency

What is the evidence regarding economies of scale, economies of scope and X-efficiency with regard to bank performance?

Individually or in combination, economies (diseconomies) of scale and scope in universal banks will either be captured as increased (decreased) profit margins or passed along to clients in the form of lower (higher) prices resulting in a gain (loss) of market share. They should be directly observable in cost functions of financial services suppliers and in aggregate performance measures.

Studies of scale and scope economies in financial services are unusually problematic. The nature of the empirical tests used, the form of the cost functions, the existence of unique optimum output levels, and the optimizing behavior of financial firms all present difficulties. Limited availability and conformity of data also present serious empirical problems. Moreover, the conclusions of any study that has detected (or failed to detect) economies of scale and/or scope in a sample selection of financial institutions do not necessarily have general applicability.

Many such studies have been undertaken in the banking, insurance and securities industries over the years (see Exhibit 4). Estimated cost functions form the basis of most of these empirical tests, virtually all of which have found that economies of scale are achieved with increases in size among small banks (below $100 million in asset size). More-recent studies have shown that scale economies may also exist in banks falling into the $100 million to $5 billion range. There is very little evidence so far of scale economies in the case of banks larger than $5 billion. An examination of the world's 200 largest banks [Saunders and Walter, 1994] found evidence that the very largest banks grew more slowly than their smaller peers among the large banks during the 1980s, but that limited economies of scale did appear among the banks included in the study. Overall, the consensus seems to be that scale economies and diseconomies do not result in more than about a 5% difference in unit costs. So, for most universal banks, scale economies seem to have relatively little bearing on shareholder value in terms of Exhibit 2.

With respect to supply-side economies of scope, most empirical studies have failed to find such gains in the banking, insurance and securities industries, and most of them have also concluded that some diseconomies of scope are encountered when firms in the financial services sector add new product-ranges to their portfolios. Saunders and Walter [1994], for example, found negative supply-side economies of scope among the world's 200 largest banks—as the product range widens, unit costs seem to go up.

Exhibit 4: Economies of Scale and Scope in Financial Services Firms—The Evidence

Study	Economies of Scale Beyond Small Levels of Output (size)	Economies of Scope among Outputs
Domestic Banks		
Benston et al., 1983	No	No
Berger et al., 1987	No	No
Gilligan and Smirlock, 1984	No	Yes
Gilligan, Smirlock, and Marshall, 1984	No	Yes
Kolari and Zardkoohi, 1987	No	No
Lawrence, 1989	No	Yes
Lawrence and Shay, 1986	No	No
Mester, 1990	Yes	No
Noulas et al, 1990	Yes	?
Shaffer, 1988	Yes	?
Hunter et. al., 1990	Yes	No
McAllister and McManus, 1993	No	?
Pulley and Humphrey, 1993	?	Yes
Foreign Banks		
Yoshika and Nakajima, 1987 (Japan)	Yes	?
Kim, 1987 (Israel)	Yes	Yes
Saunders and Walter, 1991 (Worldwide)	Yes	No
Rothenberg, 1994 (Eur. Community)	No	?
Thrifts		
Mester, 1987	No	No
LeCompte and Smith, 1990	No	No
Life Insurance		
Fields and Murphy, 1989	˙Yes	No
Fields, 1988	No	?
Grace and Timme, 1992	Yes	?
Securities Firms		
Goldberg et al., 1991	No	No

Source: Saunders, A., 1996.

As shown in Exhibit 4, scope economies in most other cost studies of the financial services industry are either trivial or negative. However, the period covered by many of these studies involved institutions that were rapidly shifting away from a pure focus on commercial banking, and may thus have incurred considerable costs in expanding the range of their activities. If this diversification effort involved significant sunk costs, which were expensed on the accounting statements during the period under study, undertaken to achieve future expansion of market-share or increases in fee-based areas of activity, then we might expect to see any strong statistical evidence of diseconomies of scope between lending and non-lending activities reversed in future periods. If the banks' investment in staffing, training, and infrastructure in fact bear returns in the future commensurate with these expenditures, then neutrality or positive economies of scope may well exist. Still, the available evidence remains inconclusive.

It is also reasonable to suggest that some demand-related scope economies may exist, but that these are likely to be very specific to the types of services provided and the types of clients involved. Strong cross-selling potential may exist for retail and private clients between banking, insurance and asset management products (one-stop shopping), for example. Yet such potential may be totally absent between trade-finance and mergers and acquisitions advisory services for major corporate clients. So demand-related scope economies are clearly linked to a universal bank's specific strategic positioning across clients, products and geographic areas of operation [Walter, 1988]. Indeed, a principal objective of strategic positioning in universal banking is to link market-segments together in a coherent pattern—what might be termed "strategic integrity"—that permits maximum exploitation of cross-selling opportunities, and the design of incentives and organizational structures to ensure that such exploitation actually occurs.

With respect to X-efficiency, a number of authors have found very large disparities in cost structures among banks of similar size, suggesting that the way banks are run is more important than their size or the selection of businesses that they pursue [Berger, Hancock and Humphrey, 1993; Berger, Hunter and Timme, 1993]. The consensus of studies conducted in the United States seems to be that average unit costs in the banking industry lie some 20% above "best practice" firms producing the same range and volume of services, with most of the difference attributable to operating economies rather than differences in the cost of funds [Akhavein, Berger and Humphrey, 1996]. Siems [1996] finds that the greater the overlap in branch-office networks, the higher the abnormal equity returns in U.S. bank mergers, while no such abnormal returns are associated with increasing concentration levels in the regions where the bank mergers occurred. This suggests that shareholder value in the mega-mergers of the 1990s was more associated with increases of X-efficiency than with reductions in competition.

Specifically with respect to X-efficiency in universal banking, Steinherr [1996] has assessed the profit performance and earnings variability of segmented and universal financial institutions worldwide during the late 1980s. Segmented and universal banks are found to have achieved roughly the same profit levels, but universal banks were found to have both lower cost levels and (interestingly) lower credit losses, which the author attributed to better monitoring of their clients based on private (non-public) information that universal banks may enjoy over their segmented counterparts. One explanation for this finding may be that *Hausbank* relationships, which represent an important aspect of universal banking in some countries, include the periodic conversion of bank debt to equity as part of credit workouts of non-financial clients in trouble, thus obviating the need to realize the full extent of credit losses.

Taken together, these studies suggest very limited scope for cost economies of scale and scope among major universal banks. Scope economies, to the extent they exist, are likely to be found mainly on the demand side, and tend to apply very differently to different client segments. It is X-efficiency that seems to be the principal determinant of observed differences in cost levels among banks.

Perhaps contrary to conventional wisdom, therefore, there appears to be room in financial systems for viable financial services firms that range from large to small and from universal to specialist in a rich mosaic of institutions, as against a competitive landscape populated exclusively by 800-pound gorillas.

4.8 Absolute Size and Market Power

Still, conventional wisdom may win out in the end if large universal banks are able to extract economic rents from the market by application of market power—an issue that most empirical studies have not yet examined. Indeed, in many national markets for financial services, suppliers have shown a tendency towards oligopoly but may be prevented by regulation or international competition from fully exploiting monopoly positions. Financial services market structures differ widely among countries, as measured for example by the Herfindahl-Hirshman index,[5] with very high levels of concentration in countries such as the Netherlands and Denmark and low levels in relatively fragmented financial systems such as the United States. Lending margins and financial services fees, for example, tend to be positively associated with higher concentration levels. So do cost-to-income ratios. Shareholders naturally tend to gain from the former, and lose from the latter.

Certainly in global wholesale banking, there is very little evidence so far that size, as conventionally measured, makes much difference in determining market share. Of the 1998 top 10 firms in terms of fixed-income and equity underwriting, loan

---

[5]*The Herfindahl-Hirshman index is the sum of the squares of market shares based on, for example, deposits, assets, or capital and is given by $H=\Sigma s^2$. If market shares are expressed in percentage points, $0<H<10,000$. H rises as the number of competitors declines and as market-share concentration rises among the largest firms among a given number of competitors.*

syndications and M&A mandates, only one, Credit Suisse/First Boston, is a universal bank (see Exhibits 5 and 6). This has been the case for over a decade. Still, there are plenty of universal banks in the top-20 and virtually all have a stated objective of top-10 status in the next five or ten years. This suggests a hypercompetitive global wholesale market, prevailing well into the future, as universal banks and more specialized independent investment banks struggle for position in dealing with increasingly sophisticated wholesale issuer and investor clients, and with the emergence of a highly profitable "global bulge bracket" — limited to the privileged few—far less than a sure-thing. So shareholders of universal banks looking for large risk-adjusted excess returns from their global wholesale banking operations would do well to fasten their seat belts. On the other hand, major universal banks may also be in a better position to lobby for favorable regulatory structures, so that it is not only competitive *structure* but also competitive *conduct* that may turn out to be favorable to their shareholders. This was seen in the impact on market-to-book values of British banks after the U.K. clearing cartel was created in the 1920s, followed by market-to-book value erosion after the cartel was abolished in the 1970s. Differences in competitive structure are also illustrated in Exhibit 7, which compares the price-to-book ratios of U.S. money center banks to major regional banks, with the latter operating in substantially less competitive markets than the former.

4.9 The Value of Income-Stream Diversification

Saunders and Walter [1994] carried out a series of simulated mergers between U.S. banks, securities firms and insurance companies in order to test the stability of earnings of the "merged" as opposed to separate institutions. They evaluated the "global" opportunity-set of potential mergers between existing money-center banks, regional banks, life insurance companies, property and casualty insurance companies and securities firms, and the risk-characteristics of each possible combination. The results were reported in terms of the average standard deviation of returns, along with the returns and risk calculated for the minimum-risk portfolio of activities. Their findings suggest that there are potential risk-reduction gains from diversification in universal financial services organizations, and that these gains increase with the number of activities undertaken.

Exhibit 5: Global Wholesale Banking and Investment Banking, 1998

Firm (a)	Global Securities Underwriting & Private Placement (b)	Global M&A Advisory (c)	International Bank Loans Arranged	Medium Term Notes Lead Managed (d)	Total	% of Top 25
Goldman Sachs	388.8	1,067.3	16.4	54.4	1,526.8	13.9%
Merrill Lynch	549.8	692.9	11.0	129.6	1,383.3	12.6%
Morgan Stanley	404.5	635.6		32.7	1,072.8	9.8%
Citigroup	366.3	483.8	107.6	51.4	1,009.1	9.2%
CS First Boston	290.5	431.8	19.1	60.2	801.5	7.3%
JP Morgan	250.1	324.2	115.7	27.5	717.4	6.5%
Chase	122.6	172.9	307.1	20.4	623.0	5.7%
Lehman Brothers	264.3	225.4	26.3	49.0	565.0	5.1%
Deutsche Bank/BT	158.7	147.9	53.8	84.4	444.8	4.1%
UBS	201.8	143.7	17.0	53.8	416.3	3.8%
Bank of America	58.0	83.7	200.1	42.3	384.0	3.5%
Bear Stearns	140.6	184.8		17.6	343.0	3.1%
DLJ	111.5	217.6	12.6		341.7	3.1%
ABN AMRO	127.1	34.1	16.3	125.3	302.8	2.8%
Paribas/Soc. Gen.	153.6	54.5		11.4	219.5	2.0%
Lazard Houses		160.8			160.8	1.5%
Barclays Capital	81.2		14.5	6.4	102.1	0.9%
Dresdner Kleinwort	54.6	37.4		8.3	100.3	0.9%
Rothschild Group		84.3			84.3	0.8%
Nomura Securities	59.0			14.6	73.6	0.7%
Schroder Group		69.2			69.2	0.6%
BankBoston		49.9	19.1		69.1	0.6%
First Union	25.0		21.6	20.0	66.6	0.6%
PaineWebber	57.6				57.6	0.5%
HSBC	57.3				57.3	0.5%
Top 25 Firms	3,922.9	5,301.6	958.1	809.2	10,991.9	
Top 10 as % of Top 25	**76.4%**	**81.6%**	**70.3%**	**69.6%**	**77.9%**	
Top 20 as % of Top 25	**96.4%**	**97.8%**	**95.8%**	**97.5%**	**97.1%**	

(a) *Full credit to book running manager only. All values, except percentages, in $ billions.*
(b) *Global rankings, top 25 completed deals only, including all U.S. private placements.*
(c) *By market value of completed global transactions, equal credit to both advisors if acting jointly.*
(d) *Equal credit to both book runners if acting jointly.*
Data: Securities Data Corp.

Exhibit 6: Global Wholesale Banking—Market Concentration

	1990	1991	1992	1993	1994	1995	1996	1997	1998
Top Ten									
% of Market	40.6	46.1	56.0	64.2	62.1	59.5	55.9	72.0	77.9
Herfindahl Index	172	231	328	459	434	403	465	572	716
No. of firms from:									
USA	5	7	5	9	9	9	8	8	7
Europe	5	3	5	1	1	1	2	2	3
Japan	0	0	0	0	0	0	0	0	0
Top Twenty									
% of Market			80.5	75.6	78.1	76.0	81.2	93.3	97.1
Herfindahl Index			393	478	481	440	518	621	764
No. of firms from:									
USA			8	15	15	14	14	13	11
Europe			11	4	5	5	6	7	8
Japan			1	1	0	1	0	0	1

Exhibit 7: Price to Book Ratios of U.S. Money-Center and Major Regional Banks

	3Q/96	2Q/96	1Q/96	4Q/95	3Q95
Money Center Banks					
Average	**191**	**166**	**165**	**152**	**150**
BankAmerica	172	159	151	134	135
Bank of Boston	222	170	163	153	173
Bankers Trust	157	138	135	124	123
Chase Manhattan	196	169	170	155	137
Citicorp	246	214	216	186	174
First Chicago	183	149	161	150	149
JP Morgan	164	162	160	159	156
Major Regional Banks					
Average	**221**	**188**	**217**	**205**	**199**
BancOne	219	178	185	179	179
Corestates Financial	258	219	220	226	229
First Union	218	193	187	179	153
Fleet Financial	200	169	187	174	144
Nations Bank	199	181	174	147	158
Norwest Corp.	276	228	250	229	225
Wells Fargo	177	150	313	299	308

Source: Goldman Sachs & Co., 1996.

The main risk-reduction gains appear to arise from combining commercial banking with insurance activities, rather than with securities activities.[6] In the two-activity case, the best (lowest risk) merger partners for U.S. money-center banks were property and casualty insurers. In the three-activity case, the lowest-risk merger combination turned out to be between money center banks, regional banks and property and casualty insurers. In the full five-activity case (an average of 247,104 potential merger combinations among financial firms in the database), the standard deviation of returns was .01452, well below the average risk level for money center banks (.02024) on a stand-alone basis.[7]

Such studies, of course, may exaggerate the risk-reduction benefits of universal banking because they ignore many of the operational costs involved in setting up these activities.[8] Moreover, to the extent that these *ex-post* risk measures reflect existing central-bank safety nets, they may underestimate the *ex-ante* risk in the future. At best, such results may be viewed as illustrative of the risk-reduction potential of universal banking.[9] It seems unlikely that the diversification benefits in terms of risk-reduction outweigh the negative earnings implications of less-than-optimum intra-firm capital allocation from the perspective of universal bank shareholders.

4.10 Access to Bailouts

It is certainly possible that the purported advantages of universal banking structures can result in a competitive landscape dominated by a small number of large institutions. In such a case, failure of one major institution is likely to cause unacceptable systemic problems, and the institution will be bailed-out by taxpayers —as has happened in the case of comparatively much smaller institutions in the United States, Switzerland, Norway, Sweden, Finland, and Japan during the 1980s and early 1990s. If this turns out to be the case, then Too-Big-To-Fail ("TBTF") guarantees create a potentially important public subsidy for universal banking organizations and therefore implicitly benefit the institutions' shareholders.

---

[6] *Boyd, Graham and Hewitt (1990) using a similar methodological approach have reached much the same conclusions.*

[7] *Boyd, Graham and Hewitt (1990) using a similar methodological approach have reached much the same conclusions.*

[8] *That is, only the financial firms in existence for the full 1984-88 period are considered.*

[9] *However, White (1986) has shown that there were actual risk-diversification gains to banks' engaging in securities activities via affiliates (pre-1933 in the U.S.), i.e., before the Glass-Steagall Act of 1933 required a separation of commercial banking from investment banking (securities activities).*

On the other hand, "free lunches" usually don't last too long, and sooner or later such guarantees invariably come with strings attached. Possible reactions include intensified regulation of credit- and market-risk exposures, stronger supervision and surveillance intended to achieve early closure in advance of capital depletion, and structural barriers to force activities into business units that can be effectively supervised in accordance with their functions even at the cost of lower levels of X-efficiency and scope economies. The speed with which the central banks and regulatory authorities reacted to the 1996 Sumitomo copper trading scandal signaled the possibility of safety-net support of the global copper market, in view of major banks' massive exposures in highly complex structured credits. The fact is that Too-Big-To-Fail guarantees are alive and well for all large banks—not only universal banks—as is public concern about what restrictions on bank activities ought to accompany them.

4.11 Conflicts of Interest

The potential for conflicts of interest is endemic in universal banking, and runs across the various types of activities in which the bank is engaged. The matrix presented in Exhibit 8 provides a simple framework for a taxonomy of conflicts of interest that may arise across the broad range of activities engaged in by universal banks. The major types of conflicts include the following:[10]

- *Salesman's stake.* When banks have the power to sell affiliates' products, managers will no longer dispense "dispassionate" advice to clients. Instead, they will have a salesman's stake in pushing "house" products, possibly to the disadvantage of the customer.

- *Stuffing fiduciary accounts.* A bank that is acting as an underwriter and is unable to place the securities in a public offering—and is thereby exposed to a potential underwriting loss—may seek to ameliorate this loss by "stuffing" unwanted securities into accounts managed by its investment department over which the bank has discretionary authority.

- *Tie-ins.* A bank may use its lending power activities to coerce or tie-in a customer to the "securities products" sold by its securities unit. For example, it may threaten to credit-ration the customer unless it purchases certain investment banking services.

- *Third-party loans.* To ensure that an underwriting goes well, a bank may make below-market loans to third-party investors on condition that this finance is used to purchase securities underwritten by its securities unit.

---

[10]*For a detailed discussion, see Saunders & Walter [1994], Chapter 6.*

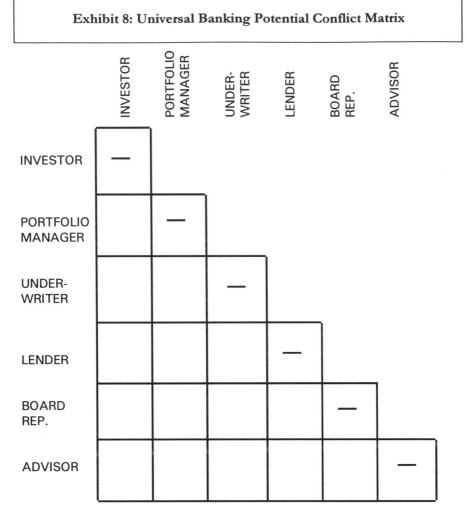

Exhibit 8: Universal Banking Potential Conflict Matrix

- *Bankruptcy-risk transfer.* A bank with a loan outstanding to a firm whose bankruptcy risk has increased, to the private knowledge of the banker, may have an incentive to induce the firm to issue bonds or equities—underwritten by its securities unit—to an unsuspecting public. The proceeds of such an issue could then be used to pay-down the bank loan. In this case the bank has transferred debt-related risk from itself to outside investors, while it simultaneously earns a fee and/or spread on the underwriting.[11]

---

[11] *A recent example is the 1995 underwriting of a secondary equity issue of the Hafnia Insurance Group by Den Danske Bank, distributed heavily to retail investors, with proceeds allegedly used to pay-down bank loans even as Hafnia slid into bankruptcy. This case is now before the courts. See Smith and Walter [1997B].*

- *Information transfer.* In acting as a lender, a bank may become privy to certain material inside information about a customer or its rivals that can be used in setting prices or helping in the distribution of securities offerings underwritten by its securities unit. This type of information-flow could work in the other direction as well—i.e., from the securities unit to the bank.

Mechanisms to control conflicts of interest—or more precisely, disincentives to exploit such conflicts—may be either market-based, regulation-based, or some combination of the two. Most universal banking systems seem to rely on market disincentives to prevent exploitation of opportunities for conflicts of interest. The United States has had a tendency since the 1930s to rely on regulations, and in particular on "walls" between types of activities. In most countries, however, few impenetrable walls exist between banking and securities departments within the universal bank, and few external firewalls exist between a universal bank and its non-bank subsidiaries (e.g., insurance).[12] Internally, there appears to be a primary reliance on the loyalty and professional conduct of bank employees, both with respect to the institution's long-term survival and the best interests of its customers. Externally, reliance appears to be placed on market reputation and competition as disciplinary mechanisms. The concern of a bank for its reputational "franchise" and fear of competitors are viewed as enforcing a degree of control over the potential for conflict exploitation.

Shareholders clearly have a stake in the management and control of conflicts of interest in universal banks. They can benefit from conflict-exploitation in the short term to the extent that business volumes and/or margins are increased as a result. On the one hand, preventing conflicts of interest is an expensive business. Compliance systems are costly to maintain, and various types of walls between business units can have high opportunity costs because of inefficient use of information within the organization. Externally, reputation losses associated with conflicts of interest can bear on shareholders very heavily indeed, as demonstrated by a variety of recent "accidents" in the financial services industry. It could well be argued that conflicts of interest might contribute to the MVE/ABVE ratios of universal banks falling below those of non-universal financial institutions.[13]

---

[12] For a comprehensive catalog of potential conflicts of interest, see Gnehm and Thalmann [1989].

[13] A detailed discussion is contained in Smith and Walter [1997A], Chapter 8.

4.12 Conglomerate Discount

It is often alleged that the shares of multi-product firms and conglomerates tend (all else equal) to trade at prices lower than shares of more narrowly-focused firms. There are two reasons why this "conglomerate discount" is alleged to exist.

First, it is argued that, on balance, conglomerates use capital inefficiently. Recent empirical work by Berger and Ofek [1995] assesses the potential benefits of diversification (greater operating efficiency, less incentive to forego positive net present value projects, greater debt capacity, lower taxes) against the potential costs (higher management discretion to engage in value-reducing projects, cross-subsidization of marginal or loss-making projects that drain resources from healthy businesses, mis-alignments in incentives between central and divisional managers). The authors demonstrate an average value-loss in multi-product firms on the order of 13-15%, as compared to the stand-alone values of the constituent businesses for a sample of U.S. corporations during the period 1986-91. This value-loss was smaller in cases where the multi-product firms were active in closely allied activities within the same two-digit standard industrial code (SIC) classification. The bulk of the value-erosion in conglomerates is attributed by the authors mainly to overinvestment in marginally profitable activities and cross-subsidization.

In empirical work using event-study methodology, John and Ofek [1994] show that asset sales by corporations result in significantly improved shareholder value for the remaining assets, both as a result of greater focus in the enterprise and value-gains through high prices paid by asset buyers. Such findings from event-studies of broad ranges of industry may well apply to the diversified activities encompassed by universal banks as well. If retail banking and wholesale banking are evolving into highly-specialized performance-driven businesses, one may ask whether the kinds of conglomerate discounts found in industrial firms may not also apply to universal banking structures as centralized decision-making becomes increasingly irrelevant to the requirements of the specific businesses themselves.

A second possible source of a conglomerate discount is that investors in shares of conglomerates find it difficult to "take a view" and add pure sectoral exposures to their portfolios. Shareholders in companies like General Electric, for example, in effect own a closed-end mutual fund comprising aircraft engines, plastics, electricity generation and distribution equipment, financial services, diesel locomotives, large household appliances, and a variety of other activities. GE therefore presents investors who may have a bullish view of the aircraft engine business, which they would like reflected in their portfolio selection, with a particularly poor choice compared with Rolls Royce, for example, which is much more of a "pure play" in this sector. Nor is it easily possible to short the undesirable parts of GE in order to "purify" the selection of GE shares under such circumstances. So investors tend to avoid such stocks in their efforts to construct efficient asset-allocation profiles, especially highly performance-driven managers of institutional equity portfolios under pressure to outperform equity indexes.

The portfolio logic of the conglomerate discount should apply in the financial services sector as well. A universal bank that is active in retail banking, wholesale commercial banking, middle-market banking, private banking, corporate finance, trading, investment banking, asset management and perhaps other businesses, in effect, represents a financial conglomerate that prevents investors from optimizing asset allocation across specific segments of the financial services industry.

Both the portfolio-selection effect and the capital-misallocation effect may weaken investor demand for universal bank shares, lower equity prices, and produce a higher cost of capital than if the conglomerate discount were absent—this in turn having a bearing on the competitive performance and profitability of the enterprise.

4.13 Non-financial Shareholdings

The conglomerate issue tends to be much more serious when a universal bank owns large-scale shareholdings in non-financial corporations, in which case the shareholder obtains a closed-end fund that has been assembled by bank managers for various reasons over time, and may bear no relationship to the investor's own portfolio optimization goals. The value of the universal bank itself then depends on the total market value of its shares, which must be held on an all-or-nothing basis, plus its own market value.

There are wide differences in the role banks play in non-financial corporate shareholdings and in the process of corporate governance [Walter, 1993]. These are stylized in Exhibit 9).

- In the equity-market system, industrial firms are "semi-detached" from banks. Financing of major corporations is done to a significant extent through the capital markets, with short-term financing needs satisfied through commercial paper programs, longer-term debt through straight or structured bond issues and medium-term note programs, and equity financing accomplished through public issues or private placements. Research coverage tends to be extensive.   Commercial banking relationships with major companies can be very important—notably through backstop credit lines and short-term lending facilities—but they tend to be between *buyer and seller*, with close bank monitoring and control coming into play mainly for small and medium-size firms or in cases of credit problems and workouts. Corporate control in such "Anglo-American" systems tends to be exercised through the takeover market on

Exhibit 9: Alternative Bank-Industry-Government Linkages

1. The Equity-Market System

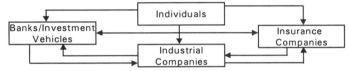

2. The Bank-Based System

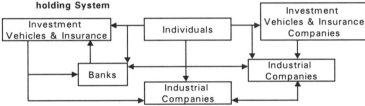

3. The Bank-Industrial Cross-holding System

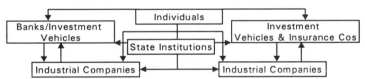

4. The State-centered System

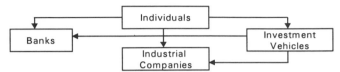

the basis of widely available public information, with a bank's function limited mainly to advising and financing bids or defensive restructurings. The government's role is normally arm's length in nature, with a focus on setting ground-rules that are considered in the public interest. Relations between government, banks and industry are sometimes antagonistic. Such systems depend heavily on efficient conflict-resolution mechanisms.

The second, bank-based approach centers on close bank-industry relationships, with corporate financing needs met mainly by retained earnings and bank financing. The role of banks carries well beyond credit-extension and monitoring to share ownership, share voting and board memberships in such "Germanic" systems. Capital allocation, management changes, and restructuring of enterprises are the responsibilities of non-executive supervisory boards on the basis of largely private information, and unwanted takeovers are rare. Mergers and acquisitions activity tends to be undertaken by relationship universal banks. Capital markets tend to be relatively poorly developed with respect to both corporate debt and equity, and there is usually not much of an organized venture capital market. The role of the state in the affairs of banks and corporations may well be arm's length in nature, although perhaps combined with some public-sector shareholdings.

- Third, in the so-called "crossholding approach," inter-firm boundaries are blurred through equity crosslinks and long-term supplier-customer relationships. Banks may play a central role in equity crossholding structures—as in Japan's "keiretsu" networks—and provide guidance and coordination as well as financing. There may be strong formal and informal links to government on the part of both the financial and industrial sectors of the economy. Restructuring tends to be done on the basis of private information by drawing on these business-banking-government ties, and a contestable market for corporate control tends to be virtually non-existent.

- The state-centered approach—perhaps best typified in the French tradition—involves a strong role on the part of government through national ownership or control of major universal banks and corporations, as well as government-controlled central savings institutions. Banks may hold significant stakes in industrial firms and form an important conduit for state influence of industry. Financing of enterprises tends to involve a mixture of bank credit and capital markets issues, often taken up by state-influenced financial institutions. Additional channels of government influence may include the appointment of the heads of state-owned companies and banks, with strong personal and educational ties within the business and government élite.

These four stylized bank-industry-government linkages make themselves felt in the operation of universal banks in various ways. The value of any bank shareholdings in industrial firms is embedded in the value of the bank. The combined value of the bank itself and its industrial shareholdings, as reflected in its market capitalization, may be larger or smaller than the sum of their stand-alone values. For example, firms in which a bank has significant financial stakes, as well as a direct governance role, may be expected to conduct most or all significant commercial and investment banking activities with that institution, thus raising the value of the bank. On the other hand, if such "tied" sourcing of financial services raises the cost of capital of client corporations, this will in turn be reflected in the value of bank's own shareholdings, and the reverse if such ties lower client firms' cost of capital. Moreover, permanent bank shareholdings may stunt the development of a contestable market for corporate control, thereby impeding corporate restructuring and depressing share prices that in turn are reflected in the value of the bank to its shareholders. Banks may also be induced to lend to affiliated corporations under credit conditions that would be rejected by unaffiliated lenders, and possibly encounter other conflicts of interest that may ultimately make it more difficult to maximize shareholder value.

4.14 Franchise Value

The foregoing considerations should, in combination, explain a significant part of any difference between the adjusted book value of equity and the market value of equity of a universal bank. But even after all such factors have been taken into account and priced-out, there may still be a material difference between the resulting "constructed" value of equity and the banks' market value (see Exhibit 2). The latter represents the market's assessment of the present value of the risk-adjusted future net earnings stream, capturing all known or suspected business opportunities, costs and risks facing the institution. The residual can be considered the "franchise" value of the bank. Much of it is associated with reputation and brand-value. Franchise value may be highly positive, for example, as in the case of Coca-Cola. Or, it could be significantly negative, with a firm's stock trading well below its constructed value or even its adjusted book value; for example, if there are large prospective losses imbedded in the bank's internal or external portfolio of activities.

Demsetz, Saidenberg and Strahan [1996] argue that the franchise-value of banks also serves to inhibit extraordinary risk-taking. They find substantial evidence that the higher a bank's franchise value, the more prudent management tends to be. This suggests that large universal banks with high franchise values should serve shareholder interests (as well as the interests of the regulators) by means of appropriate risk management as opposed to banks with little to lose.

4.15 From Market Value of Equity to Potential Value of Equity

The market capitalization of a universal bank is what it is, a product of a broad spectrum of quantifiable and not-so-quantifiable factors such as those discussed in the previous section. Looking ahead, managing for shareholder value means managing for return on investment, in effect maximizing the "potential value of equity" (PVE) that the organization may be capable of achieving. In the merger market this would be reflected in the "control premium" that may appear between the bank's market capitalization and what someone else in a position to act thinks the bank is worth.

The Chase is Dead. Long Live The Chase. Take the case of Chase Manhattan. The bank had suffered for years from a reputation for under performance and mediocrity, despite some improvement in its results, better strategic focus, improved efficiency levels and a cleaned-up balance sheet. In January 1995, Chase's stock price was $34, with a return on assets a bit under 1%, a return on equity of about 15%, a price-to-book ratio of about 1.2 and a price to earnings multiple of 7.0. Exhibit 10 shows Chase's stock price performance relative to the S&P 500 and the S&P Money Center Banks during 1991-94.

In April 1995, investment manager Michael Price, Chairman of Mutual Series Fund, Inc., announced that funds under his management had purchased 6.1 percent of Chase's stock, and that he believed the Chase board should take steps to realize the inherent values in its businesses in a manner designed to maximize shareholder returns. At the bank's subsequent annual meeting, Price aggressively challenged the bank's management efforts: "Dramatic change is required. It is clear that the sale of the bank is superior to the company's current strategy...unlock the value, or let someone else do it for you."[14] Chase's Chairman, Thomas Labreque, responded that he had no intention of selling or breaking-up the bank. By mid-June 1995 the Mutual Series Fund and other institutional investors, convinced that Chase stock was undervalued, were thought to have accumulated approximately 30% of the bank's outstanding shares and the stock price had climbed to about $47 per share. Labreque announced that the bank was continuing its efforts to refocus the bank's businesses and to reduce costs.

During June and July of 1995, Chase and BankAmerica talked seriously about a merger in which the BankAmerica name would be retained. Then BankAmerica suddenly backed-out for reasons that were not totally clear to outsiders at the time.[15] Chemical Bank followed quickly with a proposal for a "merger of equals." According to Chemical's chairman, Walter Shipley, "This combined company has the capacity to perform at benchmark standards. And when we say benchmark standards, we mean the best in the industry."[16] Labreque agreed, and the negotiations were completed on August 28, 1995. Chemical would offer to exchange 1.04 shares of its stock for every Chase share outstanding, an offer reflecting a 7% premium over the closing price of Chase shares on the day before the announcement.

---

[14]*The Wall Street Journal, May 19, 1995.*

[15]*Institutional Investor, November, 1995.*

[16]*ABC Evening News, August 28, 1995.*

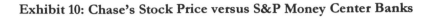

Exhibit 10: Chase's Stock Price versus S&P Money Center Banks

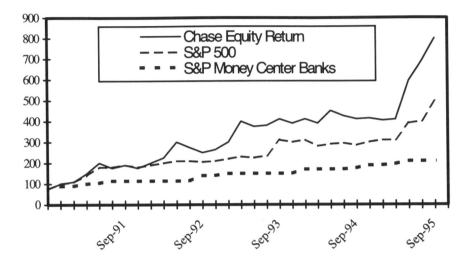

The combined bank, retaining the Chase name, thus became the largest bank in the United States and 13th largest in the world in terms of assets. The new Chase also became the largest U.S. corporate lending bank, one of the largest credit card lenders, and the largest player in trust, custody, and mortgage servicing. Shipley became chief executive, and Labreque became president. Substantial cost-reduction efforts were quickly launched (including large-scale layoffs and branch closings) aimed at reducing the combined overhead of the two banks within three years by 16%. In the month following the announcement of the merger, Chemical Bank's stock rose 12%.

Labreque denied that shareholder pressure had anything to do with the merger. Michael Price asserted that he had not played a major role, but was happy to have been in the "right place at the right time." Nevertheless, adjusting for the exchange offer and the post-merger run-up in Chemical's share price, Chase shares more than doubled their value in a little over six months based on the market's assessment of the potential value imbedded in the merger. What was the source of the added value?

4.17 Realizing the Potential Value of Equity

Clearly, merger transactions in contestable markets for corporate control are—as in the case of Chase Manhattan—aimed at unlocking shareholder value. The intent is to optimize the building-blocks that make up potential value of equity, as depicted in Exhibit 2, through realizable economies of scale, economies of scope, X-efficiency, market power, and TBTF benefits, while minimizing value-losses from any diseconomies that may exist as well as avoiding to the extent possible conflict-of-interest problems and any conglomerate discount. Evidently the market agreed in this case, amply rewarding shareholders of both banks, especially those of the old Chase.

At least in the United States, bank acquisitions have occurred at price-to-book value ratios of about 2.0, sometimes as high as 3.0 or even more. In eight of the eleven years in a recent study [Smith and Walter, 1996], the average price-to-book ratio for U.S. banking industry acquisitions was below 2.0, averaging 1.5 and ranging from 1.1 in 1990 to 1.8 in 1985. In two years, the price-to-book ratio exceeded 2.0—in 1986 it was 2.8 and in 1993 in was 3.2. These values presumably reflect the opportunity for the acquired institutions to be managed differently and to realize the incremental value needed to reimburse the shareholders of the acquiring institutions for the willingness to pay the premium in the first place. If in fact the value-capture potential for universal banks exceeds that for U.S.-type separated commercial banks; then this should be reflected in higher merger premiums in banking environments outside the United States.

An active and contestable market for corporate control may not, of course, trigger pressure for shareholder value optimization, but it probably helps. Comparing cost, efficiency, and profitability measures across various national environments that are characterized by very different investor expectations and activism suggests that external pressure is conducive to realizing the potential value of shareholder equity in banking. In terms of Exhibit 2 and the empirical evidence available so far, the management lessons for universal banks appear to include the following:

• Do not expect too much from economies of scale.

• Do not expect too much from *supply-side* economies of scope, and be prepared to deal with any diseconomies that may arise.

• Optimize X-efficiencies through effective use of technology, reductions in the capital-intensity of financial services provided, reductions in the work force, and other available operating economies.

- Exploit *demand-side* economies of scope where cross-selling makes sense, most likely with retail, private and middle-market corporate clients.

- Seek-out imperfect markets that demonstrate relatively low price-elasticity of demand, ranging from private banking services, equity transactions that exploit "fault lines" across capital markets, and leading-edge emerging-market transactions that have not as yet been commoditized, to dominant "fortress" market-share positions in particular national or regional markets, with particular client-segments, or in particular product-lines. The half-lives of market imperfections in banking differ enormously, and require careful calibration of delivery systems ranging from massive investments in infrastructure to small, light, entrepreneurial and opportunistic SWAT-teams. The key managerial challenge is to accommodate a broad array of these activities under the same roof.

- Specialize operations using professionals who are themselves specialists.

- Where possible, make the political case for backstops such as underpriced deposit insurance and TBTF support. Although this is a matter of public policy, shareholders clearly benefit from implicit subsidies that don't come with too many conditions attached.

- Pay careful attention to limiting conflicts of interest in organizational design, incentive systems, application and maintenance of Chinese walls, and managerial decisions that err on the side of caution where potential conflicts arise.

- Minimize the conglomerate discount by divesting peripheral non-financial shareholdings and non-core businesses, leaving diversification up to the shareholder. The gain in market value may well outweigh any losses from reduced scope economies and earnings-diversification. Pursuing this argument to its logical conclusion, of course, challenges the basic premise of universal banking as a structural form.

- Get rid of share-voting restrictions and open-up shareholdings to market forces.

- Pay careful attention to the residual "franchise" value of the bank by avoiding professional conduct lapses that lead to an erosion of the bank's reputation, uncontrolled trading losses, or in extreme cases criminal charges against the institution. It's never a good idea to cut corners on compliance or on building an affirmative "culture" which employees understand and value as much as the shareholders.

Exhibit 2 shows some of these as a "recapture" of shareholder-value losses in universal banks associated with diseconomies of scale and scope, conglomerate discount not offset by the benefits of a universal structure, and potential conflict-of-interest and reputational losses. The balance of any further potential gains involves ramping-up key elements of the production function of the bank, capitalizing on market opportunities, and an intense focus on maximizing franchise-value and reputation. If a strategic direction taken by the management of a universal bank does not exploit every source of potential value for shareholders, then what is the purpose? Avoiding an acquisition attempt from a better-managed suitor who will pay a premium price, as in the case of Chase Manhattan, does not seem as unacceptable today as it may have been in the past. In a world of more open and efficient markets for shares in financial institutions, shareholders increasingly tend to have the final say about the future of their enterprises.

References

1. Akhavein, J. D., A. N. Berger and D. B. Humphrey. 1996. The Effects of Megamergers on Efficiency and Prices: Evidence from a Bank Profit Function. Paper presented at a *Conference on Mergers of Financial Institutions*, New York University Salomon Center.
2. Benston, G. 1994. Universal Banking. *Journal of Economic Perspectives*, 8(3).
3. Benston, G., G. Hanweck and D. B. Humphrey. 1982. Scale Economies in Banking. *Journal of Money, Credit and Banking*, 14.
4. Berger, A. N., D. Hancock and D. B. Humphrey. 1993. Bank Efficiency Derived from the Profit Function. *Journal of Banking and Finance*, April.
5. Berger, A. N., G. Hanweck, and D. B. Humphrey. 1987. Competitive Viability in Banking. *Journal of Monetary Economics*, 20.
6. Berger, A. N., W. C. Hunter and S. J. Timme. 1993. The Efficiency of Financial Institutions: A Review of Research Past, Present and Future. *Journal of Banking and Finance*, April.
7. Berger, P. G. and E. Ofek. 1995. Diversification's Effect on Firm Value. *Journal of Financial Economics*, 37.
8. Clark, J. A. 1988. Economies of Scale and Scope at Depository Financial Institutions: a Review of the Literature. *Federal Reserve Board of Kansas City Review*.
9. Demsetz, R. S., M. R. Saidenberg and P. E. Strahan, Banks with Something to Lose: The Disciplinary Role of Franchise Value. *Federal Reserve Bank of New York Policy Review*, October 1996.
10. Economides, N. Network Economics with Application to Finance. *Financial Markets, Institutions and Instruments*, Vol. 2, No. 5, 1993.

11. Fields, J. A. and N. B. Murphy. An Analysis of Efficiency in the Delivery of Financial Services: The Case of Life Insurance Agencies. *Journal of Financial Services Research*, 2, 1989.
12. Gilligan, T. and M. Smirlock. An Empirical Study of Joint Production and Scale Economies in Commercial Banking. *Journal of Banking and Finance*, 8, 1984.
13. Gilligan, T., M. Smirlock and W. Marshall. Scale and Scope Economies in the Multi-Product Banking Firm. *Journal of Monetary Economics*, 13, 1984.
14. Gnehm, A. and C. Thalmann. 1989. Conflicts of Interest in Financial Operations: Problems of Regulation in the National and International Context. *Working Paper*, Swiss Bank Corporation, Basel.
15. Goldstein, S., J. McNulty and J. Verbrugge, Scale Economies in the Savings and Loan Industry Before Diversification. *Journal of Economics and Business*, 1987.
16. Hawawini, G. and I. Swary. 1990. *Mergers and Acquisitions in the U.S. Banking Industry*. North Holland, Amsterdam.
17. John, K and E. Ofek, Asset Sales and Increase in Focus. 1995. *Journal of Financial Economics*, 37.
18. Kellner, S. and G. F. Mathewson. 1983. Entry, Size Distribution, Scale and Scope Economies in the Life Insurance Industry. *Journal of Business*.
19. Kim, H. Y. 1986. Economies of Scale and Scope in Multiproduct Financial Institutions. *Journal of Money, Credit and Banking*, 18.
20. Kolari, J. and A. Zardhooki. 1987. *Bank Cost Structure and Performance*. Heath Lexington, Lexington, MA.
21. Lawrence, C. 1989. Banking Costs, Generalized Functional Forms, and Estimation of Economies of Scale and Scope. *Journal of Money, Credit and Banking*.
22. Mester, L. 1987. A Multiproduct Cost Study of Savings and Loans. *Journal of Finance*.
23. Mester, L. 1990. Traditional and Nontraditional Banking: an Information Theoretic Approach. Federal Reserve Board *Working Paper*, No. 90-3.
24. Murray, J. D. and R. S. White. 1983. Economies of Scale and Economies of Scope in Multiproduct Financial Institutions. *Journal of Finance*.
25. Noulas, A. G., S. C. Ray and S. M. Miller. 1990. Returns to Scale and Input Substitution for Large U.S. Banks. *Journal of Money, Credit and Banking*.
26. Saunders, A. 1996. *Financial Institutions Management*, Second Edition, Richard Irwin, Burr Ridge, IL.
27. Saunders, A. and I. Walter. 1994. *Universal Banking in the United States*. Oxford University Press, New York, NY.
28. Saunders, A. and I. Walter (eds.). 1996. *Universal Banking: Financial System Design Reconsidered*. Richard Irwin, Burr Ridge, IL.
29. Shaffer, S. 1988. A Restricted Cost Study of 100 Large Banks. Federal Reserve Bank of New York *Working Paper*.
30. Thomas F. S. 1996. Bank Mergers and Shareholder Value: Evidence from 1995's Megamerger Deals. *Federal Reserve Bank of Dallas Financial Industry Studies*.

31. Smith, R. C. and I. Walter. 1996. Global Patterns of Mergers and Acquisitions in the Financial Services Industry. Paper presented at a *Conference on Mergers of Financial Institutions*, New York University Salomon Center.

32. Smith, R. C. and I. Walter. 1997A. *Global Banking*. Oxford University Press, New York, NY.

33. Smith, R. C. and I. Walter. 1997B. *Street Smarts: Leadership and Shareholder Value in the Securities Industry*. Harvard Business School Press, Boston, MA.

34. Steinherr, A. 1996. Performance of Universal Banks: Review and Appraisal. In A. Saunders and I. Walter (eds.). *Universal Banking: Financial System Design Reconsidered*. Richard Irwin, Burr Ridge, IL.

35. Tschoegl, A. E. 1983. Size, Growth and Transnationality among the World's Largest Banks. *Journal of Business*.

36. Walter, I. (ed.). *Deregulating Wall Street*. John Wiley & Sons, New York, NY.

37. Walter, I. 1988. *Global Competition in Financial Services*. Ballinger-Harper & Row, Cambridge, MA.

38. Walter, I. 1993. *The Battle of the Systems: Control of Enterprises in the Global Economy*. Kieler Studien Nr. 122, Institut für Weltwirtschaft, Kiel.

39. Yoshioka, K. and T. Nakajima. 1987. Economies of Scale in Japan's Banking Industry. *Bank of Japan Monetary and Economic Studies*.

Chapter 5

Redefining Customer Relationships in the Age of the Ascendant Consumer

Thomas L. Monahan, III
Corporate Executive Board Company

5.1 A Marriage Made in Heaven?

Socrates once observed that relationships were like cities under siege: everyone on the outside, wishing to get in, those on the inside, wishing to get out. We are a little hesitant to begin an article by disputing Socrates, but the retail financial services business, particularly retail banking, has powerful economic incentives to develop relationships with retail customers.

This insight has not been lost on the industry. In fact, if there is any topic that banks around the world uniformly agree on, it is the importance of relationships. Figure 1 contains a series of quotes to that effect from the annual reports of a number of leading institutions. Banks around the world are concentrating on relationships: creating them, sustaining them, building them up, continuously improving them, and perfecting them. We would get virtually the same picture if we plotted insurance companies, or stockbrokers, or fund managers.

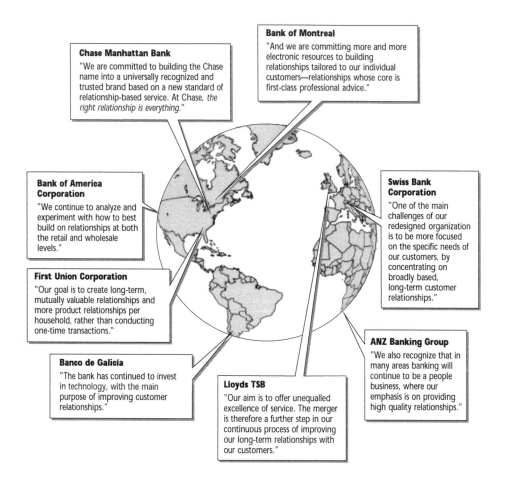

Figure 1

A Universal Language

Bank of Montreal

"And we are committing more and more electronic resources to building relationships tailored to our individual customers—relationships whose core is first-class professional advice."

Chase Manhattan Bank

"We are committed to building the Chase name into a universally recognized and trusted brand based on a new standard of relationship-based service. At Chase, *the right relationship is everything.*"

Bank of America Corporation

"We continue to analyze and experiment with how to best build on relationships at both the retail and wholesale levels."

Swiss Bank Corporation

"One of the main challenges of our redesigned organization is to be more focused on the specific needs of our customers, by concentrating on broadly based, long-term customer relationships."

First Union Corporation

"Our goal is to create long-term, mutually valuable relationships and more product relationships per household, rather than conducting one-time transactions."

Banco de Galicia

"The bank has continued to invest in technology, with the main purpose of improving customer relationships."

ANZ Banking Group

"We also recognize that in many areas banking will continue to be a people business, where our emphasis is on providing high quality relationships."

Lloyds TSB

"Our aim is to offer unequalled excellence of service. The merger is therefore a further step in our continuous process of improving our long-term relationships with our customers."

Source: Council on Financial Competition research.

According to research performed by Unisys – in 1995, over 90% of all banks in the US listed customer retention and cross selling products as top priorities. In 1997, when we interviewed 100 members across the globe about their strategic priorities, every one had establishing or developing "relationships" as their number one or number two objective. These are not mere platitudes; we found powerful evidence that investment dollars are supporting these objectives. In

1996, for example, investment in relationship building support was far and away the largest focus of discretionary spending on technology, garnering over 35% of the industry's elective spending.

5.2 Looks Great on Paper

In abstract terms, this focus on relationships is quite sensible. *Theoretically,* substantial benefits should accrue to those who foster strong relationships. For example, the cost of a sale can be significantly reduced if an institution can sell more products to existing customers. (See Figure 2.) Compared to a base cost of $116 to sell the average product to an average stranger, when we sell to a repeat customer we save $39 on marketing and $14 on account set up, for a total reduction of $53 or a whopping 46%.

Figure 2

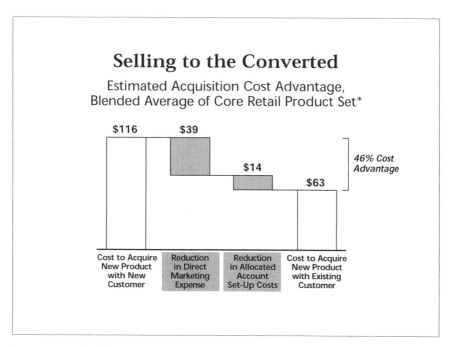

* Assumes direct mail solicitation, on-site closure and set-up. Does not include underwriting.

Source: Wharton Financial Institutions Research Center; Blades Bank; Oliver Wyman & Company; Council on Financial Competition research and estimates.

Banks also get a boost if they can translate a relationship into an increase in key customer retention. For a typical retail financial institution, a five percentage point difference in the retention rate of Tier One customers (those in the top 20% by contribution) can boost annual profits by as much as 25% after five years.

A third theoretical benefit is that loyal customers are less affected by price changes, allowing institutions to sustain higher and more consistent margins. One leading institution, which we will call Leslie Bank, found that its relationship management expertise translated into far-reduced price sensitivity on the part of its customers. Analysis indicated that when Leslie lagged the market on rates, it suffered only one third the customer runoff of leading competitors. Leslie and other leading institutions have begun to consider their ability to command a price premium a key indicator of relationship health. Their reasoning is quite simple: if a consumer brings an institution business merely because of pricing, this doesn't qualify as much of a relationship.

Stepping back from the individual details, it is no exaggeration to say that theoretical benefits of a relationship *pull every lever* of the NPV equation—cost–to-acquire, price, volume, tenure and even reduced risk—as institutions gain more information about their customers. So, in theory, a good relationship should be a worthy corporate aspiration.

Perhaps the brightest ray of golden light shining on the theory of relationships is that retail customers claim to want them. Facing an increasingly complex world with a huge increase in the variety of providers, the sophistication of products, and the complexity of delivery methods, consumers report feeling a bit overwhelmed. When asked if they would be better off with all of their needs met by one financial institution, in 1996 almost two thirds (61%) agreed or strongly agreed with that sentiment.

5.3 Trouble in Paradise

But despite all of the terrific theory that surrounds relationship strategies, most retail financial institutions find that in the real world the relationships they have with customers differ substantially from the ideal relationships evident only in theory. Several phenomena suggest that forging viable economic relationships with customers is far more difficult than theory suggests.

The first is what we have called the paradox of primacy. By that we mean that consumers do not reward the institution which *they* consider to be their *prime* provider with any extra business.

When consumers were asked for their primary provider of financial services an overwhelming majority—81 percent—said it was their bank or thrift. Forty-two percent said they gave their prime provider their transaction account. Yet only 10% did the *majority* of their deposit or investment business with their "primary provider." And a paltry 2% did the majority of their borrowing from their primary provider. So earning the designation of primary relationship provider does not necessarily translate to earning a significant share of the customer's business (see Figure 3).

Figure 3

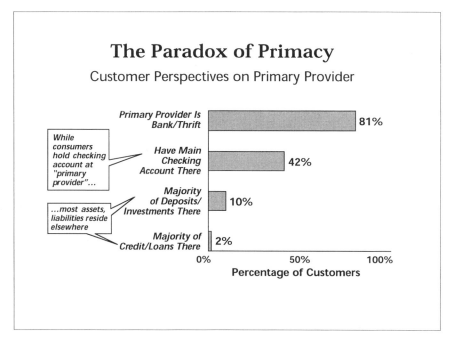

Source: BAI National Payments System Symposium.

The second concern stems from the economic performance of such "relationships." Strong evidence suggests that, if improperly designed, some relationships can hurt providers. The results from a First Manhattan Consulting Group (FMCG) study shown in Figure 4 mirror findings many institutions shared with our research team.

Figure 4

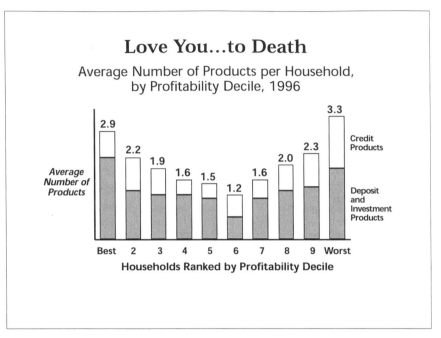

Source: First Manhattan Consulting Group; Council
on Financial Competition research.

This FMCG study indicated that a bank's most profitable customers purchase an average of 2.9 products. Its *least* profitable customers buy an average of 3.3 products. This strange phenomenon is due to the perverse economics of most financial products. Unlike most other businesses, banks and financial providers do not necessarily make money when customers buy products, but rather when they use products profitably. Hence, even customers who buy a number of products from the same institution can be unprofitable, for a variety of reasons. The reasons most often center on incorrect pricing at the front line, expensive usage patterns (e.g., many branch visits for low-balance accounts), or simple failure to use a product, as is often the case with dormant consumer credit. The irony is that the tools most institutions use to "enhance" relationships— preferential pricing for customers with multiple products, cross-selling campaigns, "bundled" products—have deteriorated the economics of their existing relationships

Third, and closely related, many institutions have observed that we actually lose money on a large number of our relationships. Figure 5 shows data from a member disguised as Colleton Bank, showing three very different customer profiles. On the left, on 22% of their total customer base, it averages $829 per year in profit. In the middle group, 40% of their total customer base, they earn an average of $8 in profit. And, on the right, on the remaining 38%, they lose an average of $193 per customer annually.

Figure 5

Colleton Bank Retail Profitability Tiers

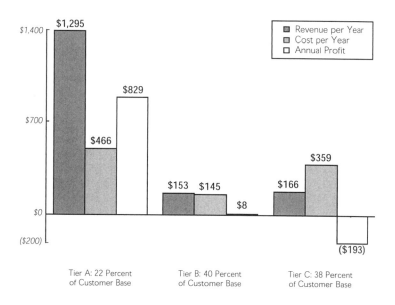

Fully 38% of their customers are significantly unprofitable, a relatively common condition for banks. Due to loopholes in the price/service offering, these customers are able (intentionally or not) to capitalize on the tremendous cross subsidies inherent in the product set. Institutions that face profitability skews like this have begun to ask which group of customers they want to have a relationship with: that small group of customers whose exaggerated profits fund the institution? Or, those who would happily beggar the institution through a pattern of cross subsidy?

This data begs a larger question: what is the definition of relationship? Across the industry there were dozens of definitions of relationship in use. Most institutions defined a relationship as selling a number of products to a customer or retaining a customer for a long period, despite clear evidence that these achievements do not always result in fair economic return.

A few pioneering institutions profiled in this research had defined relationships with retail customers in a fundamentally different manner. One executive we interviewed defined a relationship as "a mutually beneficial set of economic arrangements that span multiple consumer needs and multiple accounting periods." By that rigorous definition, most institutions can claim to have few real relationships, despite the powerful theoretical appeal of the concept.

While the industry bemoans the economics of its current relationships, there is powerful evidence that a desire for mutually beneficial relationships has not been at the forefront of most institutions' strategies. Some of this is driven by industry history.

Across the 700-year history of the financial services industry the core of the business has been a process known as reserve banking, or balance sheet banking. The process is straightforward. Banks borrow money (take deposits) at less than the market rate, lend it for more than the market rate, and keep the difference.

This is a closed system: the amount that banks can pay depositors is strictly capped by what banks can charge borrowers. Every financial benefit that a bank gives to its consumers affects its bottom line.

Banks have reacted to this win-lose proposition predictably over time. In Figure 6, we have plotted the historical relationship between rates on a number of products, including one unique to banks, the savings account. When rates climbed, in 1988 and again in 1992, savings rates were not able to match those increases. Savings accounts are more liquid than other instruments, and thus we would expect consumers to pay a small liquidity premium. But the institutions that viewed this data, were troubled at the industry's eagerness to re-price when rates were falling and hesitance to move rates on this product when base rates were rising.

Figure 6

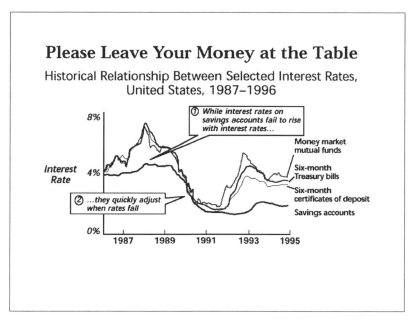

Please Leave Your Money at the Table

Historical Relationship Between Selected Interest Rates,
United States, 1987–1996

Note: The data are monthly. Rates derived
from commercial banks. Savings accounts
include money market deposit accounts.

Source: Federal Reserve Board statistical
releases H.6 and H.15.

5.4 The Ascendant Consumer

Consumers have responded to this situation in a predictable way. Rather than relying on a single provider, they are seeking a variety of alternatives to optimize their financial well being. In this quest, they have some powerful allies. Three factors in particular are coming to their assistance. First, consumers have increasingly direct capital markets access. Second, search costs for alternatives are falling rapidly, and third, the cost to switch providers is also falling.

The first dynamic is a steady migration of consumer assets and liabilities away from institutions' balance sheets and into the capital markets. The device that brought this to the consumer market is asset securitization, first widely used in the U.S., and now an increasingly global technology. As a result, today Countrywide Mortgage, MBNA or Discover Card can lend substantial volumes without needing to gather bank deposits to fund them.

A corollary event has been the opening of the investment markets to consumers. Mutual funds allow even small savers to invest in diversified portfolios of stocks under professional management and gaining access to equity upside at an acceptably low transaction cost. The money market account allows small sums of transaction dollars and to enjoy returns close to the wholesale cost of funds. As a result, Charles Schwab or Merrill Lynch can gather hundreds of billions of dollars of "deposits" and not have to make loans.

The impact of this technology on competitive position has been profound. Figure 7 shows the growth of securitized consumer credit and the attendant increase in market share of the non-bank finance and loan companies. Paralleling the growing acceptance of securitization is a spike in market share by companies not reliant on traditional deposit gathering.

Figure 7

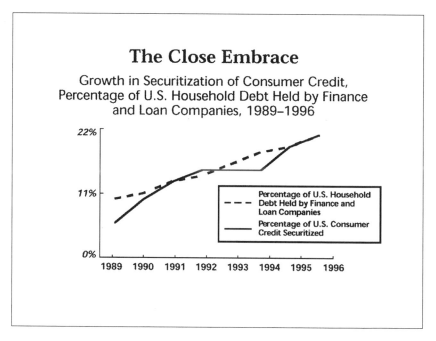

The Close Embrace

Growth in Securitization of Consumer Credit,
Percentage of U.S. Household Debt Held by Finance
and Loan Companies, 1989–1996

- - - Percentage of U.S. Household Debt Held by Finance and Loan Companies
—— Percentage of U.S. Consumer Credit Securitized

Source: Federal Reserve; Council on Financial Competition research.

Perhaps more than any other factor, this de-coupling of deposit taking and lending has fostered the rise of best-in-class, narrowly focused product companies who are in turn giving consumers the options—and the reason—to diversify the majority of their borrowing and investing away from their primary provider. As these alternatives become available, it is increasingly easy for consumers to find them. Here technology is driving massive change. Heavy investments in phone centers and computer systems make it easy and cheap for a consumer to search across a range of alternatives, find, and move to the best product available.

But it isn't just the availability of options that has empowered the customer, it is the ease with which they can find and select these options. Figure 8 shows how technology has eroded the time required to shop for a high rate CD: from 300 minutes to shop in person (which a decade ago was the only alternative) to less than 30 minutes to shop by phone and now all the way down to about a minute to shop using an agent on the World Wide Web. When it took five hours only the most miserly or bored would go shopping for such a mundane product. At one minute, consumers almost can't afford not to shop.

Figure 8

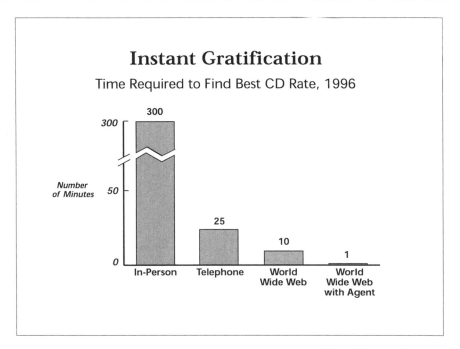

Instant Gratification

Time Required to Find Best CD Rate, 1996

Source: McKinsey & Company; Council on Financial Competition research.

Even as search costs plummet, switching costs are also in free fall. In a truly transparent market where the consumer can examine all options, it is increasingly difficult to charge someone for the privilege of opening an account. As a result, the average load required to invest in a mutual fund has fallen by almost 50% from 1980 to 1994, from 8.5% to 4.5%, and front-end fees and prepayment fees are disappearing across the product set.

Aided by these new financial and information technologies, consumers are becoming increasingly selective and diversifying their business at unprecedented rates. This is happening even as institutions gain enhanced regulatory powers and mount ever-more intensive "cross-selling" efforts. Figure 9 displays the answer to the question "How many financial providers do you currently hold relationships with?" 35.1% of respondents were loyal to a single provider in 1993, 30.2 in 1996. So one in six of the loyal group became "promiscuous" in the intervening three years. Even more striking, the number of truly diversified households, those holding relationships with four or more providers, has doubled, from 10.5% to 21.1%.

Figure 9

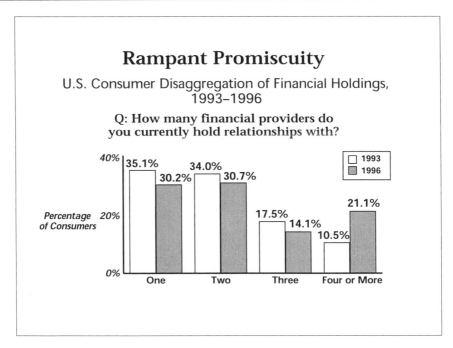

Rampant Promiscuity

U.S. Consumer Disaggregation of Financial Holdings,
1993–1996

**Q: How many financial providers do
you currently hold relationships with?**

Source: Unidex, *Customer Loyalty Among
Financial Institutions*, 1996.

Across the four bars, over 37% of those surveyed now do business with more providers than they did three years ago. It is this migration which has fueled the paradox of primacy we noted earlier.

5.5 Endgame for an Unhappy Compromise

So more options have become available for consumers looking to diversify their financial holdings across an array of providers. Some industry observers have suggested that this phenomenon has the power to render relationship strategies obsolete. If consumers were perfectly happy with this state of affairs, that might be the case, but when consumers piece together their financial products from an array of providers, they lose a substantial amount of convenience in the process. Data from PSI presented in Figure 10 shows that while more than 54% of consumers claim it would simplify their life to do business with one provider, nearly 57% fear that by consolidating they would lose access to best-in-class pricing. On its face, this seems like an unwanted compromise.

Figure 10

Forced Compromise

Perceived Benefits and Drawbacks of Consolidating All Financial Accounts with One Institution, 1996

While consumers yearn for simplicity of single provider...   *...most see risk in not "shopping around"*

Benefits (Among households using more than one institution)	Rank	Pctg.	Drawbacks (Among households using more than one institution)	Rank	Pctg.
It would be convenient to deal with one institution	1	54.2%	The institution may not offer me the best prices	1	56.7%
It would be easier to deal with one institution (would simplify my life)	2	45.7%	The institution may not offer all the products my household needs	2	46.6%

Source: PSI, 1996.

Consumers have to make a trade-off: they can either get the best product if they go to multiple sources *or* they can have a single relationship but suffer from higher prices or ill-fitting products. Consumers are diversifying to get better products, but they recognize explicitly that they are forfeiting convenience in the process.

In Figure 11, we show the compromise as it has actually been made by consumers over time. On the horizontal axis we show the relative product choice available to consumers and we approximate the notion that choice is increasing as time goes by. On the vertical axis we show the percentage of financial business involving the primary provider. You can see the tough choice being made over time as the consumer gains increased product choice, yet suffers a decline in the convenience of a concentrated relationship.

Figure 11

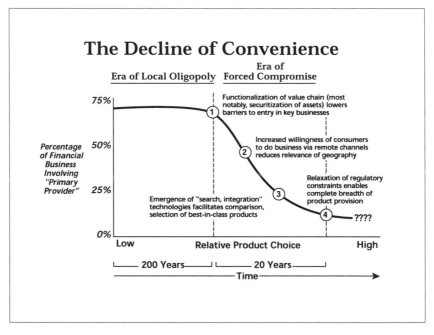

Source: Council research.

We have marked just a few milestones in this migration from (relative) reliance on one provider to a dispersion of financial activity. Despite giving them access to a variety of outstanding products, and choice of world-class providers for every need, this migration has forced customers to make a tough compromise. Our message to them has been simple. Pick an evil: either select convenient access to under-performing products, or select the best product, and grossly complicate your life

The market will not be able to force that compromise for much longer. Figure 12 shows the determinants of industry structure, as described by Michael Porter of the Harvard Business School. At the bottom are those factors that Porter observed drive buyer power. As we have documented, relative choice is rising and switching costs are falling. The buyer has more information to guide his actions. And finally, the buyer is increasingly able to backward integrate, to do some of the work himself (consider here Quicken.com or any of the multitude of web sites that offer self-service advice). This rise in buyer power strongly suggests that this compromise between convenience and access will not stand for long.

Figure 12

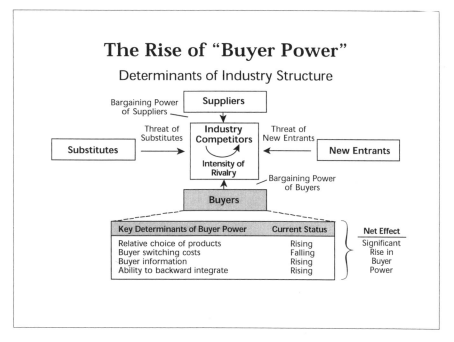

Source: Adapted from Porter, Michael E., *Competitive Advantage,* New York: Free Press, 1985.

In Figure 13, we add three more milestones to the chart in Figure 11 showing the dispersion of consumer financial business across an array of providers.

Figure 13

The Rise of the Relationship Provider

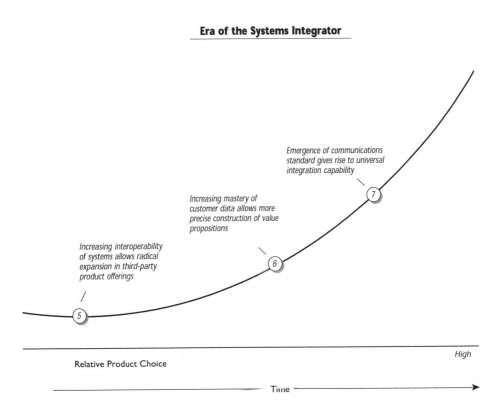

Era of the Systems Integrator

Emergence of communications standard gives rise to universal integration capability

⑦

Increasing mastery of customer data allows more precise construction of value propositions

⑥

Increasing interoperability of systems allows radical expansion in third-party product offerings

⑤

High

Relative Product Choice

Time ———▶

In stage five, the increasing interoperability of systems enables third parties to integrate the best products from a number of providers to give customers access to a range of best product in one place. The Schwab OneSource product set was perhaps the harbinger here. Here the primary provider starts to play an integration role, bringing together products it "manufactures" with information about, and access to, products held elsewhere.

At stage six, ironically, in exchange for offering a broader variety of products, the integrator is paid in the currency of information. More information about consumer financial activities, gleaned via provision of a larger set of financial needs, pays off in the ability to provide more robust solutions and better advice.

At stage seven, the last piece to fall into place will be the establishment of integrated messaging standards which will enable relationship providers to seamlessly provide every product as if it was their own. We have seen strong competitors in our industry hunting this Holy Grail for some time, and given consumers' powerful appetite for both convenience and access, it will continue to be a high priority for industry leaders.

Contrary to pessimistic projections, the prospect of a "relationship" between a financial services customer and an institution is alive and well. But the type of relationship likely to prosper will be fundamentally different from what most providers envision today. Rather than one institution simply cross-selling its own products, a primary institution will now integrate information about its products with real-time information about competitors' products. Institutions will facilitate payments and movements of cash between providers. And it may offer any number of relationship features, including advice, on top of the integration platform.

Such a relationship obviously has enormous attraction for consumers, as they can (at last) access world-class product variety and integrated information. And while, in draft form, such a future might not appeal to institutions currently using "relationship" as a euphemism for monopoly pricing, it will allow institutions to design pricing and servicing strategies that rectify the troubled economics of today's relationship strategies.

In the year we spent conducting this research, we were constantly surprised that this future is not nearly as far off as it seems. In interviews with our membership, which includes 300 leading retail financial services providers, we found dozens of experiments underway, each of which aimed at redefining relationships in accordance with the new rules of engagement. In our published report, we document about 20 best demonstrated practices for beginning to break the compromises faced by most consumers. The migration path followed by industry leaders has the following three major components:

1. *Repairing Relationship Equilibrium.* Institutions are using tactical methods such as profit-based price concessions, or enhanced relationship management platforms to reallocate discretionary investment dollars toward their most valuable relationships.

2. *Responding to the New Consumer.* Institutions are beginning to integrate non-proprietary products into their relationship management platform, providing choice among competing product sets and establishing themselves as navigators among complex offerings. This activity, which began in the mutual fund business, is rapidly moving to incorporate mortgage lending, credit cards, insurance, and other products.

3. *Embedding Accountability to the Customer.* Institutions are fundamentally reorganizing themselves around new capabilities for establishing and maintaining relationships with retail customers, including brand management, consumer segment management, and customer information analysis. These new models—already in evidence at a number of institutions—are predicated on the idea that better alignment between customer goals and institutional goals is the only possible platform for a relationship strategy. As a result they have even rethought corporate structure and executive pay in accordance with their ambition of enhancing relationship health.

Chapter 6

Out of the Fog: Creating Value by Assembling and Managing a Portfolio of Services

Praveen R. Nayyar
New York University

6.1 Introduction

As I write this chapter, I look out of my window and see a dense early-spring fog obscuring the rolling green landscape that I know lies not far from my home. I know that this fog will clear when the sun rises higher and the wind sets in. Engulfed in a fog, many scholars and most managers commit a trilogy of errors plus one. First, they do not consider important differences between cost-reduction and revenue-enhancing strategies when analyzing and planning diversification strategies. Second, they ignore important differences among services – leading to erroneous beliefs about expected benefits from different diversification strategies. Third, they do not account for implementation hurdles that reduce the benefits that a firm can expect from different diversification strategies. The plus one error is that they tend to "see" synergies in diversified firms when there can be none.

The purpose of this chapter is to clear the fog surrounding the analysis and practice of diversification strategies in financial services firms. Services firms have diversified rapidly since the early 1980s. More recently, financial services firms have been on a diversifying spree and now there are calls to remove regulatory restrictions on financial services firms preventing them from offering inter-state banking and insurance, among other things. Of course, some financial services firms have succeeded in circumventing some regulations by forming bank holding companies while other firms are more directly seeking the removal of many restrictions on banks. An example of the latter is the recent merger of Citicorp with The Travelers Group to form Citigroup.

Most such diversification moves are motivated by expected synergies from either reduced costs or increased revenues. However, I have found that many such diversification moves by services firms have destroyed shareholder value. In particular, expected cost-reduction is seldom realized because it requires substantial changes in the way businesses are organized and managed. And, expected revenue enhancement is often simply wishful thinking because it arises only under very special conditions that are generally ignored when diversification moves are contemplated.

I present and discuss the results of studies I conducted to examine the performance effects of cost-reduction and revenue-enhancement driven diversification strategies in services firms (Nayyar, 1990, 1992a, 1992b, 1993a, 1993b). Tests using accounting-and stock-market-based performance measures revealed that revenue-enhancement diversification strategies created value while some cost-reduction diversification strategies destroyed value. These results depended upon the type of service involved. The revenue-enhancement strategy was particularly valuable for firms offering services whose quality cannot be determined until after purchase and, even then, with some difficulty, such as for asset and risk management services. For services whose quality can be determined prior to purchase, such as for tax return processing, consumer finance, and mortgage lending, cost-reduction strategies created value. However, for services whose quality cannot be determined before purchase, cost-reduction strategies *destroyed* value.

I also discuss appropriate organization structures needed to attain the desired benefits from diversification by services firms. (For details see Nayyar & Kazanjian, 1993.) Since each source of benefits is based on different underlying mechanisms, attaining each benefit requires adopting an appropriate organization structure. For example, attaining cost-reduction benefits requires structuring organizational divisions based on the particular resources shared between different services. In contrast, attaining revenue-enhancement benefits requires structuring organizational divisions based on the particular customers shared between services.

6.2 Promises, Promises: Potential Benefits from Diversification Strategies

Services firms can pursue two sources of benefits by diversifying. These are (1) information asymmetry and (2) economies of scope. The mechanisms underlying each benefit differ greatly.

6.3 Information Asymmetry Benefits

Buyers purchase services after comparing the price and quality of available alternatives. However, service quality is difficult to evaluate because services are intangible and often simultaneously produced and consumed. This makes service choice decisions difficult for buyers. Hence, buyers gather information about service quality to make informed choices. Service sellers often have more information than buyers do about service quality. This information asymmetry can result in moral hazard for sellers, or encouragement for them to exert less than full effort in service design and delivery. For buyers, information asymmetry can result in "adverse selection," or their picking a poor quality service supplier. Of course, the potential for repeated transactions can attenuate these problems somewhat. Thus, both sellers and buyers have an incentive to engage in repeated transactions, whether for existing services or for new services.

When choosing services providers, buyers can reduce information acquisition costs by simply using any currently satisfactory providers of other services. Therefore, service providers can sell additional services to existing satisfied buyers more easily than they can sell services to entirely new buyers. This "reputation effect" reduces some adverse consequences of information asymmetry for buyers. Hence, diversified services firms can gain a competitive advantage by selling multiple services to existing satisfied buyers (Nayyar, 1990). Information asymmetry cuts both ways. Not meeting buyer and employee expectations about new services can affect existing services negatively. Unfavorable reputations for existing services can also affect new services negatively.

Service characteristics

Services are not a homogeneous set. Information asymmetry varies with three service attributes -- search, experience, and credence qualities (Darby & Karni, 1973). Search qualities are attributes such as color, style, price, fit, feel, hardness, and smell that can be evaluated before purchase. These attributes are usually determined by tangible components of services such as facility layout and features, equipment, uniforms, consulting reports, structural plans, and presentation material. Intangible attributes include service descriptors such as the term, interest rate, rate cap, approval time, and monthly payments of a mortgage loan.

Experience qualities are attributes such as taste, purchase satisfaction, convenience, safety, security, speed, reliability, level of comfort, and a seller's attention to buyer's needs and feelings that can be evaluated only after purchase or during consumption. Credence qualities are intangible attributes such as the degree of service providers' professionalism and knowledge, and the advantages of certain repair or medical care procedures that buyers are unable to evaluate even after purchase and consumption.

Each service comprises a mix of search, experience and credence qualities. However, one of these attributes is dominant for each service. To examine the effect of service characteristics on information asymmetry it is sufficient to only distinguish search services from experience and credence services. Therefore, below I refer to search and experience services only.

By definition, information asymmetry between buyers and sellers is higher for experience services than for search services. Higher information asymmetry results in greater difficulties for buyers (Darby & Karni, 1973). Therefore, buyers' incentives to favor current service providers are stronger for experience services than for search services. Thus, *potential* information asymmetry benefits for diversified services firms are greater for experience services than for search services (Nayyar, 1990).

Diversified services firms with favorable reputations can seek potential information asymmetry benefits in many situations. Public accounting firms often sell management consulting to their audit customers. American Express sells financial services to buyers of its travel related services. Humana, Inc., a health insurance firm, also runs hospitals, and legal services firms also offer financial services to their clients.

6.4 Economies of Scope

Economics of scope result when the costs of producing multiple outputs together are less than the sum of the costs of producing each output alone. Such cost benefits arise when businesses share some unique factor of production, whether it is a management or distribution system, a product or process technology, or plant and equipment. Under certain market conditions when an efficient market in the shared factor does not exist, potential economies of scope provide a diversification motive (Teece, 1980).

Resource sharing among businesses requires that the shared resource be allocated to each business. Thus, the amount available for other businesses is constrained. However, economies of scope also can arise when multiple businesses of a diversified firm *independently use* the same significant resource. Such multiple use does not require any resource allocation among businesses because using a resource in one business does not reduce its availability for other businesses. For example, technology is often *not shared* among businesses. Common technologies are, however, *independently used* in multiple businesses. Similarly, unique managerial capabilities, which are often considered to be distinctive or core competencies (Prahalad & Bettis, 1986; Prahalad & Hamel, 1990), are used to manage multiple businesses in some diversified firms.

Diversified services firms can seek potential economies of scope in many situations. Firms primarily in the hotel business apply their expertise in efficiently meeting travelers' boarding and lodging needs and providing similar services to hospital and nursing home patients. ARA Services, a large, diversified U.S. firm, maintains municipal vehicles using its vast underutilized fleet maintenance facilities, and Delta Airlines services the aircraft of other airlines using spare capacity at its maintenance facilities at many airports.

6.5 From Promises to Reality: Implementation Hurdles in Diversification Strategies

Potential information asymmetry benefits and economies of scope are not always *realized*. Diversification strategies face many implementation hurdles. Realizing potential information asymmetry benefits requires that firms minimize image contamination costs (Carman & Langeard, 1980; Heskett, 1986; Nayyar, 1990; Normann, 1984). Realizing potential economies of scope requires that firms establish working relationships among business units to share resources (Haspeslagh & Jemison, 1991; Hill & Hoskisson, 1987; Hoskisson & Hitt, 1988; Jones & Hill, 1988; Kanter, 1989; Porter, 1985).

Image contamination costs

An image is a mental representation of reality (Boulding, 1956). Image is "an information tool whereby management can influence staff, clients, and other resource holders whose actions and perceptions of the company...are important for market positioning and cost efficiency" (Normann, 1984, p. 21). Image is important because it provides additional information to evaluate service quality and because it guides and controls employee behavior that determines delivered and perceived service quality (Carman & Langeard, 1980; Heskett, 1986; Normann, 1984).

Image conflicts result when a firm offers services of differing quality or when it serves customers drawn from dissimilar market segments (Carman & Langeard, 1980; Heskett, 1986; Normann, 1984). For instance, the provision of "luxury" service by a "no-frills" airline creates an image conflict because customers' attractions and expectations, vary for each service. Each service also demands different employee actions. Since image helps to guide and control employee behavior during service delivery, image conflicts cause employee confusion that leads to service quality variations (Normann, 1984; Schneider & Bowen, 1985). Image conflicts among services confuse buyers. This makes service quality evaluation even more difficult (Heskett, 1986; Normann, 1984). These undesirable consequences of image conflicts are image contamination costs.

Service characteristics affect image contamination costs. Image contamination costs are low for search services because image does not provide valuable additional information for search services. In contrast, image contamination costs can be high for experience services because image is a valuable source of information for such services (Nayyar, 1993a, b).

The source of benefits sought affects image contamination costs. Potential information asymmetry benefits exist only when image conflicts are absent. Buyers transfer favorable reputation effects across multiple services only when there are no image conflicts. Image conflict raises buyers' information acquisition costs and eliminates any information asymmetry benefits. Buyers do not transfer any reputation effects across multiple services offered by diversified services firms when image conflicts exist (Nayyar, 1990).

Pursuing potential economies of scope mixes service management systems and it targets new customers. Mixing service management systems confuses employees and customers about a firm's true image. This confusion is likely to be high for experience services and low for search services. Therefore, when economies of scope are sought, image contamination costs are likely to be high for experience services and low for search services.

Internal transaction costs

Transaction costs are the costs of negotiating, monitoring, and enforcing contracts such as those needed to share resources underlying potential economies of scope. They arise because contracts are incomplete (Williamson, 1975, 1985). Firms adopt costly organizational structures, systems and processes to deal with internal transactional difficulties (Galbraith, 1973; Gupta & Govindarajan, 1986; Jones & Hill, 1988; Porter, 1985; Riordan & Williamson, 1985; Williamson, 1985).

Such managerial actions may not maximize resource sharing among businesses. Although firm-level cooperation benefits may be recognized, there are few instances of actual cooperation in daily managerial decision making (Kanter, 1989). Adding services to corporate portfolios cause anxiety. Such changes cause non-rational behavior from a firm's perspective although its managers may be acting rationally from their own limited perspectives (Buono & Bowditch, 1989; Mirvis, 1985; Riordan & Williamson, 1985; Williamson, 1985). Protecting turf may take precedence over expanding the corporate pie (Gupta & Govindarajan, 1986).

Internal transaction costs depend on the extent of cooperation and coordination required among businesses. Pursuing information asymmetry benefits requires little, or no, cooperation and coordination among businesses in diversified services firms. These benefits arise from sources outside the firm, i.e., the buyers. Internal transactions are few and internal transaction costs are low when potential benefits from information asymmetry are sought. In contrast, internal transaction costs are high when potential economies of scope are sought because they require many internal transactions to share resources.

Other organizational barriers

There exist several other organizational barriers to achieving cooperation in organizations. These are:

1. Lack of communication within a firm about intentions to seek joint benefits (Kanter, 1989).
2. Lack of a detailed action plan for achieving joint benefits (Kanter, 1989).
3. Perceived, or real, loss of independence and autonomy that sharing resources may bring about (Bastien, 1987; Buono & Bowditch, 1989; Gupta & Govindarajan, 1986; Mirvis, 1985; Napier, 1989; Porter, 1985).
4. Resistance to business-level compromises although they would actually result in a global optimum (Jemison & Sitkin, 1986).
5. Organizational learning difficulties that impede entry into new domains of activity (Ghoshal, 1987; Kazanjian & Drazin, 1987).
6. Difficulties associated with technology transfer if a new business is expected to gain from using highly specific technology (Adler, 1989; Gartner & Naiman, 1978; Gruber & Marquis, 1969; Rumelt, 1982; Teece, 1980; Tornatzky et al. 1983).
7. Inappropriate accounting conventions for allocating joint costs (Dearden, 1978) and benefits (Porter, 1985).

Organizational barriers hinder cooperation and coordination among businesses. Firms use valuable resources in overcoming barriers. This increases implementation costs thereby reducing the net gain from a strategy. Attempts to implement the chosen strategy fail if organizational barriers are not overcome.

Seeking potential information asymmetry benefits demands little cooperation and coordination within diversified services firms. This keeps organizational barriers low and greatly increases the probability of realizing benefits. In contrast, seeking potential economies of scope requires cooperation and coordination within diversified services firms. This raises organizational barriers and reduces the probability of realizing benefits.

6.6 Promises, Promises Revisited: Realizable Benefits from Diversification Strategies

Services firms seeking to diversify make two choices:

1. To pursue either information asymmetry benefits or economies of scope.
2. To offer either search or experience services.

Each quadrant in Table 1 depicts a diversification strategy based on these choices. In each quadrant are listed the expected potential benefits and implementation hurdles for each strategy.

Comparing and contrasting strategy pairs in Table 1 helps to estimate the relative achieved benefit from each strategy. To make these comparisons, assume without loss of generality that *high* potential economies of scope are equal in magnitude to *high* potential information asymmetry benefits in diversified services firms. In other words, assume that services firms are indifferent between the two benefits sources when evaluated based on *potential* benefits before considering service characteristics and implementation hurdles because there is no reason to believe otherwise.

Consider strategies C and D. Strategy C offers low potential information asymmetry benefits because it involves search services. These benefits could arise from encouraging trial for new services among existing buyers. Strategy D offers high potential benefits from information asymmetry because it involves experience services. Since both strategies C and D seek information asymmetry benefits both face low image contamination costs. Both strategies require little cooperation and coordination among businesses and, therefore, face low internal transaction costs and organizational barriers. Thus, the achieved benefit from strategy D exceeds that from strategy C. This can be represented as D > C.

Hypothesis 1: Ceteris paribus, pursuing information asymmetry benefits results in better firm performance for experience services than for search services.

Table 1: Potential Benefits And Implementation Hurdles		
Source of Benefits	Type of Service	
	Search	Experience
Economies of Scope	**A.** Potential Benefits: High Implementation Hurdles: • Low Image Contamination Costs • High Internal Transaction Costs • Many Organizational Barriers Examples: • UPS (Air freight) • Marriott Hotels (In flight services) • Sears (Information services)	**B.** Potential Benefits: High Implementation Hurdles: • High Image Contamination Costs • High Internal Transaction Costs • Many Organizational Barriers Examples: • Consulting firms (Executive placement services) • ARA Services (Fleet maintenance services) • Hyatt Hotels (Managing health care facilities)
Information Asymmetry	**C.** Potential Benefits: Low Implementation Hurdles: • Low Image Contamination Costs • Low Internal Transaction Costs • Few Organizational Barriers Examples: • Merrill Lynch (Conference centers) • Ogden Allied Services (Janitorial and building maintenance services) • AT & T (Consumer credit)	**D.** Potential Benefits High Implementation Hurdles: • Low Image Contamination Costs • Low Internal Transaction Costs • Few Organizational Barriers Examples: • American Express (Financial services) • Accounting firms (Management consulting) • Humana, Inc. (Health insurance)

Next, consider strategies A and B. Both strategies seek potential economies of scope. Hence, internal cooperation and coordination among businesses is required. This creates high internal transaction costs and high organizational barriers resulting in a low probability of achieving potential benefits. For strategy B, which involves experience services, image contamination costs are high. In contrast, for strategy A, which involves search services, image contamination costs are low. Hence, the achieved benefit from strategy A exceeds that from strategy B. This can be represented as A > B.

> *Hypothesis 2: Ceteris paribus, pursuing economies of scope results in better firm performance for search services than for experience services.*

Next, consider strategies A and C. Strategy A offers high potential economies of scope. It faces low image contamination costs because it involves search services. It results in high internal transaction costs and high organizational barriers that reduce the probability of achieving potential economies of scope. Strategy C offers low potential benefits from information asymmetry since search services are involved. It faces low image contamination costs, low internal transaction costs and low organizational barriers that greatly increase the probability of achieving potential information asymmetry benefits. In sum, strategy A offers high potential economies of scope, but it encounters high internal transaction costs that reduce benefits and high organizational barriers that lower the probability of achieving them. In contrast, although strategy C offers only low potential benefits from information asymmetry, they are virtually certain to be achieved. Therefore, the achieved benefit from strategy C exceeds that from strategy A. This can be represented as C > A.

Therefore, since D > C and C > A, we have D > C > A. Further, since A > B, we have, D > C > A > B. This means that achieved information asymmetry benefits (strategies C and D) exceed those from achieved economies of scope (strategies A and B) in diversified services firms.

> *Hypothesis 3: Ceteris paribus, pursuing information asymmetry benefits results in better firm performance than that from pursuing economies of scope.*

Methods

I used a standard event-study methodology to determine stock market reactions to the four diversification strategies discussed above. Since realized and potential benefits can differ due to implementation hurdles (Nayyar, 1992a), I identified actual, rather than potential, business relationships in diversified services firms using primary data collected from firms. Once relationships among businesses were established, I found the date on which a firm had announced its intention to enter each related business. I used the market-adjusted returns approach (MARA) to assess the impact of an event on a firm's common stock value by measuring the difference between actual and expected stock returns during a specific time-period surrounding each event.

I selected a random sample of 513 U.S. services firms. Their activities spanned the full range of Standard Industrial Classification (SIC) codes assigned to nonmanufacturing industries excluding utilities, government and noncommercial educational, scientific, and research organizations. The sample firms ranged in size from $250 million to over $15 billion in annual revenues in 1987, with an average of $1.98 billion. Therefore, the sample comprised large U.S. services firms.

I mailed a pre-tested, self-administered, structured questionnaire to the chief executive officers (CEOs) of the sample firms in late 1987 and received 80 usable responses, representing an effective response rate of about 16 percent. Table 2 lists the primary industries in which the sample firms participated. I collected data to classify each diversification event as resulting in either information asymmetry benefits or economies of scope. For more details see Nayyar (1993b).

Table 2: Primary Industries Of Sample Firms	
Industries	Number of Firms
Air transport	4
Amusement and recreation services	3
Banks	6
Business services	3
Communication	4
Consulting services	3
Eating places	5
Financial services	5
Health services	7
Hotels	7
Insurance	5
Personal services	3
Real estate	2
Repair and maintenance services	1
Retailers	9
Transport (except air) and transportation services	6
Wholesalers	7
Total	80

Service characteristics

Two independent expert raters familiar with the information economics literature, where search and experience qualities are discussed (Darby & Karni, 1973; Holmstrom, 1985; Wilde, 1981), categorized all services listed in the 4-digit SIC classification into either the search or the experience category

(Appendix A). Table 3 contains criteria used to classify services. The two raters agreed in their classification for over 95 percent of the SIC codes. Disagreements were resolved by referring to the services marketing and management literatures (Bowen & Jones, 1986; Shostack, 1977; Zeithaml, 1981) and by discussions among us.

Table 3: Classifying Services		
Criteria	Search Services	Experience Services
Difficulty in evaluation	Low	High
Mix of tangible and intangible elements	Tangible dominant	Intangible dominant
Need for joint provision of diagnosis and service	Low	High
Examples	Janitorial services Building maintenance services Data processing services Tax return processing Communication services Retail/Wholesale services Aircraft and Airport services Consumer finance Motion picture theaters Fast food restaurants Mortgage lending	Security services Pest control services Software development Systems integration Consulting Risk management Aircraft maintenance Hotels Insurance Motion pictures Hospitals Asset management Child care services Advertising services Legal services Automobile repair

I identified a primary SIC code for all businesses of each sample firm by comparing the businesses listed on the questionnaires with each firm's 10-K reports and segment data in COMPUSTAT. I used these SIC codes to classify each of the 163 business entries by the 80 firms in my sample as primarily involving either search or experience services. 69 entries were in search services and the remaining 94 were in experience services.

6.7 Promises and Reality: Value Creation and Destruction by Diversification Strategies

Market-adjusted abnormal returns over the period Day (-1, 0, +1) for each diversification strategy are in Table 4. Overall, all 163 business entries created value with a 0.62 percent 3-day abnormal return. A 1% 3-day abnormal return is equivalent to an annual return of 137%. A 1% abnormal return for an average firm on the *Business Week 1000*, with a market value of $3.8 billion on March 5, 1993, results in an increase in market value, after adjusting for overall market movements, of $38 million in 3 days. Diversification moves seeking information asymmetry benefits involving experience services (D) created value with a 1.24 percent 3-day abnormal return. This return was significantly greater than the 0.77 percent 3-day abnormal return created by moves involving search services (C). Diversification moves seeking economies of scope involving search services (A) created value with a 0.46 percent 3-day abnormal return. However, diversification moves seeking economies of scope involving experience services (B) *destroyed* value with a -0.99 percent 3-day abnormal return. Diversification moves seeking benefits from information asymmetry (C and D) created far greater value than those seeking economies of scope (A and B) did (1.06 percent versus only 0.16 percent).

Table 4: Market-Adjusted Abnormal Returns To Diversification Strategy

Source of Benefits	Search Services	Experience Services	Total
Economies of Scope	(A) 0.46* (0.54) 36	(B) -0.09* (0.22) 43	0.16* (0.48) 79
Information Asymmetry	(C) 0.77* (0.50) 33	(D) 1.24* (0.64) 51	1.06* (0.63) 84
Total	0.61* (0.54) 69	0.63* (0.83) 94	0.62* (0.72) 163

Note: *In each cell, the top number is the average market-adjusted abnormal return as a percentage. The number in parentheses is the cross-sectional standard error of the mean. The third number is the number of occurrences (business entries) for that cell.*

* *Bonferroni t-tests with a family-wise error rate of 0.05*

6.8 Organization Design: Unlocking Potential Benefits for Diversified Services firms

Appropriate organization designs are needed to unlock potential information asymmetry benefits and economies of scope for diversified services firms. Nayyar and Kazanjian (1993) suggested how organizations should be structured to realize these benefits. When a service firm diversifies it generally creates distinct organizational divisions. Such divisions are self-contained, generally organized around businesses, products, brands or geographic lines, and responsible for profits or some other performance measure (Hill & Hoskisson, 1987; Hoskisson & Hitt, 1988; Jones & Hill, 1988; Williamson, 1975).

Figure 1 shows some alternative divisional structures. Panel A shows a diversified service firm offering two independent services, S1 and S2, each sold to different sets of buyers, B1 and B2, and each produced from different sets of resources, R1 and R2. Self-contained divisions minimize coordination costs and may be structured around different services or sets of resources or sets of buyers. Forming divisions for this firm is relatively simple.

Panel B depicts a firm where a set of buyers, B1, buys both services S1 and S2, thus providing potential information asymmetry benefits. In addition, another set of buyers, B2, buys service S2 only. Separate divisions could be organized for each service and buyers purchasing both services would interact with both divisions, which would coordinate actions so that potential information asymmetry benefits are not compromised. Alternatively, two divisions could be organized so that each independently meets the needs of each set of buyers B1 and B2. One division offers services S1 and S2 to buyers wishing to buy both and another division offers only service S2 to buyers B2. Or, only one division could be organized containing both resources R1 and R2 and offering both services S1 and S2 to both sets of buyers B1 and B2.

Panel C depicts a diversified service firm in which two businesses share resources seeking potential economies of scope. Separate divisions could be organized for each service with the shared resource R1 contained within one of these divisions. The second division, which also needs resource R1 to produce service S2, would coordinate its needs for R1 with the first division. Alternatively, a separate division could be organized for the shared resource R1 and its output "sold" to two service divisions. Or, resources R1 and R2 could be organized into one division offering both services S1 and S2 to both sets of buyers B1 and B2.

Figure 1: The Pursuit Of Information Asymmetry Benefits And Economies Of Scope

---

RESOURCE   SERVICE   BUYER   EXAMPLES

A.   No commonality between services

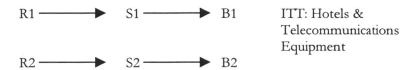

R1 ———▶ S1 ———▶ B1   ITT: Hotels &
                                    Telecommunications
                                    Equipment
R2 ———▶ S2 ———▶ B2

B.   Common buyers between services

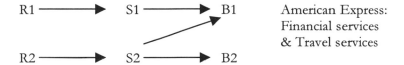

R1 ———▶ S1 ———▶ B1   American Express:
                                    Financial services
                                    & Travel services
R2 ———▶ S2 ———▶ B2

C.   Shared resources between services

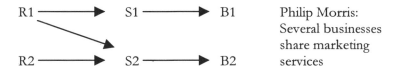

R1 ———▶ S1 ———▶ B1   Philip Morris:
                                    Several businesses
                                    share marketing
R2 ———▶ S2 ———▶ B2   services

Each arrangement of divisions has advantages and disadvantages. The primary purpose of organization design is to help realize business objectives with minimum coordination costs (Williamson, 1975; Jones & Hill, 1988). Thus, organization design is a constrained optimization problem. The objective is to minimize the sum of coordination costs subject to the presence of organizational linkages needed to achieve different business objectives such as information asymmetry benefits and economies of scope.

The business objective of a diversified services firm seeking information asymmetry benefits is to meet buyers' multiple needs so that they reduce information acquisition costs by buying multiple services from the firm. Similarly, the business objective of a diversified services firm seeking economies of scope is to share resources among services so that costs are reduced compared with when resources are not shared.

Assume that

1. The business objective is to seek a primary benefit, i.e., either information asymmetry benefits or economies of scope.
2. All non-coordination costs are constant across alternative organization structures.
3. Each link between organizational units has equal costs irrespective of business objectives.
4. Horizontal coordination among units is achieved by one level above in the organizational hierarchy.
5. Only organizational levels and units directly involved in seeking information asymmetry benefits and economies of scope are considered.
6. Firms produce two services.

Further, use the following notation:
CO   =   Corporate office
BSDi   =   Business Divisions
RDi   =   Resource Divisions
BDi   =   Buyer Divisions
Ri   =   Resources providing economies of scope
Bi   =   Buyer-Interface Unit. These are marketing, customer service, design and engineering, equipment installation, or service delivery departments whose actions could influence buyers' purchase decisions

6.9 Unlocking Information Asymmetry Benefits

A diversified services firm obtains information asymmetry benefits when buyers buy multiple services from it. Buyers transfer reputation effects among multiple services offered by a diversified services firm to economize on information acquisition costs when evaluating difficult-to-evaluate services. To facilitate this, a diversified services firm can organize in four different ways as shown in Figure 2.

Figure 2: Organizing For Information Asymmetry Benefits

A.

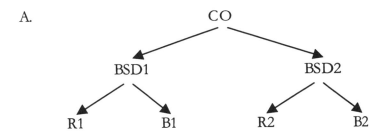

Number of links = 6

B.

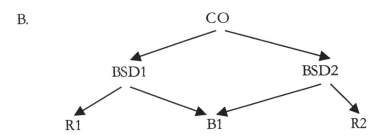

Number of links = 6

C.

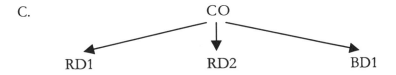

Number of links = 3

D.

Number of links = 2

CO = Corporate office, BSD = Business division, RD = Resource division,
BD = Buyer division, R = Resource unit, B = Buyer-interface unit

Panel A of Figure 2 shows a diversified services firm with two business divisions, BSD1 and BSD2. Each division includes resources R1 and R2 and buyer-interface units B1 and B2 needed to independently produce and deliver the two services to a common set of buyers. To ensure that information asymmetry benefits are realized each division designs and delivers their service considering the needs of other services the common buyers purchase. This requires inter-divisional coordination by the corporate office, CO. This requires 6 organizational links. Panel B of Figure 2 also shows two business divisions, BSD1 and BSD2. Now a buyer-interface unit, B1, is shared by the two divisions to better serve common buyers. This also requires 6 organizational links.

Panel C of Figure 2 shows a diversified services firm with two resource divisions, RD1 and RD2, and one buyer division, BD1. The corporate office, CO, coordinates the three divisions. This requires 3 organizational links. Panel D of Figure 2 shows a diversified services firm with only one buyer division, BD1, that includes both resources, R1 and R2, needed to produce and deliver the two services to a common set of buyers. This results in internally independent divisions requiring only 2 organizational links, which is the lowest possible number. Thus, diversified services firms seeking potential information asymmetry benefits should be organized into buyer divisions with each division designing and delivering all services required by its buyers. This minimizes organizational coordination costs for realizing potential information asymmetry benefits.

Many large commercial banks are organized as commercial, retail and private-banking divisions on the basis of services that sets of buyers purchase. It is possible that this organization design may result in some duplication of effort resulting in increased costs if each division does not take full advantage of any available economies of scale. However, if economies of scale are significant, then the primary business objective of the firm should be to realize them instead of information asymmetry benefits.

Unlocking Economies of Scope

A diversified services firm obtains potential economies of scope by sharing resources across services. To achieve potential economies from shared resources, production and delivery of multiple services offered by a firm must be coordinated. To facilitate this, a diversified services firm can organize in four different ways as shown in Figure 3.

Figure 3: Organizing for Economies of Scope

A.

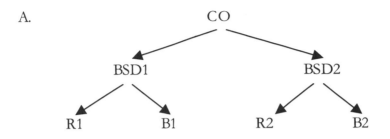

Number of links = 6

B.

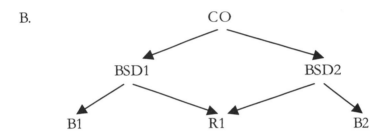

Number of links = 6

C.

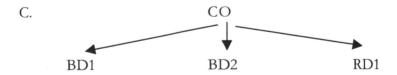

Number of links = 3

D.

Number of links = 2

CO = Corporate office, BSD = Business division, RD = Resource division,
BD = Buyer division, R = Resource unit, B = Buyer-interface unit

Panel A of Figure 3 shows a diversified services firm with two business divisions, BSD1 and BSD2. Each division includes resources, R1 and R2, and buyer-interface units, B1 and B2, needed to independently produce and deliver the two services to two different sets of buyers. Since resources are not shared, potential economies of scope cannot be realized by this structure. Panel B of Figure 3 also shows two business divisions, BSD1 and BSD2. Now the two divisions share the resource, R1, to obtain economies of scope. This requires 6 organizational links.

Panel C of Figure 3 shows a diversified services firm with two buyer divisions, BD1 and BD2, and one resource division, RD1. The corporate office, CO, coordinates the three divisions. This requires 3 organizational links. Panel D of Figure 3 shows a diversified services firm with only one resource division, RD1, that includes both buyer-interface units, B1 and B2, needed to serve each independent set of buyers. This requires only 2 organizational links, which is the lowest possible number. Thus, diversified services firms seeking potential economies of scope should be organized into resource divisions with each resource division designing and delivering all services effectively and efficiently. The demands of each service on shared resources can then be coordinated to maximize economies of scope without congestion (Panzar & Willig, 1981). This minimizes organizational coordination costs for realizing economies of scope.

Most large airlines have a separate aircraft maintenance division to maintain their aircraft and also maintain the aircraft of other airlines. Some large airlines have a separate flight-crew training division that not only trains their own flight-crew but also offers training services to other airlines. Some hotels have a separate food service division managing airline, airport and school food service. Some food companies have a separate food service division coordinating sales and service to the food service industry for all products.

Thus, unlocking potential information asymmetry benefits and economies of scope requires appropriate multidivisional organizational structures that minimize coordination costs while achieving business objectives. Divisions should be structured on the basis of the particular source of benefits being sought by diversified services firms.

> *Proposition 1: Realizing potential information asymmetry benefits in diversified services firms will be facilitated when divisions are organized around unique independent sets of buyers.*
>
> *Proposition 2: Realizing potential economies of scope in diversified services firms will be facilitated when divisions are organized around unique shared resources.*

6.10 Conclusions

The pursuit of potential information asymmetry benefits and economies of scope results in two *different* related diversification strategies for services firms. They differ in the underlying mechanisms generating potential benefits. Their effectiveness varies depending upon the type of services involved. Their potential benefits are not always realized fully due to implementation hurdles.

In particular:
1. Diversification strategies seeking information asymmetry benefits are valued more highly by the stock market than strategies seeking economies of scope.
2. Diversification strategies seeking information asymmetry benefits when experience services are involved are valued more highly by the stock market than when search services are involved.
3. Diversification strategies seeking economies of scope when search services are involved are valued more highly by the stock market than when experience services are involved.
4. Diversification strategies seeking economies of scope when experience services are involved are valued *negatively* by the stock market.

It is clear that service characteristics and implementation hurdles make a difference in the performance impact of different diversification strategies. Information asymmetry between buyers and sellers of services, which is a demand-side phenomenon that does not directly affect the production cost function, fundamentally alters the relative attractiveness of strategic options based on potential economies of scope.

The pursuit of economies of scope is not indicated when experience services are involved due to the detrimental consequences of image contamination that Carman and Langeard (1980) and Normann (1984) described. But, when search services are involved, these dangers are substantially reduced and, therefore, services firms might fruitfully seek potential economies of scope in this case.

The detrimental consequences of mixing service management systems referred to by Normann (1984) appear to be much less important when diversified services firms seek potential information asymmetry benefits. Consequently, the pursuit of potential information asymmetry benefits is valued more highly by the stock market than the pursuit of potential economies of scope. Information asymmetry benefits for diversified services firms are greater for experience services than for search services.

Analysts of diversified services firms also face some daunting tasks in determining whether diversification strategies will yield realized benefits. The presence of implementation hurdles makes an external examination of the business portfolios of diversified services firms inaccurate because it does not reveal the *achieved* relationships existing among the various businesses of such firms. Diversified firms might participate in several potentially related businesses but might never gain any benefits from doing so. If this deviation of achieved relatedness from potential relatedness is large, it presents a difficult analytical problem because connecting diversification strategies to firm performance requires measuring *achieved* relatedness within diversified services firms. Furthermore, diversified services firms differ substantially in their abilities to implement diversification strategies thereby attaining different levels of achieved relatedness for the same level of potential relatedness.

The particular source of benefits being pursued by diversified services firms cause variations in the multidivisional form of organization. Treating the multidivisional organizational structure as a monolithic category masks important differences within such organization designs crucial to successful realization of potential relatedness benefits. It is, perhaps, this tendency in previous research and analysis that has contributed to the lack of understanding about why diversification strategies often result in no gains for firms (Porter, 1987) and the growing confusion about diversification strategies in the literature (Reed & Luffman, 1986; Ramanujam & Varadarajan, 1989).

Returning to the fog I see engulfing the analysis and practice of diversification highlights some popular value-destroying misconceptions in financial services firms. An example of one unfortunate consequence of being engulfed in this fog is that the terms "universal banking" and "conglomerate banking" are so imprecise. The former suggests "all things to all customers" but surely it does not imply that retail banking, commercial banking and investment banking are to be offered to the same customers or by using the same firm resources. Similarly, the latter suggests "unrelated banking services" thereby implying the absence of synergies. Even "one-stop shopping" does not tell us why it yields benefits.

Services are not all alike. Some are search services and some are experience services. Cross selling is likely to be successful for the latter but not for the former. This distinction has implications for whether there exist any potential benefits from diversification for financial services firms. For example, commercial, or wholesale, banking seems to have little in common with retail banking. Thus, I am hard pressed to suggest potential benefits from such diversification moves. Similarly, commercial and retail banking seem to have little in common with investment banking. Although the "client firm" for both may be the same entity, suggesting information asymmetry benefits, the actual buyers of each service are likely to be different and motivated by different concerns. Thus, I see no potential benefits from such combinations.

When such combinations fail to deliver their "promised" benefits, implementation efforts and "cultural differences" are often blamed. Culture conflicts may indeed be present between commercial and investment bankers. However, without the presence of any potential benefits from combining these two services, such combinations cannot claim to have been crafted to seek synergies. Thus, I do not see their failure as an indictment of diversification strategies.

Another manifestation of operating in a fog is the notion of financial services firms trying to attract customers to have multiple relationships with them. It is thought that such customers are "more profitable" than those who have relationships with multiple financial services firms. Hence, it is believed that financial services firms must diversify into a large number of product lines. However, this line of reasoning is flawed because it ignores a basic tenet of competition. Wide product-lines are not a substitute for basic strengths in the primary businesses that comprise a diversification strategy. Wide product-lines do not necessarily make diversified financial services firms better at providing value than their more focused competitors. Ultimately, all firms need to compete and succeed in the many product-markets in which they have a presence by providing value to customers. Thus, the smart buyers may be the ones who buy from the best purveyor of each individual financial service rather than buy all the services they need from a one-stop purveyor of many mediocre financial services.

Clearing some of the fog surrounding diversified services firms, my studies of such firms for the past 15 years show that appropriately assembling and managing a portfolio of services creates shareholder value. Diversification strategies do work for services firms but only under very special conditions. Financial services firms would do well to let the sun and the wind swallow the fog surrounding their diversification strategies.

References

1. Adler, P. S. 1989. When knowledge is the critical resource, knowledge management is the critical tool, *IEEE Transactions*, 36(2), pp. 87-94.
2. Bastien, D. T. 1987. Common patterns of behavior and communication in corporate mergers and acquisitions, *Human Resource Management*, 26(1), pp. 17-33.
3. Boulding, K. 1956. *The Image*, University of Michigan Press, Ann Arbor, MI.

4. Bowen, D. E. and G. R. Jones. 1986. Transaction cost analysis of service organization - customer exchange, *Academy of Management Review*, 11(2), pp. 428-441.

5. Buono, A. F. and J. L. Bowditch/ 1989. *The Human Side of Mergers and Acquisitions*, Jossey-Bass Inc., San Francisco, CA.

6. Carman, J. M. and E. Langeard. 1980. Growth strategies for service firms, *Strategic Management Journal*, 1(1), pp. 7-22.

7. Darby, M. R. and E. Karni. 1973. Free competition and the optimal amount of fraud, *Journal of Law and Economics*, 16(April), pp. 67-86.

8. Dearden, J. 1978. Cost accounting comes to service industries, *Harvard Business Review*, 56(5), pp. 132-140.

9. Galbraith, J. R. 1973. *Designing Complex Organizations*, Addison-Wesley, Reading, MA.

10. Gartner, J. and C. S. Naiman. 1978. Making technology transfer happen, *Research Management*, pp. 34-38.

11. Ghoshal, S. 1987. Global strategy: An organizing framework, *Strategic Management Journal*, 8(5), pp. 425-440.

12. Gruber, W. H. and D. G. Marquis. 1969. *Factors in the Transfer of Technology*, MIT Press, Cambridge, MA.

13. Gupta, A. K. and V. Govindarajan. 1986. Resource sharing among SBUs: Strategic antecedents and administrative implications, *Academy of Management Journal*, 29(4), pp. 695-714.

14. Haspeslagh, P. C. and D. B. Jemison. 1991. *Managing acquisitions*, The Free Press, New York.

15. Heskett, J. 1986. *Managing in the Service Economy*, Harvard University Press, Boston, MA.

16. Hill, C. W. L. and R. E. Hoskisson. 1987. Strategy and structure in the multiproduct firm, *Academy of Management Review*, 12(2), pp. 331-341.

17. Holmstrom, B. 1985. The provision of services in a market economy. In R. P. Inman (ed.), *Managing the Service Economy: Prospects and Problems*, Cambridge University Press, Cambridge, U.K., pp. 183-213.

18. Hoskisson, R. E. and M. A. Hitt. 1988. Strategic control systems and relative R & D investment in large multiproduct firms, *Strategic Management Journal*, 9(6), pp. 605-621.

19. Jemison, D. B. and S. B. Sitkin. 1986. Corporate acquisitions: A process perspective, *Academy of Management Review*, 11(1), pp. 145-163.

20. Jones, G. R. and C. W. L. Hill. 1988. Transaction cost analysis of strategy-structure choice, *Strategic Management Journal*, 9(2), pp. 159-172.

21. Kanter, R. M. K. 1989. *When Giants Learn to Dance: Mastering the Challenges of Strategy, Management, and Careers in the 1990s*, Simon and Schuster, New York, 1989.

22. Kazanjian, R. K. and R. Drazin. 1987. Implementing internal diversification: Contingency factors for organization design choices, *Academy of Management Review*, 12(2), pp. 342-354.

23. Mirvis, P. H. 1985. Negotiations after the sale: The roots and ramifications of conflict in an acquisition, *Journal of Occupational Behaviour*, 6(1), pp. 65-84.
24. Napier, N. K. 1989. Mergers and acquisitions, human resource issues and outcomes: A review and suggested typology, *Journal of Management Studies*, 26(3), pp. 271-289.
25. Nayyar, P. 1990. Information asymmetries: A source of competitive advantage for diversified service firms, *Strategic Management Journal*, 11(7), pp. 513-519.
26. Nayyar, P. 1992a. On the measurement of corporate diversification strategy: Evidence from large U.S. service firms, *Strategic Management Journal*, 13(3), pp. 219-235.
27. Nayyar, P. 1992b. Performance effects of three foci in service firms, *Academy of Management Journal*, 35(5), pp. 985-1009.
28. Nayyar, P. 1993a. Performance effects of information asymmetry and economies of scope in diversified service firms, *Academy of Management Journal*, 36(1), pp. 28-57.
29. Nayyar, P. 1993b. Stock market reactions to related diversification moves by service firms seeking information asymmetry benefits and economies of scope, *Strategic Management Journal*, 14(8), pp. 569-591.
30. Nayyar, P. and R. K. Kazanjian. 1993. Organizing to attain potential benefits from information asymmetries and economies of scope in diversified service firms, *Academy of Management Review*, 18(4), pp. 735-759.
31. Normann, R. 1984. *Service Management: Strategy and Leadership in Service Businesses*, John Wiley and Sons, New York.
32. Panzar, J. C., & Willig, R. D. 1981. Economies of scope, *American Economic Review*, 71, pp. 268-272.
33. Porter, M. E. 1985. *Competitive Advantage: Creating and Sustaining Superior Performance*, The Free Press, New York.
34. Porter, M. E. 1987. From competitive advantage to corporate strategy, *Harvard Business Review*, 65(3), pp. 43-59.
35. Prahalad, C. K. and R. A. Bettis. 1986. The dominant logic: A new linkage between diversity and performance, *Strategic Management Journal*, 7(6), pp. 485-501.
36. Prahalad, C. K. and G. Hamel. 1990. The core competence of the corporation, *Harvard Business Review*, 68(6), pp. 79-91.
37. Ramanujam, V., & Varadarajan, P. 1989. Research on corporate diversification: A synthesis, *Strategic Management Journal*, 10, pp. 523-551.
38. Reed, R., & Luffman, G. A. 1986. Diversification: The growing confusion, *Strategic Management Journal*, 7, pp. 29-35.
39. Riordan, M. H. and O. E. Williamson. 1985 Asset specificity and economic organization, *International Journal of Industrial Organization*, 3(December), pp. 365-378.
40. Rumelt, R. P. 1982. Diversification strategy and profitability, *Strategic Management Journal*, 3(4), pp. 359-369.

41. Schneider, B. and D. E. Bowen. 1985. Employee and customer perceptions of service in banks: Replication and extension, *Journal of Applied Psychology*, 70(3), pp. 423-433.

42. Shostack, G. L. 1977. Breaking free from product marketing, *Journal of Marketing*, 41(2), pp. 73-80.

43. Teece, D. J. 1980. Economies of scope and the scope of the enterprise, *Journal of Economic Behavior and Organization*, 1(3), pp. 223-247.

44. Tornatzky, L. G., J. D. Eveland, M. G. Boylan, W. A. Hetzner, E. C. Johnson, D. Roitman, and J. Schneider. 1983. *The process of technological innovation: Reviewing the Literature*, National Science Foundation, Washington, DC.

45. Wilde, L. L. 1981. Information costs, duration of search, and turnover: Theory and applications, *Journal of Political Economy*, 89(6), pp. 1122-1141.

46. Williamson, O. E. 1975. *Markets and Hierarchies: Analysis and Antitrust Implications*, The Free Press, New York.

47. Williamson, O. E. 1985. *The Economic Institutions of Capitalism: Firms, Markets, and Relational Contracting*, The Free Press, New York.

48. Zeithaml, V. A. 1981. How consumer evaluation processes differ between goods and services. In J. H. Donnelly, and W. R. George (eds.), *Marketing of services*, American Marketing Association, Chicago, pp. 186-190.

Appendix A: 4-Digit SIC Codes Classified Into Search And Experience Categories									
Search Services					Experience Services				Combined SIC Codes
4221	5064	5211	5931	6143	4011	6531	7542	8651	4119
4222	5065	5231	5941	6144	4013	6541	7549	8661	4226
4224	5072	5251	5942	6145	4111	6552	7622	8711	4459
4225	5074	5261	5943	6146	4121	6611	7623	8712	4469
4231	5075	5271	5944	6149	4131	6711	7631	8713	4619
4311	5078	5311	5945	6153	4141	6722	7641	8721	4784
4582	5081	5331	5946	6159	4142	6723	7692	8731	4789
4583	5082	5334	5947	6162	4151	6724	7694	8732	4899
4612	5083	5399	5948	6163	4171	6725	7813	8734	4939
4613	5084	5411	5949	6172	4172	6732	7814	8741	4959
4712	5085	5412	5961	6231	4212	6733	7819	8742	5039
4742	5086	5422	5962	6532	4213	6792	7911	8743	5149
4743	5087	5423	5963	7211	4214	6793	7922	8744	5159
4782	5088	5431	5982	7212	4411	6794	7929	8748	5199
4783	5093	5441	5983	7213	4421	6795	7941		5599
4811	5094	5451	5984	7214	4422	6798	7948		5999
4821	5099	5462	5992	7215	4423	7011	8011		6029
4832	5111	5463	5993	7216	4431	7021	8021		6059
4833	5112	5499	5994	7217	4441	7032	8031		6399
4891	5113	5511	5995	7218	4452	7033	8041		6519
4892	5122	5521	6011	7332	4453	7041	8042		6799
4911	5133	5531	6022	7341	4454	7221	8051		7219
4922	5134	5541	6023	7342	4463	7231	8062		7299
4923	5136	5551	6024	7374	4464	7241	8063		7319
4924	5137	5561	6025	7394	4511	7251	8069		7339
4925	5139	5571	6026	7396	4521	7261	8071		7349
4931	5141	5611	6027	7512	4722	7311	8072		7369
4932	5142	5621	6028	7513	4723	7312	8081		7379
4941	5143	5631	6032	7519	6211	7313	8111		7399
4952	5144	5641	6033	7523	6221	7321	8211		7539
4953	5145	5651	6034	7525	6281	7331	8221		7629
4961	5146	5661	6042	7823	6311	7333	8222		7699
4971	5147	5681	6044	7824	6321	7351	8241		7999
5012	5148	5699	6052	7829	6324	7361	8243		8049
5013	5152	5712	6054	7832	6331	7362	8244		8059
5014	5153	5713	6055	7833	6332	7372	8321		8091
5021	5154	5714	6056	7932	6351	7391	8331		8249
5023	5161	5719	6112	7933	6361	7392	8351		8299
5031	5171	5722	6113	7992	6371	7393	8361		8399
5041	5172	5732	6122	7993	6411	7395	8411		8699
5042	5181	5733	6123	7996	6512	7397	8421		8999
5043	5182	5812	6124	7997	6513	7531	8611		
5051	5191	5813	6125	8231	6514	7534	8621		
5052	5194	5912	6131		6515	7535	8631		
5063	5198	5921	6142		6517	7538	8641		

1. See *1987 Industry and Product Classification Manual* for titles and a definition of SIC codes.
2. When a 4-digit SIC code included 5- or 6-digit SIC codes that could not all be classified into a single category, the 5- or 6-digit SIC codes were separately classified as needed.
3. Combined SIC codes include businesses not given a unique code. Descriptions of businesses in the *1987 Industry and Product Classification Manual* were used to classify them.

Chapter 7

Challenges of Product Delivery in Emerging Markets

Akshaya Bhargava
Citibank, Czech Republic

7.1 Background

Commercial banking today is very much an international industry. Factors such as advances in technology, the decreasing relevance of political boundaries, and international consolidation of production capabilities as well as distribution and sales channels of a bank's corporate customers have contributed to rapid developments in financial products both on the supply as well as on the demand side.

In this environment, the biggest strategic choice for any bank with international aspirations is its overall business positioning. Since wholesale financial services products are regarded by many as almost commodity products, it would lead us to expect a high level of uniformity in business strategies adopted by banks and very strong linkages between overall business goals and individual product strategies.

This chapter examines this aspect with a specific focus on international commercial banks in emerging markets and seeks to examine strategic choices available to them in light of their objective of building business revenues that are sustainable in the long term.

7.2 Long term Business Strategy versus Marketplace Performance

Global commercial banks have either adopted niche strategies to focus on specific product families (JP Morgan, Morgan Stanley Dean Witter, State Street) or specific markets (Standard Chartered Bank, Deutsche Bank) or more broad-based strategies (Citibank, Hong Kong and Shanghai Banking Corporation (HSBC), ING Group, Chase). While the bank's global strategy is an important statement, a compelling strategic vision does not always result in a sustainable competitive advantage or a superior competitive position. This is because a strong business strategy does not automatically result in an explicit strategy for product delivery, where tactical considerations often overshadow concerns of long-term competitive positioning. It is the contention of the author that many business strategies fail precisely because they do not succeed in making a clear and logical linkage between the overall business strategy and sub-strategies for individual products.

The central reason behind this phenomenon is that it is relatively easy for a corporate customer to buy financial products in an "unbundled" manner from a bank. This is in part due to intense competition which compresses margins to the extent that it becomes expedient to limit investments (usually with an adverse long term impact), in part due to the ease with which a financial product can be reverse engineered which causes new product margins to fall very rapidly; and in part due to the fact that there is often a conflict between that bank's overall strategy and the minimum capability required to compete effectively in the long term.

Unbundled buyer behavior also leads to excessive focus on augmentation of features and functions to defend market share and can lead to an artificially narrow perspective of the competitive arena, making niche strategies appear to be far more attractive because it is easier to achieve a superior position in individual products. This may well be a good option in developed markets, but it is inappropriate in emerging market-economies where markets are still rapidly developing. This chapter seeks to demonstrate that the pace of development in emerging markets make niche strategies inappropriate.

To illustrate this point, the cash management product family has been used as an example. Various strategic alternatives for building a cash management business are examined to determine which alternative represents superior long-term revenue streams.

As a starting point, it is important to look at

- what is required to be a long-term player in a particular product family (e.g. cash management) and
- are these requirements consistent with bank's overall business strategy.

7.3 What is Cash Management?

Cash management, from a bank's standpoint, is a product family that consists of all products and services that are provided by the bank that allow its customers (in this case only corporate and institutional) to

- manage their receivables and payables
- integrate their operational processes with that of their banks'
- optimize transactional risk and associated costs

As a result, some of the specific products that form cash management are:

- Depository Services (Current Accounts, Time Deposits)
- Payments
- Collections
- Electronic Services (Electronic Banking, EDI, e-commerce)
- Liquidity Management (Pooling, Netting)

Cash management products are usually one of the three most significant revenue streams for any commercial bank (others being lending and treasury). While these products tend to be specifically sold and explicitly priced in developed markets, they are considered a part of the operating business of the customer and are often very loosely priced (sometimes not at all), with account balances being used to compensate the bank.

As there is no direct linkage between product usage and price, cash management is often seen as a part of "operations" and many banks do not focus on it as a product set in which they can differentiate themselves. Payments, collections, deposits etc. are seen as something that are a result of other products being sold to the customer. Some banks, on the other hand, have taken an opposite view and have been successful in differentiating themselves in cash management.

Before we develop this argument further, it is important to understand the revenue dynamics of cash management. Unlike some other banking products, cash management is both a "flow" business as well as a "stock" business. It is a "flow" business because of the payment flows that a customer generates through his bank account (as he pays his suppliers and collects from his customers). This generates fee income for the bank, which is an explicit income for the bank and an explicit cost for the corporate customer.

It is simultaneously a "stock" business because some portion of the flow stays with the bank in the form of account balances or time deposits. These provide liquidity and generate interest income for the bank. For the bank this is clearly income and although this is not as explicit for the corporate customer, it is very much a financial cost.

While both revenue streams represent income for the bank, in most environments (particularly so in emerging markets), it is the customer account balances that generate most of the revenues. However, since depository products are by their very nature commodities (and therefore very price sensitive), banks try to differentiate themselves by offering superior "flow services" such as collections and payments and electronic integration.

Clearly, it is in the interests of the bank to bundle both flow and stock products to the extent possible. This is often done with banks pricing the flow products very aggressively (sometimes not at all) in order to get greater revenues from the depository products. (This is analogous to shaving products where the razor is deliberately priced low and the bulk of the margin comes from the cartridges.)

7.4 Cash Management in Emerging Markets - The Traditional View

A global bank has many inherent advantages in operating in emerging markets. First, it has a natural customer base in multinationals that enter emerging markets. These customers are familiar with international banks and usually have relationships with the bank in another country. This allows them to leverage that relationship to gain pricing or risk advantages in the new country.

Second, international banks have access to proven technology. It is true that many of these systems are today considered legacy and do not always use the latest available technology, but they have one major advantage – they work. These systems are usually robust, their operational requirements are well understood, application bugs have been discovered (and fixed) over the years and are accompanied by a set of people who understand these systems.

Finally, these banks have a management experience base that extends beyond one country. Most foreign banks in emerging markets are staffed by a core staff of expatriate managers who have worked with the bank in more than one country and can apply lessons learned in one environment to another – once again, giving them an edge over local competitors. This is not to say that local banks do not have advantages. Local banks usually offer much larger branch networks, access to large primary deposits and have a greater share of the government business, but international banks can and do compete effectively for attractive business in emerging markets.

Even so, these factors do not automatically ensure business success and a global bank that wants to be a significant player in cash management needs to consider several factors before establishing a product delivery capability. The important questions with respect to cash management are:

- which customers segments should the bank deal with?
- what products should be provided to these customers?
- what level of transaction volumes will be handled?

These choices are usually a function of the financial infrastructure available in the country (including the local clearing and settlement systems) and are primarily driven by the bank's customer base. Given a global bank's natural affinity for top tier corporate customers, product delivery efforts revolve around the needs of these customers. Even within this customer segment, global banks tend to be unwilling to undertake manpower intensive activities (cash counting, payroll payments) due to the fact that these activities require headcount and large fixed investments.

Local banks, on the other hand, are more than happy to provide such services as these activities utilize their existing infrastructures better and contribute to a lower unit cost. As a general statement, it is safe to say that international banks involved in cash management in emerging markets tend to:

- select a relatively small (usually top tier) corporate customer base.
- have a relatively small branch network in any one country.
- stay away from products that involve manual processing.
- not have large volume processing capabilities.

It is both interesting and important to note the difference in approaches between an international bank and a local bank operating in the same market. The former tends to take a position where investment in fixed infrastructure is seen as undesirable whereas the latter already has a large (usually too large!) infrastructure and sees it more as capacity utilization. This has a direct bearing on the cash management business as we examine the elements it consists of.

7.5 Cash Management - The Flow Matrix

The cash management market is best understood in terms of the payment flows in the economy. These payments are represented in a simplified form in the flow matrix below:

| | | To | | |
		Corporate	Government	Consumer
From	**Corporate**	**1** **Purchase of** **Goods and** **Services**	**3** Taxes, Duties, Tariffs, Goods and Services	**6** Payroll, Benefits
	Government	**2** Purchase of Goods and Services	**5** Purchase of Goods & Services, Taxes	**8** Payroll, Social Security, Pensions, Insurance Claims
	Consumer	**4** Taxes, Investments, Purchase of Goods and Services	**7** Taxes, Pension contributions, Insurance premia, utility payments	**9** Not considered in this paper

7.6 The Flow Matrix and its Implications for Product Delivery

Box 1

The flows in Box 1 represent payments made by corporations to other corporations. This is a very important component as 35% - 50% of flows (by value) in any economy lie within this category. This box also represents the most attractive segment for any bank, especially for foreign banks in emerging markets because it allows them to capture maximum value with minimum investment and minimum customer acquisition. Therefore, accessing payment flows in Box 1 would represent the most efficient utilization of the bank's resources.

However, this is true for every bank in the market and as a result, Box 1 also represents the area of greatest competition and therefore yields the lowest margins. This is another reason banks are forced to price "flow" products for top tier corporate customers very aggressively.

If the bank's chosen strategy is only to operate in Box 1, then from a product delivery standpoint, the bank needs to:

- handle mostly high value payments and collections which do not require a substantial volume handling capability

- have only a single branch presence in a country that allows access to local clearing systems

- maintain close integration with its global network to cater for the cross border flow of payments and collections for its corporate customers.

This is the most common position taken by global banks in emerging markets.

Boxes 4/7 and 6/8

These boxes represent the other end of the spectrum from Box 1. Whereas Box 1 contains high value but low volume payments, Boxes 4 and 7 represent high volume (and low value) collections whereas boxes 6 and 8 represent high volume (and low value) payments from the viewpoint of the bank's corporate customers.

Usually, these payments also represent the areas of greatest difficulty for corporate customers (payment of payroll, dividends, coupon interest on bonds etc.) and while individual fees (and therefore margins) on the payments are low, in aggregate these payments represent another 30% - 45% of flows in an economy. Competitive behavior in these boxes is also significantly different from Box 1. While banks are very aggressive for the business in Box 1, they usually shy away from business in Boxes 4/7 and 6/8 and only agree to handle these services when compelled to do so. Corporate customers frequently try and "bundle" *their* flows by forcing the banks to take the high volume business along with their high value business.

If the same global bank were to aim to build a cash management business in boxes 4/7 and 6/8 (in addition to Box 1), this would have profoundly different implications for product delivery than offering only those services represented in Box 1. Some important consequences are that:

- a local, in-country "network" for payments and collections becomes critical. The cost to build such networks is usually prohibitive. This makes it essential to create strategic partnerships with network providers.

- in emerging markets, boxes 4/7 usually mean large volumes of paper which require manual (or partially automated at best) forms of data capture leading to higher headcount.

- boxes 7 and 8 require a global bank to deal with quasi government or public sector organizations.

- volume handling and logistics management become the required core competencies.

It is evident that the impact of the above choice on the product delivery strategy is dramatically different from the first scenario. It is also important to note that this is a rare choice by any international bank.

7.7 Which Strategy?

Clearly there is a choice to be made here. The alternatives are not close to each other but are actually at opposite ends of the spectrum.

High value, low volume business	↔	Low value, high volume business
Small and manageable production infrastructure	↔	Elaborate and complex (often expensive) production capabilities
Small country presence	↔	Wide geographic coverage
Immediately verifiable business results	↔	Invest for the longer term with a much longer (and uncertain) payback

To answer these questions, we need to consider three factors.

First, we need to go back to the one fundamental fact about buyer behavior for banking products discussed at the start of this chapter – which is the increasing ability of the corporate customer to buy financial products in an "unbundled" manner from a bank.

If the customer's buying behavior is towards an unbundled purchase then price becomes the most important differentiator. This implies a need for lower production costs. In order to achieve lower costs in the long term, scale is important. If scale is important, then the greater the throughput, the better the capacity utilization and the lower the unit price. If lower unit cost is important, then a fixed cost base is far better than a variable one as it will allow for economies of scale.

Cash management, the best example of a scale business in banking, can only achieve economies of scale if the bank's strategy calls for it to compete in Boxes 4/7 and 6/8. It will never achieve critical mass or any long-term economics of processing if the bank chooses to compete only in Box 1.

Second, since features and functions of any individual financial product can be reverse engineered in almost no time, the only long term competitive barrier (other than price) therefore becomes the quality of service. While quality is a function of many things, it is also primarily a function of scale. If the bank does not have scale, it will neither be in a position to apply process disciplines to product delivery nor will it be able to commit high quality people resources to make a difference over time.

Third, we need to consider the impact of these alternative strategies over time. If the bank chooses to remain in Box 1 as the economy develops (which happens much more rapidly in emerging markets than in the developed world), it faces the risk that local banks (who grow with the economy) will begin to make large investments in infrastructure and technology and therefore, achieve scale. As local banks acquire scale they not only get better at managing the business in Boxes 4/7 and 6/8, but they also use that advantage to compete for business in Box 1. A bank that only competes for the business in Box 1 will have no such advantage and it will tend to lose market share over time.

If we follow this line of thinking it becomes obvious that in a scale business such as cash management, it is essential to participate meaningfully in Boxes 4/7 and 6/8, without which there is no long-term advantage for the bank.

In reality there is no real choice in the long term other than to build a business in all 8 segments of the flow matrix, otherwise

- it will not reach critical mass in terms of business volume.

- this will make investments in upgrading local product delivery (leading to lower long term unit costs) uneconomic.

- this lack of investment will make it impossible to gain critical mass by way of market share.

In terms of timing of investment, in the emerging markets context, it is also historically accurate to assume that as the economy develops, local banks will find investing in their own capacity for product delivery more attractive. Therefore, unless a global bank undertakes a similar pre-emptive investment, it may find that barriers to entry become much too high, and the only way to gain market share is by acquisition (as is the case in developed markets).

7.8 Beyond Cash Management

Cash management is but an extreme illustration of the general conclusion from this argument, which holds true for all products. Unless the global bank has scale, it will not find it attractive to make investments; unless it makes those very investments, it will not be able to gain economies of scale; if it does not gain economies of scale, someone else (usually a local bank) will; if other competitors gain scale then banks without scale will see their market share diminish over time.

Recent developments in technology and networking do not in any way take away from this theme. Let us consider two major factors – the Internet and regional processing.

With the advent of the Internet as a channel for delivering/facilitating "banking" transactions, it is logical to believe that it will require less and less infrastructure to offer banking services. It necessarily follows that banks will see greater competition. Under this scenario, if all banks can offer similar (or close) products, the only long-term advantage is the quality of customer relationships and the inelasticity of customer behavior (assuming high standards of service) will become the primary driver for market share. Stated differently, this is another argument for scale.

Regional processing centers are another important factor that can affect economies of scale as it can be argued that regionalizing production capabilities will create scale even in markets where the domestic economies are much too small. Clearly, the greater the level of international business that a bank has, the greater the opportunities for regionalization. This is indeed correct and there are several examples of successful regional operations centers run by international banks.

However, if scale is viewed in the context of having a large enough share of a customer's business in order to leverage either a pricing advantage or a more inelastic customer behavior, then scale acquires a different implication. This view would require a bank to get involved in customer businesses that are not easily amenable to regional processing (e.g. Box 7 - payments made by individual consumers to utility companies). In this context the only economies of scale possible are those that can be achieved within a single country environment.

Perhaps an even more important consideration is whether the bank's overall business strategy calls for scale. This is often not the case as many global banks do not have the investment appetite to achieve and maintain scale. In such a case, regardless of how well articulated a bank's overall strategy is, loss of market share over time is an inevitable consequence. In other words, the bank needs to take a much broader view of its destination positioning beyond niche successes and this needs to be driven not by mere corporate ambition but by a fundamental understanding of the strategic necessity of achieving such a position.

Chapter 8

Modeling Services of Financial Institutions in Emerging Markets

Edward L. Melnick
New York University

8.1 Introduction

The success of financial institutions expanding into emerging markets is a function of the services provided. Competitive positioning of institutions relative to competitors includes location of customer access, services provided, and timing and quality of service. The methodology described in this chapter is intended to infer strategies that will optimize management's objectives and indicate changing dynamics in the marketplace.

Access to financial services can be either physical or through an electronic network. Since the focus of this chapter is on emerging markets, the discussion will be limited to physical location sites.

Financial institutions have been expanding into emerging markets with mixed success. Bhargava (chapter 7, this volume), for example, describes different strategies of global commercial banks that include focusing on specific products, specific markets, or a broad base approach. The most efficient strategy, however, depends not only upon the institution's objectives, but also on the social, economic, and political environments of the markets. Therefore, it is important to develop a methodology for understanding the effect of local environmental factors upon the activities of a financial institution in an emerging market. With this knowledge, mathematical models can be developed for suggesting optimal strategies that an institution should adapt. Along with this, an updating procedure is required that will suggest modifications in the policies as the environmental factors evolve through time. This paper proposes such a methodology and an updating procedure.

In an ideal world, performance variables would be defined by the institution and a series of experiments would be designed to determine the effect of environmental factors upon performance. Since running experiments is not feasible, we propose that information from recorded studies be used as surrogate experiments. The objective is to develop contour lines of constant performance on a graph whose dimensions are the environmental factors. From these plots, optimal (or, nearly optimal) strategies could be suggested for an institution within a particular market. Then, building upon the evolutionary operations literature, simulations can be conducted that will suggest policy modifications as environmental factors change.

8.2 Facility Location

The location of facilities that provide services to a spatially dispersed population is a capital-intensive commitment that also influences the demand for services. The location must be in areas where management can react to changing economic conditions. Although widely discussed in the academic literature, location allocation models have rarely been used by financial institutions.

Simple deterministic location models are based on maximizing (profit or distance from competitors) or minimizing (traveling or construction costs) measures within the context of locating a single facility. These models are usually of little value in multi-site studies and in the presence of competition. Further, for some services competitive clustering has been observed to increase demand when compared to isolation.

The next level of complexity is to add a spatial demand component to the model. This is difficult to measure historically. More important, and less well studied are models with changing demand patterns, for example, the demand for services based on new technologies and expected competitive location centers. Although the number of facilities and their locations are important decisions for the management of financial institutions, modeling of the decision process is difficult because of the lack of information and counterintuitive (e.g., competitive clustering) observations.

8.3 Services

The specific financial services, and associated costs, required by customers differ. Low-income customers might, for example, need assistance paying bills and balancing checkbooks, whereas high-income customers might need to capitalize a loan or require investment information. The heterogeneity of the customer base makes it difficult to predict the type and frequency of services required. Attempts to segment the potential customer population have been proposed, but the methodology does not allow for changing needs nor can it be applied to emerging markets where there is little historical experience. Thus, in a problem with little formal structure and great complexity, it is not possible to construct a useful model a priori. Instead a strategy is proposed that uses designed experiments to obtain data that implicitly forms a mathematical model upon which management decisions can be made.

In the following sections a methodology is proposed based on response surface methodology within an EVOP (Evolutionary Operation) framework. The starting point of the analysis is that each market has its own characteristics and each institution has its own unique objectives and areas of specialization. Local banks tend to have many branches and specialize on personal contact and the needs of small businesses for the local population. International banks, on the other hand, specialize on technology and high income customers with international relationships. Given the diversity and limited knowledge of emerging markets, the strategy in this chapter is to approach the modeling process as a controlled experiment, and, as the information base grows, the implied experimental design will emerge as a model.

8.4 Response Surface Methodology (RSM)

Experimental Environment

To begin, assume that an objective, Y, can be clearly stated (e.g., maximize profit, maximize customer base or attraction to a facility, maximize services provided, or maximize a mean-variance measure of profit) and the independent variables, ξ_i, are under the control of the experimenter. For each set of values of ξ_i, there is a corresponding value of Y, yielding a surface above the $\xi_1, ..., \xi_k$ plane. An example of this procedure is provided in section 8.5. Connecting all points with the same yield produces contour lines of constant responses called contour plots. Ideally, the optimal Y can be determined for specific values of $\xi_1, ..., \xi_k$.

The general form of the model is

$$Y = f(\xi_1,\ldots,\xi_k) + \varepsilon$$

where the function f is unknown and ε is the variability not explained by f. A popular form of f is a second order polynomial in which the parameters can be estimated by least squares (or the maximum likelihood procedure).

RSM begins with a determination of the relevant independent variables. In the context of defining strategy planning for financial institutions a set of variables must be proposed that might optimize the Y variable. These variables might include a distance measure from a population center, distance measure from a competitive institution, number of branches to be built, services to be provided, or cost associated with services. The determination of the important variables may be addressed using either one model or a series of structural models. For example, the first stage model may determine the number of branches and the second stage may be used to determine their locations.

Once a model is proposed, it is necessary to check that it only includes the variables important to optimizing Y. This is determined by applying the methodologies developed in the statistical regression literature. The analysis of variance is used for testing the importance of the slope coefficients in the model. These tests are useful when searching for explanatory variables that influence Y. Once a set of variables is identified, statistical procedures such as stepwise regression and/or the C_p statistic can be used to find the best subset. The next step in an analysis is the determination of data subsets that greatly influence the derived model. These subsets may be clusters of outliers that indicate inadequacy of the model, or leverage points in the ξ space that greatly influence the values of the estimated parameters, or a combination of Y values and ξ that influence the development of the model as measured by the Cook Distance Function proposed by Cook (1997). This function is a weighted distance measure between the regression coefficients obtained from the full data set and the coefficients computed by deleting the ith observation. Large values of this measure (greater than 1) indicate observations that have great influence on the regression results.

Finally, in a series of controlled experiments, the response surface can be mapped. Optimality is obtained by applying an optimization technique such as the method of steepest ascent to plan new experiments and move the process to its optimum. Experimental protocols usually associated with RSM are the factorial or fraction factorial designs with additional experiments to indicate possible nonlinear structure. Computing efficiency is obtained if the ξ_i values are standardized to coded variables x_i that are dimensionless with mean zero and variance one.

In the context of modeling services for financial institutions, multiple objectives must be satisfied. One set of goals might be to service a maximum number of local industries with a minimum number of branches while maximizing profit. An ad hoc solution for this problem is to address singularly each objective, overlay the three contour graphs, and select the ξ_i that comes the closest to optimizing all objectives. More formal algorithmic solutions are based on a value of Y that is a weighted function (weights reflecting relative importance) of the objectives.

Exploratory Environment

The modeling of service in an emerging market is, by definition, very difficult since there are little available data, a situation that does not lend itself to a statistically designed study. The solution proposed here is an extension of the idealized problem discussed above. Issues to be addressed are the determination of the influencing independent variables, the size of a surrogate data file, and design or lack of design used to capture that data. The steps of the proposed methodology are:

i. Develop a response surface with the surrogate data.
ii. Find the region of optimality with the derived surface.
iii. Design experiments within the markets of interest, and
iv. Modify the response surface with the newly captured data.

One approach to dynamically developing a response surface model is based on the ideas of Taguchi (1987). He proposed separating the independent variables into two groups: the control factors that are the variables controlled by the experimenter and the noise factors that are the uncontrolled variables affecting the dependent Y variable. For example, control factors might include services to be offered and location of branches, whereas the noise factors might reflect local political climate, and strength of the economy. The uncontrolled noise variables cause most of the variability around optimality. In the problem defined in this chapter, the noise variables are included in the set of independent variables. Taguchi's focus is to determine robust parameters. His proposal is to categorize the response variable as a function of levels of the noise factors and select the levels of control factors with minimal response variation as a function of noise and then optimize the response variable. To this end he proposes signal-to-noise ratios for selecting the levels of the independent variables that maximize/minimize or achieve a target value for Y. Myers and Montgomery (1995) extended the methodology by proposing mean-variance functions that could be used to generate response surfaces. These general functions allow a determination of the independent variables that affect dispersion and interact with the noise factors.

Evolving Environment

RSM was developed for determining factors that optimize a process. The underlying assumption is that the environment is static and data can be generated from a series of carefully planned experiments. Evolutionary operation (EVOP) is a related methodology proposed by Box (1952). Its purpose is to continually monitor and improve a process. In the context of modeling services, the initial data are obtained from similar studies and are used to define the initial services provided by a financial institution. EVOP is introduced by making small changes in the levels of the control variables. These changes should be sufficiently small as to not create dramatic changes in the market but large enough to result in some behavioral changes. The changes are made on each control variable following the points of a predetermined design. At the completion of each cycle the response variable is analyzed for changes and a decision is made to change the basic operating conditions. Although EVOP can theoretically be applied to all variables, it cannot be applied to location variables and, in practice, rarely applied to more than three variables. The evaluation of the output data is based on standard analysis of variance tests. Tests of the model discussed earlier were within the context of classical regression models. These same tests can be applied to output from EVOP, but the interpretations differ. Here, tests for goodness-of-fit of the model are used to confirm that data used from related studies were reasonable surrogates for the new markets. If this test fails, EVOP must be performed with the objective of striving for efficiency while developing a database.

Once sufficient data are obtained, the process must restart with a search for a minimum set of important control variables. This search is enhanced by identifying the x data with high leverage since they indicate the variables and direction with greatest impact on model formation. In regression analysis it is important to identify points in the x-space that have great influence in determining model properties. High leverage points are of concern because these few observations overwhelm the information content of the entire data file. Since EVOP is based on perturbing the design matrix, it is important to learn which changes (and direction) have the greatest influence on the Y variable. Finally, the identification and study of the outliers will not only indicate the volatility of the Y data, but also more importantly indicate deficiencies in the model such as non-linearity.

8.5 An Illustrative Example

Assume that a financial institution is planning to expand into an emerging market. The institution would like to maximize the size of its local customer base, and therefore must determine the number of branches it will open, the location of the branches, and the percent of activities it will dedicate to services for low-income (local) customers. Further, assume the institution has been able to capture information on experiences where financial institutions have entered into 17 emerging markets. The data are shown in Table 1.

Table 1: Illustrative Historical Market Profile Data				
Market	Size of Customer Base	Percent Activity for Low Income Services	Number of Branches	Average Customer Traveling Time (min.)
1	11250	62.25	21	10
2	6240	54.53	16	11
3	7545	53.87	15	10
4	11190	61.14	25	9
5	7785	63.35	12	11
6	9405	57.83	11	14
7	9810	61.14	16	15
8	10455	58.93	21	13
9	7620	64.46	12	6
10	9330	56.72	12	7
11	8355	60.04	24	12
12	10620	62.25	16	4
13	6975	60.04	8	10
14	10710	57.83	19	8
15	9570	62.25	12	14
16	9330	62.25	13	7
17	11025	61.14	21	11

The notation in this example is

Y = Size of customer base

ξ_1 = Percent activity for low income services

ξ_2 = Number of branches

ξ_3 = Average customer traveling time

The first step in the analysis is the representation of the independent variables into a dimensionless form with mean zero and variance one. This is accomplished by forming:

$$x_{ij} = \frac{\xi_{ij} - \overline{\xi}_i}{S_{\xi_i}}$$

where

ξ_{ij} is the jth observation of variable i

$$\overline{\xi}_i = \frac{1}{17} \sum_{j=1}^{17} \xi_{ij}, \text{ the sample mean}$$

$$S_{\xi} = \left[\frac{1}{16} \sum_{j=1}^{17} \left(\xi_{ij} - \overline{\xi}_i \right)^2 \right]^{\frac{1}{2}}, \text{ the sample standard deviation.}$$

A first order approximating model of the data with low order interaction terms is:

$$Y = \beta_0 + \beta_1 \xi_1 + \beta_2 \xi_2 + \beta_3 \xi_3 + \beta_{11} \xi_1^2 + \beta_{22} \xi_2^2$$
$$+ \beta_{33} \xi_3^2 + \beta_{12} \xi_1 \xi_2 + \beta_{13} \xi_1 \xi_3 + \beta_{23} \xi_2 \xi_3 + \in$$

where $\in$ is the random error term. This model was fitted to the data with the independent variables expressed in standard form. The best derived model is:

$$\hat{Y} = 10827 - 923X_1^2 + 712X_2 - 742X_2^2 + 534X_1 X_2.$$

The residuals for this model satisfy the required properties, the model is statistically significant, and the R^2 statistic (proportion of variation in Y explained by the independent variables) is 0.75. The maximum customer base can be estimated by the usual techniques of calculus, in which the first partial derivatives are used to determine the stationary points and the second partial derivatives are used to determine whether these stationary points are maximum, minimum, or saddle points. In this example,

$$\frac{\partial \hat{Y}}{\partial X_1} \overset{set}{=} -1846X_1 + 534X_2 = 0$$

$$\frac{\partial \hat{Y}}{\partial X_2} = 712 - 1484X_2 + 534X_1 \overset{set}{=} 0$$

so that

$$X_1 = 0.1549, \ X_2 = 0.5355, \ \hat{Y} = 11018..$$

More importantly, the model indicates that the maximum customer base occurs when ξ_1, percent activity for low-income services, is 60 and ξ_2, number of branches, is 19. Based on this analysis the customer traveling time to the branch does not significantly (in a statistical sense) affect the size of the customer base. Below is a contour plot of the derived model:

Figure 1: Contour Plot

Contour Plot of Size of Customer Base

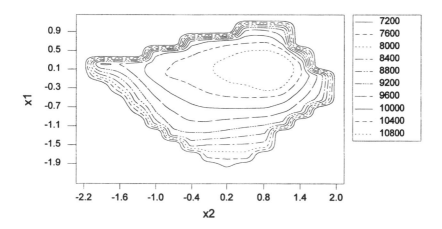

Because every point on the contour plot has a standard error, the true optimum point may not be correctly indicated on the graph. Nevertheless, the graph provides useful input for designing the original strategy and the next set of experiments.

8.6 Conclusions

Modeling services in an emerging market should be based on response surface methodology within the context of an evolving economy. Taguchi and Wu (1980) had introduced robust parameter design, Box (1957) introduced evolutionary operations, and Myers and Montgomery (1995) demonstrated how these concepts could be addressed within response surface methodology.

Time and cost limit the number of control variables that can be considered. This issue is somewhat resolved by making decisions in stages. For example, the first decision might be the number of branches, followed by the choice of location of the branches, and then the services to be offered. Once the location of the branches is determined, the remaining questions focus on the quality of services to be offered.

A second problem is the high level of noise in the system. This, however, is the reason for designed experiments. Replicating results and averaging the data reduce variability. It might also indicate the combinations of control variables that are less volatile.

Finally, as noted by Myers and Montgomery (1995), EVOP appears to be in conflict with the principles of quality control, which advocate not changing (tampering with) a process because it introduces variability. This too is not a problem since the objective is to optimize the success of financial institutions, not to eliminate unpredictable relationships with the institutions.

The goal is to define success for a financial institution and then develop a model that presents strategies for achieving that success. This chapter describes a process that will result in such a model.

References

1. Box, G. E. P. 1957. Evolutionary Operations: A Method for Increasing Industrial Productivity. *Applied Statistics*, 6, 81-101.

2. Cook, R. D. 1977. Detection of Influential Observations in Linear Regression. Technometrics, 19, 15-18.

3. Myers, R. H. and Montgomery, D. C. 1995. Response Surface Methodology: Process and Product Optimization Using Designed Experiments. John Wiley & Sons, Inc., New York.

4. Taguchi, G. 1987. System of Experimental Design: Engineering Methods to Optimize Quality and Minimize Cost. UNIPUB/Kraus International, New York.

5. Taguchi, G. and Wu, Y. 1980. Introduction to Off-Line Quality Control. Central Japan Quality Control Association, American Supplier Institute, Michigan.

SECTION II:

CUSTOMER VALUE FOCUSED SERVICES

Chapter 9

Creating Value: Evolution and Management of Financial Derivatives

John O. Matthews
Cathy A. Rusinko
Villanova University

9.1 Introduction

Financial derivatives have been in the headlines over the past decade as the source of generous profits for many financial and non-financial firms. However, during the same period, derivatives have been a source of dramatic losses for a few users. While derivatives have created much more financial value than financial loss overall, this chapter describes some of the problems that caused losses in order to illustrate how derivatives problems are solved through the efforts of what is known in the management literature as the technological community (Van de Ven, 1993), and also through learning by firms. The problems encountered with development and sales of derivatives are those typically encountered with new product development and sales. This chapter shows how the technological community, via learning, systematically develops solutions to the sets of problems that emerge as the financial services industry evolves and extends its use of this relatively new product--financial derivatives.

There have been three different sets of problems in the derivatives area. The initial set of problems were those associated with management and control issues, including: (1) lack of standards for derivatives; (2) lack of definition of public and private sector responsibilities with respect to derivatives; (3) lack of a framework for management control which led to unauthorized trading; and (4) lack of clarification of the responsibilities that derivatives sellers (dealers) have toward derivatives buyers (end-users). Losses by Gibson Greeting Cards and Proctor and Gamble ($23 million and $157 million, respectively, both in 1995) are examples of these first types of problems.

Another set of problems emerged that were related to the management of firms' portfolios of derivatives and the related issue of the model risk associated with using complex computer models as the basis of asset trading. Many of the derivatives trading operations of both dealers and end-users employ these complex computer models to find profitable trading opportunities. Model risk refers to the potential for errors to exist in the models themselves or in the data that is used as input to the models. Examples of model failure are the Union Bank of Switzerland's loss of $412 million in 1997 from derivatives, partly because of incorrect prices fed into an equity derivatives pricing model, and NatWest Capital Market's loss of $112 million in 1997 from mispricing a portfolio of German and British interest rate options (Business Week, 1998).

The third and most recent set of problems with derivatives can be viewed as a hybrid of the first two sets of problems – both a lack of disclosure and a lack of adequate management of portfolio positions. It involves the great losses sustained by hedge funds, following the upheaval in international financial markets in August 1998. These losses were the result of excess leverage used by firms, combined with the failure of the firms' financial models. Part of the turmoil was due to the Russian government's suspension of bond and currency trading on August 14, 1998. As a result, Long Term Capital Management (LTCM), saw its portfolio fall in value by 44 percent in August of 1998, contributing to a loss of $2 billion for the first three quarters of the year. Through leverage, the firm had controlled $125 billion in financial assets with a capital stake of $2.6 billion (Wall Street Journal, 1998a). The firm was able to borrow so much from banks and other lenders because of its prior superior performance attributable to computer-based trading strategies, and its list of financial superstars on the payroll. Between its inception in March 1994 and the end of 1997, the hedge fund had nearly tripled the wealth of its investors.

The technological community, the group of public and private stakeholders that develop, commercialize, standardize, and regulate financial derivatives, addressed all three types of problems. However, before addressing the technological community, the section below provides a brief background of derivatives and their role in the financial world.

9.2 Background

The Derivatives Market

Derivatives are an innovation that has redefined the financial services industry and created new markets with billions of dollars in value. They are one of the recent product innovations that has allowed the U.S. to maintain the most profitable financial markets in the world (Matthews, 1994). Derivatives are financial instruments or contracts whose value is linked to, or derived from, changes in the value of more traditional financial instruments including stocks, bonds, commodities, and currencies. Derivatives are used for hedging, speculating, arbitraging price differences, and adjusting portfolios. Derivatives allow end-users to more effectively manage the risks associated with holding increasingly larger portfolios of diverse financial assets. There are four basic types of derivatives: (1) futures, (2) forwards, (3) options, and (4) swaps.

These four basic types can be combined to create even more complex derivatives, or hybrids. Since there are virtually hundreds of different types of derivatives and they are all introduced as new products in a similar fashion, this article refers to the general family of derivative products rather than any one specific type of derivative. Derivatives can be further categorized according to whether they are standardized, or customized to meet specific end-users' needs. Standardized derivatives are traded through organized exchanges and are called exchange-traded derivatives. Customized derivatives are privately negotiated by the parties involved and are called over-the-counter (OTC) derivatives.

The Magnitude of the Global Derivatives Market

The Bank for International Settlements in Basle, Switzerland released statistics on open positions in the global over-the-counter (OTC) derivatives market as of June 1998. The data were collected from 75 large market participants representing nearly 90 percent of total market activity. The statistics include the notational amounts and gross market values outstanding of the worldwide consolidated OTC derivatives exposure of major banks and dealers in the G-10 countries. They cover the four main categories of market risk: foreign exchange, interest rate, equity, and commodity.

After adjusting for double-counting resulting from positions between reporting institutions, the total estimated notional amount of outstanding OTC contracts stood at $70 trillion at the end of June 1998. This was 47 percent higher than the estimate for the end of March 1995. However, after adjusting for differences in exchange rates and the change from locational to consolidated reporting, the increase over the period was about 130 percent. The most recent data confirm this predominance of the OTC market over organized exchanges in the financial derivatives business.   Interest rate instruments remain the largest OTC component (67 percent, mainly swaps) followed by foreign exchange products (30 percent, mostly outright forward contracts and forex swaps) and those based on equities and commodities (with two percent and one percent, respectively).

At the end of June 1998, estimated gross market values stood at $2.4 trillion, or 3.5 percent of notational amounts. Allowing for risk reduction arrangements, the derivatives-related credit exposure of reporting institutions was $1.2 trillion. U.S. commercial banks' share of this global market was about 25 percent, and U.S. investment banks accounted for another 15 percent. While the U.S. firms" 40 percent share exceeded that of dealers from any other country, the OTC markets are truly global, with significant market share held by dealers in Canada, France, Germany, Japan, Switzerland, and the United Kingdom.

How Derivatives Create Value

The reason that there has been such dramatic growth in derivatives is that these financial instruments are increasingly important vehicles for unbundling risk. Derivatives enhance the ability to differentiate risk and allocate it to those investors most able and willing to take it. This unbundling improves the ability of the markets to engender a set of product and asset prices far more calibrated to the value preferences of customers than was possible before derivative markets were developed.   The product and asset price signals enable entrepreneurs to finely allocate real capital facilities to produce those goods and services most valued by customers, a process that has improved national productivity growth and standard of living.

Non-banks, as well as bank users of these new financial instruments, have increasingly embraced them as an integral part of their capital risk allocation and profit maximization. It is no surprise that the profitability of derivatives products has been a major factor in the dramatic rise in large banks' non-interest earnings and doubtless is a factor in the significant gain in the overall finance industry's share of American corporate output during the past decade. In the view of Alan Greenspan, Chairman of the Federal Reserve Board, the value added by derivatives is based on their ability to enhance the process of wealth creation (Greenspan, 1999).

While the value of risk unbundling has been known for decades, the ability to create sophisticated instruments that could be effective in a dynamic market had to await the last decade's development of computer and telecommunications technologies. The ability to create and employ sophisticated financial products also encouraged the academic community to develop increasingly complex models of risk management.

Derivatives have very practical benefits for institutions that hold large portfolios of financial assets. First, by providing commitments to prices or rates for future dates, or providing protection against adverse price movements, derivatives can be used to reduce the extent of financial risk. Second, depending on the derivatives instrument, it may cost less to execute a transaction in the derivatives market in order to adjust the risk exposure of an institution's portfolio to new economic information than it would cost to make that adjustment in the cash market. Third, transactions can generally be completed faster in the derivatives market. Fourth, some derivatives markets can absorb a greater dollar transaction without an adverse effect on the price of the underlying instrument, so the derivatives market may be more liquid than the cash market.

The next section explains the role of the technological community in developing and advancing derivatives markets, and addressing the three types of problems (and solutions) that developed among derivatives traders and users. The sequence of problems and solutions show the technological community to be a learning community: it systematically develops solutions to the sets of problems that emerge as the financial services industry evolves and extends its use of this relatively new product. The solutions are generally developed by private sector stakeholders in the community with the oversight of government regulators. The analysis suggests that government regulators can rely on members of the technological community to develop solutions without the need for inappropriate government regulation that could stifle innovation in the industry. Rusinko and Matthews (1996) discuss the benefits of industry self-regulation in the financial services industry.

9.3 The Technological Community Framework

Rusinko and Matthews (1997) used the technological community framework (e.g., Rappa and Debackere, 1992; Van de Ven, 1993) to broadly examine the development and commercialization of financial derivatives. The technological community can be defined as the group of stakeholders, both public and private, that develop, commercialize, standardize and regulate a new product. This group transcends the boundaries of individual firms, industries and populations, and includes public and private sector actors. According to Van de Ven (1993), this community perspective on the emergence of innovations includes three different events that are necessary to develop and transform basic scientific knowledge into commercially viable products or services: (1) resource endowments (or basic research activity); (2) proprietary functions (or firm activities to transform basic R&D into proprietary knowledge); and (3) institutional arrangements (or standardization and regulation). (See Figure 1.) While these three events tend to occur chronologically (particularly at the start of the innovation and product development process), they are also interdependent. That is, they influence one another, or they "co-produce" one another.

Figure 1: The Technological Community

Resource Endowments

- Basic Research Events
- Financing Events
- Education & Training Events

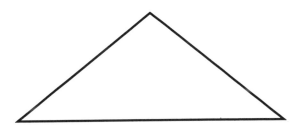

Proprietary Functions

- Applied R&D Events
- Testing & Evaluation Events
- Manufacturing & Sourcing Events
- Marketing & Distribution Events

Institutional Arrangements

- Legitimation Events
- Regulation Events
- Technology Standards Events

Source: From Rusinko, C.A. & Matthews, J. Evolution of a technological community: A case study of financial derivatives. Journal of Engineering and Technology Management. 14(1997) 315-336.

Results of the earlier application of the technological communities framework to financial derivatives (Rusinko and Matthews, 1996; 1997) confirmed two propositions about how technological communities, and hence, innovations evolve: (1) that the success of developing a technological innovation (here, financial derivatives) is largely a function of the extent to which the entire technological community is established, including resource endowments, proprietary functions, and institutional arrangements; and (2) that technological innovations (here, financial derivatives) do not emerge as the result of a few events performed by a few actors, but rather, through many interrelated resource endowments, proprietary events, and institutional arrangements involving many public and private sector actors over time (Van de Ven, 1993).

Since the components of the technological community are interdependent, gaps or under-development in one part of the community can cause problems in other parts of the community. For example, as was the case early on with derivatives, gaps in institutional arrangements (e.g., standards) can create problems with respect to some proprietary functions (e.g., legitimacy and subsequent sales of derivatives). Correspondingly, problems in one part of the community can inspire: (1) solutions by the community; and (2) additional problems within the community, which may arise from the solutions in (1) above. Hence, early on, the technological community was responsible for the emergence of private sector standards setting organizations that solved problems and enabled the industry to achieve legitimacy and to grow.

First Set of Problems: Standards and Management Issues

Since OTC derivatives are customized contractual arrangements (e.g., a traditional financial instrument combined with a futures or options component) that are not traded on exchanges, they represent a significant new technology for the financial sector. The tools necessary for valuing OTC derivatives contracts are complicated, computer based, mathematical models that factor in estimates of movement and volatility for interest rates, currencies, stock prices and bond prices. It is difficult, if not impossible, to value some of these complex contracts without the use of sophisticated computer models.

Dealers have developed these costly models on a proprietary basis to create and trade derivatives. To gain a competitive advantage, dealer firms update their models with the latest approaches developed by financial theorists and financial engineers. Naturally, dealers are reluctant to give outsiders access to their proprietary systems. Dealers' proprietary "secrets" would be difficult to keep if outsiders were allowed easy access to dealers' models.

Many end-users that have lost money on derivatives claimed that they did not understand the risks to which they had been exposed. They also claimed that they had been misinformed and misadvised by dealers, whom, according to end-users, had a fiduciary obligation to educate the client. For example, one end-user claimed that they were prisoners of a secret, proprietary, multivariate pricing model (Fortune, 1995). However, dealers argued that they had no such fiduciary obligation since end-users are financially sophisticated and should be responsible for ensuring that the end-user's staff is trained and competent in the management of derivatives.

Another important problem for end-users was related to the inability of end-users (and also dealers) to monitor the activities of their own derivatives traders. Because of the dramatically new technology that derivatives represented, the old system of management control based on traditional products was inadequate. One part of the problem was that upper management did not understand derivatives and the risks associated with large derivatives portfolios (Hu, 1993). No clear management guidelines were in place to ensure that operating level traders were not taking risks inappropriate for the firm. Also, the value of derivatives portfolios could change in a very short time. In addition, Miller (1994) argues that incentives existed in the system for traders to take excessively risky trading positions. He argues that the gambler's utility function is a relevant way to look at the incentives the trader faces. If the trader makes an unauthorized trade and loses a substantial amount of money for the firm, there is a high probability the trader will get fired. So the trader might as well increase the bet the next time around and try to win back what he or she has lost plus something extra. If the trade works out, the trader is a hero. If the new bet does not work out, the penalty is the same; the trader is fired. Therefore, since derivatives are difficult to value, and since risk monitoring and managing systems had not been very well developed, some traders had been able to take very risky positions without their supervisor's knowledge or approval. It has been alleged that Nick Leeson at Barings Bank lost more than a billion dollars by engaging in unauthorized trading. A sound management control system prevents the trader from facing these choices.

Derivatives blow-ups tend to destroy confidence or trust in derivatives products. Lack of trust can undermine the success of any new product. For example, under conditions of product uncertainty, "lemons" (inferior products) often drive high quality products out of the market because of the negative reputation they create for other industry products (Akerlof, 1970). Successive customers require greater assurances to purchase a product in the event that initial customers find the product to be a lemon.

One of the ways trust can be created, restored, or maintained is through institutional legitimating devices such as the adoption of industry standards. Industry standards can also form the foundation for valuation practices and management control systems. Standards are developed through industry councils, technical committees, and trade associations. These industry associations, in turn, approach, educate and negotiate with other institutions and government units to obtain endorsement of these standards and the development of regulatory procedures (Maitland, 1982). In the derivatives industry, these industry institutions emerged in the 1980s and 1990s.

Solutions

An important role in solving the initial problems with derivatives was played by three standard setting organizations that emerged from the private sector: The International Swaps and Derivatives Association, The Group of 30, and The Derivatives Policy Group. The emergence of these private sector groups is a predictable outcome of the technological community framework.

Standardizing Derivatives Instruments. In the early days of swap derivatives, each bank wrote its own wording for swap contracts. This lack of standardization introduced potentially injurious delays into the approval of contracts as well as unnecessarily large legal expenses. In March 1985, a group of large New York banks established the International Swaps and Derivatives Association (ISDA) to standardize derivatives contracts. Over time, the ISDA has expanded its membership and taken on additional tasks such as negotiating with government regulators to come to agreements on other procedures and practices that relate to the derivatives businesses.

Defining Responsibilities of Public and Private Sectors. The Group of 30 (G30), a group formed by the largest and most influential international banks, and the Derivatives Policy Group (DPG), formed by six of the largest investment banks in New York, both played roles in defining these responsibilities and proposing controls. Both groups have established frameworks that recommend that: (1) policy and decision making for derivatives be made at the highest levels of the organization; (2) derivatives be valued at market, at least for risk management purposes; and (3) end-users and dealers quantify market risk under adverse market conditions. By having firms implement these recommendations, the need for an extensive set of additional governmental regulations for derivatives activities is not necessary.

One of the most important issues for regulators was the determination of the riskiness of firms' derivatives portfolios, and the implication of that risk for the required regulatory capital. To meet expanded regulatory reporting requirements, firms were to provide the Securities and Exchange Commission (SEC) and the Commodities and Futures Trading Commission (CFTC) with net revenue data for the various derivatives product lines or business units. Certain other information would also be supplied to the SEC and the CFTC in the context of the evaluation of risk in relation to capital.

Evaluating the Risk of Derivatives Portfolios. In relation to capital, the DPG came to the view that the preferred methodology to be used to estimate the risk to capital consisted of the calculation of changes in portfolio values based on the firm's quantitative models. However, because the models are proprietary, they may differ from firm to firm. Thus, the DPG had to develop a method to ensure that the performance characteristics of all models used for these purposes would be broadly similar and rigorous. This was achieved by the development of minimum standards and an audit verification criteria that all models would have to satisfy in order to be used for performing the calculations designed to estimate the "capital at risk" associated with OTC derivatives activities.

Clarifying Sellers' Responsibilities. Some derivatives end-users who incurred large losses (e.g., Procter and Gamble who lost $125 million) argued, that the dealers did not fulfill their fiduciary obligations to ensure that end-users fully understood the risks of their derivatives portfolio. The position of the dealers has been that the end-users are financially sophisticated entities and that dealers do not have a fiduciary obligation to educate their customers about the risks of derivatives. The DPG specifically addressed this issue by taking the position that derivatives transactions are predominantly an arm's length relationship in which each party to the transaction has a responsibility to review and evaluate transactions and to obtain necessary information or professional assistance.

Second Set of Problems: Valuation and Model Risk

The Problem of Valuation. In addition to improvements in management and control, holders of derivatives had to decide: (1) what approach to use to assess the riskiness of the derivatives positions held; and (2) how to judge the impact of these positions on the regulatory capital required to be held by financial firms.

Solutions: Value at Risk (VaR). To address the second set of problems, members of the technological community (e.g., J.P. Morgan, Bankers' Trust) developed software that enabled implementation of VaR by derivatives dealers. VaR calculates the amount of risk inherent in any financial portfolio at any given time based on the expected volatility of the financial assets in the portfolio. A computer-based model calculates the maximum amount a portfolio could possibly lose, for example, in the next 24 hours, with a confidence level of say, 95 percent. It also sheds light on how risk exposures in different parts of a portfolio can either amplify or cancel each other out. To calculate VaR, one needs to choose a common measurement unit, say the dollar, as well as a time horizon and a probability. The chosen probability of loss usually ranges between one and five percent. The time horizon can be any length, with the most common holding periods of one day, one week, or one month (Jorion, 1997).

VaR has benefits that go beyond the ability to calculate the potential change in the value of a portfolio. Suppose a bank's portfolio VaR suddenly increased by 50 percent. This could happen for a number of reasons such as market volatility could have increased overnight, a trader could be taking an inordinate risk, a number of the firm's traders could be positioned on the same side of a news announcement, or an error could have been made in recording a position. Any of the factors should be cause for further investigation, which can be performed by reverse engineering the final VaR number. Without this VaR approach, it is difficult for an institution to get an estimate of its overall risk portfolio. Each firm following a number of different routes develops VaR approaches. Some have adopted and modified risk management systems developed and made available by J.P. Morgan (RiskMetrics) and Bankers Trust (RAROC). Others have hired consultants to set up systems. Still others have developed the systems in house, which involves substantial training for the firm employees.

Limitations of VaR. While VaR has attracted substantial support, this approach can only be used with a full understanding of its limitations. There is a danger that relying too much on VaR can give risk managers a false sense of security or lull them into complacency. VaR suffers from the same fundamental problems associated with computer models. That is: (1) it can be "gamed" or manipulated by traders who understand how it works; and (2) it cannot account for unpredictable financial events.

Therefore, most firms use VaR together with stress testing, since these methods can complement one another. Since stress testing allows simulation of unpredictable financial events, it can help decrease the probability of unforeseen surprises. If analysts have sufficient foresight to choose relevant scenarios, stress testing can be effective. However, stress testing is not foolproof since it is highly subjective and depends on the choice of scenarios. An excellent example of how a major bank—Chase Manhattan—uses its VaR system can be found in Labrecque (1998).

The Problem of Model Risk. As financial derivatives mature and become more widely used, problems in managing these products go beyond the issue of risk estimation, and to the heart of the models themselves. These problems are referred to collectively as model risk. Given the range of models, assumptions, and data used by each holder of large derivatives portfolios, it would appear that many firms might have an unfortunate event lurking somewhere in the firm's computers. Model risk covers at least two distinct areas: (1) the choice, testing, and maintenance of the mathematics and computer codes that forms a model; and (2) the choice of inputs and the calibration of the model.

Choice, Testing and Maintenance of Models. These models have been built by the new generation of "financial engineers" who are technically trained in the new financial theories developed in the academic community, but not necessarily conversant with how these models are used by traders on the trading floor. Therefore, the most important step is to develop a way to test each of these models, preferably before they are in use (Elliott, 1997). In addition, traders may develop their own models or enhance those developed by financial engineers. For example, as the derivatives securities become more complicated, longer in term, and less liquid, traders may develop their own views about how these products will trade. If the models used by financial engineers and traders are not the same, there will be internal control problems and a potential for unexplained profit and loss differences.

Choices of Inputs and Calibration of Models. Most of the problems do not occur in the program code, but in the data, inputs, or calibration of the model. According to consultants, few organizations make sure that all their traders use the same database. Firms use data from many sources and it is not unusual that testing of a model is done using historical data that may not match the details of data feeds available today. Therefore, some model users may be using current data sources and incompatible historical information. In at least one case, part of a large loss resulted from models and procedures that were not kept current. Since using poor data can ruin the benefits of sophisticated analytical models, consultants generally recommend that firms set up a centralized data capture mechanism.

Solutions: Model Management Issues. In order to understand how models affect a firm's business, the firm must carefully track all the models they use. This means records of which models are used, how they are used, and who uses them. Problems result when someone changes the logic of an approved model and others are unaware of the change. Therefore, while models should evolve and improve over time, there is a need for firms to establish a procedure to change the model's code and verify the improvement.

Within the technological community, large derivatives holders are increasingly turning to independent consultants for risk management checks that include model audits. The consultants come in with a broader range of models than are used by a single firm, and the models may be more current in terms of finance theory. The consultants can then tell if the model used by the firm is theoretically wrong or using a different approach than that assumed by the firm. Either problem would result in the firm mispricing securities.

Third Set of Problems: Use of Excessive Leverage

Because the excess leverage problem is so clearly illustrated by the LTCM case, this situation will be discussed in detail. In August 1998, LTCM revealed that it had lost about $2 billion, primarily due to unexpected turmoil in the financial markets. Since its founding in 1994, LTCM had a prominent position in the world of hedge funds for a number of reasons, including: (1) a large initial capital stake; (2) two partners who are Nobel Prize-winning financial economists; (3) one partner who was former vice chairman of the Federal Reserve; and (4) several superstar traders from Wall Street.

LTCM's reputation was enhanced by its performance during its first three and one half years with average annual returns exceeding 40 percent. LTCM appears to have earned those returns principally by making judgments on interest rate spreads and the volatility of market prices. To find high returns, LTCM levered its capital through securities repurchase contracts and derivatives transactions, relying on sophisticated models of behavior to guide those transactions. As long as the configuration of returns generally followed their historical patterns, LTCM's mathematical models could be used to find temporary price anomalies. LTCM's trading both closed such price gaps and earned return on capital. But it is the nature of the competitive process driving financial innovation that such techniques would be emulated, making it more and more difficult to find market anomalies that provide shareholders with a high return. The very efficiencies that LTCM brought to the overall financial system gradually reduced the opportunities for above-normal profits (Greenspan, 1998).

To counter the diminishing opportunities, LTCM apparently reached further for returns over time. The firm began to employ more leverage and increased its exposure to risk, a strategy that was destined to fail. Unfortunately, LTCM chose this strategy just as financial market uncertainty and investor risk aversion began to increase around the world. In this environment, which was so at odds with the historical data built into the models, LTCM incurred stunning losses.

The failure of LTCM resulted from a lack of transparency and external oversight in a business that shrouds itself in secrecy. Hedge funds by their nature don't want anyone—even the clients—to learn what they are doing, at least until their bets are in place. And LTCM was more scrupulous about secrecy than most hedge funds. Unlike other funds, LTCM would not disclose the nature of their trades even after it made money on them. Investors who inquired about the details of the trades were told that the firm did not disclose that information. Only the top insiders of LTCM knew before its near collapse the extent of its highly levered global bets—and just who has backed them and with how much money. Therefore, apparently, no one outside LTCM knew the full extent of the firm's global portfolio bets. So it was impossible for anyone on the outside, including LTCM's creditors, to assess the full set of risks facing LTCM. The Wall Street Journal reported that in late August, 1998, LTCM was supporting a balance sheet of $125 billion in assets, about 54 times its capital base of $2.3 billion (Wall Street Journal, 1998a).

Both private and public members of the technological community collaboratively developed both short-term and long-term solutions to the LTCM situation.

Solutions to LTCM's Situation

Shorter-term Solution. In mid-September 1998, LTCM was teetering on the edge of collapse, with lenders pressing claims for billions owed to them. Top executives of 16 commercial and investment banks gathered at the New York Federal Reserve Bank headquarters to put together a rescue package. The outcome of their efforts was $3.5 billion in capital that was put into LTCM to recapitalize the firm in exchange for a 90 percent stake in the hedge fund. Eleven of the firms attending the meeting contributed $300 million apiece and four others contributed $100 million to $125 million (Wall Street Journal, 1998b).

Longer-term Solutions. In early 1999, The Basle Committee on Bank Supervision issued supervisory guidance with the aim of improving bank's policies and practices with regard to highly leveraged institutions (HLI). The Basle Committee, which is comprised of bank supervisors from the G-10 countries, develops supervisory policies for internationally active banks. While the Committee does not have formal enforcement powers, its conclusions and recommendations are widely implemented, both in G-10 countries and many other nations. The recent recommendations related to the relationship between banks and HLI's are an example of the international technological community at work. The Committee's recommendations went beyond those of the G-30 or the DPG in that the banks were to closely monitor not only their own derivatives portfolios, but also those of their HLI counterparties (McDonough, 1999).

The goal with the recent recommendations was to provide a framework for identifying: the broader issues raised by the LTCM episode; the policy responses of supervisors; and some key management challenges for the banking industry going forward. The Committee's report revealed a number of deficiencies in banks' practices, including an imbalance among the key elements of the credit risk management process, with too much reliance upon collateral to protect against credit losses. This undue emphasis, in turn, caused many banks to neglect other critical elements of effective credit risk management, including in-depth credit analyses of counterparties, effective exposure measurement and management techniques, and the use of stress testing.

The Committee found that banks did not obtain sufficient financial information to allow for a full assessment of how much and what types of risk had been taken on by large HLI's. The banks did not have sufficient information to understand the HLI's concentrations in particular markets and risk categories, or their exposure to broad trading strategies. Also, banks did not sufficiently understand the ability of HLI's to manage their risks. Because risk profiles can change dramatically from day to day, it is necessary for an HLI's counterparties to be certain that the HLI can effectively manage its business operations and risks on an ongoing basis.

The Committee also concluded that banks should develop better measures of the credit exposure resulting from different types of trading activities. In particular, banks must develop more effective measures of what is called "potential future exposure." Potential future exposure measures the credit exposure between a counterparty and a bank, and how this exposure could change as market prices fluctuate. Unfortunately, methods for calculating potential future exposure have not kept pace with the growth and complexity of HLIs. As we have seen, under volatile market conditions, a bank's exposure to HLIs can increase quickly. In most instances, banks request HLIs to post collateral to cover their exposures. However, a bank that does not use a realistic measurement of potential future exposure to decide how much collateral to require can find its collateral holdings to be grossly inadequate. The Committee expects the industry to develop more effective ways to measure and manage potential future exposures, and supervisors will closely monitor progress to insure that this occurs.

Stress Testing. The Committee's report also indicates that banks must develop measures that better account for credit risk under extreme market conditions. This can be achieved through stress testing where the banks conduct "what if" analyses of how credit exposures to a single counterparty could grow under these market conditions. These might include a rise or fall in interest rates or a major change in an exchange rate. More rigorous stress testing could have given some banks at least some warning of the types of exposures they faced last fall.

Sound Practice Recommendations. The Basle report is accompanied by sound practices documents that set forth an important set of standards that will guide both banks and their supervisors. Among other things, banks are called upon to take five actions, including: (1) establish clear policies governing their involvement with HLIs; (2) adopt credit standards addressing the specific risks associated with HLIs; (3) establish meaningful measures of potential future exposures; (4) establish meaningful credit limits, incorporating the results of stress testing; and (5) monitor exposure on a frequent basis. Banks generally tightened the credit risk management standards for their HLI exposures after the near collapse of LTCM. However, it is important that supervisors ensure that progress continues.

In addition to the work by the Basle Committee on banks, the International Organization of Securities Commissioners (IOSCO) focuses on securities firms' dealings with hedge funds and the ways in which risk management and market transparency can be improved, which complements the Basle Committee's work on banks. At their meeting in February 1999, the Group of Seven (G-7) countries' finance ministers issued a statement endorsing both the Basle Committee and the IOSCO efforts. The Board of Governors of the Federal Reserve fully endorses the Basle documents. The Basle guidance has been incorporated into Federal Reserve Guidance by direct reference in their

Supervisory and Regulation, "Supervisory Guidance Regarding Counterparty Credit Risk".

9.4 Past Lessons And Future Implications: A Learning Community

The three sets of problems and solutions by the technological community for financial derivatives manifest the iterative nature of new product development, commercialization, and maturation. Likewise, the history and evolution of the technological community for the derivatives industry also manifests that which is vital to survival in a complex and competitive world – learning. The technological community is a learning community.

Over the past several years, much has been written with respect to learning organizations (e.g., Senge, 1990). According to Crossan, et. al. (1995), learning occurs on three levels: individual, group, and organization. Individual learning can be defined as the generation of new insights. Group learning can be defined as the development of shared understanding, based on those insights. Organizational learning can be defined as the institutionalization of new learning into the system, structure, strategy, and procedures of the organization.

Therefore, in the financial derivatives industry, learning takes place at all three levels. For example, at the individual level, financial engineers develop new financial products. At the group level, valuation and model risk management strategies are developed in order to effectively trade derivatives. At the organization level, controls and policies are put into place to try to insure that, for example, traders are not taking inappropriate risks. In addition, learning takes place beyond the level of the organization, at the level of the community. For example, community members – including national and international organizations – come together in order to make recommendations and lobby for their implementation, in order to facilitate efficient and effective development and commercialization of new financial products and processes, as well as to support innovation in the financial industry.

While there is no single view of what a learning organization is, it can be defined as "…. an organization skilled at creating, acquiring, and transferring knowledge, and at modifying its behavior to reflect new knowledge and insights" (Garvin, 1993). According to Garvin (1993), learning organizations are skilled at five main activities: (1) systematic problem solving; (2) experimentation with new approaches; (3) learning from their own experiences;

(4) learning from others' experiences and best practices; and (5) transferring knowledge quickly throughout the organization. While Garvin's focus is at the organization level, in this chapter, we prefer to view these practices at the level of the community.

The technological community for financial derivatives has participated in all of these activities to some degree; however, further participation would minimize the number of future blowups and other problems, and increase the efficiency with which innovative products and processes are introduced to customers by the industry. In addition, further participation in learning activities would tend to decrease the threat of inappropriate regulation that might have a stifling effect on the industry. According to Garvin (1993), participation in *systematic problem solving* and *knowledge transfer* includes tools and training for all organization members. Correspondingly, the technological community has provided tools and training for many of its members, and should continue to do so. For example, training takes place through seminars that bring together academics, dealers, end-users, and regulators on a regular basis throughout the year. Also, a number of universities – including Columbia, Chicago, and MIT – have introduced programs to train financial engineers (Mehta, 1998).

Experimentation, or systematically searching for and testing new knowledge, is practiced regularly by financial engineers and others who develop new products within the community. However, this presents a challenge for managers who must strike a balance between maintaining accountability and control of experiments on one hand, and supporting and promoting creativity on the other hand. In the technological community for derivatives, this balance is maintained by organizations including the private standard setting organizations, as well as individual controls within each organization. The industry needs to continue to work with these organizations; they are vital as standard bearers, and to prevent inappropriate regulation that could stifle innovation and learning in the industry.

For *learning from past experiences and learning from others' past experiences*, Garvin (1993) advocates reviewing past successes and failures; he adds that knowledge gained from past failures is often instrumental in achieving subsequent successes. The derivatives community learned from all three sets of problems (either firsthand or as observers). These lessons resulted in improved control systems in individual firms, private standard setting organizations within the community, more sophisticated valuation and risk assessment technology, and support by community members such as the Federal Reserve and the G-7 Finance Ministers. This kind of learning and quick response by the entire community is vital to maintain industry success and competitiveness. As

Federal Reserve Governor Lawrence Meyer has stated, "...the lessons stemming from this episode (LTCM) have not gone unlearned..." (Meyer, 1999).

Historically, we have seen the technological community address three different sets of problems with three different types of approaches.   Each set of problems resulted in technological community solutions, as well as learning at the individual, group, organization, and community levels.   Correspondingly, each succeeding set of problems was met and resolved by a more mature and better-developed technological community.   Therefore, it is essential that the technological community for derivatives continue to engage in learning activities in order to be able to address future generations of community problems.   While it is true that gaps or problems in one part of the technological community tend to negatively affect other parts of the community, it is also true that learning in one part of the technological community can positively affect other parts of the community.

Additional Learning Applications: Derivatives Markets in Emerging Economies. Given the great potential for wealth creation that financial derivatives represent, some experts suggest that they may be able to play a pivotal role in developing economies. What follows is a very short list of some considerations on this topic. A more thorough exploration will be the focus of a future study.

Since evolution of financial derivatives markets is dependent upon evolution of the corresponding technological community, successful development of derivatives markets in any economy is a direct function of evolution and continued operation of all three dimensions of the community: (1) resource endowments; (2) proprietary functions; and (3) institutional arrangements (See figure 1).   As was stated above, underdevelopment or problems in one dimension of the technological community will have a negative effect on the other two dimensions, and ultimately, upon the entire community and the success of the derivatives market.   Correspondingly, the technological community framework might be used as a type of template for the development of derivatives markets in emerging economies. With respect to financial derivatives, it can provide lessons for all community members, including derivatives developers, dealers, end-users, and policy makers.   A major lesson that emerges is that the success of financial derivatives markets is largely a function of collaborative, community standardization and regulation – primarily by private standard setting groups, and with government playing an oversight role. That is, as is the case with most new products, inappropriate and heavy-handed government regulation can stifle innovation and learning, and diminish the success of developing derivatives markets.

An equally valuable lesson is the importance of a highly educated set of professionals to develop, market, and customize derivatives products and hence, develop the technological community itself. Education is also essential for end-users.

Of course, since derivatives have substantial flexibility and can be customized to manage risky portfolios, the products themselves may be beneficial in accelerating wealth creation in emerging economies. However, as was stated above, education is essential for developers, traders, and users of derivatives.

References

1. Ackerlof, G. A. 1970. The market for lemons: quality, uncertainty, and the market mechanism. Quarterly Journal of Economics, 84: 488-500.
2. Business Week. 1998. Failed wizards of wall street. September 26: 114-20.
3. Crossan, M., Lane, H., White, R. E., & Djurfeldt, L. 1995. Organizational learning: dimensions for a theory. International Journal of Organizational Analysis, 3: 337-60.
4. Elliott, M. 1997. Controlling model risk. Derivatives Strategy, 2:18-23.
5. Fortune. 1995. Cracking the Derivatives Case. March 20: 50-68.
6. Garvin, D. A. 1993. Building a learning organization. Harvard Business Review, 74: 78-91.
7. Greenspan, A. 1998. Testimony on the private sector refinancing of the large hedge fund, long term capital management, before the Committee on Banking and Financial Services, U.S. House of Representatives, October 1.
8. Hu, H.T.C. 1993. Misunderstood derivatives: the causes of informational failure and the promise of regulatory incrementalism. The Yale Law Journal, 102: 1457-1513.
9. Jorion, P. 1997. In defense of VaR. Derivatives Strategy. 2: 20-22.
10. Labrecque, T. G. 1998. Risk management: one institution's experience. Economic Policy Review - Federal Reserve Bank of New York. 4:237-40.
11. Maitland, I. 1982. Organizational structure and innovation: The Japanese case. In S. Lee and G. Schwendiman (Eds.), Management by Japanese systems. New York: Prager.
12. Matthews, J. O. 1994. Struggle and survival on wall street: the economics of competition among securities firms. New York: Oxford.
13. McDonough, W.J. 1999. Statement before the Subcommittee on Financial Institutions and Consumer Credit, U.S. House of Representatives, March 24.
14. Mehta, N. 1998. Fast track to wall street. Derivatives Strategy, 3: 10-12.

15. Meyer, L.H. 1999. Testimony on hedge funds before the Subcommittee on Financial Institutions and Consumer Credit, U.S. House of Representatives, March 24.
16. Miller, M. 1994. Financial derivatives and the regulators. Videotaped speech given at Widener University, October 12.
17. Rappa, M. A. & Debackere, K. 1992. Technological communities and the diffusion of knowledge. R&D Management, 22: 209-20.
18. Rusinko, C.A. & Matthews, J. O. 1996. Standards setting for derivatives by the industry's technological community. The Journal of Financial Engineering, 5: 229-42.
19. Rusinko, C.A. & Matthews, J. O. 1997. Evaluation of a technological community: a case study of financial derivatives. Journal of Engineering and Technology Management, 14: 315-36.
20. Senge, P. 1990. The Fifth Discipline: The Art and Practice of Learning Organizations. New York: Doubleday/Currency.
21. U.S. Department of the Treasury. 1998. Declaration of G7 finance ministers and central bank governors. October 30: 1-6.
22. U.S. General Accounting Office. 1994. Financial derivatives: actions necessary to protect the financial system. Washington, D.C.: 196 pp.
23. Van de Ven, A.H. 1993. A community perspective on the emergence of innovations. Journal of Engineering and Technology Management, 10: 23-51.
24. Wall Street Journal. 1998a. A hedge fund falters, and big banks agree to ante up $3.5 billion. September 24: A1-8.
25. Wall Street Journal. 1998b. How a big hedge fund marketed it expertise and shrouded its risks. September 25: A1-8.

Chapter 10

Electronic Commerce and Financial Services: Going for Broke

Andrew Hosking
Ajit Kambil
Amanda Lister[1]
Andersen Consulting

10.1 Introduction

From every perspective, growth in online investing is astounding. Online transactions are estimated to comprise approximately 25% of all brokerage transactions. Assets held in online brokerage accounts grew to over $420 billion by the end of 1998.[2] The number of online brokerage accounts continued their rapid climb, more than doubling from the end of 1996 to 3 million at the end of 1997 and then again to over 7 million by the end of 1998.[3] The average daily transaction volume doubled from approximately 150,000 in the fourth quarter of 1997 to over 330,000 in the fourth quarter of 1998.

---

[1] Authors are listed in alphabetical order.
[2] According to Piper Jaffray analyst.
[3] Recent figure according to Piper Jaffray analyst.

This growth can be attributed to three factors: technological advances, changes in individual investor attitudes, and favorable market conditions. The marked rise in the use of the Internet (from 13.9 million users in 1995 to nearly 100 million users in 1998)[4] as an efficient broad communications mechanism, has given individual investors new capabilities to transact? This includes improved access to information (such as highly current company information, economic news and securities prices) previously only accessible by professionals, as well as greater convenience to trade at any time of the day. The rapidly declining costs and improving performance of computers and communications have also led to a major decline in the costs of trading. Today online commissions are as low as $8, but average $15 per trade. This compares to $50-100 at a discount broker and $100-$150 at a full-service broker.[5] Online investors have the opportunity to review news, financials, historical values, competitor valuations, commentary (often through discussion groups or chat rooms), and, increasingly, review fundamental research on the investment target. The online investor can choose how much or how little of such information s/he wishes to access, depending upon interests and time constraints. The delivery of the information is immediate, as opposed to traditionally waiting for information to be forwarded by mail. Online investors can place orders outside of business hours for execution during the next market session, although few online investors provide forums for after-hours market trading (though innovations in this area have begun to be publicized). The online investor need not wait until business hours and the opportunity to actually speak to his broker to place an order for a trade. As few investors can devote business hours to trading their personal accounts, the ability to evaluate and order investments after-hours is an important development. For the self-directed investor, the ability to order a trade without encountering the appropriation of a good idea by a broker, the ridicule of a broker for a bad idea, or a broker's conflicting agenda greatly reduces the friction associated with making and executing independent investment decisions.

Accompanying increased investor capability is an increased interest in individual financial planning. This results partially from the perceived crisis in the social security system giving rise to concerns that relying on government retirement planning will prove insufficient for meeting the financial needs of future retirees. Reinforcing the need for individualized retirement planning is the decline of traditional defined benefit pension funds for most employees and the rise of defined-contribution, 401-K retirement plans. These generally involve self-selected asset allocations. High levels of investor confidence have also lead to increased investment, as the market (measured by the Dow Jones Industrial Index) has nearly tripled in value since 1994.

---

[4] Piper Jaffray Equity Research. Online Brokerage Report, October, 1998.
[5] Commission data for discount and full-service brokers derived from data in SmartMoney broker ratings. November, 1998.

The impressive industry growth in online brokerage has attracted increased entry and price competition. The number of firms offering online retail brokerage services has climbed from 12 in 1995 to approximately 100 by the end of 1998. The intensity of price competition is indicated by the rapid decline in average online commission rates. The weighted average online trading commission dropped from $32 in the first quarter of 1997 to $16 in the fourth quarter of 1997, although average pricing has stabilized near $15 through the end of 1998.[6] These changes are dramatically transforming the dynamics of competition in the industry and undermining existing value propositions, revenue and business models. This is explored below.

10.2 The Changing Competitive Landscape

Electronic commerce, as in many other industries, is shifting the value-cost curve as illustrated in Figure 1. Three forces typically operate in this transformation[7]:

- Moore's law or the constant performance-cost improvements in computing and communications originally identified by Gordon Moore.
- Coase's law where declining communications costs reduce transactions costs and increase transaction efficiency.
- Metcalfe's law that the value of the network increases by the number or participants squared as consequence of network externalities. This in turn generates increasing returns to scale.

These forces enable new entrants (Ameritrade, Datek, etc.) to enter a market space on the new value frontier by leveraging new technologies to offer a substantially lower cost-lower value bundle proposition to the customer. If new entrants are able to grow substantial market share, it often undermines the traditional revenue models and deconstructs the value bundles offered by traditional industry incumbents. Incumbents now have to develop a strategy to reconstruct a new value bundle and position themselves on the emergent value-cost curve.

If we map the bundle of services (see Table 1) offered by a traditional retail brokerage firm and a new entrant we can see substantial differences in the range of services and offerings. Full service brokerage firms would typically rate higher on the scale, and therefore, would retain advantages through their ability to provide formalized investment advice, proprietary investment research, access to initial public offerings (IPOs) and capital commitment in positioning a particular stock, enhancing trading liquidity.

---

[6] Piper Jaffray Equity Research. Online Brokerage Report. October, 1998.
[7] See *Unleashing the Killer App:* by Chunka Mui and Larry Downes.

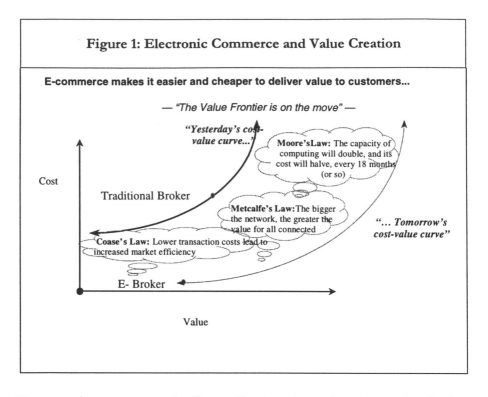

Figure 1: Electronic Commerce and Value Creation

However, the acceptance of online trading is undermining the traditional value bundle and pricing offered by full service brokers. First, new entrants selectively offer the parts of the bundle that are most impacted by the Internet, at a dramatically lower cost of a trade offered to a customer. Furthermore they leverage the customer's new capabilities to "co-create" value or "integrate" multiple value streams online. For example, as customers order trades online in a self-service model, online brokers save costs in order processing that they share with customers. Second, instead of offering advice, the online broker can rely on the customer's new capabilities to integrate information from multiple online sources to make a trading decision, thereby reducing the cost of service to the customer. As customers go towards greater self-service and leverage the new capabilities enabled by electronic commerce, it becomes more difficult to justify high expenditures on full service brokerage. As the value bundle is deconstructed by competitors, customers can arbitrage the cross-subsidies in existing bundles, getting the research for a few trades from a full service firm and trading on a low cost electronic platform. This unbundling of value consumption is forcing the traditional full service firms to rethink their value propositions and revenue models that traditionally relied on full service commissions.

Table 1: Business Models

Traditional value bundles are deconstructed and new bundles emerge.

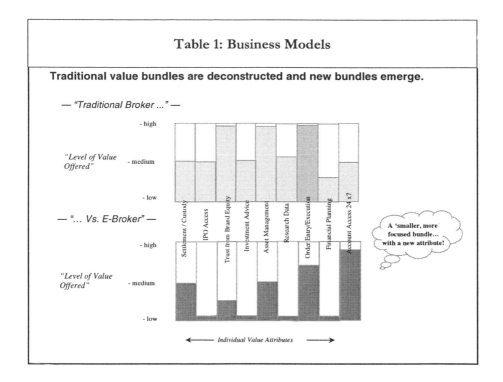

In three short years as online firms have matured, there is increasing convergence in product offerings. All leading brokers provide some free real-time quotes, provide margin lending and cash management services, expanded from trading stocks to trading stocks, bonds and mutual funds, and all provide (directly or through alliances easily enabled over the Internet) market news and links to publicly-available information.

Recently leading online brokers have developed alliances to narrow the gap with full service firms. Charles Schwab provides proprietary research from Credit Suisse First Boston and distributes IPO shares lead managed by CSFB and JP Morgan. E*Trade and other new entrants are establishing similar alliances.

Furthermore, despite a large number of new entrants, approximately 10 online brokerages have attained reasonable name recognition and dominate the online brokerage industry with over 80% market share (measured by transaction volume). These dominant firms include a mix of new firms developed to provide electronic trading services (E*Trade, Datek, Ameritrade), established discount brokers (Charles Schwab, Fidelity, Quick & Reilly, Waterhouse) adopting the online channel, and subsidiaries of well-established, full-service brokers (Morgan Stanley Dean Witter Discover and Donaldson, Lufkin &

Jenrette). Of the dominant firms online, Charles Schwab, an established discount broker, has consistently held the leading market share position. Although its market share has declined slightly over the past two years, Schwab's relative market share continues to exceed 20%. Because Schwab is one of the highest priced online brokers, this dominance is somewhat surprising on the surface, although it indicates an important trend toward segmentation in the online retail brokerage market. While the earliest adopters of online brokerage may have been highly self-directed individual investors, the later adopters that have fueled growth in the industry require greater levels of service. Newcomers to the channel are less active investors. At the end of 1997, the average customer account traded once every ten days. By the end of 1998, the average account traded once every 20 days.

The above trends suggest that online investing is not destined to be solely a commodity, where low prices and high trading volume will be the only determinants of success. The bundling of services (trading, research, bill paying, and financing) will remain important to customers. This is because a pure a la carte model assumes that finding and establishing multiple financial service and research relationships is virtually costless. However, time is becoming a scarce resource for many consumers, making high search costs unattractive. Despite the rapid growth in online brokerage, there remains a large portion of the retail investing customer base that has not converted to this lower cost, higher efficiency investment channel. This is further illustrated when extrapolating industry brokerage commission revenue of $1.3 billion[8], which is small compared to the leading full-service brokerage firms. Nevertheless, all major full-service brokers, including Merrill Lynch, have announced plans to provide online access to its customers. The delay in adoption of the online brokerage channel by traditional full-service brokers has been the need to fundamentally re-orient retail business strategy, which has traditionally been driven by commission-based retail brokers.

How should traditional and new brokerages re-orient their strategies in the emerging environment? We believe they will have to carefully select the market segments that they plan to serve, and select business and revenue models aligned with the segmentation strategy. Below we consider trends in revenue models and feasible business models.

Market Segmentation

New customer capabilities and behaviors triggered by online investing are forcing companies to revisit their market segmentation criteria. While most industry classifications of online consumers are proprietary to different firms,

---

[8] Based upon 4th quarter 1998 daily transaction volume, 250 trading days/year and $15 average online commission.

Gomez Advisors (http://www.gomez.com) provide one segmentation schema that is recognized in the industry. For this article we utilize the Gomez segmentation to illustrate the challenges of aligning revenue and operating models to these segments. While the Gomez classification is intuitive we recognize the need for empirical validation of this and other segmentation models of online customers.

Gomez Advisors classifies individual investors into four useful categories:

- *Hyper-Active Traders*: These are day-traders or other self-directed investors that trade very frequently, desire the most efficient order entry and execution systems, and are highly independent (of their broker) when making investment decisions. Hyper-Active Traders are most concerned about low commissions, ease of order entry, and reliability of execution. Many early adopters of online brokerage are Hyper-Active Traders.
- *Serious Investors*: These investors trade larger balances less frequently. These investors are largely self-directed, but undertake significant research before reaching an investment decision. Serious Investors are most concerned about the depth and integration of research sources and good portfolio information for monitoring investments and ideas. Some of the early adopters are Serious Investors, but this customer segment continues to be very appealing as it describes many of the private clients still using traditional full-service brokers today.
- *One-Stop Shoppers:* These individuals seek convenience in managing all personal financial matters and seek coordination of investing, bill payment, credit and other financial services. One-Stop Shoppers are most concerned about the breadth and integration of various financial services. Younger generations will be more adept with technology and more receptive to change in the way that brokerage services are delivered, as they will not hold the pre-conceived notions of their elders.
- *Life Goal Planner*: These individuals maintain smaller balances, are more likely to invest in mutual funds (investing by asset class rather than specific securities), and are more likely to target investing around medium-term goals (such as buying a home, sending a child to college, etc.). Life Goal Planners are most concerned about broad financial planning tools, general education regarding various investment alternatives, asset allocation tools, and mutual fund screening tools. Life Goal Planners may be less comfortable with computer technology.

While a single investor rarely fits perfectly into one of the foregoing categories, we find the Gomez framework useful in demonstrating the different customer demands placed on online brokers. Emerging customer demands are not complementary. The Hyper-Active Trader craves low cost and efficiency of execution. S/he does not want the broker's site to be complicated or slowed by extensive research or basic investment educational tools. The Hyper-Active Trader demands system reliability and speed. S/he wants the broker to focus on and invest in systems enhancement and back-up, rather than in alliances to offer research or a broad range of financial products. The Life Goal Planner may be willing to pay higher commissions for greater customer support, and may be intimidated by a site that is geared toward highly sophisticated and self-directed investors. The cost and system demands of providing real-time execution at a price may be wasted on the Life Goal Planner, who primarily invests in mutual funds priced at the end of the trading day. While greater on-site interaction would only frustrate the Hyper-Active Trader, it would likely result in higher revenue from the Serious Investor, Life Goal Planner or One-Stop Shopper.

Because of the variance in online investors' demands, successful online brokers will have to make strategic decisions as to which customer needs they will serve, and build their service delivery models accordingly. The variance in customer demands will intensify as the online brokerage industry grows. Initially, online investing was particularly appealing to self-directed individual investors who value the lower commissions, greater information access, convenience and privacy. Later adopters of the online channel are likely to be less self-directed and less technologically sophisticated investors.

Below we consider how emerging customer requirements will require brokerages to reconstruct value and transform business and revenue models. We begin with an analysis of trends in brokerage revenue models.

10.3 Brokerage Revenue Models for the Economy

Brokerage firms can earn three different streams of revenue:
- Commissions from individual investors or suppliers of investment vehicles
- Interest income from financing investors
- Fees for asset management, investment advice and other advice.

Below we investigate trends in each of these categories, and ways in which brokers can re-organize to address emergent segments.

Commission Revenue: Traditionally commission revenue was generated by the price paid by an individual investor to place a buy or sell order and have it processed, executed and cleared. Commissions comprise 50-60% of online brokers' net revenues. The efficiency of electronic commerce has resulted in the average online commissions to fall to $15, and are likely to decline further to the range of $8-10 per trade. This dramatic drop in pricing of this aspect of the broker's value bundle has undermined the traditional offering.

We expect this will lead to the further de-coupling of the price for trading and other brokerage services. Specifically, the industry average will be impacted when brokers charging higher online commissions (such as Schwab at $30 per trade) charge a reduced fee for trades with incremental charges for research access, etc. Commissions at traditional full-service brokerage firms will then decline substantially. Already, some full-service brokers have partially responded to reduced commissions available online by reducing the stated $300-500 per trade commission levels to the $100-150 per trade range for customers meeting minimum balance and minimum activity levels.

While traditional commission revenues from investors are falling, commission revenues from suppliers to online brokers are increasing. Supplier commissions are the fees paid by the manager of load-bearing mutual funds or the underwriting of stocks and bonds. Fees earned from distributing new stock and bond issues are likely to increase for online brokers from negligible amounts. For some time, the bulk of underwriting fees will remain the domain of full-service investment banks, as they will support the origination of such business with corporate finance staffs and research personnel. Several of the leading online brokers have already acted as a member of an underwriting syndicate in distributing directly to their online customers. However, emerging concepts for alternative, online distribution of new issues will almost certainly push down underwriting fees from current levels of 7%.

Net Interest Income: Brokers earn interest income primarily from financing a portion of investors' portfolios (margin financing) and from cash management of excess customer balances held by the broker. Brokers also have the opportunity to profit from the lending of non-financed customer security inventories. Net interest income already comprises 15-20% of net revenues of the leading online brokers. Increased competition may put some pressure on the interest skimmed from these sources, but the future levels of net interest income will vary much more from cyclical factors and market levels.

Asset Management Service Fees: Asset management fees are earned for making and managing investment decisions on behalf of individual investors (or groups thereof), generally within a specific asset class. The leading online broker, Charles Schwab, already sources 19% of its net revenue from managing mutual funds. Asset management fees currently comprise a similar portion of full-service brokerage revenues, although these asset management fees are largely derived from institutional, not retail investors. Retail asset management fees will grow across the industry. E*Trade has already received approval to offer its own branded asset management products. With increased competition, base management fees can be expected to decline. The form of investment vehicle will shift toward no-load funds with performance-based fees.

Investment Recommendation Fees: Investment recommendations include proprietary research and investment advice. Online brokerage firms have largely relied upon chat rooms and discussion groups with voluntary participation by their clients as a forum for advice (which is not endorsed by the broker). Such a mechanism is unlikely to foster high quality advice on a consistent basis. Full-service brokers have long touted the superiority of investing with a broker's advice, supported by proprietary firm research. Even Charles Schwab, a leading discount broker now offers a mechanism for clients with larger balances to connect with a network of independent brokers for advice. These potential revenue streams present the greatest challenge for the industry as neither investment advice nor proprietary research is currently priced appropriately, even on the institutional side of the market. Currently a percentage of the high commission cost of full-service brokers is paid to the broker for generating a customer trade. The online brokerage channel and broader circulation of investment recommendations will result in increased transparency and accountability for the quality of recommendations. Brokers will be challenged not only to establish pricing for broker interactions, but also to segregate pricing among average and excellent brokers.

Other Financial Services: Included in this area are referral fees generated by linking the brokerage customer with banking, insurance, mortgage and other financial services. Consolidation within the real-world financial services sector will ease multi-product offerings. More specialized brokers, if not acquired by banks, will likely provide these services through alliances. Referral fees are unlikely to be sustainable at any material level due to high levels of competition in all consumer financial products.

Future trends in segmentation and revenue sources as outlined above are likely to force traditional brokers to reconstruct their value propositions focusing on specific segments and revenue models. Below we examine alternative business models that may be selected to respond to the identified customer segments, and identify critical factors for their success.

10.4 Business Models for the New Market

In response to changing segmentation we expect brokerages to reconstruct value and organize to offer value through four distinct models: the trading infrastructure specialist, the brokerage services specialist, the financial portal, and the financial planner.

The Trading Infrastructure Specialist: will provide a narrow group of services that primarily cater to the hyperactive traders. These firms will focus on *leveraging new technologies* to gain efficiencies in order processing and execution of trades, to enable the offer of low cost trading to customers. Today this *technology enabled* strategy is best exemplified by Datek, which provides efficient systems to support high volumes of low cost trading and execution with great speed and reliability.

This model provides a focused product offering with few features and limits cross-subsidies that may arise across product attributes. Features such as proprietary research and extensive personalized customer service are unlikely to be offered by the trading specialist. Brokers employing this model will primarily cater to self-service customers requiring little support in making investment or financial planning decisions. Trading infrastructure specialists will compete for customers on the basis of price and reliability of trade execution. The primary revenue sources for this model will be trading commissions and net interest income. These firms will primarily differentiate themselves based on technology enabled efficiencies. For example the development of off-market trading mechanisms for more efficient execution (such as matching mechanisms among customer trades that serve to reduce bid/ask spreads) provides one method of differentiation. Ease of use and online support for more sophisticated option trading strategies (currently most online brokers require a conversation with a broker before placing such trades) provide another basis for differentiation. The critical success factors for profitability in this model will be the ability to accomplish economies of scale, and high trading volumes at low margins. Efficient producers of this service may accomplish scale by providing trading capabilities to other firms who wish to outsource such services.

A risk associated with this model is relatively low customer switching costs. The profile of hyper-active traders implies that they are highly price-sensitive investors focused on order execution costs. This limits the opportunity to develop strong customer loyalty through information based differentiation. The ownership of electronic crossing networks (e.g., Island by Datek) with sufficient liquidity may offset the above risk of customer switching.

The Online Full Service Broker: The online full service broker of tomorrow will most likely focus on the serious investor, providing a range of advisory services in addition to a means for trading. Charles Schwab best exemplifies the emerging online full-service model. Schwab has established a network of independent brokers and large-balance clients who have access to these resources the cost of which is subsidized by the net interest income generated by their high balances. Schwab's higher than average online commission levels can also subsidize the cost of its proprietary research alliances (and access to IPOs). These moves by Schwab are ironic given its heritage as a discount broker. The critical requirements for firms pursuing this strategy are sound systems, a broker service network and proprietary and other research that are integrated. Investors attracted to this vendor will expect well-integrated company information, investment screening tools and watch lists as well as advisory services. However, implementing such a strategy will require substantial changes to the current retail brokerage model.

Traditionally, retail brokers have been paid a percentage of the commission of trades executed by their accounts, creating the motivation to have customers trade actively. These brokers are usually supported by proprietary research and firm's own recommendations. This leads to a potential agency problem, whereby some traditional brokers push account activity by recommending the agenda of their employer, rather than acting in the best interests of their client. In this model proprietary research and good service are not appropriately priced or valued as they are typically bundled in the commission.

As broker relationships migrate online, there will be increased transparency of the value-added by a broker and the quality of research recommendations. Thus, the uncoupling of bundled pricing for broker services and access to proprietary research must occur. This unbundling is likely to force a fundamental change in the way that tens of thousands of retail brokers are compensated. In addition, there is likely to be a premium price for the highest quality advice and research. If a transparent mechanism is established for identifying superiority in research and investment advice, the bargaining power will shift from full-service firms employing analysts and brokers to individual analysts and brokers. As access to customers and data online become simplified, analysts and brokers who have established a favorable reputation may break away from traditional brokerage firms to establish private practices that may offer recommendations directly to individual and institutional investors. Alternatively, they may align themselves with a number of financial services firms and can even ply their skills in an asset management format, charging investors a base fee for enrollment in the program and additional fees based upon portfolio performance.

A critical challenge to online full service brokerages will be navigating the above organizational changes and implementing a sustainable revenue model. Revenues for this model can include the following: commissions, net interest income, supplier commissions, investment recommendations and some asset management fees as average customers in this segment will be among the wealthiest. However, operating costs will be greater due to the need for high quality, well-integrated resources, recommendations, and IT support.

The critical success factors of this strategy will be developing high quality information resources and a brand reputation for supporting investments. This can be done through proprietary research developed in-house or sourced externally. Second, online full service brokerage will have to build higher levels of customer service through brokers and analysts, and integrate across customer switching costs for this model. If brokers and research analysts become increasingly independent in the new economy, investor resources are likely to migrate away from the trading function into an asset management or private practice model, leaving the online full-service model stripped and ill-prepared to compete on the basis of scale. Hence the efforts by Schwab and others to further develop their own asset management services.

The Financial Portal: Financial portals will seek to tightly integrate and appropriately price a myriad of consumer finance services (e.g. financial planning, banking to brokerage) previously provided by discrete companies. The brokerage portion of financial portals will include a range of services such as trading, investor education, research and screening tools. They will also include bill paying and banking services, personal credit, mortgages and perhaps insurance products. Today Waterhouse Securities, a subsidiary of a Canadian bank, appears to exemplify this model although some traditional financial supermarkets such as Citigroup already have a range of services under one organization to implement this model. Portals will best serve the needs of One-Stop Shoppers.

One way to implement this model is to aggregate various existing components through alliances with other service providers. For example, a smaller online broker such as Ameritrade may be plugged into a platform, as might a corporate information provider like Hoovers. After finding a banking and bill-paying component, customer information may be aggregated and presented in a Quicken-like interface. Thus, creating a financial portal presents an opportunity for a number of different companies including existing portals, financial management software companies, online brokers, and banks with online services. Initially the linkages between services are unlikely to be seamless and customers will incur some switching costs in this model in transitioning among service providers across a portal. Over time, technology and portal innovations should increasingly reduce the friction of switching among a la carte services offered on the portal.

Over time, the portals can accumulate extensive customer data and a more complete understanding of an individual's preferences, financial condition, spending and investment patterns. This should enable targeted direct marketing and cross-selling of products. Firms in this segment will compete on the basis of price for the entire product range, breadth of products integrated into the portal, the integration of customer information, and the design of the customer interface. Points for differentiation might include software buyer agents that will assist the consumer in shopping for the best prices for certain services. The risk in this strategy is the inherent tension between the portal and competing service providers to reduce pricing (as customers will compare aggregate package pricing), increase service (largely providing consumer credit), and share overlapping activities (such as providing investment portfolio financing).

Revenues in this model will most likely include commissions on transactions, fee for buyer agency services, and advertising. The critical success factor in this model will be the portal's ability to aggregate an attractive bundle of goods for its clients (including non-financial services). Portals are also likely to evolve to offer more general financial guidance using software or human agents as outlined below.

The Financial Guide: will provide a higher level of service than simple portals to serve primarily the needs of Life Goal Planners. Savings banks or insurance companies (that also manage annuity products) may provide this service, with a plug-in brokerage model providing mutual funds and screening tools or as part of a portal. This model relies on employees to use the new media to provide individual financial planning. Competition in this sector will be based upon brand name recognition and trust and service levels (including high degrees of personalized, human interaction). Because the customers will generally be less self-directed investors and accumulate lower account balances, financial planning services will likely have to be offered on a subscription or fee for service basis or be subsidized through the sale of other services such as mortgages. The latter revenue stream assumes that cross-subsidies across services will be sustainable for a segment of customers seeking higher levels of service and that customer switching costs are high. We expect that the transparency of the Internet will make some cross-subsidies less feasible.

Personalized financial guidance provides further opportunity to capture valuable client information, both about investment intentions and financial resources. This creates the opportunity for targeted cross-selling of products and services (such as USAA has done with insurance, and totally unrelated products). The risk in pursuing this strategy is managing the costs of customer relationships to render them profitable. This is because most products provided to this customer group will be more basic and commodity-like, and therefore lower margin. We thus expect some subscription and usage fees to supplement revenues from cross-selling and minimize incentives for inefficient service utilization. As intelligent agent technology evolves we expect substantial levels of customer assistance to be provided through such software.

Both the financial portal and financial guide strategies will generate revenues from cross-selling products. There is debate whether banks have been successful in cross-selling products. Monahan (chapter 5, this volume) suggests otherwise, as customers are wary of putting all eggs in one basket. Firms are responding to early failures at cross-selling by becoming more sophisticated at identifying customer "intentions" around any specific service interaction[9]. For example an intention may be a broader life objective such as growing the family by having children. Such an intention should generate sub-intentions such as moving to a larger home, and various needs such as finding a home, making the move, mortgages, home insurance etc. By better understanding intentions, firms can organize "intention value networks" of fully owned and independent companies to deliver an array of services to respond to a customer's need arising from a specific intention. We expect this model to be facilitated by electronic commerce and expand such that some electronic brokerage services are part of broader "intention value networks" to fulfill customer needs.

10.5 Conclusions

Electronic commerce provides new capabilities to both customers and providers of financial services. These capabilities allow new entrants to "cherry pick" services to offer customers and allows the customer to integrate disparate services to arbitrage prior cross subsidies and undermine the traditional value propositions in the industry. By lowering the costs of trading and interactions,

electronic commerce also transforms the traditional basis of customer segmentation, such as allowing for the growth of hyperactive traders as a critical customer segment. To cope with these transitions we believe managers of traditional brokerages will have to rethink their segmentation models and reconstruct the value bundles offered in the electronic marketplace. The four models illustrated in this chapter outline one approach to segmentation and servicing customers. We believe successful brokerage in the electronic economy will require careful fit between the value proposition offered and the target market segment, execution strategy and revenue models. As investment requirements and competencies required differ across segments, firms will have to focus and specialize their model to a segment. Otherwise they will not realize the scale or specialization benefits required for competitive advantage in the new economy.

---

[9] See "Best Intentions: A business model for the eEconomy" by Joel Friedman, and Toni C. Langlinais, Outlook Magazine, January 1999, Andersen Consulting.

Chapter 11

The Internet Channel Revolution: The Case of Charles Schwab

Sanjeev Dewan
University of Washington
Haim Mendelson
Stanford University

11.1 Introduction

The Internet has spread like wild fire in the discount brokerage industry. By the end of 1998, more than ninety firms were offering online trading to over 8 million customer accounts, with commissions as low as $5 per trade, and online trading accounted for 13.7% of total equity trading volume. The online volume leader is Charles Schwab, with almost a third of the market, and a trading volume that roughly equals that of its next three competitors combined. Most trades come to Schwab through the Internet channel, and Web investors account for more than a third of Schwab's customer assets. This chapter will use Schwab as a case study that illustrates the use of the Internet channel and the role of Information Technology ("IT") and the Internet in the creation of value in financial services. We show how the Internet has come to the core of Schwab's business strategy, and draw lessons from the Schwab experience to shed light on the broader impact of online trading on the financial services industry.

Over the years, Schwab has repeatedly and successfully leveraged technology to introduce a number of product innovations – 24×7 customer access, a mutual fund "supermarket," touch-tone quotes and order entry, and software-based online trading systems, to name a few. Technology was Schwab's major advantage, but it could also become its Achilles' heel. In the mid-nineties, Schwab's dominance among discount brokers was facing the emerging challenge of the Internet. Based on open standards and scalable computing power, the Internet decreased both the fixed and variable costs of the brokerage business, and substantially lowered the barriers to entry. Electronic brokers such as Lombard (later acquired by Discover Dean Witter) and E*Trade were springing up, offering prices as low as $12 per trade (less than 10% of full-service brokerage commissions), threatening a price war, and endangering Schwab's commission revenues.

The Internet promised to change the relationship between broker and customer. Customers could easily get market information, online advice, and direct access to transactions using a Web browser. As such, the Internet had a particularly significant impact on discount brokers like Schwab, which historically used technology to lower costs and offer superior service at lower prices to investors who did not want to pay for investment advice. Indeed, the typical Internet investor was similar to the typical Schwab customer. Further, Web-based brokerage firms were attractive to Schwab's most profitable customers: those who traded often, usually through electronic channels. Thus, Internet discount brokers presented a threat to Schwab's commission revenues. Schwab's Co-CEO David Pottruck described his company's concerns as follows: "We were very worried about what [the Internet] represented as a threat to our business – the cannibalization it represented – as the prices for trading continued to drop."[1]

This chapter will examine Schwab's response to the Internet threat and, more broadly, the evolution of its business strategy from operational excellence to product leadership and, more recently, to one of customer intimacy. In what follows, the next section provides an overview of the "value disciplines" framework that we use to trace the evolution of Schwab's business strategy. We then review the brokerage industry and Charles Schwab Corporation. Next, we describe Schwab's innovations in the pre-Internet era. The following sections provide an overview of Schwab's Internet channel and the shift to a strategy based on customer

---

[1] Retail Banker International, October 7, 1998.

intimacy. We conclude with general observations about the Internet's impact on the brokerage industry.

11.2 Three Value Disciplines

Treacy and Wiersema[2] propose a framework for analyzing business strategy based on three "value disciplines" that define the value provided to a customer and how that value is delivered. Their framework is based on three distinct strategies – operational excellence, product leadership and customer intimacy – and posits that successful companies have narrowed their business focus to *one* of these strategies. Table 1 summarizes the essential aspects of the three value disciplines, highlighting three attributes in each case:

- the *business focus* that underlies each strategy;
- examples of *companies* that follow each of the three value disciplines; and
- the *role of IT* in implementing each of the value disciplines.

The last attribute – the role of IT – reflects our own view of ways in which IT can be used to create value, as we briefly explain below.

In companies that focus on *operational excellence*, the role of IT generally is to help optimize business processes for efficiency – e.g., workflow automation, elimination of intermediate steps, and squeezing out overhead costs. For example, coordinating order entry with production and distribution, using IT-enabled strategies such as build-to-order and just-in-time logistics can reduce inventory costs. Inventory cost savings can also be achieved by postponing the differentiation of products to later stages of the supply chain, when there is better information about customer demand.

The general role of IT in firms that adopt a *product leadership* strategy is to optimize business processes for speed of product development. Computer-aided design tools (e.g., CASE tools in the case of software development and CAD/CAM tools in manufacturing) can be used to automate product design and development. IT-based systems can provide information and analytic capabilities for product-related decision-making such as positioning, pricing and advertising. Information awareness (about the external environment) can facilitate the discovery of new product ideas, as can knowledge sharing and dissemination inside the organization.

---

[2] Michael Treacy and Fred Wiersema, The Discipline of Market Leaders, Addison-Wesley, 1995.

Table 1: Three Value Disciplines

OPERATIONAL EXCELLENCE

Business Focus
> Providing reliable products and services at competitive prices with minimal difficulty and inconvenience

Companies
> Wal-Mart, Federal Express, GE

Role of IT
> - Optimizing business processes for efficiency (e.g., workflow automation)
> - Substituting information systems for inventory
> - Using integrated information systems to coordinate order entry with production, distribution and service

PRODUCT LEADERSHIP

Business Focus
> Producing a continuous stream of state-of-the-art products and services that are attractive to customers

Companies
> Intel, Microsoft, Nokia, Johnson & Johnson

Role of IT
> - Optimizing business processes for product development speed
> - Providing support for quick product-related decision-making (e.g., design, pricing, advertising)
> - Information Awareness for discovering new product ideas
> - Knowledge Management for assimilating and disseminating information

CUSTOMER INTIMACY

Business Focus
> Customizing products and services to increasingly fine definitions of customer segments; moving from customer transactions to customer relationships

Companies
> Amazon.com, Merrill Lynch, Capital One, Home Depot

Role of IT
> - Enhancing relationships through the use of IT-based channels
> - Optimizing business processes for flexibility and responsiveness (e.g., intelligent call centers, flexible manufacturing systems)
> - Database marketing and other data-mining tools for customer profiling and segmentation
> - Decision Architecture empowers employees closest to the customers

Based on Treacy and Weirsema, 1995

Finally, there are several ways in which IT can support a strategy based on *customer intimacy*, allowing a firm to leverage its customer relationships. First of all, IT-based interactive distribution channels, combined with powerful data mining tools, can be used to track and model customer behavior. The resulting knowledge can be used to personalize and customize the firm's product or service offerings to increasingly fine definitions of customer segments. Business processes optimized for flexibility and responsiveness – e.g., using intelligent call centers in the case of service firms and flexible manufacturing systems in the case of manufacturing firms, enable the delivery of customized products. Customer responsiveness is also enabled by a decentralized decision architecture which co-locates decisions and information closer to the customers themselves.

In what follows, we use the Treacy and Wiersema classification to study the evolution of Schwab's strategy. We start with an overview of the brokerage industry.

11.3   The Brokerage Industry and Charles Schwab

To provide a context for the range of companies and services in the brokerage industry, we start by outlining how this industry creates value. From an investor's perspective, the investment process is a cycle consisting of four distinct steps: information acquisition, investment decision-making, order execution, and account management. We describe each of these steps below.

Steps of the Investment Cycle

- *Information Acquisition* – Investments are driven by two types of information: the investor's financial goals and portfolio positions; and market information that includes news, price quotes, transaction reports and research. Much of the information used by investors comes from their brokers, but an increasing proportion is available from public sources on the Internet.

- *Investment Decision-Making* – This step involves the formulation of an overall investment strategy, which is then translated into tactical trading decisions. The investment strategy specifies the investor's allocation across asset classes. Tactical trading decisions determine when and what securities the investor will buy or sell, and they eventually result in actual orders. Brokers assist investors in making portfolio and asset allocation decisions and they often influence or even make the final trading decisions.

- *Order Execution* – Orders are captured through one of the broker's distribution channels (such as the telephone) and are then sent via the broker's order-routing system to the appropriate financial market.

- *Account Management* – Brokers provide account management and custody services, such as updating investors' portfolios, safekeeping securities, bookkeeping, performance tracking and periodic statements and analyses.

Brokers provide a range of services to support the investment cycle and, in turn, charge their customers brokerage commissions. On May 1, 1975, the Securities and Exchange Commission deregulated brokerage commissions, spawning the discount brokerage industry. Thereafter, the brokerage industry became partitioned into two distinct industry segments: *full-service brokers* and *discount brokers*. Full-service brokers offer investment advice such as research reports, buy/sell and market-timing suggestions and even the actual management of their customers' assets. In contrast, discount brokers charge lower commissions and provide less comprehensive service support for the investment cycle; i.e., the investors make all investment decisions themselves. The first firm to discount commissions was Charles Schwab Corporation.

The Charles Schwab Corporation

Charles R. Schwab founded the company bearing his name in California in 1971 as a brokerage firm helping individual investors to trade stocks and bonds. Schwab understood that the bundling of complete brokerage services for all steps of the investment cycle increased the costs to savvy investors who felt comfortable making their own financial decisions. Schwab decided that unlike full-service firms, his company would not sell advice to customers on what and when to trade.[3] Instead, Schwab (the company) focused on providing knowledgeable investors low-cost execution services – the third step in the investment cycle. Since its inception, Schwab's primary mission has been "to provide investors with the most useful and ethical brokerage services in America."[4] Traditionally, Schwab appealed to sophisticated, independent-minded investors who are highly educated, technology-literate, comfortable trading securities without advice, and in search of low prices.

Schwab and other discount brokerage firms reduced commissions to almost one half of the prevailing rates and began stealing trading volume and market share from the larger full-service firms. This was facilitated by

---

[3] That is, Schwab would not participate in the decision-making step of the investment cycle.
[4] Schwab Annual Report, 1991.

the increase in investor sophistication, driven in part by wider access to financial information through newspapers, finance-related cable television programming and magazines. Discounters tapped into the growing population of sophisticated investors, gradually increasing their presence in the brokerage industry. In 1980, discounters accounted for only 1.3% of total industry commissions, but by 1997 that number had grown to 14.4% (See Table 2).

Table 2: Market Shares Based on Estimated Retail Commissions

| | Retail Commissions | | | | | |
Year	Schwab ($ Millions)	Discounters ($ Millions)	Estimated Industry ($ Millions)	Discounters Share of Retail	Schwab Share of Discounters	Schwab Share Of Retail
1980	--	$48	$3,788	1.3%	--	--
1981	--	$80	$3,560	2.2%	--	--
1982	--	$147	$4,008	3.7%	--	--
1983	--	$258	$5,567	4.6%	--	--
1984	--	$232	$4,730	4.9%	--	--
1985	$126	$299	$5,492	5.4%	42.2%	2.3%
1986	$203	$539	$6,982	7.7%	37.6%	2.9%
1987	$297	$718	$8,449	8.5%	41.4%	3.5%
1988	$186	$482	$5,860	8.2%	38.6%	3.2%
1989	$229	$580	$6,767	8.6%	39.5%	3.4%
1990	$244	$613	$5,919	10.4%	39.8%	4.1%
1991	$841	$758	$7,059	10.7%	110.9%	11.9%
1992	$441	$999	$7,723	12.9%	44.1%	5.7%
1993	$552	$1,283	$9,138	14.0%	43.0%	6.0%
1994	$546	$1,305	$9,003	14.5%	41.8%	6.1%
1995	$751	$1,446	$10,665	13.6%	51.9%	7.0%
1996	$954	$1,777	$12,267	14.5%	53.7%	7.8%
1997	$1,174	$2,048	$14,221	14.4%	57.3%	8.3%

*NYSE *member discounters vs. all NYSE firms*

Source: *1998 Securities Industry DataBank; Schwab Annual Report*

As shown in Table 2, full-service brokers still dominate the brokerage industry. These brokers typically cater to older customers having significant wealth, who trade less frequently, but with transactions of higher-than-average size. These customers tend to be less comfortable with technology, have limited knowledge of financial markets, or are simply too busy to invest on their own. However, the discount brokerage segment has expanded significantly over the past two decades and has changed the industry landscape, lead by Charles Schwab. In the nineties, Schwab's revenues and profits have grown by more than 25% and 45%, respectively (see Table 3). As of the end of 1998, Schwab had 5.6 million active customer accounts with $491 billion in assets through 291 domestic branch offices, and net income of $349 million on revenues of $2.74 billion (See Tables 3 and 4).

Table 3a: Schwab Operating Results, 1990-1998

	1990	1991	1992	1993	1994	1995	1996	1997	1998	Compound annual Growth rates 1990-95	1990-98
Revenues											
Commissions	$244	$349	$441	$552	$546	$751	$954	$1,174	$1,309	25%	23%
Mutual fund service fees	$46	$54	$63	$99	$157	$219	$311	$428	$559	37%	37%
Interest revenue, net of interest expense	$71	$77	$92	$120	$165	$211	$255	$354	$476	24%	27%
Principal transactions	$4	$63	$130	$169	$163	$191	$257	$258	$287	117%	71%
Other	$22	$27	$24	$25	$34	$48	$74	$85	$105	17%	22%
Total	$387	$570	$750	$965	$1,065	$1,420	$1,851	$2,299	$2,736	30%	28%
Expenses excluding interest											
Compensation and benefits	$155	$234	$307	$393	$437	$594	$766	$962	$1,163	31%	29%
Communications	$42	$57	$76	$94	$107	$129	$165	$183	$206	25%	22%
Occupancy and equipment	$43	$51	$65	$77	$88	$111	$130	$154	$201	31%	21%
Commissions, clearance and floor brokerage	$12	$21	$32	$43	$49	$77	$81	$92	$83	45%	27%
Marketing and advertising	$20	$25	$34	$41	$36	$53	$84	$130	$155	22%	29%
Other	$86	$94	$90	$110	$124	$178	$231	$331	$352	16%	19%
Total	$358	$482	$604	$758	$841	$1,142	$1,457	$1,852	$2,160	26%	25%
Operating income	$29	$88	$146	$207	$224	$278	$394	$448	$577	57%	45%
Net income	$17	$49	$81	$118	$135	$173	$234	$270	$349	59%	46%

Table 3b: Schwab Operating Results, 1990-1998

Operating Ratios	1990	1991	1992	1993	1994	1995	1996	1997	1998
Revenues									
Commissions	63%	61%	59%	57%	51%	53%	52%	51%	48%
Mutual fund service fees	12%	9%	8%	10%	15%	15%	17%	19%	20%
Interest revenue, net of interest expense	18%	14%	12%	12%	15%	15%	14%	15%	17%
Principal transactions	1%	11%	17%	18%	15%	13%	14%	11%	10%
Other	6%	5%	3%	3%	3%	3%	4%	4%	4%
Total	100%	100%	100%	100%	100%	100%	100%	100%	100%
Expenses excluding interest									
Compensation and benefits	40%	41%	41%	41%	41%	42%	41%	42%	42%
Communications	11%	10%	10%	10%	10%	9%	9%	8%	8%
Occupancy and equipment	11%	9%	9%	8%	8%	8%	7%	7%	7%
Commissions, clearance and floor brokerage	3%	4%	4%	4%	5%	5%	4%	4%	3%
Marketing and Advertising	5%	4%	5%	4%	3%	4%	5%	6%	6%
Other	22%	16%	12%	11%	12%	13%	12%	14%	13%
Total	93%	85%	81%	79%	79%	80%	79%	81%	79%
Operating income	7%	15%	19%	21%	21%	20%	21%	19%	21%
Net income	4%	9%	11%	12%	13%	12%	13%	12%	13%

Source: 1997 Schwab Annual Report, Charles Schwab Web site

Over the years, Schwab has employed a two-pronged strategy based on brand name recognition and IT-based innovation. Schwab's marketing strategy has been grounded on establishing the Schwab brand name, using its founder's congenial, trustworthy face in TV commercials, magazines, billboards and the like. The company has built a brand name in financial services at par with American Express Co. and Merrill Lynch. In 1998, Schwab spent 6% of revenues on advertising, well above the brokerage industry average (see Tables 3 and 4).

Table 4: Brokerage Industry Operating Results, 1990-1997

	1990	1991	1992	1993	1994	1995	1996	1997
Total Revenues (net of interest expense)	$31,317	$41,847	$46,857	$56,187	$47,624	$58,128	$71,053	$81,390
Expenses excluding interest								
Compensation and benefits	$17,715	$20,824	$24,162	$28,968	$27,340	$30,309	$36,768	$41,666
Communications	$2,222	$2,119	$2,282	$2,481	$2,713	$2,822	$3,089	$3,450
Occupancy and equipment	$3,092	$2,950	$3,009	$3,136	$3,170	$3,401	$3,632	$3,934
Marketing and advertising	$878	$930	$1,094	$1,279	$1,296	$1,245	$1,553	$1,842
Commissions, clearance and floor brokerage	$1,731	$1,760	$1,867	$2,306	$2,620	$2,728	$3,103	$3,673
Other	$5,841	$7,414	$8,257	$9,417	$9,357	$10,219	$11,637	$14,617
Total Expenses (excluding interest expense)	$31,479	$35,997	$40,671	$47,587	$46,496	$50,724	$59,782	$69,182
Operating income	($162)	$5,850	$6,186	$8,600	$1,128	$7,404	$11,271	$12,208

Operating Ratios

	1990	1991	1992	1993	1994	1995	1996	1997
Total Revenues (net of interest expense)	100%	100%	100%	100%	100%	100%	100%	100%
Expenses excluding interest								
Compensation and benefits	57%	50%	52%	52%	57%	52%	52%	51%
Communications	7%	5%	5%	4%	6%	5%	4%	4%
Occupancy and equipment	10%	7%	6%	6%	7%	6%	5%	5%
Marketing and advertising	3%	2%	2%	2%	3%	2%	2%	2%
Commissions, clearance and floor brokerage	6%	4%	4%	4%	6%	5%	4%	5%
Other	19%	18%	18%	17%	20%	18%	16%	18%
Total Expenses (excluding interest expense)	101%	86%	87%	85%	98%	87%	84%	85%
Operating income	-1%	14%	13%	15%	2%	13%	16%	15%

Source: 1998 Securities Industry Factbook

Schwab's advertising investment seems to have paid off. From 1992 to 1997, Schwab more than doubled its customer base to 3.2 million. The other distinctive feature of Schwab's strategy has been the emphasis on brokerage innovations, which are naturally IT-based, as Schwab's business is an information business. To analyze the evolution of Schwab's strategy and value proposition over time, we appeal to Treacy and Wiersema's framework that outlines three paths to market leadership.

11.4 From Operational Excellence to Product Leadership

Discount Brokerage and Distribution Channels

Schwab's first innovation was the concept of discount brokerage itself, as described in the previous section. Until the early eighties, Schwab's business was narrowly focused on providing smooth, reliable and low-cost execution of trades in basic stocks and bonds at competitive prices, backed up with major investments in IT. In 1980, Schwab established a 24-hour quotation service, which was expanded in 1982 to provide customer access to quotes and order entry 24 hours a day, seven days a week. Schwab was the first brokerage (whether full-service or discount) to offer such 24×7 service. The firm targeted customers who seek fast, efficient transaction services at fees that were substantially lower than those of full-service brokerage firms – that is, customers who value *operational excellence*. Indeed, Schwab's value discipline in the early years was one of operational excellence: offering low price, efficient and reliable transaction services that were accessible anytime from anywhere. Schwab could deliver high-quality transaction services at discount prices, thanks to its operating model and reliance on IT. No wonder Treacy and Wiersema feature Schwab as an example of operational excellence: "Transactions that are easy, pleasant, quick, accurate – market-leading operationally excellent service companies like Charles Schwab...design the means to achieve that end."[5] While Schwab has maintained its high operational standards over the years, its focus has shifted over time to product leadership and innovation.[6]

Starting in the mid-eighties, Schwab introduced a series of new distribution channels and asset classes, consistent with a strategy of product leadership. A key dimension of Schwab's "product" leadership has been its innovation in the use of new distribution channels. In 1989, Schwab launched *TeleBroker*, a fully automated telephone system that offered real-time stock quotes and took orders. Virtually all calls were routed to one of four call centers, which handled customers' requests on a 24×7 basis. By 1998, 73% of the 110 million customer calls received and more than 2.4 million trades were handled electronically via TeleBroker. In 1996, Schwab added *VoiceBroker*, an automated system that utilizes speech recognition

---

[5] Treacy and Wiersema, Op. Cit., p. 50.
[6] In the brokerage industry, the "product" is in fact a service, and innovation can be applied to any of its dimensions.

technology for distributing real-time quotes and accepting mutual fund trades. Actually, these phone-based systems were predated by another electronic channel – a DOS-based software trading system called *Equalizer*. This was followed by Windows-based *StreetSmart* in 1992 and Web-based *SchwabNOW* in 1996. Today, Schwab offers its customers a variety of distribution channels, including the Internet, touch-tone telephone, 24×7 live brokers at the call centers, and additionally, an extensive network of physical branches.[7]

Mutual Funds Marketplace

Schwab has also transformed the way mutual funds are sold by brokers and mutual fund companies alike. In 1992, Schwab introduced the mutual fund *OneSource* program that allows customers to buy or sell Schwab and non-Schwab no-load mutual funds without paying transaction fees. With *OneSource*, customers can purchase mutual funds using their Schwab account through any of Schwab's distribution channels. Schwab also provided customers consolidated quarterly and year-end statements, simplifying paperwork and tax reporting. Schwab charged the fund providers a 25-35 basis point (i.e., 0.25%-0.35%) fee for participating in *OneSource* and providing distribution and shareholder services. As seen in Table 3, the *OneSource* program has proven to be highly profitable for Schwab. By 1998, Schwab's *OneSource* service gave customers access to over 1,400 mutual funds from more than 200 fund families without incurring transaction fees. Customer assets in Schwab's own funds reached $82 billion by the end of 1998.

"Schwab-Style" Advice and Asset Management

Although Schwab is not directly involved in giving advice or managing customers' assets, its customers can obtain advice and asset management services indirectly through fee-based financial advisors. These advisors charge an annual fee based on customer assets, help investors manage their portfolios, and often make trading decisions on behalf of investors. Unlike commissioned brokers, whose incentives might not necessarily align with the customer's goals, fee-based advisors are more objective and less committed to pushing proprietary products. One of the features that attracted financial advisors to Schwab was *SchwabLink* – an electronic link used by financial advisors to trade and manage customer accounts, "outsourcing" the back office operations to Schwab. The vast majority of assets managed by fee-based advisors through Schwab are managed using *SchwabLink*.

---

[7] By the end of 1998, Schwab operated 291 branches in 48 states and abroad.

These independent, fee-based financial advisors have become a virtual sales force for Schwab. As Arthur Urciuoli, senior vice president for retail marketing for Merrill Lynch put it, "We don't compete with the discounters. We do compete with Schwab. They have essentially built a Merrill Lynch by proxy."[8] In this way, Schwab has created an "Information Age Business Network"[9] which enables it to deliver value to its customers through a network of partners (in this case, the fee-based financial advisors) with Schwab serving as the network's hub.

By the end of 1998, Schwab had attracted more than 5,400 fee-based advisors who had brought in $147 billion in assets, starting from zero in 1987. The partnership with financial advisors enables Schwab to expand its reach to more customers, to better leverage its brand name, and to make investment advice available to customers who value it. This is an essential element in Schwab's broadening focus; the Internet channel is another.

Schwab's Strategy Evolution: Summary

In the pre-Internet era, Schwab's business strategy has evolved from operational excellence to product leadership. More recently, Schwab's strategy has transitioned to *customer intimacy* to deal with the challenges and opportunities of the Internet era, as we explain below. First, we review Schwab's adoption of the Internet channel.

11.5 The Internet Channel

Schwab's Move to the Internet

Schwab launched its Web-based trading service, which enabled customers to trade by logging onto the Schwab Web site, on March 31, 1996. Web customers paid a flat $39.95 commission for up to 1,000 shares and 3 cents a share thereafter. Customer response to this new distribution channel was extremely enthusiastic. Schwab leveraged its brand name, marketing muscle, and wider range of product offerings to quickly overtake its rivals on the Web. While E*Trade and Lombard were offering only equities and options, Schwab introduced in close succession, trading in Treasury securities, mutual funds, and corporate bonds. Schwab's active online accounts grew from 617,000 in December 1996 to 2.2 million by the end

---

[8] Institutional Investor, April 1996.
[9] See H. Mendelson, "Organizational Architecture and Success in the IT Industry," Management Science, 1999; H. Mendelson and J. Ziegler, Survival of the Smartest: Managing Information for Rapid Action and World Class Performance, Wiley, 1999.

of 1998, representing 40% of active customer accounts. The corresponding assets acquired over the Web channel increased from $42 billion to $174 billion over this time frame.

**Figure 1: Average Brokerage Commissions
Charged By The Top-10 Online Brokers, 1996-98**

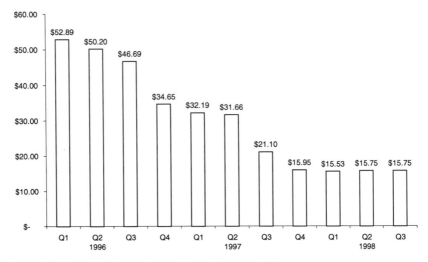

Source: Credit Suisse First Boston Research Report, November 1998.

The online brokerage industry has been the scene of vicious price wars, especially in the early stages. Since the industry had primarily targeted the customer base interested in fast and cheap trades, price-cutting was commonplace. For example, E*Trade reduced its prices seven times between 1993 to 1997, before settling down at $14.95. Figure 1 shows the evolution of the average commission charged by the top 10 – on-line brokers over 1996-8. From the beginning of 1996 through the end of 1997, the average commission charged by these brokers dropped by about 70%, from $53 per trade to $16. Since mid-1997, commissions have stabilized, and the average commission stayed flat through 1998 (see Figure 1).

Initially, Schwab offered Internet trading as a defensive move to protect its market share from low-priced on-line competitors. The price of Web trading was correspondingly set at $39.95, and dropped soon thereafter to

$29.95 – above most of Schwab's on-line competitors, but below the $49.50 Schwab charged to conduct a transaction using its earlier on-line product, *StreetSmart*. To get the $29.95 price users were required to trade through the Web, but request customer service by e-mail. Users who wanted the option of speaking to a human, could keep their regular Schwab account and still trade online, but they got only a 20% discount off the regular Schwab commission schedule. "We were trying to offer a technical product that didn't have all the rest of the services that Schwab had to offer but could offer a lower price," recalls Pottruck.

However, Schwab's customers did not want to have to choose between service and price, and Schwab soon realized that it had to alter its Internet strategy.   Starting in January 1998, Schwab offered Web trading for everyone at $29.95 for up to 1,000 shares, consistent with Schwab's strategy of positioning its products in the "middle" of the market. Most discount brokers charge commissions lower than Schwab, while full-commission brokers have started offering discounted commissions to selected retail customers. In 1998, Schwab's commissions were 60% lower than those of full-commission brokers, but they were higher than those of most discounters.

Table 5 presents a compilation of brokerage commission rates charged by the top 17 discount brokerage firms for equity trades in listed securities, via the Internet, as of February 7, 1999.[10]   There is substantial variation in prices and maximum trade sizes (for the flat commission rate), with most firms charging a premium for limit orders. While not shown in the table, most firms charge a premium for NASDAQ OTC equities as compared to exchange-listed ones. By and large, firms charging higher prices tend to offer a broader choice of investable assets, distribution channels and information. For example, Schwab, which is at the top end of Internet brokers in terms of price, can be accessed via the Internet, touch-tone phone, 24x7 live brokers and branch offices. In contrast, low-cost Datek offers only Internet and live brokers (for limited daily hours).

Schwab's Products and Services on the Internet

The Internet allowed Schwab to vastly broaden its brokerage products and services, which we describe next, following the steps of the investment cycle introduced earlier in this chapter.

---

[10] Adapted from Kiplinger's broker ratings at www.kiplinger.com, updated by the authors to February 7, 1999.

Table 5: Commission Rates for Internet Trading of Listed Equities, for the Largest Discount Brokers (as of February 7, 1999)

Broker	Market Order	Limit Order	Maximum Shares	Extra Charge Per Share
Accutrade	$29.95	$29.95	1,000	2 cents
American Express	24.95	24.95	4,000	2 cents
Ameritrade	8.00	13.00	--	--
Brown & Co.	5.00	10.00	5,000	1 cent
Bull & Bear	19.95	19.95	1,000	2 cents
Charles Schwab	29.95	29.95	1,000	3 cents
Datek	9.99	9.99	5,000	--
Discover	14.95	19.95	5,000	1 cent
DLJDirect	20.00	20.00	1,000	2 cents
E*Trade	14.95	19.95	5,000	1 cent
Fidelity	25.00	30.00	1,000	2 cents
Nat. Discount Brokers	14.75	19.75	5,000	1 cent
Quick & Reilly	14.95	19.95	5,000	2 cents
Suretrade	7.95	9.95	5,000	1 cent
Waterhouse	12.00	12.00	5,000	1 cent
Web Street	14.95	14.95	--	--

Information Acquisition
The firm provides a wide array of information resources on its Web site. Customers can obtain real-time quotes, construct watch lists, and draw performance charts to compare securities. The *Analyst Center* provides tools to research industries and individual stocks using fundamental and technical data, stock screening, charting, and earnings estimates. The resources provided by Schwab online are comparable to those on a stockbroker's desk: company and industry research reports from Standard & Poor's, earnings forecasts by First Call, daily summary and analysis of market activity and interviews with executives and industry experts from Briefing.com, data on corporate insiders' trading from Vickers, price and volume charts by BigCharts, and news stories from Dow Jones & Co. Each week, *Industry CloseUp* provides independent analyst's reports including company rankings, recommendations, and trends on eight

featured industries. *MarketBuzz* is another information tool that has a very broad collection ranging from up-to-the-minute market highlights and emerging financial news to a directory of finance-related Web sites and links to finance magazines and newspapers.

In October 1998, Schwab started offering research reports from two investment banks — Credit Suisse First Boston and Hambrecht & Quist. Schwab charges $29.95 per month for access to this proprietary information. However, the fee is waived for Schwab's most active customers. Another aspect of Schwab's information resources is investment planning. Schwab's investor tax center provides online retirement and tax planning information service including a capital gains estimator, tax strategies, and tax forecasting. Schwab introduced the *IRA Analyzer*, a tool designed to educate investors about their retirement planning choices, towards the end of 1998.

Several new features are in the pipeline for Schwab's Web site. A key feature in the pilot stage will show total returns on securities in an investor's portfolio. Also being developed are e-mail services that will alert customers when certain events are triggered, such as when their portfolio is not in balance with their asset-allocation models, or if a particular fund spends a certain amount of time in the bottom quartile of its category. It is hoped that these new features would further strengthen Schwab's relationship with its customers.

Investment Decision-Making
Schwab's *Asset Allocation Toolkit,* introduced on September 15, 1997, allows investors to easily manage their account holdings by asset class. Investors can view the allocation of their assets by account, determine the allocation that's appropriate for their investment profile, compare their current allocation to other strategies, and get help and guidance in managing their portfolio. A more recent tool, *Positions Monitor* introduced in November 1998, allows investors to easily track the performance of their portfolio (whose composition comes directly from Schwab's systems) and its components against relevant benchmark (e.g., large-, mid-, and small-cap stocks). Schwab aggregates data from sources such as Morningstar, Standard & Poor's and First Call with information about the investor's portfolio to provide performance comparisons at the click of a mouse. Another click provides more detailed information including performance figures, news, and charts or particular holdings, and projections under alternative return scenarios.

Introduced in January 1997, *Mutual Fund OneSource Online* has automated selection tools that can help an investor choose a fund and then click and buy it. Founded in alliance with fund companies, this service contains information directly from these companies. Customers have access to fund prospectuses online, and they can query the Schwab mutual fund database to search funds by different criteria, e.g., performance over one, three or five years in a particular sector. Investors can compare funds and search for funds that match their specified criteria. There is no proactive "prodding" of customers, in light of changing market conditions, although customers can request to be notified by e-mail if a particular fund spends more than a certain amount of time in the bottom quartile of the fund category.

Transactions Execution
Customers can place trade orders for stocks, mutual funds, options, treasuries and corporate bonds and choose from over 850 no-load mutual funds from *Mutual Fund OneSource* with a few clicks of their mouse on Schwab's Web site. Once an order is placed, the customers are prompted to verify their order before it goes through. Once the order is executed, an online acknowledgment is sent to the customer.

Account Services
Investors can customize their home pages to view their account information, order status, market news and quotes. They also have access to their account history. Using Schwab *MoneyLink,* they can electronically transfer funds between their Schwab account and other financial institutions.

Summary

Schwab has moved to the Web in an aggressive fashion. Using Internet tools, Schwab has managed to cover a broad range of services in all four phases of the investment cycle. The shift to the Internet has paid off for Schwab: by the end of 1998, Schwab had 2.2 million active online accounts holding assets of $174 billion, and 54% of Schwab's 141,900 average total trades each day were conducted through its online channels. This corresponds to a market share of 30% of online trading volume, roughly equaling that of its next three online competitors combined.

11.6   Customer Intimacy

In less than three years, the Internet channel grabbed the lion's share of Schwab's business — roughly 60% of daily trades by the end of 1998. "Everything is converging on the Web," says Randy Goldman, Vice President in the Electronic Brokerage enterprise, referring to the steady and rapid migration of all brokerage products and services to the Web channel.

The explosive growth of the Internet and the mounting demand from investors for help and investment advice resulted in a strategy shift at Schwab, which is getting closer to offering the functionality of a full-service firm. Thus, the Internet is catalyzing a broader business mission at Schwab and its abandonment of long-held principles. "The help and advice we are giving to customers over the Internet is the most profound change the company has ever gone through," says David S. Pottruck, Schwab's co-CEO, and "the Net is totally embedded in the center of our business."[11] The Internet allows Schwab for the first time to compete head-on with full-service providers like Merrill Lynch, following a customer intimacy strategy.

As a result of this repositioning, Schwab is now "defining [itself] as the company that redefined what 'full service' means," according to Gideon Sasson, head of Schwab's Electronic Brokerage Enterprise. However, Schwab is not planning to spoon-feed investors like full-service brokers do. Instead, it aims to coach people on investing by exploiting the interactive capabilities of the Internet channel.

Customer Relationships

As Sasson notes, Schwab's current focus is on cementing its relationships with customers:

> *[We are on the Internet to] create partnerships with our customers. It's all about relationships; it's all about taking customers to a place they couldn't get to before. It's all about education, providing tools, providing help and advice... giving them what they need so they can be in control, so they can control their transactions, so they can control their future. And how do we do that at Schwab? We have a philosophy that says, 'real e-commerce needs real people.' Strong customer relationships are made through experiences with people, not technology. I submit to you that it is impossible to create relationships with customers just with technology. You can cement relationships. You can enhance relationships. But at the end of the day, relationships happen because of people... That is what we at Schwab are all about: It's about people and the value they provide.*

Schwab cements customer relationships through "customization, personalization and communities." *Customization* means that Schwab allows each customer to create his or her own Internet experience, e.g., by

---

[11] Fortune, December 7, 1998.

creating a personalized view of Schwab's homepage. *Personalization* means that when Schwab sends information to a customer, e.g., by e-mail, Schwab tries to create the customer's value proposition based on the information it has about her. *Community* is a place for the customer to get more information, talk about problems and obtain answers for her questions—either through a discussion with other investors or from Schwab experts.

To emulate the personalized product and service offerings of full-service brokers, Schwab analyzes customer transaction data to uncover useful behavioral patterns and trends. The information from these data analyses is used to customize the services offered to the customer. For example, Schwab created the *Signature Services* program, which offers tiered services for investors who have more than $100,000 in assets or trade more than 12 times a year. Three levels of service are available in the signature services programs: "plain vanilla" "gold" and "platinum," depending on the client's assets or trades. Signature Services clients receive access to an exclusive Web site, to discussions with CEOs and money managers, to pre-screened fee-based advisors and to online research. In addition, Schwab partnered with Bloomberg to develop an exclusive analysis magazine published quarterly for Signature Services clients. Clients do not get personal brokers, but each is assigned to a small team in one of the call centers. With the help of these teams, clients can develop an investment strategy and get special response, such as a "red-hot call" when the stock market is very volatile.

Another area where Schwab customizes its services depending upon customer profile is the distribution of initial public offerings (IPOs). Historically, most IPO shares were offered by the underwriters to large institutions and to their own preferred customers. In September of 1997, Schwab partnered with Credit Suisse First Boston, J.P. Morgan and Hambrecht & Quist to distribute shares of stocks they underwrite to Schwab customers. Since 1998, Schwab has sold shares to customers who register to take part in the firm's IPO program. Schwab combs through its database of information about customers' portfolios and investment preferences to select those that it will invite to participate in specific offerings. Recently, Schwab has decided to raise its profile in the IPO business by becoming a co-manager in a number of IPOs. For example, Schwab co-managed the IPO of Select Comfort Corp., a Minnesota mattress maker, in December 1998.

Information-Age Business Network

The way Schwab provides services on the Internet is an example of an effective Information Age Business Network.[12] Such networks are bound together not by ownership and control, but by information sharing and reciprocity, and they enable a firm like Schwab to focus on what it does best and use business partners to do the rest. As a result, Schwab's approach to full service is dramatically different from that of traditional full-service brokers.   Unlike full-service firms, which provide a wide selection of their own proprietary products, Schwab is offering a broad selection of *everybody's* products. As Schwab's co-CEO put it, "Companies don't own the customer anymore, so trying to build walls around the customer is not going to work."[13]

In Schwab's view, the future belongs to those who give customers the most freedom to make informed decisions. As discussed in Section 11.5, the Internet helped Schwab provide market data, advice and asset management services by destroying the barriers to information. In the words of Gideon Sasson:[14]

> *Before the Internet, the world was the realm of the few. Few people had access to real-time quotes, to analyst reports, to real-time news, research, and other people's opinions... What the Internet did was basically democratize [information]...*

In other words, the Internet defies any institution's ability to monopolize information, enabling Schwab to unbundle the full-service brokers' products and puts the customers in control of their investments. As Chairman Charles Schwab remarks in the company's television commercials, "It's all about freedom. Now, you are in control."

Schwab-Style Advice

A key innovation that facilitates customer focus and moves Schwab products closer to those of full-service firms, while taking full advantage of its business network, is providing neutral customer advice – "Schwab-style" advice that is independent and free of pressure, and points customers towards investments without creating a conflict of interest. Customer surveys revealed to Schwab that baby boomers were moving to Schwab in record numbers. Unlike the more experienced stock selectors of the past, most of Schwab's new customers were inexperienced investors who needed help. For example, over half of Schwab's new customers in 1996 considered themselves "beginners" or "somewhat experienced" with

---

[12] See Mendelson, Op. Cit., Mendelson and Ziegler, Op. Cit.

[13] Op. Cit.

[14] San Jose Mercury News, October 4, 1998.

investing, looking for intelligent and unbiased guidance. To improve the services available to customers seeking investment advice, Schwab began in June of 1995 *AdvisorSource*, a referral service for fee-based financial advisors. The service had signed up 320 pre-screened fee-based advisors in 30 states to whom Schwab referred interested customers. In exchange, Schwab received 30% of the advisor's fees in the first year, 25% in the second year, 20% in the third year, and nothing in following years.

Multi-Channel Strategy

While the majority of Schwab's trades originate on the Web, the company recognizes the importance of maintaining a strong presence across multiple delivery channels – functionality that is valued by Schwab's customers. Rather than try to minimize channel conflict, Schwab actively supports the use of multiple channels in the belief that the more channels customers have access to, the better is Schwab's value proposition. This multi-channel approach is key to Schwab's business strategy going forward. Schwab's business model is different from pure online trading firms that narrowly focus on only Internet trades, as Schwab is seeking to take advantage of synergies across different channels. For example, Schwab still views its brick and mortar branches as a strategic asset, enabling face-to-face communications and fostering customer trust. The Internet channel is not meant to replace branch offices, but rather to complement their capabilities. In fact, Schwab uses its branches to conduct investment seminars to educate customers who are not comfortable with Internet technology.

11.7   Conclusions

In this chapter, we examined how the market leader in the discount brokerage industry – Charles Schwab – has responded to the threats and opportunities posed by the Internet. Schwab was not the first to launch Internet trading, but the company leveraged its brand name, breadth of product offerings, and IT capability to quickly vault to the top of the online brokerage market, with a 30% market share by the end of 1998. As we discussed, Schwab's focus has evolved through the three value disciplines from operational excellence to product leadership and finally to customer intimacy, exploiting the capabilities of the information-rich Internet channel. The Schwab story illustrates many of the new challenges faced by the brokerage industry in the Internet era.

First of all, investors are increasingly finance-savvy, due to the proliferation of investment-related information in newspapers, magazines, cable television and, last but not least, the Internet. Still, there is substantial variation in investment knowledge and experience across different individual investors. At one extreme are "day traders" – the speculative and aggressive traders who buy and sell stocks frequently, often in a matter of hours and sometimes in minutes. These investors do not value extra services or research tools; they are looking for rock bottom prices. At the other extreme are novice or busy investors, who are familiar with the Web and feel comfortable taking their transactions online, but are new to investing and need substantial "hand-holding" or do not wish to spend the time needed to do everything themselves. This category also includes baby boomers, who are entering their wealth-building years and are in need of financial guidance. Between these extremes are many other investor-types with different preferences for brokerage services. A key challenge for a brokerage firm is to decide which customer segments to target, which in turn has important implications for product positioning and pricing.

At the same time, the Internet is drastically reducing investor search costs – the time and effort required by investors to find brokerage products (range of services and prices) that fit their requirements. In addition to the huge amount of information that brokers place on their own Web sites, a variety of inter-broker ratings have mushroomed on the Web, including such sources as Gomez Advisors, Keynote Systems, Kiplinger, SmartMoney, and Yahoo! Finance, among many others (see e.g., www.investorguide.com). Empowered with information, investors demand a tailor-made brokerage product at the lowest possible price, and are unlikely to be loyal to any one provider. Lower investor search costs are contributing to a heightened level of price competition, increased commoditization and, consequently, reduced profitability of at least some brokerage services, such as transactions execution (see Bakos (1998) for a discussion of search costs in electronic markets).[15]

The impact of lower search costs is compounded by structural changes on the supply side, where the Internet is lowering fixed and variable costs as well as barriers to entry. For example, by the end of 1998, there were over 90 firms offering online brokerage at commissions as low as $5 per trade. Further, it is estimated that online brokerage firms spent an average of $300 on marketing and advertising to acquire each new customer.[16] Thus, the Internet is causing a "double whammy," threatening online brokerage profitability from both the demand side and the supply side.

Schwab has responded to these challenges by adopting a new business strategy based on customer intimacy as the underlying value proposition

---

[15] Y. Bakos, "The Emerging Role of Electronic Marketplaces on the Internet," *Communications of the ACM*, August 1988.

[16] See www.investorguide.com.

for the customer. This has enabled Schwab to strengthen its customer relationships, customize its products to different customer segments, build a Web-based virtual community, and generally to enhance product differentiation and lessen the effect of price competition. The Internet is clearly an essential ingredient in this new business model, along with an information-age business network of non-proprietary financial assets, advisors and asset managers.

Is this the recipe for market leadership in the new brokerage world? Yes, if you go by the collective judgement of investors on Wall Street, who at the end of 1998 raised Schwab's market capitalization past that of brokerage giant Merrill Lynch.[17]

---

[17] Schwab's market capitalization first topped that of Merrill Lynch on December 28, 1998, and has remained higher through February 1999.

Chapter 12

Lessons from Developing the Yield Book

Ernest Battifarano
Salomon Analytics

12.1 Introduction

The Yield Book is an X-based front end to Salomon's research and analytics. It is used by sales, trading, and research at Salomon, by institutional fixed-income investors, and by selected (noncompeting) regional dealers to analyze fixed income securities and portfolios. Its development, both in the literal sense as software and in the management sense as an institution within a broker-dealer, has coincided with the trend toward greater automation that is evident in, say, robotic automobile manufacture, automated banking and electronic trading, and with the trend toward easier and cheaper access to all kinds of information that was either completely unavailable outside small circles or very expensive.

The Yield Book is also an example of the sort of analytical engine used by issuers and investors to analyze and hedge complicated risks. Conceived in 1988 and born in July of 1989, it is more than an analytics program. Yield Book is the focal point for a wealth of analytics and research produced by many of Salomon's highly regarded research and trading groups. Among these are the Treasury Analysis group, Mortgage Research, the Fixed-Income Index group,

Derivatives Research, and the CMO Modeling group. Yield Book gives its user a virtual seat on Salomon's sales and trading floor so that the user can see at his desk the same analytics, data, and research available to Salomon's salesmen, traders, and analysts.

Yield Book has grown to maturity at the same time that fixed-income instruments have become much more complicated and markets have exhibited extraordinary volatility. Severe penalties have been exacted by the market on some highly regarded firms for misunderstanding or underestimating these complexities and volatility. Cautious and risk-tolerant investors alike have turned to Yield Book to help them assess market-choices and market-risks.

Yield Book was not created to fill a specific demand nor has there ever been a grand vision of its final form. Rather it has grown in ways that our customers, who, as traders, salesmen, research analysts, and institutional investors, are excellent market proxies, have asked it to grow. In this sense Yield Book is not a product at all but rather it is a process – collaborative effort by developers and customers, making it everyone's custom tool.

The Yield Book is designed to look like a book, with 'chapters', 'pages', and a table of contents because everyone knows how to use a book. When Yield Book was first released there was less familiarity, and thus, less comfort, with graphical user interfaces than there is today. A graphical interface that resembled a book proved to be a good way to overcome reluctance among senior members of the financial community to use a modern tool. They had, after all, become respected senior members by mastering very different tools.

The name and the ideas embedded in the software are descendants of the seminal work *Inside the Yield Book* by Sidney Homer and Martin Leibowitz (Prentice Hall, 1972) which explains the mathematics behind price/yield tables found in *yield books* that investors used before computers were widely available to analyze fixed-income securities. Yield Book's software descended more recently from another computer system, the now nearly retired Cash Matching and Portfolio Optimization System, "CMPOS", which was used by sales analysts on behalf of customers. Just as logarithm tables and slide rules (for those of you who remember these artifacts) have been completely replaced by contemporary computing devices, so has the Yield Book, and its computational relatives, replaced yield books.

In the following, part of the Yield Book tale, as interpreted by a software engineer, is told. The context of greater complexity of fixed-income securities is described in the first section. The Yield Book architecture, always ahead of its competitors, always under re-evaluation, and so integral a component of its success, is described in the second section. The third section gives a view of the

Yield Book's management within a broker-dealer and its relation to a potentially competing system part-owned by Salomon itself. Yield Book's history within Salomon and some of the internal debate that guided its evolution is described in the fourth section. In the next section some of the enormous synergy that Yield Book has produced is described. In the last two sections the case is made that broker-dealers in general, and Salomon in particular, are the best possible sources for such analytics software even if these institutions are not in the business of producing commercial software.

12.2 The Need For Technology

Complexity

Over the past sixteen years, the variety and complexity of fixed-income securities have increased dramatically. Many new securities, called derivatives, have been created by securitizing pre-existing assets. Two very important examples of derivative securities are collateralized mortgage obligations ("CMO"), created from the cash flows produced by home mortgage pools, and asset-backed securities ("ABS"), created from the cash flows of a variety of debt, including auto loans, credit card debt, home equity loans, equipment loans, small business loans and student loans. Since their introduction, issuance of CMO and ABS have accelerated sharply. For example, CMO issuance increased from $5 billion in 1983 to $324 billion in 1993[1].

Securitizing existing financial instruments has increased so dramatically, in part, because it benefits both issuers and investors. One advantage for issuers and investors is improved liquidity of the underlying assets. Traditional mortgage pass-through securities, for example, have long times to maturity, which means that their price are very sensitive to changes in prevailing interest rates. In addition, they are subject to prepayment risk, which makes cash flows, and therefore prices, uncertain. On the other hand, classes of CMOs can be constructed with many different times to maturity and cash flow characteristics. Some classes are less sensitive to interest rate changes than traditional mortgages while other classes are considerably more sensitive. An investor who could not, or would not, own a mortgage pass-through, might find a more predictable cash flow and shorter time to maturity among the classes of a CMO and an investor with greater risk tolerance might also find an appropriate security among the more interest-rate sensitive classes of the same CMO. In fact, some CMO classes have been custom-designed for particular investors. A second advantage of securitization is increased availability of home mortgages. This makes home ownership more easily attainable and while this does not benefit issuers or investors directly, it is generally considered a societal benefit.

---

[1]   The Handbook of Fixed Income Securities, Frank J. Fabozzi, Editor, 1997.

Another investor advantage offered by securitizing mortgage pools is the potential for a higher return than that of traditional fixed-income securities.

Advantages of derivative products come with a price: increased complexity. This is especially the case for the more interest-rate-sensitive classes of CMO and ABS. In fact, the complexity-return relation has been characterized by some as exponential – in the hope of slightly better return, one must assume significantly more complicated risk. Cash flow characteristics of CMO classes can be devilishly complicated. The cash flows for the classes of a relatively simple deal are pictured in figure 1. Intuition and back-of-the-envelope calculations are not applicable and are simply inadequate.

Figure 1: Screenshot of CMO Cash Flows

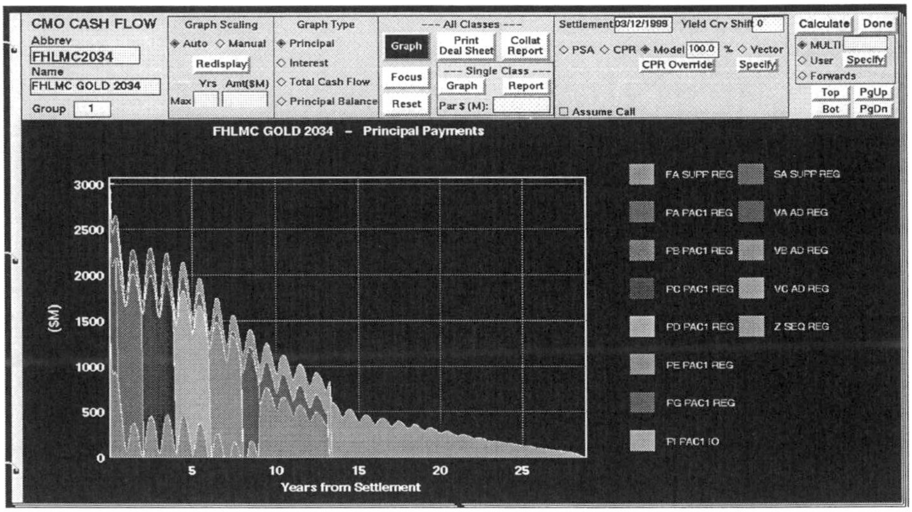

Yield Book has grown dramatically, as have some of its computational relatives, at the same time as the demand for these esoteric securities has increased. That demand for complicated securities has stimulated demand for Yield Book is very easy to accept. It is only slightly harder to accept that the existence and acceptance of analytical tools have served to increase demand for such securities by making esoteric securities less mysterious. Yield Book has benefited from this cycle.

Market volatility

During the past fifteen years, market participants have witnessed extraordinary market volatility. The equity markets in 1987, the high-yield market and regional banks in 1990, the fixed-income market in 1994, and both the equity and fixed-income markets in 1998 have all demonstrated record-setting and stomach churning volatility.

Failure to understand and manage prepayment and interest rate risks can be penalized severely by the market. In recent years there have been several well-publicized failures. (See the February 24, 1997 edition of the Wall Street Journal which details some of the failures following big interest rate moves in 1993 and 1994 and discusses the changes in investors' views between 1994 and early 1997.) For example, in 1994 interest rates moved sharply higher after having declined sharply throughout 1993. The robust growth in CMO issuance, mentioned earlier, ended abruptly in 1994 as investors first suffered from massive prepayments as rates fell precipitously in 1993 and then suffered from extending durations and declining valuations as rates rose in 1994.

At the time of this writing, September 1998, there is, once again, serious market volatility sparked by a wave of currency devaluations and outright default by one militarily important government struggling, with its conversion to a free-market economy. The benchmark U.S. treasury yield curve is moving wildly; volatility in the bond and equity markets is soaring. Spreads to the U.S. treasury yield curve of corporate bonds and mortgage-backed securities are widening, sometimes dramatically, and prices of these securities have fallen; spreads to the U.S. treasury yield curve of foreign bonds are widening to unheard of levels, and mortgage rates are trending downward and prepayments are widely expected to accelerate steeply. Some highly leveraged fixed-income hedge funds which made bets on the direction of future interest rate moves have suffered dramatic reversals. One hedge fund in particular was taken over by a consortium of fourteen investment and commercial banks, which had invested in the fund, in an effort to avert panic liquidation of its extraordinarily large and highly leveraged portfolio. Construction of the consortium of banks was orchestrated by the Federal Reserve Bank of New York which feared that a too-rapid liquidation of its holdings would lead to further world-wide instability as other hedge finds and financial institutions would also be forced to liquidate steeply discounted securities to meet margin calls.

Wild interest rate moves like these stimulate demand for tools to profile, understand, and hedge portfolio-level risks. Even successful portfolio managers in quiet times are frequently required by sponsors to explain how they achieved their returns and the risks they assumed along the way.

Getting credible answers to questions about performance, interest rate exposure, and prepayment risk requires a credible, sophisticated analytics engine.

Investors have three options when considering securities with complicated risk: just say no and pass up the opportunity for higher return, assume a rosy future and ignore all special risks, or use an analytical engine to understand and manage the risks and rewards.

Broker-dealers have only the third option. They are typically first to assume the risk of owning complicated securities and first to develop tools to manage these risks. Furthermore, by definition, market makers must make two-sided markets in a wide variety of securities, and they must do so in every type of market. Since mispriced securities remain unsold, accurate information and high quality analytics are essential for success. Risk managers at broker-dealers must mark to market all holdings daily, even hourly, and self-preservation dictates that they know the valuations of their holdings in a variety of interest rate environments.

Investors who choose to participate in contemporary fixed-income markets are well- advised to develop their own tools or use one developed elsewhere. In either case, the highest cost is that of ignorance.

How much computing power is needed to properly analyze portfolio risk? Given the exponential risk-complexity relationship mentioned earlier, increasing yield a few basis points by buying a complex security can increase the owner's computational requirements many times.

Bonds that look cheap on a yield or option adjusted spread basis may really be fairly valued, or even expensive, when the computational costs of ownership are included. Fast computers, and reliable data are required to price these instruments correctly.

Yield Book Architecture

Overview

No discussion of Yield Book can ever be considered complete without a description of its architecture, for its architecture, as much as its content, explains its wide acceptance by demanding and impatient salesman, traders and investors.

Yield Book is an excellent example of the power of client-server architecture. This design had made it possible to deliver reliably high quality analytics, data, and research to a variety of desk top computers widely distributed around the world. Furthermore, efficiencies of client-server architecture have allowed us to increase the complexity and flexibility of our software, the breadth of market coverage, the size of our customer base, and the geographical distribution of our customers with only minimal organizational change, that is, with very few growing pains.

There are four main components to current Yield Book architecture: a set of 'compute server' computers; a set of 'Yield Book server' computers; a collection of databases; and the networks which knit the components into one seamless whole.

In figure 2 is an overview of Yield Book architecture. Each box represents a set of computers, except those at the bottom which represent different financial institutions and their respective desktop machines. Arrows indicate the data flow directions.

Figure 2: Overview of Yieldbook Architecture

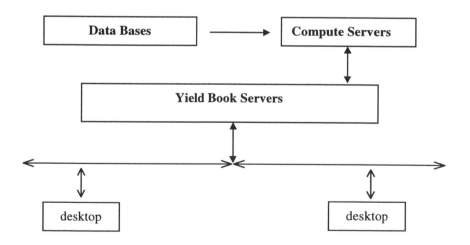

12.3 The Yield Book Server

Yield Book servers are powerful UNIX-based multi-processor computers which are the centerpiece of the architecture. The primary program, called 'Yield Book', which manages the user interface, runs on these machines. (The term "Yield Book" denotes both the whole package of machines, programs and networks and this specific 'primary' program. Before the introduction of client-server architecture, there was only one executable program which was unambiguously called "Yield Book." The meaning of "Yield Book" should be clear from the context.) Each Yield Book server supports as many as 75 concurrently running Yield Books and one database management server (data server). The data server manages as many as 60 private, read-write databases and several read-only databases, all resident on the Yield Book server, which are updated nightly with the latest yield curves, prices, and detailed, calculated valuation measures. Each running Yield Book establishes three connections (actually more, but we discuss only three here): one to a desktop computer via our wide-area network; one to the 'local' data server (that is, the data server running on the Yield Book server); and one to a load-balancing program that manages requests to compute servers for calculations and for data from one of our central databases.

The local data server provides direct access to over 20,000 fixed-income securities (U.S. and foreign corporate and government bonds, futures contracts on U.S treasuries, generic mortgages); yield curves from more than twenty international markets; five flavors of pre-computed, detailed price-yield calculations that include many measures (duration, convexity, dv01, partial dv01, carry adjusted prices, etc.) of a bond's sensitivity to changes in the treasury yield curve or its local currency yield curve; and Salomon's fixed-income indices.

The local data server further provides every user with access to a private, read-write database where it is possible to write user-generated portfolios, user-supplied prices and Yield Book-calculated valuation measures, and user-generated securities for later recall and analysis. It is very easy to move portfolios and pricing data between Yield Book and back office systems, a fact that no doubt partially explains the Yield Book's high level of integration with our customers' businesses.

Yield Book displays a graphical user interface on each desktop computer. This interface displays Yield Book output, text and graphics, and accepts user input in a variety of modes - text, mouse button clicks, and file transfer. A diagram of a Yield Book server is given in figure 3.

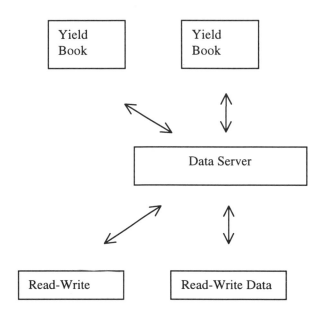

Figure 3: Diagram of Yieldbook Server

Compute Servers

The Yield Book uses a set of UNIX-based multi-processor computers, 'compute servers', specialized for floating-point arithmetic, and a set of specialized programs, many with parallel algorithms, to perform CPU-intense, security-specific calculations. For example, one program computes option-adjusted spreads ("OAS") on CMO. Some compute server programs are query processors which forward data requests to read-only databases (figure 2.) and return results to the Yield Book.

An internally-developed load-balancing program routes calculation and data requests from users to the least loaded compute server computer and compute server program so that response time experienced by customers is minimized.

The number of different valuation measures that are computed and returned to customers, the precision with which they are computed, and the speed with which results become available to users are unrivaled by competing fixed-income analytics systems.

Databases

The Yield Book provides access to a set of read-only databases in addition to those residing on Yield Book servers. Some are maintained by the Yield Book group, others by different groups at Salomon. Access to these databases is indirect, through the load-balancing program and request-handling programs that accept user requests, forward user requests to the appropriate data server, and return query results to the Yield Book display.

In the set of read-only databases are a deal-level CMO/ABS database with 8,000 deals and 1,000,000 mortgage pools and a class-level CMO/ABS database with 45,000 classes taken from the deal level database; a fixed-income database with 25,000 corporate securities in addition to those stored on the Yield Book servers; a firm-wide time series database of prices and yields; and an index returns database. Users may copy securities from the deal level or class level CMO/ABS databases, the mortgage pools database and fixed-income database to their personal, read-write, databases for fast access, to store their own pricing, or to include them in portfolios.

An example is pictured in figure 4.

Figure 4: Example of Database Usage

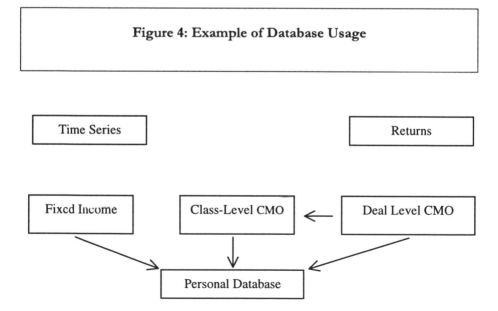

Networks

Two networks support the Yield Book's client-server architecture: a local, high-speed network for internal server-to-server communication and a wide-area network for Yield Book to desktop communication. The wide-area network consists of high-speed, dedicated telephone lines. Routers, one at our end and one at the customer end of the network, assure the integrity of the respective internal networks.

Alternatively, customers can use slower dial-up telephone lines to connect to theYield Book and they can combine dial-up lines with laptop computers to display Yield Book wherever it is needed or convenient.

Advantages of the Yield Book Architecture

Yield Book's client-server implementation has several advantages over the architectures used by competing systems. It is integrated into the client's local network so that it is conveniently viewable from the user's desktop together with all of other computer applications. Yield Book can be accessed from laptops which is useful for home-use, travel or as an inexpensive contingency-site plan. Almost no Yield Book software runs on desktop machines. Only two programs need to be installed on the client's desktop computer. One is a small program, used to initiate and authenticate connections, which, because it changes very infrequently, rarely requires re-installation. The other program is a commercially available X-server which is required to manage the graphical interface. Yield Book releases, therefore, require no customer participation. Minor software enhancements can, and do, happen very frequently, sometimes as often as daily. This gives Yield Book extraordinary flexibility and contributes significantly to its reputation for responsiveness. All CPU intensive calculations are done on large, powerful computers, not on desk top computers. Yield Book, therefore, delivers first class analytics in a small fraction of the time that would be required if calculations were performed on a desktop. No network-consuming data transfers to a client's desktop computer are required because the Yield Book program is running on the same side of the wide area network as all of its data sources. Only displayed data is transferred across the wide-area network to a desk top.

Earliest Architecture

It is not only our current architecture that explains Yield Book's market penetration but also our willingness to re-architect as hardware and networking technology change. For example, the balance between 'centralized' and 'distributed' computing pictured in figure 2 evolved from a very different one. The earliest Yield Book architecture (1989-1991, approximately) was much simpler and much more distributed than the current architecture. It was also much less scalable, that is, doubling the number of customer institutions or doubling security coverage would have required nearly twice the man-hours to maintain and software releases to many machines required days, rather than minutes, to complete.

At each customer site one UNIX workstation supported one Yield Book and one data server. Yield Books of that era not only managed the graphical user interface but also performed all calculations. The data server managed a single read-write database. Data, distributed nightly to each workstation, fed a batch process that calculated valuation measures and stored the results in the database for morning use. Yield Book had no access to any securities not in the local database. If figure 2 were modified to portray the earliest architecture, it would consist only of the bottom boxes and the connected two-pronged arrow, signifying the network joining the user's computer toSalomon.

This primitive-sounding architecture was widely applauded at the time. Internal customers were accustomed to very slow, and somewhat unreliable, access to mainframe computers. Now, nearly every security they needed was in a work station that they alone used. External customers suddenly had easy access to software that could previously be used only indirectly, with the help of a sales analyst.

Intermediate Architecture

Another architecture, adopted after our initial, single-executable one but before our current one (1991-1993, approximately), had three components: customer-site workstations; wide-area and local networks; and a set of compute servers.

This architecture was adopted shortly after the mortgage prepayment model was included in Yield Book. Customer-site workstations easily became occupied for long times with CPU-intensive mortgage calculations. While so occupied, customers could not use their Yield Books for any other tasks. This condition required a fix.

There were two alternative solutions for this problem: upgrade the hardware at each customer site or move the time consuming calculations off of the customer-site workstation and onto dedicated, more powerful computers at our site. We chose the latter alternative and when the feasibility of compute-server architecture was established for mortgage calculations, we moved additional calculation types off of the stand-alone workstation.

12.4 Yield Book History

There are several threads through the Yield Book history to follow: the view of Yield Book from sales and trading as it is perceived from within the Yield Book group; the evolution of the Yield Book architecture; and the evolution of customer support.

Yield Book's existence divides naturally into three periods corresponding approximately to three institutional states, or business plans and three architectures. The correspondence between architectural states and business plans is not exact, and border lines between periods are very fuzzy.

The Yield Book policy did not follow a straight line from its initial to its current state. Almost nothing about our current state was envisioned in the first business plan. The Yield Book has alternated between periods of rapid change and periods of relative inactivity, not as a software project because enhancement requests never abated and markets never rest from change, but as an institution within the broker-dealer.

The Yield Book architecture has influenced and been influenced by policy decisions. What is deliverable and how people value that service are definitely related. Authorization to expand is meaningless if the required infrastructure is missing or inadequate, or if your offering is not what customers want.

Customer service for a software product, which is at once very flexible and very complicated (complexity and flexibility are nearly synonymous in software), is vitally important for success, difficult to deliver, and potentially expensive. Good customer support is labor intensive and it is easy to think that a customer support group must grow at the same rate as the number of institutional customers or the number of individual users to remain effective. It has been a goal, partially met, to make usage support more efficient so that the support group grows more slowly than the customer base without sacrificing any of its often-cited responsiveness.

Motivation to build

Yield Book was conceived and initially released primarily as a marketing tool. We did not start out to develop a tool as closely linked, as it is today, to the valuation of complicated securities. Earliest versions could analyze corporate and treasury bonds and generic mortgages only; complex securities like CMO and ABS were not included on the original development agenda.

Development of Yield Book began as a consequence of a 1988 study of Salomon's business by outside consultants which found that customers valued

Salomon's research and analytics highly but they very often executed trades elsewhere. The study concluded that giving customers easier access to analytics and research would be rewarded with greater customer loyalty and more sales and trading business. Initial rollout of Yield Book in July of 1989 to a very small, carefully selected, set of salesmen (four) and their best customers (three), was intended to test this hypothesis.

Shortly after its release to this select group, Salomon's traders discovered Yield Book and almost immediately a debate, or tug-of-war, began between two groups, those favoring wide Yield Book distribution among customers and those favoring its retention as an internal-only tool. This debate persists today but now the issues separating those who argue for expansion from those who argue against expansion are different.

Earliest funding for Yield Book development came directly from the office of the chairman of Salomon which probably shielded us to some extent from the debate. Yield Book's managers were given firm deadlines and nearly complete freedom to choose hardware, to choose third-party (database and networking) software, and to manage development.

Early years: 1989-1993

The early years (all dates are approximate) are characterized by a highly distributed, single-executable architecture and its evolution to an 'intermediate architecture'; by the creation of competing software, 'UniVu,' written by the 'Electronic Joint Venture,' EJV, a consortium of six major dealers, including Salomon; by the development of a customer service group to support institutional customers directly; and by the evolution of Yield Book into a first class mortgage tool. Also, during this period, Yield Book's cost was moved from the chairman's office to sales and trading.

During the early years, consistent with the notion that Yield Book was a marketing tool, the software, the wide-area network, a high-powered (by then-current standards) workstation, a printer, and all necessary hardware, software, and usage support for this infrastructure were provided free of charge to customers.

Usage support was delivered to institutional customers initially by Salomon's sales force, not from within the Yield Book group. In fact, in July of 1989, there was no Yield Book customer support group. Our single person in a support capacity is more accurately described as sales support. His job was to teach salesmen how to use Yield Book and they, in turn, were to train customers. Conversations between salesman and customers, including those about

Yield Book usage, were supposed to improve the likelihood that transactions would be directed to Salomon rather than one of its competitors.

This customer support model was not long lived. Salesmen found ultimately that they did not have the time to handle the job of Yield Book customer support and investor usage patterns diverged widely from those of sales and trading. Investors used Yield Book for a wide variety of relatively complicated jobs, such as portfolio analytics, scenario analysis, and report generation, that salesmen did not, and so they became more sophisticated Yield Book users than their salesmen. Growing complexity of the product compounded the problem. Customer questions rapidly became too hard and too time consuming for salesmen to answer. Furthermore, changes to early Yield Book versions at major releases, generally semi-annually, were typically substantial enough to require customer-site tutorials, a chore completely beyond what the sales force, with few exceptions, wanted to do. Salesmen are, after all, compensated to sell bonds, not to train customers or perform calculations for them. Consequently, sales management asked the Yield Book group to handle customer usage questions directly. Certainly by the end of this period, all Yield Book usage support of broker dealer customers had shifted to an internal group.

Soon after it began, the rollout to external customers was slowed at the behest of internal users, especially mortgage traders. The rapid growth of the CMO market, the prodigious data requirements of CMO deals, the time consuming calculations required to model these deals and the inability of older mainframe computers to deliver all of this to impatient salesmen and traders accelerated Salomon's switch from mainframe computing to distributed computing in general and to the Yield Book in particular.

There was also a policy debate regarding the Yield Book and its use by investors. As usage among salesmen and traders increased, they came to appreciate its advantages over older systems, and more generally, the advantages of distributed computing. With greater appreciation of Yield Book's advantages, a debate began at Salomon. Was the Yield Book too valuable internally to share with customers? If transaction volume did indeed increase, would the revenue gain offset possible losses caused by the exposure of proprietary models to customers and possibly, by indirect exposure, to competitors? Could Yield Book be taken back from institutions where it was already installed?

The EJV and its UniVu product (1990) raised questions about Yield Book's future as a customer tool quite independently of other questions such as exposure of Salomon's proprietary models to investors. The EJV and UniVu are closely related, genealogically speaking, to Salomon Analytics and Yield Book. Their similar beginnings and different fates are discussed later. UniVu was supposed to provide the same functionality as Yield Book and its content providers, six broker-dealers, had enormous financial and intellectual resources. How Yield Book and UniVu were ultimately to co-exist or if they were to co-exist at all was not clear to developers.

Early in 1991, an internal analysis of customer transactions concluded that transaction growth rates were substantially higher among Yield Book customers than they were among non- Yield Book customers. Consequently, it was decided to resume and accelerate the rollout to more of the broker-dealer's customers. The size of the Yield Book user community grew sharply. From our initial release of seven licenses to four internal and three external users in July of 1989, we grew by December of 1993 to nearly four hundred internal users in sales, trading and research and to one hundred fifty of the largest, most well-known financial institutions each with a single license.

The decision to expand not-withstanding, the debate about the wisdom of sharing Yield Book with customers continued. Somewhat surprisingly, some customers joined the side opposed to releasing too many Yield Books to other Salomon customers. Customers with Yield Book realized its advantages and they felt that universal availability would hurt them. People who had mastered the intricacies of bond analytics the old fashioned way, by reading books, feared that Yield Book would turn mere novices into formidable competitors very quickly. Also, some very good customers of the broker dealer took offense at the fact that some non-customers were given Yield Book with the expectation that Yield Book would motivate them to become good customers. To discourage indiscriminate release, these customers argued that continued expansion of Yield Book's customer base would erode the competitive advantage it conferred and universal availability might, therefore, ultimately discourage Yield Book use. Subsets of sales and trading and Yield Book customers agreed that it was a good for them and Salomon to have Yield Book but that further expansion was in no one's best interest.

Meanwhile, capabilities developed to satisfy internal users, especially mortgage traders, made Yield Book even more desirable to the broker-dealer's fixed-income customers. Usage, by every measure, whether time spent running the Yield Book or CPU-seconds spent doing calculations or calls to customer support, was increasing at a high rate. Existing Yield Book customers were asking for additional licenses beyond the one envisioned in the original business plan and they wanted Yield Book more thoroughly integrated into their local networks. It is not possible to utilize Yield Book fully if it is trapped in its own stand-alone workstation and private network, they argued. Salomon's broker-dealer customers without Yield Book also wanted access.

Arguments made by customers that usage would decline as market penetration increased were proven wrong. The degree to which customers relied on Yield Book analytics, measured by those usage measures mentioned above and by anecdotal evidence provided by customers themselves, grew, and continues to grow today, at a rate far in excess of the growth rate of the customer base; not only were there more licenses but each was being used more heavily than in the past. Yield Book was becoming ever more thoroughly woven into the fabric of customers' work; it was making the transition from a "very nice" product to a necessity.

Flattering anecdotes began circulating. Some competing dealers complained that Yield Book customers would not buy a CMO that could not be modeled on Yield Book. Confirmation of this has come from customers themselves who have told us directly that only deals modeled on Yield Book are acceptable instruments for their portfolios. One regional dealer, to be eligible for Yield Book, offered to change its business plan so as not to be considered a Salomon competitor. Recently, a large institutional money manager switched to Yield Book from a competing system because, they said, 'a firm of our size and stature must have Yield Book, the people who evaluate us expect it.' One money manager was quoted recently in a prestigious investor publication as saying the 'Yield Book would have to be pried from my cold dead hands.'

Analytics Technology Corporation: 1993-1996

The period from 1993 to July of 1996 is characterized by the introduction of our Yield Book server architecture and several corollary technical and policy changes, including a name change in August of 1994 to Analytics Technology Corporation, or, ATC, a wholly-owned subsidiary of Salomon. It is also a period with two distinct sub-periods. One characterized by very rapid institutional change and one of relative dormancy which, it later was revealed, was a time during which Yield Book's business plan was reassessed.

In order to accommodate requests for multiple licenses and better integration into customer networks, we moved from one-book-per-stand-alone-workstation architecture to the full blown Yield Book server architecture described earlier. The conversion period lasted nearly eighteen months, measured from the time of our first completed installation at a technically sophisticated customer, which was regarded for quite some time as a feasibility test, to the last conversion. Most of the conversion time was spent dealing with telephone companies and complicated network issues, including data and network security, that needed to be resolved in a different way at each institution to accomplish a network upgrade.

Very few new institutional customers were added during the conversion period. The debate between expansion and contraction proponents was at something of a stalemate. Increasing the number of licenses at existing Yield Book customers was approved; providing Yield Book to new customers was not.

Simultaneous with the architecture redesign there were five additional technical and policy changes to Yield Book. We lifted the ceiling on the number of licenses that a customer was permitted; customers were required to buy their workstation and printer, at steep discounts to market prices because they were nearly fully amortized, and assume maintenance responsibility, or return them to us and provide their own desktop hardware; we upgraded our wide-area networks; we expanded our customer support group; we imposed a small charge on customers to cover the increased cost of the new, higher band-width network and the expanded customer service group; and finally we changed our name to Analytics Technology Corporation, a Salomon subsidiary solely responsible for Yield Book distribution to Salomon's fixed-income investors.

The elevated ceiling on customer licenses was not uniform. Sales force approval was still required for each additional license and approval depended on current or anticipated transactions. Some customers were granted additional licenses, others were not; some were granted several licenses, others only one.

Upgraded networks and expanded customer support were both required components of the new architecture because many customers took advantage of the elevated ceiling on licenses. With more licenses, we anticipated correctly, that more data, in the form of X, or image-related, traffic would move over the network and that more inexperienced users would call customer support with usage questions. Failure to upgrade networks or to expand customer support would have meant diminished service, not only for newcomers, but for long-time customers as well.

The trade-off between more licenses and better integration with their internal networks on the one hand, and the small charge on the other, was very well received by customers. Cancellations were negligible. Under the ATC business plan, few new institutions were added as a matter of policy not for lack of demand, but the number of licenses grew to approximately 200 because existing customers took advantage of the new licensing rules.

A very big obstacle to growth was removed when customers were required to maintain their own desktop Yield Book machines and printers. Providing hardware support to widely scattered customers was very expensive and clearly not conducive to efficient growth.

Again the rollout slowed because no one could determine whether Yield Book, which was, by 1995, a conspicuous budget item, was returning enough value to the broker-dealer. The original business model was for each of Salomon's best customers to have one Yield Book on its own workstation with a dedicated network connection to us. The hardware and support costs of this arrangement grew very quickly. Even though the ATC business model was very different from the original, and considerably less expensive per customer, it was still impossible to determine whether the broker-dealer was adequately compensated for its Yield Book expenses. The control group, non-Yield Book users who were good customers of the broker-dealer, which was used in 1991 to determine that Yield Book was, in fact, generating more transactions, was now too small to be useful as a benchmark. Sales management therefore found it very hard to see any incremental advantage for the next Yield Book. The decision making process was further clouded because many of the broker-dealer's senior managers who knew Yield Book from its beginning had left Salomon. New managers looked skeptically at Yield Book, especially its expenses. They wanted the answer to one simple question. 'Were Yield Book customers doing enough additional transactions to justify the cost?' With neither a control group of broker-dealer customers nor sufficient institutional memory, there was no way to derive a conclusive answer.

Yield Book expansion was very difficult to halt however. Salesmen wanted more of their very best customers to have Yield Book and they wanted some of their best customers to have multiple licenses. While sales management may have doubted the incremental value of the next Yield Book, individual salesmen, thinking of specific customers, very often had a different view of the next Yield Book's value. Also word of Yield Book had spread among the broker-dealers' customers from those with Yield Book to those without, and salesmen did not like the role of Yield Book gatekeeper. No salesman wants to say 'no' to a customer!

Salomon Analytics: 1996 to date

Faced with a dilemma, too much demand from valued customers on the one hand and no clear idea if continued expansion would be profitable on the other, sales management decided to let the market decide Yield Book's value by making it a commercial product. On July 1, 1996, Yield Book became a wholly owned subsidiary of Salomon, 'Salomon Analytics' with a business plan different from that of ATC. Its sole function is marketing Yield Book software to all buy-side firms and selected regional dealers, who are more partner than competitor to the broker-dealer. Decisions about which investor firms should have Yield Book and how many Yield Books an institution should have were made by the institutions themselves and these decisions were made without regard to transaction rate with the broker-dealer.

With commercialization, the software itself was charged to customers. Fees increased sharply from the network and usage-support fee imposed as Analytics Technology Corporation. The sales force was no longer charged for customer licenses; it was freed of the responsibility of getting paid for Yield Book in the form of increased transactions; and it was freed of the unpleasant job of saying no to customers who wanted additional licenses, or their first license, but who failed to meet the required transaction levels.

Reaction among customers to commercialization was surprising. Most customers approved of the new structure; generally, they liked separating Yield Book usage from broker-dealer transactions. A few institutions cancelled their Yield Book outright and a few reduced the number of licenses. Total decline in license count, from cancellations and reductions, was less than 15%. The ceiling on the number of Yield Book licenses was removed altogether and a veritable explosion in the number of licenses followed. There was obviously substantial pent-up demand for additional licenses from existing customers and from new customers who wanted their first. Before commercialization there were roughly 200 licenses at 150 institutions and today (March 1999) there are nearly 750 licenses at more than 250 institutions.

At the time of commercialization, some salesman expressed the fear that Yield Book customers really had been rewarding the broker-dealer for the Yield Book with transactions, and that, with higher Yield Book costs, customers would move their transaction business elsewhere, perhaps as punishment for the change in the fee structure, perhaps because they no longer felt an obligation to trade with the broker-dealer. An updated version of an old question was asked. Would revenue from Salomon Analytics offset potential revenue declines suffered by the broker- dealer?

There is no evidence that Yield Book customers have moved transactions to other dealers. On the contrary, many of the customers added since commercialization have been referrals from Salomon's sales force. It is reasonable to think that salesmen are acting in their own interest when they recommend Yield Book to their customers; they expect to sell more securities. Presumably then, Salomon the broker-dealer, is now paid twice for Yield Book, once under the old business model, in the form of higher transaction rates, and once under the new business plan.

Formation of Salomon Analytics has benefited all of its constituents. The broker-dealer has unambiguously determined Yield Book's value and it is being paid in at least two ways for its investment in Yield Book development. Investors have access to first class software at a very small fraction of its development and maintenance costs. Contributing Salomon groups, like Treasury Analysis, Mortgage Research, and Fixed-Income Index, for example, have gotten far more reputation-enhancing exposure to institutional investors with Yield Book than they would have without Yield Book.

12.5 Management

This enterprise has little to do with the broker-dealer's usual money-making business; one does not think of Salomon as a software start-up company. It is not even head-quartered in California. Why has Yield Book succeeded?

Given that similar broker-dealer projects were started and abandoned in the period between July of 1989 and today, Yield Book's continued existence, ten years later, is reason enough to make management questions interesting. Its apparent success makes it more interesting.

UniVu and the EJV

One particularly interesting example of a Yield Book-like product that had a very promising and very similar beginning, but which is no longer a competitor, is 'UniVu,' a system built by the EJV. UniVu began its existence in 1990 with a purchase of then-current Yield Book source code and its first release was in the middle of 1991. It was supposed to be a Yield Book-like application, but with a different look and feel, that would serve the needs of all six broker-dealers in the consortium and their customers.

The precise roles that UniVu and Yield Book were supposed to fill at Salomon was not very clear to us in the Yield Book group. According to one business plan in circulation, Yield Book and UniVu were to co-exist at Salomon as complementary systems. UniVu would be sold to non-consortium brokers and buy-side customers and Yield Book was to be Salomon's internal delivery platform. This plan is consistent with the slow-down in Yield Book release shortly after its initial release. According to another hypothesis, Yield Book's existence was merely to prove the concept and that UniVu would ultimately become the single fixed-income tool in use at the six member brokers and their customers.

UniVu, despite the head start it got with its purchase of Yield Book software and despite its generous support from the EJV, is now found at very few institutions and it is never mentioned as a Yield Book competitor among the buy-side customers we approach.

UniVu's managers complained that it was very hard for them to sell their product at the same time that Yield Book was available free. UniVu became available for sale in the middle of 1991, about one year after its start. At the time, Yield Book was available at approximately forty buy-side institutions. While it is true that Yield Book was free, UniVu had a larger development staff (something we will later maintain may not have been an advantage) and it had released some important capabilities ahead of Yield Book. UniVu also benefited from the combined resources (data, models, and funding) of six firms whereas Yield Book was solely the work of a single broker-dealer with obviously divided loyalties.

Yield Book benefited from UniVu's existence because, while the other five broker-dealers were waiting for the EJV to complete UniVu, they undertook no internal development of their own on similar projects that could have emerged as Yield Book competitors. Yield Book development, on the other hand, was unaffected by UniVu either before or after its release.

Still, UniVu could, and probably should, have been an effective competitor, especially as it commanded substantial resources in the form of money, data, and models from six major fixed- income market makers and it started its life with the source code of a product which ultimately succeeded.

Given the similar parentage, goals, and markets of Yield Book and UniVu, it is reasonable to want to explain their divergent histories. Unfortunately, we do not know, and therefore cannot comment on, UniVu's history and management, but we can provide some observations about Yield Book which may be relevant in explaining its longevity.

Company within a company

The Yield Book project has always been managed as a company within a company. We are a whole company in the sense that every expertise required to make the project work is available within the group. From the beginning, our own systems engineers maintained the hardware, our own network engineers maintained networks. Customer usage support was provided for a short time by salesmen before it too became an internal Yield Book function. With the formation of Salomon Analytics, a sales team has been created to pursue new business, whether it is a referral from the broker-dealer or another source.

Unlike other software projects at Salomon, Yield Book did not use the firm's technology office. Typically, projects at Salomon use the firm-wide database group to handle database design and maintenance, the firm-wide systems group to maintain the hardware and the firm-wide network group to handle networking. Projects so organized lack dedicated expertise available to troubleshoot problems immediately and, more importantly, to anticipate and implement architectural changes before their need becomes critical. Still worse is the additional communication costs incurred when disparate groups, each with its own priorities, need to cooperate.

Yield Book has never suffered micro-management from either broker-dealer management or from its own management. Choices of hardware platforms, operating systems, routers, network providers, and database management systems, for example, have been made with considerable freedom, sometimes adopting the firm-wide standard as our own, sometimes not, but always questioning whether the firm-wide standard was the best available to meet our particular needs. Since Yield Book's founding, for example, we have used computers produced by three different manufacturers. Only one of these was the standard Salomon platform. This freedom has allowed us to get the best price performance in existence at the time of hardware purchase.

Nearer to the actual development, there have never been top down software development standards except for the most general ones like programming languages, database management server, etc. Typically programming structure emerges, in a self-organizing way, from individual developers or small groups of developers, once features are in place. Software design and implementation decisions have always been left to individual developers. This is true today and it was even truer in the beginning. Even now, ten years after our founding and after considerable code restructuring, Yield Book code is still very much 'unstructured', that is, it does not conform to the rules of structured programming. On the other hand, Yield Book development is noted for its exceptionally short turn-around time on requests. This trade-off, taking rapid feature delivery in exchange for uniform coding standards, is clearly the right one for us to make. It is true, to some extent, that our unstructured beginning later made it more difficult than it would have otherwise been to add capabilities. However, if we had concentrated too heavily on doing it right from the very start, there may have been only the beginning and nothing beyond. Furthermore, doing it right requires a very clear statement and a presumption that these goals are immutable. However, in a market-driven business, where even the most artfully constructed program can face obsolescence, maybe before it is completed, clearly stated goals, strictly adhered to, may more realistically be a prescription for extinction rather than success. Yield Book became the tool to use because it had what people needed when markets dictated that they needed it.

Budgetary freedom, budgetary responsibility, and software development

Substitute any product you like for software and its production is very definitely related to its budget. Obviously, in the limiting case, no budget means no product. On the other had, infinitely large budgets do not guarantee success.

In the following, we offer some thoughts on the relation between budgets and software. The degree to which their relation decides success or failure for a software project cannot be determined definitively. However, we think that it may be instructive to think of the impact each has had on the other.

Periods of rapid growth and budgetary constraint, very often self-imposed, have been taken as opportunities by us to develop program efficiencies and infrastructure efficiencies. Cost containment was an ever present fact of our existence. We never lacked hardware resources and no one ever questioned our budget, to my knowledge, but this seemingly privileged position with regard to hardware was purchased with a home-grown sense of frugality. On the other hand, we have many times been subject to hiring freezes and have always worked with what appears and feels to be too few people. This attention to efficiency and cost consciousness was driven by more than our desire to retain our budgetary freedom by using it wisely. There was an innate understanding that good software development is not encouraged by easy access to hardware upgrades nor is it encouraged by easy access to developers.

To illustrate the point about developers, we use the classic fence-post-hole problem we all solved, or maybe failed to solve, in high school algebra as an analogue of software development. The problem goes like this: if one man can dig one fence post hole in one hour, how long would it take two men to dig the same fence post hole? Well, if they work at the same rate then the 'correct' answer is clearly 1/2 hour. The implicit assumption is that these two fellows work perfectly together, that there is no negative feedback when the second person begins to contribute. However, the logic used to arrive at this conclusion rapidly becomes silly when you consider adding even more people. How long would it take one thousand men to dig a single fence post hole? Obviously these men will now impede each other's work to the point that, if each of one thousand men insists on contributing, the job will take far longer than the one hour required when one man worked alone.

Software development is, in some ways, like digging a fence post hole. Software is simply a set of files, and software development, by definition, is file modification. Adding more people to the development effort implies that more people require access to the files and hence wait time increases and communication costs grow.

Increasing the number of files as the number of developers grows seems a plausible way to handle this problem, development in parallel, or, using our fence post hold again, have one thousand men dig one thousand holes. Unfortunately, creating more files is itself a time-consuming job that produces no direct customer benefit. Furthermore, subdividing existing files into smaller pieces generally increases the number of different files that need to be modified for each additional feature. Increasing the number of files to accommodate more developers is hard to do and ultimately does not change the file contention problem very much.

Another reason for a relatively small development team is that deep knowledge held by a single developer is much more efficiently used than that same knowledge shared among two or more developers, even if every one of them has the same deep knowledge. A single developer who knows the program well spends no time at all communicating. A group of two or more must communicate and communication costs grow super linearly with the number of developers. As a purely practical matter, as developers are added, each has responsibility for a smaller percentage of the overall program and so each is likely to know less about the program than his predecessors. This knowledge dilution further adds to communication costs.

Just as in the fence post hole problem, communication-induced inefficiencies grow rapidly with the number of individuals. In our fence post hole example, one thousand men digging a single hole would no doubt spend the lion's share of their time deciding how to apportion the work, and not digging the hole. In software development, it is very easy to add enough people to a project so that development time increases to unacceptable levels.

Software development, being more complicated than hole digging, also incurs a heavy educational cost as people are added. Even before new software engineers introduce inefficiencies by competing for files, new developers introduce inefficiencies by requiring an education.

A software project is very much like a foreign language or a small, isolated culture. Even if one knows the alphabet (or programming language) one cannot be conversant without study of the local idiom and the study time required grows as the life and complexity of the software project grows. A new developer cannot be handed a shovel and told 'go to work.' Educating new developers takes time from previously-educated developers and, in the best circumstance, when a developer stays with a project long after his education is complete, expense is added before real value is added. Developers who leave before they have matured are best not hired at all. On the other hand, institutional, or program, memory is very valuable

Easy access to additional developers can therefore work against a successful outcome in a software project. It fosters an environment rife with meetings, where specifications are developed and further meetings planned and no results.

Hardware and software development

Easy access to new and faster computers, if they are chosen to avoid the work of changing architecture or without specific needs in mind, can also work against success in a software project. Software inefficiencies can be hidden easily with fast computers and even worse, fast computers, if easily available, can discourage creative software development to overcome hardware constraints.

A very good example of this is the architecture redesign we undertook from our initial, single-executable one, to our compute-server architecture.

When interest in mortgage-backed securities was exploding, we included the mortgage prepayment model in the single Yield Book program running on the stand-alone workstations. This was a very big improvement, giving users access to a state of the art model. Unfortunately it also meant that Yield Book workstations could easily be consumed for ten to twelve hours performing CPU-intensive calculations on large mortgage portfolios.

An obvious solution was to upgrade the single computer at customer sites. A hardware upgrade would have been expensive, fast, feasible, and risk free. Another solution, also expensive but not risk free, not fast and its feasibility knowable only after its completion was the introduction of the compute server architecture. Mortgage calculations would not be done on the stand- alone workstation by the single program, but, instead, on a set of computers running a specialized program at our site. Calculation results would be sent back to the user's workstation. This meant, of course, buying powerful computers to do the calculations but it meant buying many fewer than the one per customer that would have been required had we simply upgraded the original computers.

Had the former solution been adopted, Yield Book would have gone down an entirely different development path. In principle this choice would not be not irreversible, but, had it been adopted, it may have changed how customers and benefactors regarded Yield Book and that different perspective may have produced unpleasant consequences.

When deciding which machine would be appropriate for the mortgage compute server, we exercised our freedom to buy the best possible computer, measured by price and performance on our specific CPU-intensive calculations, that fit into our overall budget. Several computer manufacturers enthusiastically competed for the privilege of providing these compute servers to us.

It is very hard to imagine that a firm-wide price-performance measure could be as meaningful as the very specific measure, on exactly the calculations that we needed to perform. Hardware we adopted as compute server was not standard at Salomon; we were in fact the only group using this hardware. It was, however, the best computer available at that time for our specific need. Even more important is the fact that the revised architecture has proven to be exceptionally growth-friendly or scalable and, in the long run, significantly cheaper than the alternative.

Moving mortgage calculations to compute server computers on our side of the wide-area network had another effect. Networks, before they were upgraded as part of our switch to the Yield Book server architecture, were asked to carry more data between customers' stand-alone workstations and our compute servers. This additional load on the wide-area networks did not go unnoticed by customers. It made them more aware of the importance of network performance for their work. Their later willingness to pay the small fee we imposed as Analytics Technology Corp to cover increased costs incurred by a network upgrade when we moved to our full-blown client-server model, can be explained, perhaps, by this understanding.

12.6 Efficiency

Yield Book and efficiency are nearly synonymous. Yield Book has done for the bond business, especially for mortgages and CMO, what robotics has done for automobile manufacturing. The magnitude of the impact is much smaller, but the direction, toward more efficient revenue production, is the same. Like the automobile industry, in which manufacturers and consumers have both benefited from robotics, so have Salomon and Yield Book customers benefited from Yield Book. In an industry where both time and people are dear, it has revolutionized how a wide array of analytics is delivered, streamlining the process of analyzing and selling fixed-income securities, reducing the amount of time and the number of people required to design and validate transactions.

The job of restructuring a client's portfolio, for example, requires understanding the current portfolio, understanding the constraints to be imposed on the new portfolio, finding securities that satisfy the constraints, and determining that the proposed portfolio behaves acceptably in a variety of interest-rate environments and over a variety of horizons. For at least one Salomon competitor, one of these tasks, the search for appropriate securities (a job given to an analyst) typically requires several days to complete.

Yield Book, with its powerful relational database search engines, wealth of databases and security types, and its built-in optimizer can locate bonds meeting constraints on rating, currency, duration, maturity, option adjusted spread, etc. in minutes, not days. Once securities are selected, Yield Book's powerful compute servers can be used to analyze the restructured portfolio in a variety of arbitrarily defined interest rate environments and over a variety of arbitrarily defined horizons. Moreover, Yield Book does all of this in minutes, or, in the case of very complicated, highly structured securities, hours.

In the few days that another firm without Yield Book would require simply to locate securities, a Yield Book customer, with or without the assistance of a salesman, can construct and very thoroughly analyze many different restructured portfolios.

Another example of Yield Book efficiency is the speed with which an OAS on a generic mortgage or CMO can be determined today versus the time it required before Yield Book. In the days before Yield Book, anyone (customer, trader, or salesman) who wanted to know Salomon's OAS on a mortgage would have to contact a mortgage analyst who would perform a calculation and return the result when the calculation, lengthy by today's standards, was completed. Customers, of course, requested their information through a salesman. Now, internal and external Yield Book customers compute it themselves in significantly less time than it used to require.

Yield Book advantages, like those mentioned above, over old-fashioned methods continue to grow. As the breadth of covered securities increases, and the size and sophistication of the financial tool box at users' finger tips increases, the gap between the old-fashioned way of doing business and the new way increases.

Efficiency is not only delivered to internal and external users but something we build for ourselves. In July of 1989, there were seventeen members of the Yield Book group, developers and systems engineers, supporting seven licenses. In March of 1999, there are fewer than fifty Yield Book group members, including customer support and sales, and nearly 750 external licenses and nearly 500 internal licenses. Every day we ask ourselves what can we do to double the number of licenses, to increase security coverage, to offer more research, to offer additional valuation measures, and how can we deliver these to customers faster than we do now without increasing costs.

The enormous efficiency of Yield Book in planning and analyzing transactions, explains why salesmen have been most enthusiastic providers of names of possible Yield Book customers and why customers have been adding licenses since July of 1996 at the high rate they have.

There are other efficiencies that Yield Book delivers to Salomon: the value of the whole exceeds the sum of the values of its constituents and Yield Book's development cost is less than the sum of the separate development costs that would have been incurred if separate delivery tools were built for each of its constituents. It is doubtful that separate delivery tools for mortgages on the one hand and corporate bonds and treasury securities, on the other, would be as valuable to customers or internal users, but total development and maintenance costs would, almost certainly, be greater than those of Yield Book.

Efficiencies like these are effectively a third form of compensation to the broker-dealer from its Yield Book investment. Yield Book costs are effectively reduced by the savings achieved because fewer people, and even fewer groups, are needed now that Yield Book has incorporated into one central delivery mechanism functions formerly performed by others.

Yield Book, counting only direct revenue is now modestly profitable. A more accurate measure of Yield Book's contribution to the broker-dealer's profit and loss would include revenue derived from increased transactions and efficiency driven cost reduction.

12.7 Why A Broker-Dealer?

Broker-dealers have the means and the motive to build Yield Book-like tools. Every broker-dealer is well-equipped to develop a Yield Book-like tool, better equipped than independent software development teams not closely linked to financial institutions and markets. Every broker-dealer has all, or almost all, of the required components - mortgage prepayment model, corporate option model, treasury market model, CMO/ABS modelers, time series database of prices, and high-quality, ambitious developers who possess the required technical skills. Developers excepted, these are off-the-shelf-components, used for other purposes but never used-up. Furthermore, at broker-dealers, these components have survived rigorous testing by salesmen and traders who use only tools that add value. This on-going testing by market professionals in friendly and hostile markets is invaluable. Programs with all of the same components, even with comparable - quality components, but without professional credibility have a hard time gaining space on crowded desks and crowded screens.

Broker-dealers also have motivation to build delivery tools. They are, just as Salomon is, market makers with the same exposure to interest rate volatility and it is also likely that, any broker-dealer asking outside consultants to determine how best to increase transaction volume would get a prescription similar to Salomon's: share analytics with customers. The EJV is proof. In fact, other broker-dealers typically do share analytics with customers; but, they do so in ways that are considerably less efficient, for them and their customers, than Yield Book. For example, rather than providing the analytics to customers so that portfolios can be analyzed conveniently by customers, they insist on taking delivery of portfolios and performing in-house calculations just as Salomon did with its CMPOS system or they put single-security calculators on a web site.

12.8 Why Salomon?

Salomon has specific assets, in addition to those that available at every broker-dealer, that help explain Yield Book's successful development.

Salomon's bond research department, founded by Sidney Homer, is one of the oldest and most respected on Wall Street. It has valued and used computers to evaluate fixed-income securities since they became widely available.

Success that salesmen and traders had with earlier research-built computer models and tools predisposed them to try Yield Book.

Salomon was one of the earliest broker-dealers to convert from centralized to distributed computing and the UNIX operating system, which lends itself to constructing a distributed computing environment. Salomon, also, was one of the earliest broker-dealers to develop high-speed internal networks to nourish the development of distributed computing.

Many of the components provided to Yield Book by other Salomon groups in research and trading are highly respected on their own. Among these, to risk the sin of omission, are the mortgage prepayment model, the CMO/ABS deals provided by the CMO modelers, the fixed-income indices, and the vast amount of data that comes from derivatives research.

Salomon also has had considerable success getting disparate internal groups, which normally do not cooperate with each other because they have no real need, to agree to use Yield Book as their delivery tool. Each additional desk and research department that decided to use Yield Book as its own delivery platform helped increase Yield Book's worth for internal users and, especially for, external customers.

12.9 Conclusion

Yield Book has evolved from what now looks like a humble beginning to become a highly respected, critically important piece of software in heavy use at the biggest and most well known money management firms, insurance companies, pension funds, banks, and hedge funds as well as within Salomon Smith Barney. And "evolved" is the correct way to characterize its development. This sort of success was not planned. Views of Yield Book's future were never long-ranged; there has never been a master plan with a complete list of functionality requirements for its "final state." Yield Book grew from year to year in ways that were not predicted and in many cases contrary to whatever vision there was of its future path. The Yield Book's success is in part due to the collaboration between customers and developers.

The Yield Book is a leader in a wave of democratization which is changing the financial services industry. This trend is analogous to the transformation which changed the computer hardware and software industries. Thirty years ago, the mainframe computer was the only computer. Firms providing computers also provided software and systems support. Those firms, together with the most prestigious universities, monopolized computer expertise. It was common, for example, for computer science departments to hire people with doctorates in philosophy to teach class and ultimately to perform research. Companies wanting computing power (it was unthinkable for individuals to want computing power) bought everything from one these giant providers.

Today, the computer software and hardware industries have been democratized to a degree unimaginable thirty years ago. Computing power is relatively cheap and very widely available; programming and systems expertise are also widely available. Every major corporation and many small companies have computers and the knowledge to manage them.

Financial services is evolving similarly in part because of the evolution in computing expertise. Fifteen years ago, key bond valuation parameters existed only in a research departments at major brokerage houses. Now, buy-side institutions have access, on their terms, to information that was once closely guarded. But their appetite has not been sated. Electronic dissemination of information and electronic trading will continue to evolve; the financial services industry will continue its democratization. One can imagine a future in which giant financial service firms are dominated by world-knowledgeable traders with capital to commit and technical leaders with systems to facilitate analysis and transactions. The key to good customer service will not be to provide information while retaining the position of information gatekeeper. Rather good customer service provides tools to deliver information directly and efficiently. This trend toward greater democratization is unstoppable. Successful firms will be those embracing the trend and leading the race.

Developers, especially those who remember the early days of Yield Book when success was just a vision are proud of its acceptance by, and importance to, investors and internal users. Yield Book developers recognize the intrinsic value to users and to the software that a long-term association has produced. A deep understanding of software, a particularly valuable form of institutional memory, has benefited all of Yield Book's customers, both internal and external, as well as the developers.

Acknowledgements

Yield Book benefits directly and enormously from the work of many other groups at Salomon. In many cases their work is standard-setting and highly respected in the financial community. Some of the groups whose contributions are vital to Yield Book are Treasury Analysis, Mortgage Research, CMO modeling, CMO database, Fixed Income Index, Time Series (Rover), Fixed-Income Database, and Derivatives Research. Without their contributions, Yield Book would not be the highly regarded product it is.

I would like to thank T. Klaffky, R. Moreno, B. Boyce, L. Plaza-Colon, G. Treimanis, S. Lin, M. Liang, D. Gavilan, R. Chang, J. Kuang and U. Bidkar for their substantive discussions, historical perspective and recollections, grammatical corrections and technical assistance. I would also like to thank all current and past Yield Book group members and our external and internal customers for making this project a success.

SECTION III:

CUSTOMER VALUE FOCUSED SYSTEMS

Chapter 13

Impending Revolution in Corporate Information Technology Departments

Kevin McGilloway
Lehman Brothers, Inc.

13.1 Introduction

It is old news that the Technology and Financial Services sectors are undergoing revolutionary changes in the very nature of their products, services and structures. The more current revolution is that the two sectors have mated and mutated into a new revolutionary force, e-commerce. Yet while corporate Chief Executive Officers (CEOs) and Chief Information Officers (CIOs) are attempting to address these challenges in their businesses, it is interesting to note that they often seem to completely ignore the implications to the unit in their organizations most intimately involved with dealing with these changes, namely their Information Technology (IT) departments.

This chapter proposes that the fundamental factors that are driving the massive changes in the Technology and Financial Services (FS) sectors will render similar profound changes to corporate IT departments. With e-commerce as the new battlefield for Financial Services corporations, it is clear that the companies that emerge as winners will need to find ways to have the IT departments adapt to the new realities or they will find themselves on the losing end of the war. The metaphor of the simmering frog comes to mind when assessing the current situation in corporate IT departments. As legend has it, a frog placed into a pot of boiling water will immediately attempt to jump out to save itself, while a frog placed in cool water that is slowly brought to a boil will ignore the increasing heat until it is too late. Whether this is a scientific reality or a consultant's marketing pitch, the image fits nicely when applied to corporate CIOs. The heat is clearly increasing and approaching a boiling point. Yet despite evidence[1] that the current model is not working, CIOs for the most part continue working within structures that were created in the 1960's and 1970's. This chapter suggests that, like our friend the frog, CIOs will be driven to consider radical changes if they (and their organizations) are to survive.

This chapter suggests the likely form of at least one set of these survival actions, specifically how the structure and function of corporate IT organizations may be forced to change. Predicting imminent radical change is a high-risk gambit, since the promise of revolutionary change is often over-hyped and under-delivered. (Who can forget the claims that bubble memory, neural networks and CASE tools would revolutionize IT!) In spite of this risk, the image of a boiled frog is sufficiently intimidating to justify such a speculative article in order to rally the CIO fraternity to consider structural change to our organizations. Since the Gartner Group estimates that corporate IT spending exceeds \$750 billion a year, the revolution—if it comes—could be a doozie!

The sections that follow outline the factors that have influenced the Financial Services and Information Technology revolutions, providing a framework that will be applied to corporate IT departments.

13.2 Evolutionary Revolution – Financial Services Sector

History has repeatedly demonstrated that revolutions are usually borne of long gestation periods, during which the seeds of change slowly evolve into a new environment that can support the final dramatic revolutionary surge. In the Financial Services sector, deregulation that began in the mid-1980s is generally viewed as such a seed, softening the regulatory, operational and competitive barriers to permit the emergence of global capital markets. Examples of these evolutionary seed changes include everything from the creation of facilitating entities such as SWIFT (Society for the Worldwide Interbank Funds Transfer), the erosion of the Glass-Steagall Act, and most recently the European Monetary Union.

Deregulation in turn facilitated another major change driver in Financial Services, namely, securitization. Securitization is the process of taking assets that normally sit on corporate balance sheets and packaging them into well-defined financial instruments (securities) that can be easily bought and sold.

---

[1] A separate paper would be needed to assess corporate IT effectiveness. For purposes of this article, the reference to a failing corporate IT model is supported by continued high CIO turnover, low CEO satisfaction survey levels, the continued legacy infrastructure burden, increasing IT budgets and the disruptive impact of new e-Business models that are more successfully leveraging newer technologies.

Securitization has revolutionized financial services by making balance sheets dynamic, with assets such as car loans and mortgages packaged for resale rather than absorbing corporate capital until their term expires.

The combination of these two influences has permitted the disintermediation of inefficient products and players, so far to the benefit of investment banks. Before securitization emerged (primarily in the US), traditional financial services firms managed their assets and liabilities within the limits of their own balance sheets and distribution channels. In this world, size mattered since growth was predicated on your balance sheet's absorption capacity and sales force distribution power. Regional and/or national organizations—S&Ls, insurance companies, banks, exchanges, regulatory agencies—came to dominate narrowly focused and protected specialty 'franchise' spaces. Life was good in these large 'vertical' organizations, whose infrastructures could be characterized as follows:

- Defined geographic domain
- Scheduled operational hours
- Regulated/protected
- Narrowly focused products/services
- Long product cycles
- Lifetime employment
- Self-contained operating model
- Proprietary infrastructures
- Central administration
- Balance Sheet/Fixed Asset orientation
- Hierarchical mentality
- Premium for acting as an intermediary

With deregulation and securitization representing the evolutionary base, the revolution in Financial Services has arrived today with the disruptive technology of the Web driving the new forms of e-Business. Not only can the assets be securitized, but also now the distribution of these products has become global, near real time and available to an entirely new, and massive, electronic consumer community. A horizontal 'networked' economy with 100 million users just seconds away, capable of direct interaction with suppliers and each other, is a powerful wake-up call to all firms whose fundamental function is that of intermediary. The basic business model of the large successful vertical organizations is therefore under attack, never to be the same. As IBM's CEO Lou Gerstner expertly assesses "In my discussions with senior executives around the world about the power of networked computing and electronic business, I consistently make the point that the real revolution isn't about the

technology itself. The real revolution here has to do with institutional change—
the fundamental transformation of time-honored ways of doing things."[2]

The table below demonstrates the extent of this change, with virtually every
characteristic of traditional vertical institutions now diametrically reversed:

Traditional 'Vertical' Institution	New 'Horizontal' Market Realities
Defined geographic domain	Global, borderless, ill-defined
Scheduled operational hours	Continuous operations
Regulated/protected	De-, re-, and un-regulated
Narrowly focused products/services	Broad, integrated solutions
Long product cycles	Accelerated lifecycles
Lifetime employment	Career 'resets' every 3 to 4 years
Self-contained operating model	Open, permeable model
Proprietary infrastructure	Standardized, common infrastructure
Central administration	Distributed and networked
Balance Sheet/Fixed Asset	Capital Market/Virtual Assets
Hierarchical mentality	Matrix management; alliances
Premium as intermediary	Dis- and re- intermediation

Over the last fifteen years, these dis-intermediating pressures have essentially
created a three-tier product model within the Financial Services arena. As the
table below indicates, newly created securities dominate the 'niche' product
space, with higher margins and risks arising from lower liquidity and standards.
As these products mature, the margins and risk fall until the product becomes
commoditized, with razor thin margins, total liquidity and low risk. At this
point, commodity products that are capable of being electronically represented
(alias 'bittable') are swept into the e-commerce flow with the intermediaries
eliminated.

	NICHE	MATURE	COMMODITY
Market	Complex, new	Maturing	Well-understood
FS Example	Structured Credit	Corporate Bonds	US Governments
Liquidity	Low	Medium/High	High
Margins	High	Medium	Low
CAGR	>15%	0-15%	Declining
IT Emphasis	Speed, Flexibility	Control	Efficiency

As asset class after asset class is attacked by investment bankers and moved off
institutional balance sheets into the capital market, the institutions which rely
on these mature products are not only put under increasing profitability
pressure, but also the fundamentals of their business model are challenged.
Commercial and residential mortgages, for example, were once the exclusive
domain of S&Ls and commercial banks. Today, investment banks are dominant
in mortgage-backed securities while a few specialty service providers dominate
mortgage servicing. In essence, many banks must live off origination fees,

---

[2] Think Leadership Magazine, Vol. 3, No. 2

which themselves are threatened by electronic disintermediation. In a similar fashion, the commercial banks and S&Ls were forced to relinquish their hegemony over short-term savings, with traditional savings and checking accounts supplanted by cash management accounts that offer direct access to the capital markets, most visibly in the retail sector via mutual funds.

The reality is that isolated, closed vertical institutions must reinvent themselves or perish. Convergence is the result. For some institutions, the reinvention comes in the form of merging with like institutions to dominate a commodity space, with scale and market share permitting survival of a select few. Others attempt to revitalize themselves by merging with institutions offering complementary mature products or expanded geographic markets to sustain size via cross-selling. And a few hearty souls travel the acquisition route to attempt to introduce niche investment banking and asset management skills into their more traditional cultures. It is still too early to assess the effectiveness of these strategies, but the real message is that the revolution has unquestionably arrived.

The need to radically rethink time-honored ways of doing things has in turn put enormous pressures on corporate Information Technology departments in a number of ways:

- they must accommodate the increased business demand for new *niche* products and get these products to market faster,
- they must find ways to enhance *mature* products, often by wrapping products reflecting their firm's core competency with value-added services (not always their own),
- they must find ways to lower costs on *commodity* products to remain competitive, and
- they must find ways to deliver products and interact with customers through new distribution channels that have low barriers to entry.

Before discussing how corporate IT departments are reacting to these pressures, it is worthwhile to examine the pressures and opportunities facing Information Technology itself.

13.3 Evolutionary Revolution – Information Technology

Information Technology's influence on 'electrifying' the global economy and in so doing accelerating the pace of change and raising the level of competition has already been mentioned. But Information Technology is itself undergoing a revolution that is producing equally daunting challenges to Financial Services participants and corporate IT departments. The IT revolution has many obvious parallels to the Financial Services revolution described above. Large vertical technology institutions, like their Financial Services counterparts, are being forced to reinvent themselves. Simply replace insurance with telecommunications, banking with hardware manufacturers, and technical standards with financial conventions and the story remains the same. Institutions that had dominated narrowly defined and 'franchise' spaces are being assaulted with standardization, de-regulation and new product pressures, and are concluding that they must re-invent themselves to survive. Clearly, the "time-honored" business models that supported powerful telecommunications, hardware and software franchises just ten years ago have already undergone tremendous change, which is by no means complete.

Similarly, the 'Niche-Mature-Commodity' product categorization used for Financial Services also applies to IT. Niche products are the domain of smaller start-ups, enjoying high growth and high risk while a smaller set of larger institutions dominate the mature/commodity space. Interestingly, in the IT sector, it seems that the larger institutions are a bit more effective in acquiring and melding niche cultures into institutional frameworks.

For IT, standardization is the analogue to securitization. Driven largely by market forces arising 'bottoms-up' from the Internet, an amazing standardization of telecommunication protocols, relational database access mechanisms, desktop operating environments and information exchange definitions has occurred. The discussions of what is the best 'bleeding edge' technology have given way to the most practical technology on the 'blending edge'. As a result, Microsoft has become the de facto desktop standard, TCP/IP the network protocol standard, Cisco for data routing, and SQL for relational access.[3] Today, computer users take for granted that they can exchange documents and information quite easily, using almost any "terminal" device—an ATM machine, corporate desktop, palmtop or airport lounge PC—virtually anywhere in the electronically accessible world to connect to their desired service.

With standardization and deregulation as the drivers, IT is experiencing the same convergence revolution as financial services[4]. The large vertical players are going horizontal, looking to merge with other mature players or acquire niche start-ups to provide more complete and more efficient global solutions. Add to this the convergence of core hardware, software and database technologies with consumer electronics, content providers, telecommunication services and cable companies and the potential for new products and solutions grows exponentially. And as this convergence occurs, the familiar growing pains also surface. Unsophisticated investors continue to pay irrational multiples on next year's earnings for companies that don't have a last year. Over-aggressive

---

[3] Although battles continue among the dominant players to establish their 'standard' as the standard, the market has become far less tolerant of these distractions, demanding vendor rather than user resolution.
[4] The convergence phenomenon appears to be a general business trend of the 90's, impacting many sectors beyond just IT and FS.

players, resistant vested interests and lagging leadership have also slowed the pace of change. It is important to also recognize that much of the resistance is not negative or ill-intended but simply the reflection of a very tricky problem. Consider for a moment the regulatory challenges associated with enforcing control disciplines around cyber-finance—a largely anonymous exchange medium with 100+ million participants interacting real-time across a global jurisdiction. But as is true in any revolution, the better solution usually finds a way to overcome the birthing obstacles to create a 'quantum' jump to a newer and better structure.

Chunka Mui and Larry Downes, in their book *Killer Apps*, describe the potential of new network centered products to drive this quantum leap. The authors propose that the convergence phenomena will permit the introduction of new products based on distributing information electronically to a globally networked population. Mui and Downes see the Internet as the base technology that is driving the second information distribution revolution. The first revolution occurred 500 years ago with the introduction of the printing press and was the driver for profound socio-economic (Industrial Revolution), religious (Reformation) and intellectual (Renaissance) change. They argue effectively that the potential exists for similar profound changes from the second information distribution revolution.

Another excellent insight from Mui and Downes is the observation that the new technology is introducing a 'Law of Diminishing Firms'. The thesis is that unlike the old communications technologies (telephony and telegraph) that reduced the cost of maintaining large scale organizations across wide geographical distances, new technologies such as the Internet are having the opposite impact, that is, acting as a reducing rather than expanding influence on a firm's size. The driver of this reversal is that the cost of transactions done outside a firm (via the Internet) are now often cheaper than the cost of the same transactions done inside. Their actual statement of the Law of Diminishing Firms is: "As transaction costs in the open market approach zero, so does the size of the firm."[5]

Based in part on the above described 'revolutionary' changes, it is not surprising that corporate IT departments in the financial services sector find themselves confronted with tremendous pressures to exploit the new technologies in revolutionizing ways. Financial Services CEO satisfaction surveys indicate that the increasing cost and continued legacy infrastructure 'drag' factors continue to frustrate management, with constant CIO turnover one reflection of this frustration. If CEOs need additional incentive to motivate their IT departments to action, they need only calculate the generous premiums that the investment community is applying to firms that are perceived as having

---

[5] Context Magazine, Summer 1998 Issue, p. 64.

the skills to navigate the e-commerce waters. IT departments clearly need to find a better model to respond to these challenges. The next section offers one possible course of action.

13.4 The Next Revolution – Corporate IT

The material presented above basically outlines the challenges facing corporate IT departments that have arisen from the revolutions in the Financial Services and Information Technology sectors. Using the 'Niche-Mature-Commodity' framework, corporate CIOs are being asked to simultaneously accommodate niche business and technical product demands via innovative new development while also driving down the support costs of their mature and commodity technology and business products. Unfortunately, the levers to effect this change are somewhat rusted. A typical corporate IT department allocates between 50 and 75% of the total IT budget to keeping 'lights on'. Maintenance upgrades, business shifts, mandated regulatory changes, special projects (EMU, Y2K), and an increasingly volatile and costly workforce further erode the discretionary investment pool that is needed to engineer change and meet new demand. Also of importance is that killer apps, by nature, usually require the infamous (and costly) paradigm shifts that stress rather than leverage infrastructures and cost models.

It is clear that most corporate IT departments are organized very much along the lines of the vertical closed institutional framework that is being revolutionized in the FS and IT arenas. The diagram below outlines a typical Financial Services IT organization:

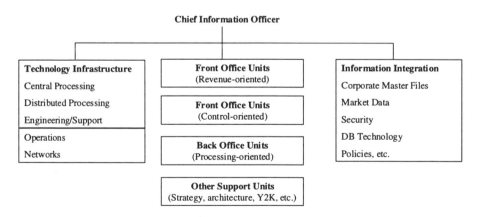

Although there are different mixes across organizations (e.g., outsourcing, matrixing to businesses, shadow organizations) the fact remains that most CIOs are asked to directly provide the bulk of the IT functions for their company. Using the financial services sector metaphor, corporate IT managers are holding all of their IT assets within their own balance sheet although many of the asset classes are inefficiently managed. In addition, like financial services businesses, CIOs have enjoyed a protected franchise, with only token competitive pressure placed on essentially closed infrastructures. It is also true that the IT investment food chain that sustains IT organizations has rightfully been driven by business priorities. As a result, front and middle office functions (and their associated information needs) tend to receive better financial support than back office and technology infrastructures, creating a natural drag factor that delays addressing legacy infrastructures.

As was said about the financial services sector, life was not too bad for CIOs since there are few meaningful performance metrics to assess IT effectiveness and even fewer CEOs who feel comfortable in discussing technology in any detail. But that was before the business and IT revolutions, and e-commerce, arrived. Today, technology is viewed as a central success/survival factor for most financial services firms. As a result, businesses are now demanding stronger partnership relationships and better accountability for their IT investments. CIOs are now valiantly struggling to understand their basic cost parameters (witness the rise of Total Cost of Ownership studies), competitive benchmarks and performance metrics to provide an empirical basis for IT management.

The lack of understanding of the IT function by business managers and the paucity of metrics to measure IT effectiveness have made the re-engineering challenge more difficult, explaining in part why the vertical closed organization structures of corporate IT units have survived so long. This is not to say that certain commodity subsets of the IT organization, particularly those that lend themselves to metrics (networks, data centers), have not experienced some change (most notably, outsourcing). Unfortunately, traditional outsourcing has two negative aspects for financial services IT departments:

1) Service level agreements tend to be rigidly defined and with rapid service level change requests difficult and costly to implement. By nature, outsourcers desire to standardize and commoditize their services to exploit scale, which at times conflicts with the customers desire to differentiate and innovate. This is clearly not the support model needed to meet the demands of a Financial Services business revolution. (To be fair, a number of outsourcers recognize this dilemma and are modifying their service contracts to provide greater flexibility).

2) The economics of traditional outsourcing—standardized service within a fixed price contract that over the contract's life exploits price-performance improvements and carefully monitors and charges for

unanticipated change—is particularly unattractive to the outsourced customer during a technology revolution.

So what can the corporate CEO and CIO do to fix the corporate IT model that is under such tremendous pressure? The answer, in part, is to embrace the convergence phenomenon of the financial services and IT sectors. Specifically, the open nature of the standardized FS and IT arenas, abetted by the new Internet-based 'killer apps', offers tremendous opportunities for CIOs to '*shrink and link*'.

The shrinkage should come from reducing costs by driving to higher efficiency standards and by building collaborative relationships with low cost, third party commodity service providers (who will work within more flexible and performance base service level agreements). It is difficult to predict whether a new and better set of metrics will surface to facilitate these relationships. Experience suggests that creating industry-wide metrics in fast-paced and innovative sectors like FS and IT are difficult. A new approach to metrics will therefore be required, especially to permit new forms of service level agreements. It is likely that the new service level agreements will be a hybrid of better, more precise measures for mature, commodity services along with more relaxed, practical economics for niche areas (e.g. floors and ceilings set on service provider income within 'open book' accounting). This shift of direct corporate IT commodity expenses to providers, which by their scale and specialization should be more efficient and effective in commodity spaces, could over time reduce direct IT staffs by 25% to 50% and costs by half that much.

The linkage should come from building collaborative relationships with internal front and middle office users as well as with external entities, including customers, regulators, exchanges and competitors. Specifically:

- Front end users will require increasing control and involvement in their revenue related technologies (in which distribution and the products themselves are technology-intensive) and will therefore more tightly link with IT groups, providing more integrated teams to address niche challenges. Although the business units will have a more direct control of their solutions, the CIO will be responsible to ensure that the flow of information is seamless (straight-through) across front, middle and back office processes.

- Middle office control functions will increasingly go electronic, becoming the business linkage gearbox that coordinates information flows and ensures compliance with business standards surrounding compliance, corporate guidelines (risk, funding, credit, etc.) and information management (security, recoverability, etc.). This middle office will also be the point from which regulatory interaction is coordinated.

- Regulators, in addition to enhanced linkage to corporate middle office functions, will require increased direct front and back office interaction to subject transactions and portfolios to compliance reviews.

- Customers, counter-parties, exchanges, utilities etc, will require real-time, interactive electronic links in which information and services are exchanged routinely. Signs of previously unthinkable collaborations of this sort are surfacing, especially in the mature and commodity product spaces (both technical and financial), where collaboration is a scale and efficiency alternative to the merger/bigness route. EBS (a consortium of FX dealers) and TradeWeb (a consortium of fixed income dealers) are recent examples of how competitors have come together to form a common technical, legal and business framework to provide a single service to a shared customer set for commodity products.

Obviously, this shift will bring some relief to the 'war for talent'. More leverage with business unit staff will also reduce some of the demands for IT staffs. New service relationships with commodity service providers will stabilize turnover for these staffs (since they hopefully will have compensation tied to long term success of their profit center), improve services (via specialty skills focus) and reduce costs (via efficiency and scale). The diagram below shows the reduced corporate IT profile that will result from this shrinkage and linkage.

A number of more subtle changes, again very similar to those experienced in Financial Services, are also likely to occur:

- The size of corporate IT departments will become less significant. In fact, smaller organizations with more adaptive cultures and more permeable boundaries will have an advantage over larger 'bricks and mortar' organizational models.

- IT assets such as information, applications, knowledge modules, and service techniques will become more valuable and leverage-able as standardization continues. This will introduce new opportunities for converting these IT assets to competitive advantage, especially with customers via IT-enhanced business relationships.

- IT expertise (functionality, reliability, flexibility) will become an important differentiator in the e-commerce space, particularly in valuation versus competitors.

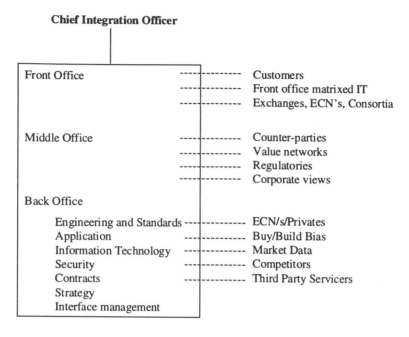

Chief Integration Officer

Front Office	Customers
	Front office matrixed IT
	Exchanges, ECN's, Consortia
Middle Office	Counter-parties
	Value networks
	Regulatories
	Corporate views
Back Office	
Engineering and Standards	ECN/s/Privates
Application	Buy/Build Bias
Information Technology	Market Data
Security	Competitors
Contracts	Third Party Servicers
Strategy	
Interface management	

- IT competitive barriers to entry will diminish for commodity and mature products, since large portions of the required infrastructure will be available through third party arrangements. For example, day trading firms can enter the market relatively easily by creating value-added front offices (assuming branding and the requisite capital and customer management capacities) leveraging third party clearance and technology platforms.

- Corporate IT departments will mobilize their own balance sheets, identifying opportunities to create more liquidity (in this case discretionary investment funds) by essentially securitizing and selling off costly assets that constrain growth and licensing value-added components (that don't compromise competitive positioning).

In effect, the Chief Information Officer's role will shift to Chief Integration or Coordination Officer, with relationship management and managing application, information and technology standards and architectures the principal focus to keep the entire flow coherent. CIOs will also become more like asset managers and Chief Investment Officers, viewing the IT portfolio as a series of assets with different valuations, risks and opportunities depending on market circumstance (and therefore requiring a much more real-time portfolio management approach).

It is also interesting to observe that if this new structure does emerge, much of the infrastructure related laboratory work done within financial services firms on bleeding edge arenas over the last 15 years (e.g. UNIX administration, global distributed databases, real-time market data feeds into spreadsheets) will shift to service providers. Corporate IT infrastructures will in effect shift from the bleeding edge to the blending edge.

Although it is difficult to estimate how long it will take for this transformation to manifest itself, it is likely that the initial pressure will arise shortly after the turn of the millennium. Once the Y2K issue is nailed down, corporations will be forced to address the legacy systems and FS/IT revolutionary pressures. Combining these factors with the backlog of demand that EMU and Y2K have created suggests that economic drivers will in all likelihood overcome the entrenched resistance. IT groups will be forced to finds ways to increase their discretionary investment pools by leveraging their commodity service expense bases, in effect, by making their IT balance sheets more dynamic. As mentioned before, metrics, although difficult, and in some cases unavoidably subjective will have to surface to allow for more manageable service agreements, alliances, partnerships and collaborations. As was true for the other revolutions, there will be birthing pains but the economics and benefits will force solutions.

13.5 Conclusion

Talking about revolutions can be exciting, but the reality is that massive shifts in sectors actually manifest themselves via hundreds of smaller evolutionary changes. In a similar way, corporate IT will in all likelihood evolve over the next few years into their new structure through a series of complementary alliances, formal and informal partnerships and new contractual relationships based on experimental metrics. This chapter has attempted to identify the general direction of these changes and to provide a discussion framework that might assist CEOs, CIOs and other potential participants to anticipate and prepare for the potential structural shifts. What is clear is that the revolution is upon us and that smart frogs will start thinking about making a quantum jump.

Ultimately, the change will come in whatever form the market dictates. Although this chapter has focused on corporate IT departments in financial services, everyone will be touched by the exciting changes of the 21st century. The following quote from Marcel Proust's *Remembrance of Things Past* captures the essence the upcoming revolution:

> We do not succeed in changing things according to our desire, but gradually our desire changes. The situation we hoped to change because it was intolerable becomes unimportant. We have not managed to surmount the obstacle, as we were absolutely determined to do, but life

has taken us round it, led us past it, and then if we turn
round to gaze at the remote past, we can barely catch sight
of it, so imperceptible has it become.

Whether referencing the meta-physical Proust or the very physical frog, the
message is the same: the revolutionary waters are roiling and the only clear
expectation is that of change.

Chapter 14

Financial Service Networks: Access, Cost Structure and Competition

Uday S. Karmarkar
Anderson School at UCLA

14.1 Introduction

Customer access is an intrinsic aspect of all services, since services involve processes that are initiated by customer requests. Financial services are no exception; in making contact with a service provider, customers must access the provider at some point. Access may occur physically, as when a customer visits a bank branch, or through some information channel, as when a customer executes an on-line transaction with a brokerage. In either case, of course, the nature of the transaction is that it involves the exchange of information. New information technologies are thus changing not only the "back room" in the financial service sector, but more recently, the "front office" as well. There are many facets to these changes, ranging from simple issues of higher processing capability, to strategic questions involving new service designs and even new industries.

In this chapter, we address the impact of new technologies on customer access and the interaction between the customer and the service provider. In fact we will for the most part, focus on access from the perspective of simple transactions. As such, we are most concerned with financial services where access plays an important competitive role. Consumer (retail) banking, brokerage, insurance, credit extension, mortgage and lending, accounting and tax services, are some examples. In much of what follows, consumer banking (or a simplified version of it) will be used as a running example. Actually, much of the discussion will apply to any service where access for the purpose of information exchange and transaction execution, plays a large part.

In many of the financial services we have mentioned, the service provided may have more than one component. For example, a retail bank provides security against theft (from a storage perspective), money management services (such as checking and bill payment), financial intermediation in both directions (from deposits to loans, as well as loans and investments in financial instruments), credit extension (including credit cards), and advisory services. For the sake of simplicity, we will often consider a more simplified model of retail banking, typically addressing only one or two of these many bundled services in a given model.

14.2 Access in Service Chains and Networks

Gaining access to a service typically represents a cost to the customer. If physical access is required, the customer must travel to the nearest access point provided by the service provider. If access for a transaction can be achieved through a third party system (such as phone, mail or the internet), the customer may not have to travel. However there may be some fixed and variable costs associated with each access occasion. In addition to travel costs, access costs may also include the costs of time due to waiting. Of course, these costs depend not only on the location of access points, but also on the service capacity available. These are not independent, since increasing the number of locations can increase service capacity as well. We will here primarily address the location aspects of the system. The costs of access can be thought of as reducing the demand for the service. Thus if the cost of access is \$c per transaction, we might think of the demand for transactions (Q) as being a function such as

$$Q = a - (p+c)\, b,$$

where p is the price per transaction and a, b are parameters of the demand function. Equivalently the demand curve can be usefully written in inverse form as

$$p = (a' - c) - b'Q,$$

where a' and b' are appropriately defined.

To facilitate customer access, service systems have tended to be geographically more widely distributed than manufacturing systems. Unlike manufacturing, service provision often cannot be centralized into a few large plants, and economies of scale may have to be foregone. This gives rise to structures like service chains (as in retail or fast food) and service networks (as in communication and transportation systems). Generally, the term "chain" simply suggests multiple, somewhat independent locations, while "network" implies that there are events in the system that involve two or more locations. However, the distinction between chains and networks is not very strong. There are clearly cases, where the network structure is a crucial characteristic of the service, as in transportation. However, even in say, a retail chain, there are usually some network features in the system (such as stock transfers between locations). Be that as it may, we are here primarily concerned with the issue of access, and the consequent pressure for geographical distribution.

In the case of retail banking, access could be improved by placing branch locations close to customers. Historically, regulations on intra-state and inter-state banking affected which banks could open branches in which locations. For our purposes, we will shelve the issue of regulation (and de-regulation or re-regulation). With the development of computer technology, the automation of teller functions became possible. Automated teller machines permitted the improvement of access in terms of both location and time, since they could operate 24 hours a day.

With the linkage of computers and communication systems, the use of any computer as an access point for on-line banking has become feasible. The development of on-line services and subsequently the Internet has greatly expanded remote access to retail banking services. In effect, on-line banking uses communication services that are already in place, to provide improved access to services. More recently, phone banking has also become more widespread and popular, though in point of fact it was technologically quite feasible long ago. In Europe, the minitel system in France, and tele-text systems on TV in other countries have provided other access channels for information services including banking. Figure 1 sketches some of the alternative forms of access for retail banking.

It should be noted that on-line banking is a pure information service, which lacks the physical means to accept deposits (checks) or to deliver cash to the customer. On the other hand, a considerable expansion of the degree of automation, as well as the range of services provided, is made possible by the computational power available with desktop computers and networked servers.

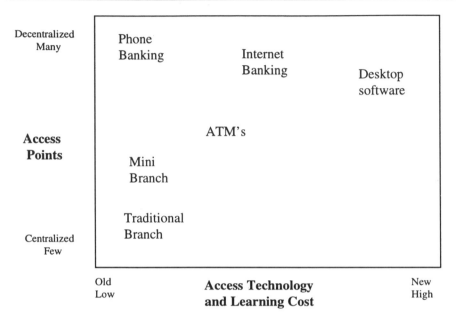

Figure 1: Access Characteristics Of Alternative Service Channels For Retail Banking

The advent of service access through communication networks has decreased the cost of access to many financial services for those customers who have invested in the necessary hardware, software, on-line access and of course, the necessary learning. For some customer segments, these fixed costs are not justified by the benefits to be gained. In many cases, the costs of learning, exacerbated by distaste for the technology, may be a significant portion of the cost. For some customers, the human contact in the conventional system has benefits that override the possibly higher access costs. In Table I, we compare the costs of alternative service channels and access mechanisms. It is apparent that there is a general pattern of movement from systems that are costly to the provider, and well understood by the user, to systems that have improved access for the user, but may be more costly for the user to employ due to initial and continuing costs to the user to adopt, install, upgrade and learn about new or changing technologies.

From a competitive perspective, the lower fixed costs associated with some types of channels have the potential for creating more intense competition due to greater levels of entry. On the other hand, the reduced costs of access could increase the demand for transactions; this has clearly been the case with on-line stock trading. One of the most important consequences of on-line access to services, however, is the uniformity of access to competing service providers, and the reduction in switching costs. Furthermore, since the new "facades" for these services are now web-sites, the potential for differentiation of service facilities may be diminished, as would the benefits of scale and investment in physical facilities. In the very least, the race for differentiation has been restarted, and (to mix a metaphor) the playing field has been leveled.

Table I: Relative Costs Of Different Service Access Mechanisms For Retail Banking Service Providers And Customers					
Relative Costs of Access Mode	Back-room fixed costs	Site fixed cost	Variable production cost	Customer's access cost	Customer's fixed cost
Traditional Branch	High	High	High	High	Very low
Mini-branch	High	Medium	Medium	Medium	Very low
ATM	Medium	Low	Low	Low	Low
Phone Service	Medium	Low	Medium	Very low	Very low
Internet Banking	Medium	Very low	Low	Very low	Medium
PC Banking	Medium	Very low	Very low	Low	High

In the remainder of this chapter we explore a number of issues related to access, location and competition, with retail banking as an illustrative example. In the next section we discuss a simple model of competition in a traditional setting with physical service sites that must be accessed by customers (such as traditional bank branches, and ATM's). Next we discuss the consequences of on-line access, and the distinction between Internet based banking and PC or desktop banking. We then address the issue of market segmentation based on customer preferences, costs and benefits. Finally, we discuss some possible directions for the evolution of financial service systems, and strategies to cope with the changes.

14.3 Traditional Branch Access and Localization

The traditional service network, where customers must access a nearby branch of their choice, leads to localized competition. Distant branches are not visited, because the access costs become prohibitive. Co-location of competitors is typically not desirable, since it leads to more intense competition. This concern may be over-ridden, when there is an especially attractive location such as a mall. Furthermore, the fixed costs of physical sites lead to a certain density of branch locations, that is related to the density of demand as well as factors such as access (travel) costs in a region.

A stylized model of this situation assumes that customers are uniformly spread across a geographical region. All branches are identical, and that each requires the same fixed cost, F, to establish. Competitors each enter with a single branch, and entry continues up to the point where the marginal entrant would cause excess investment, which would then not be recoverable. We assume that branches are then located uniformly across the region, and each branch has its own service area, which consists of those customers for whom that branch is the closest. The costs of access increase linearly with distance, and the demand curve is assumed to take a linear form (as above). There are a few other details, but a model with these simplified assumptions yields some clear analyses. A simpler model can be developed for the case where there is a single monopolist entrant, who can open several branches and choose prices to maximize total profits.

First note that once the locations are chosen, each branch is effectively a monopolist in its service area. It thus turns out that for a given number of locations, n, the price charged for service in either the monopolistic or competitive case is the same, and has the form

$$p(n) = c - d/\sqrt{n},$$

where n is the number of locations in a given area, and c and d depend on other parameters of the problem. At first glance it may seem counter-intuitive that price increases as the number of branches increases. However, this happens because more branches means smaller service areas. Thus customers are on average closer to branches, and their access costs are lower. As a result, total demand is increased. Since branches act as local monopolies, they are able to set higher prices to extract some of this benefit. Of course, the profits earned by firms in the competitive case decline as the number of entrants (locations) increases.

Naturally, the actual number of locations n*, varies for the two cases. The number of entrants under monopolistic conditions is proportional to $(1/F)^{2/3}$. In the case with competition and open entry, n* is roughly proportional to $(1/\sqrt{F})$ for a large number of entrants, and more like $(1/F)^{2/3}$ when there is a small number of entrants. However, the number is always higher than for a monopoly.

While fixed costs have similar consequences for the number of locations in these cases, the effect of access costs is rather dissimilar. As the access cost rate (in terms of cost/distance traveled) increases, the number of locations in the competitive case decreases while it increases in the monopolistic case. The reason is that in the former case, increasing access costs decrease the level of demand and the profit margin, leading to less entry. In the latter monopolistic case, of course, there is a single entrant. Here it turns out that increasing the number of branches to shrink service areas and reduce access distances for the customer, together with an increase in the price charged for the service, maximizes monopoly profits.

14.4 ATM's and Mini-branches

In assessing the impact of ATM's two kinds of fixed costs have to be considered. First, the fixed cost of creating a service access site is reduced. The implied result is that there will be more branches in both competitive and monopolistic cases. Furthermore, the model suggests that service prices will rise in both cases, though total profits in the competitive case will tend to fall. In the early days of ATM introduction, there was no significant incremental service charge for ATM use. However, today such charges are common. It may be that increased competition is making service providers more sensitive to declining margins, and the possibilities for improving them.

In order to create a network of ATM's, it is also necessary to make a substantial fixed investment in centralized transaction processing facilities and communication networks, as well as in physical collection and distribution systems for cash and deposits (these systems do scale with the number of ATM's to some degree). The implication is that the number of competing ATM networks will not be anywhere near as high as the number of ATM sites. In fact, the economies of scale inherent in the fixed costs have meant that third party networks provide ATM services, which is most efficient from an overall perspective.

Mini-branches or in-store branches in grocery stores, bookstores and cafes are becoming increasingly common. They represent an alternative to ATM's for certain segments of the market in terms of convenient access (combined with other shopping trips) as well as higher appeal in terms of personalization. Unlike ATM's they do not incur significant new "back-room" costs, and belong to banks themselves, rather than to third parties, so that they are really extensions of the traditional bank branch networks.

14.5 On-line Service Access

Now consider the case where banking (or other financial) services can be accessed via some on-line remote mechanism. In this case, the actual location of the "bank" becomes relatively unimportant. While there may be an access cost, it is independent of the location of the customer, and of the bank. Furthermore, it is likely to be the same across customers and service providers. As a result there is no localization phenomenon. To put it in the current vernacular, "all branches are equidistant in cyberspace".

While localization entry is competitive, post-entry price competition is not as intense, since the supplier captures the demand in the local service area. With on-line access, price setting is also competitive since customers can select any service provider and also easily switch providers. As a result, prices in the second stage are lower, and the profitability per site or "branch" is relatively lower. This alone would suggest that there would be fewer entrants in this case. Furthermore, it is the case today that not all customers for a service are ready to incur the fixed costs of operating on-line. Hence the number of entrants is also limited by the size of the on-line market. However there are several countervailing factors. One is that a web bank or web service site has lower fixed costs than a physical branch. Another is that since access costs are lower on-line, the demand for service is higher at any price. The variable "production" costs of handling transactions are lower in the on-line case, with automation and the substitution of labor. This acts to reduce prices and increase demand levels and profitability (which is then reduced by entry). One could also add the qualifier that the on-line segment will grow.

The net effect of all of these factors depends on the relative values of parameters for a given service sector. For a country as large as the United States, where there is considerable scope for geographic localization, it would appear that the number of service providers would decrease, as the size of the on-line segment becomes larger. Service prices are likely to be much lower, despite the fewer number of entrants, because of the greater intensity of post-entry competition. Furthermore, the discussion up to this point has not considered the effects of market segmentation and consumer choice behavior, fully. We examine these issues in later sections.

14.6 Intermediation, Entry and Competition

Financial service providers are primarily intermediaries. For example, although retail banks provide other services, they would not be able to function on the same scale without the intermediation role. The case of retail banks is perhaps unique in that unlike other financial intermediaries, consumers do not appear to go to banks consciously for their intermediary role; in other words, they are not actively playing (or even aware of) their role as suppliers of loan capital. Of course, customers are certainly conscious of the interest rates offered to them, though they may not always think about the other side of the market.

To examine the effect of changing conditions of entry and competition, consider the following simple model. Assume that a particular sector of service providers mediates between suppliers and buyers of a financial instrument or investment (possibly cash) which can be thought of as a commodity. The demand for the commodity is given by a demand function, which we take to be linear. In inverse form the demand curve is

$$p = a - b\, Q.$$

On the supply side, the supply curve is also assumed to be linear. In inverse form,

$$p' = e + d\, Q'.$$

If intermediation were unnecessary, the clearing price and quantity in the market would be determined by the intersection of the two curves. Equating prices gives

$$a - b\, Q = e + d\, Q,$$

or

$$Q^* = (a - e)/(b + d)$$

and hence,

$$p^* = (ad + be)/(b + d).$$

The intermediary role may be needed for a variety of reasons, including information management, transaction management, matching, risk pooling, risk management, loan evaluation, and so on. We consider the case where the intermediary is more efficient than individuals in matching demand for loans with the supply of deposits. We capture this efficiency as a reduction in the effective price to the demand side, or equivalently by an upward shift in the demand curve. Specifically the demand now becomes

$$p = a' - b\, Q, \quad a' > a.$$

Creating this efficiency requires investments on the part of the intermediary (bank). Suppose that each intermediary requires a fixed investment of F, to set up the mechanisms and systems for managing the supply of (through say deposits) and demand for (through loans or mortgages) the commodity. In addition there may be a variable cost of operations, v. We will presume that (a' - v) > a, so that the net effect for the marginal (first) demander is favorable.

Suppose that there are n entrants and assume that a Cournot model of competition is adequate. Each intermediary decides to make a certain quantity of the commodity available, and the price is determined by the total quantity provided by all intermediaries, to the demand side. The intermediaries pick quantities so as to maximize their post-entry profits. Of course, the price to be paid for acquiring the commodity on the supply side is also affected by the quantities chosen, and this effect must be included. It can be shown that if there are n entrants, and if the variable cost of service production for the intermediary is v, then the intermediary demand for the commodity is given by

$$Q = A - B\,p'$$

where

$$A = (a' - v),$$

$$B = [(n + 1)/n]b.$$

Note that as n becomes very large, B = b. Equating quantities with the supply curve, gives

$$p' = (Ad + Be)/(B + d),$$

which reduces to the earlier expression when n is large and v = 0. The effective shift of the demand curve is shown in Figures 2a and 2b. The former shows a case where prices and quantities are higher with intermediation; that is, lower interest rates are available to depositors, and the supply drops. Figure 2b shows a case in which prices and quantities are smaller. Either case is possible in principle. However, as the number of intermediaries increases, the former case will generally hold.

Note that in these figures, the intersection points with the derived (intermediary) demand curves, no longer represent prices on the demand (loan) side. It can be shown that the price on the demand (loan) side (marginal revenue for the intermediary) is given by

$$p^* = \left(\frac{1}{n + 1}\right) a' + \left(\frac{n}{n + 1}\right)(v + p')$$

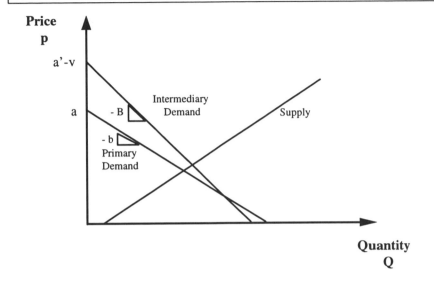

Figure 2a: Demand Curves In Primary And Intermediated Markets; Price And Quantity Both Increase With Intermediation

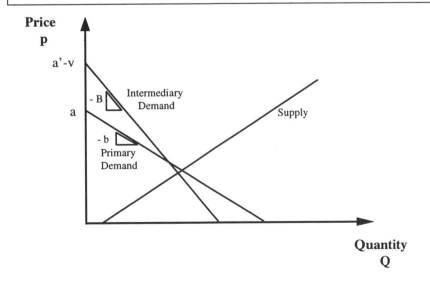

Figure 2b: Demand Curves In Primary And Intermediated Markets; Price And Quantity Both Decrease With Intermediation

Again, for very large n, no change in a, and v=0, this reduces to the earlier expression. The operating profit made by each intermediary when there are n entrants (not including fixed cost F), is

$$R(n) = \frac{1}{b}\left(\frac{a' - v - p'}{n + 1}\right)^2.$$

Therefore entry will occur until the marginal entrant is unable to cover the fixed cost of entry. Hence, the number of intermediaries is given by the n^* that satisfies

$$R(n^* + 1) \leq F \leq R(n^*).$$

Note that p' in the expression for $R(n)$ also depends on n. To get a better intuitive sense about the number of entrants, consider the continuous approximation to this condition, $R(x) = F$. This gives the number of entrants approximately as

$$x^* = \frac{(a' - v - p')}{(bF)^{1/2}} - 1.$$

If n is fairly large, then the dependence of p' on n can be ignored. This shows that the number of intermediaries is roughly proportional to the inverse of the square root of the fixed cost of entry. The price to the final demand (loan) side is approximated for large n (small F and b) by

$$p^* \approx p' + v + \sqrt{bF}.$$

This model permits us to think about the implications of access and technology changes for competitive intermediation. As the fixed and variable costs of intermediation decrease with on-line access technologies, it appears that the number of intermediaries should increase. To examine this case, suppose that the variable cost decreases from v to v', where $v'<v$. With the concurrent decrease in fixed costs, and the increase in the number of entrants, suppose that the slope of the resulting effective demand curve is now changed from the -B to -B', where $B'<B$. The result is higher prices and quantities for the supply (deposit) side as shown in Figure 3. However, for the demand side (loans) the price p^* will drop as suggested by the expression above. Again, market segmentation and the distribution of market volume will complicate the complete picture across different segments that prefer different access modes or channels. Commoditization and branding issues will also play a role.

Figure 3: Demand Curves In Old (traditional) And New (e.g., on-line) Intermediary Markets; With Lower Fixed And Variable Costs, And More Intermediaries, Price And Quantity Both Increase

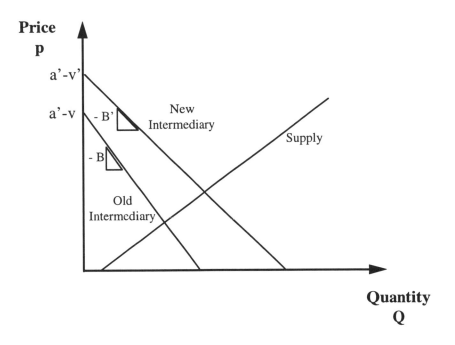

14.7 Market Segmentation

In most service markets, the costs of access are not the same for all customers. If nothing else, the opportunity costs of time will vary across customers. In addition, there may be issues like barriers due to learning costs and attitudinal differences towards new technologies. For example, in the case of retail banking, the use of on-line services may be difficult for customers who do not already use such services. Some customers may prefer the human contact in traditional teller or phone banking to automated systems in conducting banking transactions. There may also be significant differences in the volume and mix of services that are demanded. For example, more wealthy customers may need advisory and services, financial management and credit services, while others are primarily interested in simple transactions related to money management.

Consider an example of how market segmentation could be analyzed for the case of retail banking. Suppose that we restrict our attention to three kinds of transactions:

- "standard" deposits and withdrawals
- money management (e.g. bill pay and credit services), and
- investment services (investment options and advisory services)

Furthermore suppose that we consider the following access and service configurations:

- conventional (teller) banks
- mini branches
- ATM's
- phone banking, and
- on-line banking (using desktop software)

For illustrative purposes, assume that the customer population can be adequately described in terms of two parameters: wealth (W) and aversion to technology (R), where R is an index varying between 0, denoting no aversion, and 1 denoting very high aversion. Of course, this is not the only choice possible. For example, we could have used age as one demographic characteristic instead of aversion to technology. However, while age is correlated with aversion to technology, it is also correlated with wealth, and can cause some confounding of variables.

Each banking mechanism has differential costs of providing alternative kinds of service. These differences will be reflected in the prices and charges to customers. Furthermore, the costs of access in each case, depend on wealth (through the opportunity costs of time) as well as the degree of aversion to technology. Finally the benefits obtained from each form of service from each configuration as well as the demand level for each, will also differ across the population of customers depending on W and R. Assume that the costs and benefits for a customer (w,r) can be computed in dollar terms.

Now, if we are given the prices charged to customers for various services and transactions for each mechanism, we can compute the net benefit (net of costs) and the demand level from each customer for each service. By comparing across services, we can determine which customer would pick which form of service, assuming that such a choice needed to be made. The result, for some specific numbers, might look like Figure 4. Note that the segments that appear represent regions of choice. The number of customers in each segment is not necessarily related to the area on the graph, but rather depends on how the population is distributed in terms of the segmenting variables.

Figure 4: Segmentation Regions For Alternative Banking Mechanisms For A Customer Population Characterized By Wealth (W) And Aversion To Technology (R)

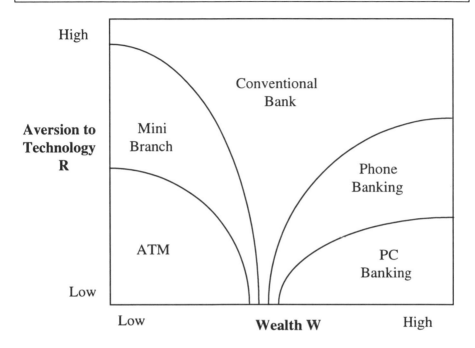

The simple analysis described above is far from complete. The distribution of the population will affect the volume in each segment. This in turn affects the costs of service provision (through scale and scope effects). Costs and volumes will determine pricing decisions, which will themselves cause shifts in segmentation. Pricing will also depend on the degree of entry and competition in each type of system, which will in turn depend on the fixed costs and other barriers to entry for the alternative service technologies. The interaction of all these factors leads to a fairly complex model, which cannot be represented by simple equations or closed form results. However, numerical computations for a given case (with data on populations, distributions, characteristics, costs and benefits) are quite feasible. The results of such computations look qualitatively much the same as in Figure 4, though of course the specific locations and sizes of segments may vary with the setting.

The figure shows several features of the service landscape. First, several types of banking mechanisms can co-exist. If we take horizontal slices of the market at differing levels of technology aversion (R), we see that the size of the conventional segment is higher for high R, while the reverse is true of the other mechanisms. Similarly vertical slices suggest that phone and PC banking for higher wealth levels supplant ATM and mini branches. Of course, this is due to the assumptions made about differential time costs as well as the benefits of more complex services that cannot be provided by the simpler systems.

The figure is also suggestive of what is likely to happen as the characteristics of the population with respect to technology use change. It seems apparent that the future of banking is in remote access and on-line mechanisms. Of course, some possibilities are not represented in this figure. For example, a simpler form of automated phone banking, that substitutes for ATM functions, could well take over the role of ATM's for simple transactions.

14.8 Gateway Competition and Commoditization

As suggested above, on-line banking is likely to be a significant portion of the retail banking market. As TV set-top boxes or other means of simple on-line access become available, the costs of use of on-line channels will decrease. One of the consequences is that localization of banking services will tend to disappear. Even now, a primary factor in localizing banking has to do with the security, trust and validation issues surrounding the opening of accounts. However, this is a transient phase since there is no fundamental reason that prevents remote establishment of accounts. Clearly, switching costs for changing providers will also be very low, even without incentives for switching. A major remaining factor for many people might be the use of safety deposit boxes for securing physical assets. However, it may be feasible to unbundle this service from others.

Whatever the eventual condition may be, it is clear that remote banking in various forms will capture a significant portion of the market. In all these cases, the access point is only weakly identified with any particular bank. With increased remote access, the same access point (phone, on-line service or web site) is likely to act as the common gateway for a number of financial services. This is especially true for PC banking, using commercial financial management software that becomes the gateway to the market, while the services recede into the background. In such a situation, undifferentiable services, become commodities. Again, this is particularly true of phone and background on-line services. It may be less true for web services or direct on-line service, where there is some opportunity for differentiation through "look and feel". However, the significant differentiation and localization created by physical sites and large buildings, go away, as do the opportunities for scale economies and entry cost barriers.

In this situation, where the service becomes close to a pure commodity, the extent of entry and the degree of competition will be decided purely on cost structure. Since both fixed and variable costs are reduced, the price of the service will drop, and so will profitability. This situation is not an attractive one for services such as retail banks. The best prospect for them is to find ways to differentiate services or to find some way to establish a different image.

14.9 Branding, Bundling and Differentiation

The problem of commoditization is not unknown to retail banking. Even without on-line access, there is little difference between banks in terms of many of their basic services and their intermediary role (at least in the absence of regulation). Physical access may cause some localization, but competition is still intense, since service areas may be quite small, and banks can almost co-locate. However, as the problem is exacerbated by on-line access, more creative solutions or new accommodations are being sought.

It is a seeming paradox that branding is especially effective in commodity markets, where one might expect that there is little on which to base a unique brand identity. Yet, when one thinks of a commodity product like table salt, there is just one brand name that occurs to most people. While establishing a brand image is difficult, it is also very valuable. In a world of on-line and remote banking, it is safe to predict that branding strategies will be increasingly crucial. While economies of scale in location and operation might be reduced to servers and back room information systems, there are scale effects in branding as well. Service providers with high name visibility and brand image due to historical reasons of scale and presence, could very well benefit from this useful legacy. Over time, as the brand legacy fades, new ways will have to be sought. It is also safe to predict that there will be increasing investments in the new "locations" of banks, whether web-sites or call centers, to attempt to differentiate them. These investments will also serve to create some entry barriers.

An alternative way to build scale in the future will be through bundling services and building scope. The scale advantages arise in the back room while scope benefits will accrue from the advantage of offering users a range of services.

It bears noting that some of the bundled services are likely to be seemingly trivial. However, gifts of a toaster or trick key chain for opening an account, while sometimes dismissed as shallow gimmickry, can be surprisingly effective in an undifferentiated market, particularly for certain market segments. The point is that bundling creates differentiation even when it does not create scale economies. Some consulting firms have built significant practices in consumer banking services around such methods.

14.10 Industry Dynamics and Evolutionary Strategies

The major trends that will affect financial services in the near future include:
- consumers who are more familiar with computers and on-line access
- increasing simplicity in methods for accessing on-line resources
- high penetration of on-line access and of broad-band services to the home
- increasing levels of transaction automation (e.g. voice response)
- higher customer expectations for integrated services with easy access
- increasing comfort levels with the use of electronic payment methods (despite some negative recent results with smart cards and digital cash)
- higher transaction volumes due to easy access and lower transaction costs.

It is apparent that more customers will access most financial services on-line through simple interfaces and will demand integrated services. It is also likely that changes in technology and the competitive landscape will permit some new entrants into service businesses. However, these changes will not necessarily be rapid, since many customers who are used to older systems, will still be customers for two or three decades. Consequently there is time for those existing firms that are adaptable, to survive by exploiting their legacy positions. One of the dangers for such firms could be a hesitation to give up tried and true methods, especially when it is the expertise of the most senior managers that must be discarded. In the near term it looks as though there will be some searching for niches possibly with polarization towards the extremes of high tech, and traditional access. However, this is likely to be a transient phase.

Integration and commoditization are likely to force continuing consolidation both within and across financial sectors. Consolidation is also an exit strategy for weaker players. This pattern is already visible. Advertising expenses are likely to be high and increasing as commoditization forces conscious brand building. In the near term, when it is not yet clear what technologies and channels will dominate, we are likely to see many co-existing forms and systems, sometimes in the same firm.

14.11 Conclusion

In this chapter we have discussed a number of issues related to the impact of new technologies on access mechanisms for financial services. There are several other technological advances on the horizon that will keep the financial service sector in flux, as it races to accommodate the consequences. We are already seeing some of these today, and they will exacerbate the trends described above:

- The complete conversion of financial services to a pure information industry as various forms of electronic cash and credit become the norm. Fundamentally, all that is needed is an identification of individuals and entities with a secure record of credit. This may happen more rapidly in certain countries in Europe and Asia than in the US.
- The increased use of automation in both the front office and the back room as well as increased outsourcing and the use of off-shore resources, as information and transactions chains are reengineered. The consequence will be huge reductions in employment levels, of the kind seen in manufacturing over the last two decades.
- Competition for the customer will shift physically to the customer's person as the use of mobile devices increases. This has implications for "gateway competition" since the makers of mobile computing and communication appliances, as well as suppliers of telecommunication services could start to play gatekeeping roles.
- The use of voice response and intelligent interfaces that permit customization down to the single customer. Examples such as Wildfire Communications demonstrate what is commercially viable already.
- The "high touch" segment, now being seen as mini-branches in bookstores, will probably translate to the home. Here there is a likely trend to immersive, experiential 3D interfaces that may provide mild barriers to entry as well as some switching costs.

Finally, the changes that are most visible in consumer markets (such as banking and brokerage) will start to impact commercial services very soon. The pace of change in those sectors is likely to be rapid, since it will be driven more by rational decision making and less by attitudinal issues. It promises to be, as the saying goes, an interesting life.

Appendix A: Notation

The notation used in this chapter is summarized below:

p:	price ($)
Q:	Quantity or number of transactions
c, v :	variable costs
a, b, c, d, e:	parameters in demand and supply functions
F:	fixed cost of establishing a service location, or of entry into an industry
n:	the number of locations or of entrants into an industry

Appendix B: Reference Notes

Chase (1978) identified the central role of customer contact in services. Even earlier, Fuchs (1968) took the more technical view that services often required "joint production"; i.e. the production function for services required inputs on the part of both the provider and the consumer. Contact itself can require several steps including access, diagnosis and production. In information based services, the economics of the service process are changing for all these steps. For a discussion of these issues and their impact on service quality and competition see Apte and Mason (1995), Apte et al. (1997) and Karmarkar and Pitbladdo (1995).

The discussion on competitive location and service areas in section 3 is based on Choi (1998), and on our continuing joint research on these problems. The underlying models are competitive, multi-agent generalizations of the min-cost single agent model described by Geoffrion (1978). There is of course, a large literature on competitive location, which we cannot review here, but see Eiselt, Laporte and Thisse (1993) for a recent survey. The classic paper on the subject is by Hotelling (1929). An example of a recent paper addressing the specific issue of search in information industries is Bakos (1997).

The intermediation model of section 6 is a simplified version of some results from ongoing work with my colleague Charles Corbett (1999). In this research, we also look in more detail at entry and oligopolistic competition on the supply side, rather than just taking the supply curve to be given. The expressions for prices and derived demand for an oligopolistic intermediary market are based on models by Karmarkar and Pitbladdo (1993, 1994). For other models of financial intermediation, see Williamson (1987).

The segmentation discussion in section 7 also follows Choi (1998), which is in turn related to Bashyam (1996) and Bashyam and Karmarkar (1996). For other discussions of competitive segmentation and positioning, see Moorthy (1988), or Choi et al. (1990).

Finally, two outstanding accessible sources that address the economic analysis of information-based industries and electronic commerce, are the books by Choi, Stahl and Whinston (1997) and Shapiro and Varian (1998).

References

1. Apte, U. M. and R.. O. Mason. 1995. Global Disaggregation of Information-Intensive Services. Management Science. 41, 1250-1262.

2. Apte, U. M., U. S. Karmarkar and R. Pitbladdo. 1997. Quality Management in Services, in Lederer, P. and U. S. Karmarkar (eds.). *The Practice of Quality Management*. Kluwer Academic Publishers, Boston.

3. Bakos, J. Y. 1997. Reducing Buyer Search Costs: Implications for Electronic Marketplaces. Management Science. 43, 1676-1692.

4. Bashyam, T. C. A. 1996. Service Design and Competition in Business Information Services. Unpublished Ph.D. thesis, Anderson School of Management (UCLA).

5. Bashyam, T. C. A. and U. S. Karmarkar. 1996. Service Design, Competition and Segmentation in Business Information Services. Anderson School Working Paper, submitted for publication; being revised.

6. Chase, R. 1978. Where does the Customer Fit in a Service Operation. Harvard Business Review. November- December, 138-149.

7. Choi, D. Y. 1998. Service Competition in Retail Banking. Unpublished Ph.D. thesis, Anderson School of Management (UCLA).

8. Choi, S., D. O. Stahl and A. B. Whinston. 1997. *The Economics of Electronic Commerce*. McMillan Technical Publishing, Indianapolis, Indiana.

9. Choi, S. C., W. S. DeSarbo and P. T. Harker. 1990. Product Positioning under Price Competition. Management Science. 36, 175-198.

10. Corbett, C. and U. S.Karmarkar. 1999. Information Intermediaries and Market Structure. In preparation.

11. Eiselt, H. A., G. Laporte and J.-F. Thisse. 1993. Competitive Location Models: A Framework and Bibliography. Transportation Science. 1, 44-54.

12. Fuchs, V. 1968. *The Service Economy*. NBER, Columbia University Press, New York.

13. Hotelling, H. 1929. Stability in Competition. Economic Journal 39, 41-57.

14. Karmarkar, U. S. and R. Pitbladdo. 1995. Service Markets and Competition. Journal of Operations Management. 12, 397-411.

15. Karmarkar, U. S. and R. Pitbladdo. 1993. Internal Pricing and Cost Allocation in a Model of Multiproduct Competition with Finite Capacity Increments. Management Science. 39, 1039-1053.

16. Karmarkar, U. S. and R. Pitbladdo. 1994. Product-line Selection, Production Decisions and Allocation of Common Fixed Costs. International Journal of Production Economics. 34, 17-33.

17. Shapiro, C. and H. R. Varian. 1999. *Information Rules*, Harvard Business School Press, Boston, Mass.

18. Moorthy, K. S. 1988. Product and Price Competition in a Duopoly. Marketing Science. 7, 141-168.

19. Williamson, S. D. 1987. Recent Developments in Modeling Financial Intermediation. Federal Reserve Bank of Minneapolis, Quarterly Review.

Chapter 15

The Potential for Virtual Work to Enhance Value in Financial Services Firms

Roger L.M. Dunbar
Raghu Garud
New York University

15.1 Introduction

In the past people knew that before they could initiate a financial transaction, they first had to have a physical meeting with their potential partners to exchange ideas about mutual interests and possibilities. Similarly in the past, firms kept their records at specific locations and employees knew they had to visit these sites to access this information. Recent advances in information processing technology have removed these location constraints. Financial transactions today can be initiated, executed and recorded no matter where the participating parties are located. Equipped with a computer and a modem, people can also access information records from anywhere (Sproull and Kiesler, 1991; Raghuram, 1996). This ability has introduced massive flexibility and new organizing options for financial services firms. The way firms exploit this flexibility is an important but complex source of value creation.

Financial service firms have responded to advances in information technology and the removal of location constraints in many different ways. Skandia AFS well illustrates how the possibilities can be used. Skandia AFS in the US has grown rapidly by utilizing Internet distribution and communication capacities while investing comparatively little in physical facilities (Bartlett and Mahmood, 1996; Hedberg, Dahlgren, Hansson and Olve, 1997). More generally, financial services firms can successfully create value by utilizing new information processing technologies to add services and at the same time eliminate real estate investments. Though the general outline of this value creation strategy is simple, its implementation can prove difficult. This is because many financial services firms, their managers and their employees are highly committed to products and services that are bound to fixed locations and rely on tried-and-true approaches to operations. Proposals to change these established practices may generate skepticism and resistance rather than enthusiasm.

The specific example we focus on to explore these issues concerns proposals to use virtual office work environments to create value in financial services firms. Such proposals seek to exploit recent advances in information technology and the associated relaxation of location constraints. Yet such proposals also imply changes in operations and in the ways managers and employees work. Some may perceive such proposals as important efforts in value creation. Others may anticipate the disruptions and potential chaos such changes may generate and be reluctant to participate for fear the initiative will lead to value destruction.

We use interview data from people involved in virtual work programs in financial services firms to illustrate how these concerns emerge as management issues. We show how such value creation efforts are ongoing processes leading to important organizational transitions. The issues that emerge reflect the way people interpret the opportunities offered by new information processing technologies. We argue that a managerial understanding of why these issues emerge, and how they can be managed, is the key to success in any value creation effort based on introducing a virtual office environment.

15.2 Alternative Approaches to Understanding Value Creation in Financial Services Firms

Financial services firms exploit the options associated with organizational flexibility in different ways. Walter (1999) noted for example how banks that are "roughly the same size and providing roughly the same range of services may have very different cost levels per unit of output." Berger, Hancock and Humphrey, (1993) concluded that these types of differences do not reflect funding costs. Rather, they reflect important contrasts in operating economies, i.e., in how firms are organized to create value.

In assessing value creation efforts in financial services industries, there are at least two possible approaches. One approach is to identify possible sources of value creation and then to adopt the perspective of an outside observer and examine objective historical data to determine whether these sources have resulted in realized operating economies (Berger, Hunter and Timme, 1993 Newman and Shrieves, 1993). Walter (1999) adopted this approach, proposing that economies of scale and scope might be sources of operating economies. Similarly, Cutler (chapter 23, this volume) examined whether initiatives intended to improve productivity actually created value. Their respective analyses based on objective data suggested that neither economies of scale or scope, nor specific productivity initiatives actually explained operating performance differences in their samples of financial services firms.

An alternative approach is to adopt the perspective of an organizational insider and examine how processes of value creation unfold in different firms (Dunbar and Ahlstrom, 1995, Garud and Ahlstrom, 1997). Such an approach is likely to uncover the variety of paths along with the forward movement and backtracking that are typical of firms attempting value creation efforts through the use of new technologies. An additional concern is that in addition to enhancing firm productivity, such value creation initiatives also affect employees in many ways. A focus on firm productivity measures can obscure the broader consequences of ongoing change efforts for employees. The advantage of an insider standpoint is that it allows the complexity of the value creation process to be recognized along with how it proceeds on multiple fronts while affecting multiple organizational levels. We adopt the perspective of an organizational insider in exploring the potential of the virtual office environment to create value in financial services firms.

15.3 The Potential of the Virtual Office Environment

The introduction of a virtual office environment often reflects ongoing and broader corporate change efforts. While these change efforts are usually driven by corporate level concerns, their implementation requires employee cooperation. Hence, success depends on the combination of organizational drivers and employee reactions and their interaction over time. If employee reactions to a virtual office initiative are negative, for example, the effort may be effectively stalled. There is also no clear view of what success may mean in such an evolving scenario. Success is usually something emergent that becomes apparent as a firm eventually moves a significant proportion of its operations to a virtual basis as a result of the many steps that have to be taken to react to and resolve employees' ongoing concerns (Garud, Dunbar and Accrocco, 1997).

To understand value creation efforts around the virtual office from an insider's perspective, one must explore the evolving nature of the implementation process and the issues it raises. This includes understanding what the firm's initiatives are and how employees react to them, and the initiatives that employees themselves may take. One of the interesting things about this process is that understandings of the same events can differ in different parts of the same organization. This usually serves to temporarily stall the initiative. As perspectives become consistent again, mutual agreement on appropriate ways forward can emerge and value creation can continue. We attempt to identify the nature of the evolving path that unwinds in an organization as a result of efforts to introduce a virtual office environment and thereby create value.

The flexibility offered by advances in information processing technology and the associated relaxation of location constraints has opened up the value creation potential of the virtual work environment for financial services firms. People involved in introducing virtual office work environments, however, don't usually talk directly about this flexibility or its wide range of strategic implications. Rather, they recognize that how this flexibility is used is a basic strategic issue and how to proceed must be determined by top management. The middle managers we have met have made many proposals concerning the potential value creation implicit in a virtual work environment but to determine what is actually done, they must wait for top managers in the financial services firm to provide direction.

> "There have been many initiatives in the past to develop alternative office strategies. Each one tended to develop in its own way and so they often reinvented everything. It was a long time before there was any organizational coordination and support for such efforts even though it was clear they offered all sorts of benefits."

A Financial Service Firm Manager

If top management decides on the establishment of a virtual work environment, discussions lower down focus immediately on implementation. Implementation is guided by the juxtaposition of corporate and employee concerns (Salancik and Pfeffer, 1977). At the corporate level, the driving concern is most often for increased cost efficiency. Specifically, firms believe they can save on real estate costs and achieve the same output by equipping employees to work out of a home office (Dunbar and Garud, 1998). To facilitate this transition, firms invest in technical support for those working from a home office and provide hoteling facilities for virtual employees visiting corporate premises. Firms prepare financial plans showing how investments in employees' home office technology and corporate hoteling facilities are more than off-set by the anticipated savings in firm real estate costs. Such cost savings are significant for firms in exclusive downtown or high rent districts and as office, hoteling and home office equipment costs are all known, they are also usually clearly identifiable and predictable.

> "At the top, they want to know about financial savings. Usually this is 'avoided costs' that would have been necessary if people had to be provided the usual office. We reckon it costs around $14,000 per year

to house a person in an office. Our calculations show that to house them at home costs about $9,000. Hence, every time we make a new hire and they don't give them an office, or a person leaves an assigned office and makes it available, we get $5,000 in avoided costs on our budget."

A Financial Services Firm Manager

Voluntary Involvement in a Virtual Work Environment

Employee concerns differ depending on their reaction to the opportunity to work at home. Employees volunteering to work virtually do so because their usual driving concern is a lack of time to do everything they want to do. They often have important life interests outside of the work place. Fulfilling these obligations in addition to doing their work puts them under stress and leads to other quality of life concerns. They wish to satisfy both their work and these other obligations but find themselves prevented from doing so by a long commute to a central work place and work place interruptions that many view as a waste of time. They believe they can satisfy their obligations by eliminating their office commute and better organizing their work at home. With the new freedom, they can develop a schedule that allows them to fulfill their work obligations and also pursue their other life interests.

> "Being out of the office, you're not dragged into meetings at a moment's notice when you may not be really needed. There's no extraneous business you have to concern yourself with."

A Virtual Office Employee

As the firm's efforts to reduce real estate costs are juxtaposed with the quality of life concerns of busy employees, there is a mutuality of interests in the introduction of a virtual work environment that allows value creation to occur for both the firm and the volunteering individual. The firm reduces its real estate costs. Employee productivity increases with estimates being usually in the 15-30% range. Employees can better schedule themselves to satisfy their work and other obligations. Volunteer virtual workers often feel very grateful to the firm for the opportunity to work virtually. They have high levels of life satisfaction and many express high levels of loyalty towards their employers.

> "It's really up to us to make it work. If we're not successful in getting our jobs done and meeting our requirements, then it's just not going to work. We need to prove that it does work."

A Virtual Worker

Required Involvement in a Virtual Work Environment

Some firms require their employees to work virtually. Several reasons can persuade a firm to make this requirement. In setting up a virtual work environment, for example, firms invest in hoteling and related facilities and minimum levels of participation are needed to ensure that these investments are cost effective. The anticipated cost savings may also be something that a firm's financial leadership believes it should capture. But required participation in a virtual work program raises new motivation issues. In a voluntary program, motivation was often not an issue because of the anticipated personal benefits. With required participation, there may be no anticipated personal benefits and the proposed change may threaten accustomed lifestyles in a variety of ways. Firms must convince their employees of the desirability of a virtual work environment in which participation is required.

> "They offered this program to about 430 people within the CSP group. An even larger population was initially in the proposed virtual program but somehow, it dwindled to the 22 who are actually doing it."

> A Financial Services Firm Manager

Persuading employees and managers to involve themselves in a virtual work effort can be difficult. Employees often feel that there is a personal compact between themselves and the firm that established a mutual basis for their relationship and that the compact should not change. If it is to change, it requires mutual consent. In financial services, employees often expect their firms to provide workspaces. The introduction of virtual work environment challenges this expectation. Employees are still given limited workspace for temporary use when the employees visit corporate offices. Otherwise, they are to provide the workspace at their homes and they are also expected to remain totally committed to their employer.

By not providing corporate workspace, a firm may significantly change the nature of work as both employees and managers perceive it. Working in a corporate office, one comes in contact with peers, superiors and subordinates daily, one is included in ongoing discussions, one has an awareness of and an influence over ongoing issues, and one has opportunities to draw attention to oneself, claim credit and influence how firm rewards are distributed. These social experiences allow employees to develop a work presence that may be an important aspect of their self-identity (Wiesenfeld, Raghuram and Garud, 1999a). Working out of a virtual environment, however, workers are almost certainly cut off from these experiences and may fear their firm no longer knows their needs. They may also be concerned about career consequences, fearing that their superiors will forget about them if they are not physically present and overlook them as candidates for promotion or other rewards (Raghuram, Garud and Wiesenfeld, 1999b). Superiors in contrast may fear that as their subordinates are out of view, the superior no longer knows what they are doing. They may not know what their employees' needs are nor how they should manage them or respond to their concerns.

> "I just feel totally isolated out here. I never hear from my manager. I went into the city for a meeting with him and his group. It took three and a half hours for me to get there and three and a half hours to drive back. All he did was present a schedule he could have sent by email. I'm not going to put up with inconsiderateness like that. At the same time you feel so lost and out of it."

> A Virtual Worker

> "That's another thing for managers to think about. They don't necessarily see it as a reasonable request that I have a space to go to when I come in."

> A Virtual Worker

In other words, a requirement that employees work virtually automatically raises many questions of fear and trust for both the virtual workers and their managers (Garud, 1997; Garud and Lucas, 1998). To effectively implement such a program, a firm must overcome these fears by establishing mutual trust within the new work context that is established by the virtual environment. Line managers are often not aware of these issues and have not considered how they might be handled.

> "The more information you give our managers, the more they are going to push it away. They just feel the virtual office employees take up more of their time. We need a focus group with Human Resources present — senior Human Resources."

> A Virtual Worker

> "Senior management generally just doesn't get it."

> A Virtual Worker

Establishing the Trust Necessary to make a Virtual Environment Work

Managers responsible for introducing a virtual work environment, however, are usually very aware of the issues of trust and mutuality that are raised. Their first effort at establishing a sense of trust is through their efforts to make the technical transition from a regular corporate office to a home office as simple and painless as possible. This involves extensive checklists explaining to employees what they have to do and, in addition, a range of internal and external support services to make sure any problems are quickly overcome. The fear at this stage is that if employees should find the process of simply moving from a corporate office to a virtual office environment difficult, it will confirm any underlying doubts encouraging them to immediately demand a return to their regular office.

> "For the most part the transition was good. It was a stage process. It didn't inhibit my productivity. Hal and his staff were very helpful. As my group was moving I had to ship my stuff home sooner than my desk was ready. There was a time lag getting the desk delivered from Staples. As soon as it was there, the Tech people had my equipment installed. Everything went smoothly."
>
> A Virtual Worker

A firm must also move to establish organizational beliefs and values that ensure virtual workers will not be discriminated against due to their remote locations. Managers and their attitudes are often the main stumbling block here. Rules are needed to guide managers to prevent them from converting virtual workers into second class corporate citizens. Reward and promotion policies must visibly demonstrate that both office and virtual workers receive the same recognition for equivalent work.

> "Q. What would your manager say is negative about the virtual program?
>
> A. She'd say it's no good because I'm not at her beck and call. My biggest concern is whether I can continue to work Virtual Office and still get promoted. My manager said that if I'm not in the office, my chances were not good. I didn't even put in for it."
>
> A Virtual Office Worker

With these types of managerial attitudes, employees perceive it as risky working virtually. If any unexpected difficulties arise, employees interpret them as indications of a developing second class status. There are often opportunities for misunderstandings. As employees feel "out of the loop" in their virtual offices, for example, they may interpret it as indicating their manager is ignoring them. As they miss collegial feedback confirming the value of work they have done, they start to doubt whether they can evaluate whether their work is satisfactory or not. As they feel ignored, they also have doubts as to whether they will be appropriately rewarded. As many of these are new programs, they are often subject to sharp scrutiny, especially from people concerned that the new possibilities have the potential to disrupt their established ways of working. Often these people are most interested in finding indications that the new virtual work environments are failing.

> "There had been a mindset that if you're not there in the office, you can't be productive all of the time. But I'm proving otherwise."

> A Virtual Worker

Consequences of Working Virtually

If a virtual work environment is mandated, managers who remain in regular offices and those who work out of virtual offices often need training to become aware of the nature of the new relationship and associated approaches to work. The main change seems to be that by removing the location constraint, managers and virtual workers both become more conscious and often more critical about how they and others allocate their time. In a virtual world, interruptions can still occur but people question the need to tolerate them. Meetings can still be held and messages and requests for an immediate response can still be sent. But people are more likely to ask, "How does this help? Is this really necessary?" This more critical attitude may help explain the unanimous view that virtual work environments significantly increase productivity. This new self-consciousness is part of the new work approach and associated value system that a virtual work environment creates.

> "People are still reluctant to call me because they know I'm at home. Yet I feel just as involved as I did at downtown. The difference is I get a lot more done."

> A Virtual Worker

> "I'm a director and I work for a VP who's remote. I've had reviews over the phone. It's been no problem."

> A Regular Worker

Most people working virtually are home two to four days a week and come to the corporate offices at least once a week for meetings, to see colleagues, and to catch up on firm developments. The sense of having one's identity partially embedded in a specific location is attenuated for many virtual workers. Instead, they have a more independent perspective based on diverse commitments that can lead to a more complex, self-managed work identity that may differ from that of a regular office worker. This more distanced perspective may provide a firm with access to new ideas and possibilities that can facilitate value creation on many different, unanticipated fronts.

> "Some jobs are just cheaper to run on Sunday night in half the time"

> A Virtual Worker

Satisfied virtual workers are often convinced that the process of working virtually is an enormous improvement and benefit for themselves and their employer. Many attribute it to a sense of mutual trust and respect in a situation where there are also many opportunities to be mistrustful. Distrust emerges when virtual workers think many corporate managers, including top management, do not appreciate the managerial implications of new information processing technology. A number of the workers interviewed described virtual work as something permitted rather than promoted by top management. Yet the fact that it was not forbidden also had value, for many virtual workers were well aware that most other firms did not yet offer such opportunities.

> "This is definitely a company I want to stay with. Virtual work has increased my loyalty tremendously. My job satisfaction is through the roof."

> A Virtual Worker

> "The X-bank has no flexibility at all. They made me an offer and I closed the door on the opportunity when they wouldn't even entertain the idea of telecommuting. This is a huge source of advantage to this company.

> A Virtual Worker

Virtual workers often use the opportunity to build a more enriched personal life (Raghuram, Garud and Wiesenfeld, 1998). This may include more involvement with family and children or it can also mean more time to devote to other life interests. This extracurricular involvement does not seem to come at the expense of the employing firm even as virtual workers report that their personal quality of life has vastly improved. Instead, associated with this improvement, a new respect, trust and loyalty develop for their employer.

> "I was planning to move. Virtual Office made it easy for me to move all the way out. I feel I missed some things for my first two kids but now I can do things for my third child. It's a good feeling to be home. It changes your inner feelings. I find everything is less stressful and I'm more productive in every way"

A Virtual Worker

> "My bank has a lot of trust that I'm not out shopping all day. I feel good that they're confident in me that I can produce even when I'm not under their eyes."

A Virtual Worker

> "I live in central New Jersey. If there's bad weather, it's rough commuting. But I always know I'm going to be productive at home. There I can keep on top of all my projects. I have a two to three hour commute. I'd say five days a year, now."

A Virtual Worker

> "When you're working at home there are no sidebar conversations. I'm getting on the computer earlier and staying later."

A Virtual Worker

15.4 Reflections on the Process

Virtual work environments offer the potential of value creation on many dimensions for firms in the financial services industries. It is top management who usually approves the introduction of a virtual work program and their decision is usually based on promises of anticipated and specific cost savings. Yet authorization of a virtual work environment not only permits "economies of substitution" (Garud and Kumaraswamy, 1995) but also launches implicit value creation potential in the more critical assessments of time allocations that appear as inevitable consequences of virtual work environments.

Virtual work programs are usually implemented at the middle management level. Managers directing such efforts usually realize the magnitude of such a value creation effort and how a virtual work environment can change the way a firm does business. As a result, they are not so surprised as they encounter successes and setbacks, enthusiasm and resistance. To move forward, they must work with individuals at all levels and serve as a bridge to line specialists to reduce feelings of threat and establish a sense of trust that can then be used to convert the potential of virtual work to a reality.

To facilitate this process, managers introducing virtual work environments must work to make the shift to a virtual office as painless as possible (Wiesenfeld, Raghuram and Garud, 1999b). They must provide continuous technical support because they know that many employees are still uncertain about whether this new way of working will prove effective. These doubts stem from the fact that many executives still assume they need office space in a corporate building to do their work. As employees hold these views, they resist or ignore the possibilities opened by new information processing technologies. Such resistance is always lurking and remains a continuous challenge to these value creation efforts.

Thus, those responsible for introducing virtual work environments often need to "deframe" (Dunbar, Garud and Raghuram, 1996) the mindset of those moving to a virtual work environment. The persuasion process does not seem to proceed in a predictable manner. Rather, it seems to require coalitions of managers and employees just strong enough to get a virtual office environment established and then later, to sustain its implementation. Sustaining a virtual office initiative requires reports of positive experiences that invite other parts of the organization to explore the new possibilities. Negative reports, however, can threaten future experiments along with the total virtual office initiative. Managers who successfully introduce virtual office environments are consistently supportive of their virtual workers and report positive experiences to a broader corporate audience.

Given the weakly understood potential of a virtual work environment, introductions within financial services firms often proceed uncertainly. Progress may seem rapid as plans are made that a particular section of a firm will go virtual. As some people hesitate in the implementation process questioning whether they want to embrace the new approach, the introduction may slow or become bogged down. At this point, negative and positive reports are examined, sources of available support are reexamined, and firm employees and top management all reconsider their priorities. Then a new corporate section becomes a target for the introduction of a virtual work environment.

15.5 Conclusion

Progress at introducing virtual work environments into financial services firms has consistently been slower than top management has expected. This apparently slow progress reflects the complexity of the process that goes far beyond the real estate cost savings that may have originally justified the initiative. Specifically, working in a virtual environment involves new organizing approaches that challenge the way many people in financial services industries think about management and work. Given the broad resistance to such a change, managing the introduction of a virtual work environment usually requires firms to provide maximal support for those exploring the new approach. Success experiences must be communicated back to build a new coalition of experimenters amongst employees who often remain nervous about the prospects of working virtually. Through this step by step process, financial services firms are slowly exploiting the value creation potential of virtual work environments.

Assessing progress in value creation efforts via the virtual office is probably best understood from the standpoint of insiders rather than relying on a more objective outside perspective. This is because historical measures of realized cost savings probably tell little about continuing efforts at value creation. In these ongoing efforts, the value that has been captured is simply not the main concern. Potentially much more important is the unrealized value creation associated with ongoing initiatives. As one interviewee explained, of the 430 employees in positions that could do their work virtually and were offered the possibility to do so, 22 accepted the opportunity. This leaves very substantial potential value creation as unrealized. Finding out why this occurs is a main concern for financial services firms. The fact is that working virtually means that both employees and managers must change their assumptions about work and management in order to take advantage of the potential value creation implicit in virtual office initiatives.

References

1. Bartlett, C. A., & Mahmood, T. (1996) Skandia AFS: Developing intellectual capital globally, Boston: Harvard Business School Case # 9-396-412

2. Berger, A. N., Hancock, D. & Humphrey, D. B., (1993) Bank efficiency derived from the profit function, *Journal of Banking and Finance*, pp. 317-347.

3. Berger, A. N., Hunter, W. C. & Timme, S. G., (1993) The efficiency of financial institutions: A review and preview of research past, present, and future. *Journal of Banking and Finance*, pp. 221-249.

4. Dunbar, R. L. M. and Ahlstrom, D. (1995) Seeking the institutional balance of power: Avoiding the power of a balanced view, *Academy of Management Review* 20 (1): 171-192

5. Dunbar, R. L. M. & Garud, R., (1998) Best practices in the virtual workplace, *STERNBusiness* (Summer) pp. 15-17.

6. Dunbar, R. L. M., Garud, R., and Raghuram, S. (1996) Deframing in strategic analyses *Journal of Management Inquiry*, Vol. 5, No.1 pp. 23-34.

7.   Garud, R. (1997) Trust and Virtual Systems, *STERNBusiness*, Vol. 4 (1): 33-35.
8.   Garud, R. and Ahlstrom, D. (1997) Technology Assessment: A socio-cognitive perspective, *Journal of Engineering and Technology Management*, Vol. 14, pp. 25-48.
9.   Garud, R., Dunbar, R. L. M, & Accrocco, D., (1997) Local, regional and global maxima and the valleys in between: Lessons from NCR's virtual work initiative, *The Academy of Management Conference*, Boston (August)
10. Garud, R. and Kumaraswamy, A. (1995) Technological and organizational designs to achieve economies of substitution *Strategic Management Journal*, Vol. 16, pp. 93-110.
11. Garud, R. and Lucas, H. (1998) Virtual Organizations: Distributed in Time and Space, New York University Working Paper.
12. Hedberg, B, Dahlgren, G, Hansson, J & Olve, N-G, (1977) *Virtual Organizations and Beyond: Discover Imaginary systems*, Chichester, Wiley.
13. Newman, J. A. & Shrieves, R. E., (1993) The multibank holding company effect on cost efficiency in banking. *Journal of Banking and Finance*, pp. 709-732.
14. Raghuram, S. (1996) Knowledge creation in the telework context. *International Journal of Technology Management*, 11, 859-870.
15. Raghuram, S., Garud R. & Wiesenfeld B. (1998) Telework: Managing distances in a connected world *Journal of Business and Strategy*, # 10, pp. 7-9.
16. Sproull, L. & Kiesler, S. (1991) Connections: New ways of working in the networked organization. The MIT Press: Cambridge, MA.
17. Salancik, G & Pfeffer, J. (1977) Who gets power – and how they hold on to it: A strategic-contingency model of power, *Organizational Dynamics*, (Winter) pp. 2-21.
18. Walter, I. (1999) Universal Banking: A shareholder value perspective, In: *Creating Value in Financial Services*, Chapter 4.
19. Wiesenfeld, B. M., Raghuram, S., & Garud, R. (1999a) Communication patterns as determinants of organizational identification in a virtual organization. *Journal of Computer-Mediated Communication*, 3, #4, and *in Organization Science* (In press)
20. Wiesenfeld, B. M., Raghuram, S., & Garud, R. (1999b) Managers in a virtual context: The experience of self-threat and its effects on virtual work organizations. In C. L. Cooper & D. Rousseau (Eds.), *Trends in Organizational Behavior*. (In press)

Chapter 16

Designing Electronic Market Institutions for Bond Trading[*]

Ming Fan
Jan Stallaert
Andrew B. Whinston
Center for Research in Electronic Commerce
The University of Texas at Austin

16.1 Introduction

Recently, there has been a growing interest in electronic bond trading. Unlike for stocks, there does not exist a central exchange for bonds. The markets for debt securities, including U.S. Treasury securities, municipal bonds, and corporate bonds have trailed the equity markets in the use of technology (SEC, 1998b). The efficiency of the bond market is of great importance to all aspects of the economy. The significance of today's bond market is demonstrated by its sheer size. U.S. Treasury securities outstanding alone account for more than $3.4 trillion, and for trade of more than $200 billion per day in 1998, compared to the daily trading value of about $28 billion on the New York Stock Exchange (NYSE) in 1998 (SEC, 1998a). But, it is estimated that only one to three percent of the U.S. Treasury securities are traded electronically (Wall Street & Technology, 1997). Most of the brokers/dealers in the bond market execute trades by using the telephone and fax machine. This "people-intensive"

---

[*] We acknowledge the financial support of the IBM Institute for Advanced Commerce, Lucent Technologies, and Intel Corporation. We thank John Hund at the University of Texas at Austin for many helpful suggestions and comments.

trading is not very efficient and hinders real-time market information collection and dissemination.

The current bond market structure is experiencing major changes. According to a 1997 survey conducted by the Bond Market Association, the majority of respondents believed that most dealers would offer electronic trading to institutional customers within two years. About 75% of the respondents also expect institutional investors to demand access to multi-dealer systems within two years (The Bond Market Association, 1997). In 1998, several multi-dealer bond markets were launched with a few more under development. These markets are fundamentally different from the previous single dealer systems, where competition is weak, and will significantly improve market transparency. However, issues such as market efficiency are rarely raised in the exchange market design. Most exchange markets are, in fact, developed by software engineers and traders, and are not necessarily based on economic principles. The rapid advances in information technology have created a unique opportunity for researchers to design electronic markets based on economic principles.

This chapter outlines our research in designing an electronic market institution for bond trading. We propose designing an auction market with the presence of dealers, combining the advantages of both an auction market and a dealer market. In order to facilitate financial engineering to provide customized solutions to real world complex financial problems, we introduce a bundle trading mechanism that can trade bundle orders or portfolios. This mechanism is shown to be efficient when investors desire a portfolio of securities that have strong complementarity. The balance of the chapter is organized as follows: Section 2 describes the background of the current U.S. bond market with emphasis on the U.S. Treasury market. Section 3 analyzes the issues of market transparency and electronic trading in the fixed-income market. In Section 4, we discuss market institution design. Section 5 provides motivational examples to illustrate that in many cases investors in a fixed-income market seek a portfolio or a bundle of bonds with strong complementarity in order to meet their investment objective. Section 6 discusses the theory of bundle market mechanism we propose for the fixed-income market. Section 7 addresses the computing platform to implement the electronic market. The last section is the conclusion.

16.2 The U.S. Bond Market

The bond market raises capital for the U.S. government as well as for private corporations. The modern U.S. bond market, with more than $11 trillion in outstanding debt obligations in 1996, is the world's largest securities market (The Bond Market Association, 1998a). It is larger even than the U.S. stock markets, which had a combined market value of about $8.9 trillion through the end of 1996. By the second quarter of 1998, the total value of the U.S. bond market reached $12.7 trillion (Table 1). Over one-third of the total market value belongs to U.S. government debt securities, which include Treasury securities and federal agency securities. With a large outstanding volume and high liquidity, the U.S. Treasury securities market is the world's most important debt market. It includes discount securities, with initial maturities of 3-month, 6-month, and 1-year, and coupon securities, with initial maturities of 2, 3, 5, 10, and 30 years. The initial issuance of U.S. Treasury securities, also known as the primary market, is conducted through auction. The U.S. Treasury auctions have a regular cycle. The 3-month and 6-month treasury bills are auctioned every Monday. The 1-year bills, and the 2- and 5-year notes are auctioned monthly. In addition, the 3-year, 10-year, and 30-year treasury securities are auctioned quarterly Fabozzi and Modigliani, 1996).

Table 1. Size of U.S. Bond Market* (in trillions)	
Government Securities	$4.5
Treasury Securities	$3.4
Agency Securities	$1.1
Municipal Bonds	$1.4
Corporate Bonds	$2.3
Mortgage and Asset Backed Securities	$2.6
Money Market Instruments	$1.9
Total	**$12.7**
Source: The Bond Market Association, 1998.	
* By the second quarter of 1998.	

Table 2. Daily Averages Trading Value by Primary Dealer in U.S. Treasury Securities for Week of October 7, 1998 (In Billion)	
Treasury bills	$32.286
Coupon securities	
Due in five years or less	$140.677
Due in more than five years	$117.183
Treasury inflation index securities	$2.375
Total	**$292.521**
Source: Federal Reserve Bank of New York, 1998.	

The secondary market for U.S. Treasury securities is largely an over-the-counter (OTC) market. The market is organized through primary dealers, which are large investment banks and commercial banks with which the Federal Reserve

Bank of New York interacts directly. The primary dealer system was established in 1960 and began with 18 primary dealers. Over time, the number of primary dealers changed. As of October 1, 1998, there are 32 primary dealers including firms such as Citicorp, Goldman Sachs, and Lehman Brothers. The U.S. Treasury market is the most liquid security market in the world. According to the Federal Reserve Bank of New York, daily average trading volume for all Treasury securities by primary dealers for the week of October 7, 1998, was about $292.5 billion (Table 2), about 10 times the daily trading value on the NYSE.

Unlike the OTC market for stocks, which is highly automated through NASDAQ, trading in the OTC Treasury market is very people-intensive. Investors, including institutional investors or individuals, have to buy and sell bonds through individual dealers without formal consolidation of orders or trading. Although there have been some advances in electronic information dissemination and trading, e.g. the development of GovPx and NASD's Fixed-Income Pricing System (FIPS), there does not exist a comprehensive electronic network like NASDAQ that displays real-time quotations for all the trading activities and allows dealers to compete for the orders. In terms of order transmission and trade execution, most of the trades are conducted through the telephone and fax machine. When trading with each other, the dealers go through intermediaries called brokers. Brokers enable speedier transactions and they keep the identities of the dealers involved in trades confidential. There are six inter-dealer brokers: Cantor Fitzgerald Securities, Garban Ltd., Liberty Brokerage, RMJ Securities, Hilliard Farber, and Tullet and Tokyo Securities. In the inter-dealer market, dealers can view other dealers' indications of interest for trades through their computers that are connected to the broker's proprietary system. But dealers still have to submit orders to brokers through either phone or fax.

In corporate and municipal bond markets, we have seen a sharp increase in the level of outstanding debts in the past decade. For example, since 1985, outstanding corporate debt has more than tripled, from $720 billion in 1985 to $2.3 trillion today. During the same time, the outstanding municipal debt bond total has grown from $860 billion to $1.4 billion (The Bond Market Association, 1998a). The trading of corporate bonds can occur at an exchange market (NYSE and American Stock Exchange) or the OTC market. The latter has the bulk of the trading volume and is organized through dealers and brokers. Unlike U.S. Treasury securities, which are owned mostly by institutional investors, municipal bonds are primarily held by individual investors, who hold about 75% of all outstanding issues. A new issue of a municipal bond is usually underwritten by investment banks or commercial banks on a competitive basis. A secondary market for municipal bonds is made by dealers and brokers as well.

16.3 Advances in Information Dissemination and Electronic Trading

Significant progress has been made in U.S. bond markets in using information technology to enhance market transparency and efficiency in recent years. GovPx was created in 1991 to collect and disseminate quotes and transaction prices on government securities. In the municipal bond market, the Municipal Securities Rulemaking Board started to develop an automated system to report transaction data in 1995. Now the system reports inter-dealer transaction data and will include dealer-customer transaction information in the future. In the corporate bond market, market information for bonds that are traded on exchanges are reported. Subscribers of the Automated Bond System (ABS) at NYSE can view bond quotation and trade information through proprietary terminals. The ABS also allows electronic order entry and automatically executes trades for matching buy and sell orders (SEC, 1998b). In the corporate bond market, FIPS provides quotations and summary transaction information for a group of high-yield bonds. But the majority of the bond trading that occurs at the OTC market does not have an electronic price disclosure system. As for electronic trading, the development of single dealer trading systems started in the early Nineties. Recently, several multi-dealer markets have been launched. We focus our discussion on the development of GovPx, FIPS, single dealer systems (SDS), and multi-dealer markets.

GovPx

Encouraged by the Securities and Exchange Commission, GovPx was founded by primary Treasury dealers and inter-dealer brokers to disseminate real-time prices on U.S. Treasury securities. Prior to GovPx, the inter-dealer market data was only available to dealers, who were reluctant to allow the general public access to the information. GovPx provides 24-hour, worldwide distribution of securities information as transacted by the primary dealers through five of the six inter-dealer brokers for all active and off-the-run Treasury securities. The data include the best bids and offers, trade price and size, and aggregate volume traded for all Treasury securities. GovPx currently extends its market coverage to provide worldwide distribution of information regarding the interest rate swaps market. This service, known as SwapPx, provides real-time, benchmark rates, data and analytics for U.S. medium term swaps, basic swaps, and spot/forward swaps ranging from 90 days to 30 years. Although GovPx has been a big improvement in market transparency, it is believed that significant gaps still exist in the current system. For example, large market dealers can easily hide a trade from the public by dealing directly with one another.

FIPS

FIPS was created in response to the 1980s junk bond market collapse and began operating in April 1994. FIPS is a screen-based system that collects, processes and displays quotes and summary transaction information for certain high-yield corporate bonds. The system now lists prices on a group of 50 high yield bonds, reporting the high and low prices and volume every hour during trading. The FIPS 50 list represents some of the most active and liquid issues currently trading. The list is periodically updated to replace called and matured issues, and to reflect changes in the market. As a particular issue no longer represents its sector or industry, it is replaced with more representative issues. Information disseminated through FIPS includes bids and offers communicated by dealers and brokers, as well as a calculation of an inside market that includes the best bid and the best offer for each FIPS security appearing in the system. A trade summary of transaction reports entered into the system during operating hours is disseminated on an hourly basis. This information includes high execution price, low execution price, and accumulated volume in all transactions reported in that hour for FIPS securities. An updated daily summary is also disseminated each hour, listing that day's cumulative high/low volume up to that hour. FIPS provides an easy access to market information for the high-yield bond market and enhances market transparency. In the future, NASD plans to add all corporate and municipal bonds and provides real-time trade reporting.

Single Dealer Systems

Of the estimated one to three percent of the bond market that utilizes electronic trading, most of the trades go through single dealer systems (SDS). Table 3 lists SDS operated by different companies. Through SDS, customers can view the quotes and enter orders using computer terminals rather than telephones and fax machines. For example, CS First Boston's GovTrade system started in 1992 and can be accessed through Bloomberg's terminals. To trade, an investor selects from a Bloomberg screen menu an issue that has First Boston's bid and offer quotes. The investor then fills out a "ticket" that pops up on the screen, and the order is transmitted to First Boston's traders. Companies that offer electronic trading to their customers believe that SDS offer convenience to customers and increase the speed of order execution. Instead of using telephones and fax machines, investors can access price quotes and enter orders from the same computer terminal. Meanwhile, SDS enable bond traders to focus more on market research, analytics, and trading strategies, rather than just taking orders. However, SDS have not really taken off in the marketplace. SDS have only changed the order entry process but have not fundamentally improved the way bonds are traded. As long as investors can only interact with one dealer through the SDS, they do not have strong incentives to use the system. Investors feel they can use telephones to call different dealers and negotiate better prices.

Table 3. Single Dealer Trading Systems		
System and Company	**Securities Traded**	**Trading Medium**
Auto Execution Ragen MacKenzie	Treasury, Agency	Bloomberg
Autobahn Deutsche Bank	Treasury, Mortgage-Backed Securities (MBS)	Bloomberg, Proprietary Network
Bear Sterns	Treasury	Bloomberg
Fixed Income Securities	Treasury, Agency, MBS, Corporate, Repos	Internet
Fuji Securities	Treasury	Bloomberg
Goldman, Sachs	Commercial Paper	Bloomberg
GovTrade, ADNTrade etc. CS First Boston	Treasury, Agency, Commercial Paper, CD, Repos	Bloomberg
LMS Merrill Lynch	Treasury, Corporate, Municipal, MBS	Bloomberg, Proprietary Network
MSZeros Morgan Stanley Dean Witter	Treasury Strip Securities	Bloomberg
Spear, Leeds & Kellogg	Treasury, Agency, Municipal, Corporate	Internet, Bloomberg
Winstar Government Securities	Treasury	Internet, Proprietary Network
Zions GovRate/Odd-Lot Machine Zions Bank Capital Markets	Treasury	Telnet, dial-up, proprietary network

Multi-Dealer/Exchange Markets

Several electronic trading systems with multiple dealers have been launched recently with a few more being developed (Table 4). The fundamental difference between a multi-dealer/exchange market and SDS is that the former allows competitive quotes by different dealers. This is the same idea behind NASDAQ, in which multiple dealers can compete with one another, thereby leading to narrow bid-ask spreads and "best" prices for investors. In some markets, investors can trade directly with each other without going through dealers. TradeWeb, which started operation in the first quarter of 1998, offers real-time trading, price information and research for U.S. Treasury securities. Currently, five primary government dealers – CS First Boston, Goldman Sachs, Lehman Brothers, Merrill Lynch and Salomon Smith Barney – are participating in the electronic market. TradeWeb users can view the quotes from different dealers and reach the dealers simultaneously. According to James Toffey, president of TradeWeb, the company is doing about $1 billion worth of trades a day (Pensions and Investments, 1998). A similar system, Chicago Board of Brokerage's (CBB) MarketPower started in July 1998. CBB is a joint venture between Chicago Board of Trade (CBOT) and Prebon Yamane. CBB will have multiple dealers as market participants as well. Both markets only trade U.S. Treasury securities right now.

Table 4. Multi-Dealer/Exchange Markets for Bond Trading			
System	**Company**	**Securities Traded**	**Trading Medium**
Automated Bond System	NYSE	Treasury, Agency, Municipal, Corporate	Proprietary Network
Bond Connect	State Street	Treasury, Agency, MBS, Corporate	Bridge Telerate
BondLink	Trading Edge	Corporate	Internet
BondNet	The Bank of New York	Corporate	Proprietary Network, Internet (Java Applets), Bloomberg
BondTrader	Bloomberg	Treasury	Bloomberg
InterVest	InterVest	Treasury, Municipal, Corporate	Internet, Dedicated Line
LIMITrader	LMITrader Securities	Corporate	Internet
MarketPower	Chicago Board Brokerage	Treasury, Repos,	Proprietary Network
MuniAuction	MuniAuction, Inc.	Municipal	Internet
PARITY	Dalcomp-Thomson	Municipal	Proprietary Network
QV Trading	QV Trading Systems	Treasury, Municipal, Corporate	Internet, Dedicated Line
TradeWeb (1998)	TradeWeb, LLC	Treasury, Agency	Internet, Proprietary Network

Source: The Bond Market Association, 1998 and research conducted by others.

But in the long run, CBB will link to CBOT's Treasury futures and options. Currently, several other bond-trading systems are under development. For example, Bloomberg is developing its own multi-dealer system and plans to roll it out in 1999. State Street Corp. plans to launch Bond Connect, an electronic bond market, in 1999 as well. Bond Connect will be available through Bridge Telerate and it implements a call market mechanism that is developed by Net Exchange. In corporate and municipal bond markets, there has been a similar development. For example, BondNet, which started in 1995 and was recently acquired by the Bank of New York, offers customers anonymous trading of corporate bonds. MuniAuction is a recent startup specializing in municipal bonds and provides real-time auctions of new municipal bond issues.

Even though many believe electronic bond trading is the future, the success of an individual market relies on a lot of factors such as market liquidity and technology. InterVest, an electronic bond market launched in 1996, ran into problems because it was not able to generate much trading volume. In early

1998, Bloomberg terminated InterVest at Bloomberg's terminals. Currently, InterVest is battling with Bloomberg in court, accusing Bloomberg of having reneged on their agreement under pressure from bond dealers who were concerned that an electronic exchange would reduce the profitability of their fixed-income operations (The Bond Buyer, 1999). InterVest now is trying to develop an Internet-based trading system that can reach traders directly and does not rely on any proprietary technologies.

It will be interesting to see how multiple bond markets coexist and compete with each other in the future. Liquidity will be a key factor in determining the success of a market and is a huge factor in inter-market competition. Liquidity tends to increase with the number of traders in a market. If prices are "better" in more liquid markets, there should be a natural incentive for traders to converge on one market rather than split their trades across markets (O'Hara, 1994). Although some believe providing liquidity is the primary role of the market maker, liquidity cannot be viewed as an isolated issue. In fact, market liquidity relates closely with market efficiency and transparency. Obviously, a market with high operation and price efficiency and great transparency will attract more traders and thus enhance market liquidity.

16.4 Electronic Market Institution Design

An exchange market is a unique economic institution that matches buyers and sellers, and provides liquidity and a price discovery mechanism for the traded assets. Efficiency, transparency, and liquidity are the top priorities of the market. Traditionally, traders and software engineers usually design exchange markets. With the rapid advance of computer and communication technology, especially the Internet, the exchange market is increasingly becoming a digital marketplace with digital products and digital processes (Whinston et al., 1998). Technology and business will become more inseparable. In this section, we will discuss the impacts of technology on financial markets and alternative market institutions that might be adopted for bond markets.

Information Technology

Technology is dramatically changing the way financial securities are traded. Computer and communication technologies have provided unprecedented opportunities for innovations in all market processes, including information dissemination, order transmission, and matching and price discovery. Today, the Internet is revolutionizing the dynamics of financial markets. Investors have more access to financial markets than ever before in history. Retail investors can now easily access real-time market information, analytic tools, and electronic trading. At brokerage firms, online trading increases the efficiency of operations, which leads to lower commissions and increased volumes. The marketplace is becoming a more level field for all types of investors.

In organized exchanges, major changes are taking place. All exchanges now have automated systems that allow their members to electronically route orders to the exchange floor. Recently, the American Stock Exchange (AMEX) has permitted its members to use wireless communication devices to communicate with one another from different points on the trading floor (Wall Street & Technology, 1996). AMEX and the Chicago Board of Options Exchange (CBOE) have plans to offer hand-held trading terminals to their members. These are tremendous advances compared to traditional communication methods on the trading floor such as hand signals and telephones. In the long run, electronic trading and clearing systems may totally restructure the way financial markets operate. Traders can submit orders through their computer terminals without the necessity of maintaining a presence on the trading floor of the exchange. More and more exchanges will find it more efficient to close their trading floors and operate in the more efficient screen-based cyber-markets. Automated trading and execution systems will not only handle large trading volume and speed up the clearing process, but also introduce more efficient market matching and price discovery mechanisms that are impossible to perform by human auctioneers. Recently, many alternative trading systems have been developed. The Arizona Stock Exchange has implemented an automated call auction that brings traders together at the same time and allows orders to transact at a single price. The Pacific Exchange will adopt an automated trading system developed by OptiMark. The OptiMark matching system will match traders' satisfaction preferences over different prices and sizes to establish an execution price. Recently, several brokerage firms including E*Trade and AmeriTrade announced the intention to form the International Security Exchange, a fully electronic options marketplace with an auction market mechanism. In equity markets, the organized exchanges will soon realize that they cannot be a natural monopoly forever and have to operate and compete like any other business. In fixed-income markets, electronic markets will bring similar, revolutionary changes as well.

Auction and Dealer Markets

Auction and dealer markets are the two major types of financial markets. In auction markets, all outstanding orders are transacted at a single price via a centralized mechanism, while in dealer markets, orders are placed with individual dealers, who execute the orders at preset quoted prices. An auction market can either be a call market or a continuous market. In a call market, orders are accumulated over time and are executed at a particular point in time. In a continuous market, orders are being executed continuously and prices are formed over time. The opening of NYSE and Tokyo Stock Exchange are implemented as call markets while CATS (Computer Assisted Trading System) in Toronto, CAC (Cotation Assistee en Continu) in Paris, and NYSE (after the opening) are examples of continuous auction markets. Examples of dealer markets are NASDAQ and London Stock Exchange's SEAQ. In an auction market, public investors' orders can cross directly. But in a dealer market, all orders have to go through dealers. A dealer has an affirmative obligation to quote bid and ask prices at which he is willing to trade up to a specified size. Small orders in a dealer market can be electronically routed to a dealer and get executed. Large orders are normally executed through telephones. In a dealer market, traders always have to pay the bid-ask spread even if a matching order is available. In return, dealers provide services to the market by holding inventories and providing immediacy to the market when there are temporary imbalances.

Auction markets are generally more transparent than dealer markets (Pagano and Roell, 1996). In an auction market, more information can be made directly available to all market participants. It thereby enhances both pre-trade and post-trade transparency. Pre-trade transparency, i.e., the visibility of the best price an incoming order can be executed at, is better in an auction market. In electronic auction markets, market makers can view the entire limit order book and see exactly at what price an order would be executed. In contrast, the quotes in dealer markets only give a vague indication of the real transaction prices. Post-transparency, i.e., the visibility of recent trading history, tends to be lower in dealer markets. Technically, orders that have been executed by dealers in a distributed manner take longer to be reported to the exchange and to be published. Additionally, stock exchange authorities tend to grant long publication delays to large transactions (Pagano and Roell, 1996). Because dealers have less information about recent trading information, they are forced to set spreads that are wider on average than in auction markets (Pagano and Roell, 1992).

An Auction Market with the Presence of Dealers

In designing an electronic market institution for bond trading, we have to consider the current market structure and the goals we want to achieve in the new electronic market. The existing dealer-oriented system will continue to play an important role in the future electronic bond market. Without the presence of dealers, the market will not have enough liquidity to attract orders and eventually will fail. There are two basic options in designing an electronic market institution. We can design an electronic quotation system like the NASDAQ. Dealers have to quote bid and ask prices and investors can view current quotations on any securities. An alternative is an auction market with the presence of dealers. We opt for the latter. We discuss the major features for the proposed market.

Auction market. Orders from dealers and other non-dealer investors will be consolidated in the auction market. The market will employ an automated double auction mechanism that matches orders continuously and forms prices for the securities over time. The prices will reflect all the information that is available in the market and provide fair valuations of the securities. Automated order matching and execution will also reduce human errors and speed the clearing process. All limit orders are recorded in the electronic order book, which can be selectively revealed to dealers and public investors. By consolidating all the orders and the execution in one market, we expect enhanced market transparency by providing both pre-trade and post-trade information to public investors as well as dealers.

The role of dealers. Certified dealers in the market are obligated to provide liquidity to the market by placing limit buy or sell orders. Having limit orders trading with a liquidity trader in an equity market is desirable because transaction price changes due to the arrival of a liquidity trader are temporary and reversible (Grossman and Miller, 1988). In contrast, having a limit order execute against such price changes is undesirable since transaction price changes due to the arrival of an informed trader are irreversible. Differently from how it works in equity markets, public information plays a dominant role in bond price adjustment (Fleming and Remolona, 1996). Dealers will find it desirable to place limit orders and provide liquidity to the market. To compensate for the risks they take, dealers may be granted access to the limit order book. Dealers are not restricted to participate in certain markets. They should be free to participate in other competing markets or trade with their own customers in the OTC market.

Order handling. Amihud and Mendelson (1985) view the trading system as consisting of three related subsystems: (1) the order execution subsystem; (2) the clearing and settlement subsystem; and (3) the portfolio subsystem. Orders in the form of prices and order quantities, which serve as inputs to the order execution subsystem, are the outputs of the portfolio subsystem. An integration of these subsystems will soon become a reality in the electronic market. Based on market information, an individual investor's preference, and his portfolio positions, the portfolio system will suggest orders that the investor can trade. Basically, a trader can trade market orders, simple limit orders (e.g. buy/sell x shares at price y), or more complicated conditional orders such as bundle orders that reflect investors' portfolio objectives.

A market order submitted to the auction market will be executed immediately at the currently best bid or offer price. A limit order submitted to the market will be recorded in the electronic order book. Order execution rules for limit orders follow price and time priority. A buy (sell) order with higher (lower) price has a higher priority. When price is the same, priority is on a first-come first-served basis. While information on individual limit orders is not revealed to the general public, the market does report the best bid and ask prices and price and quantity information for the last executed orders.

We propose a bundle order trading mechanism for electronic bond trading. Parameters of a bundle order comprise bundle composition (b vector), limit price (v), and the number of bundles (N). For example, $\{b'=[2, 1, 1], v=\$400, N=1000\}$ represents an order to buy *1000* bundles at *$400* per unit, for a total of *2000* shares for bond 1 and *1000* shares for both bond 2 and 3. The limit price represents the buyer's valuation of the bundle. A positive price signals a willingness to pay while a negative price signals a willingness to sell. A bundle does not have to consist of pure buy or sell orders. It can have mixed buy and sell orders. A bundle order reflects a trader's complex trading strategy to optimize his portfolio performance. We believe bundle orders have many advantages. Trading using market orders requires that traders constantly monitor the market information and make real time trading decisions. An alternative is to use limit orders. However, most of the markets do not even allow limit orders condition on each other, which prohibits traders from submitting orders that capture their portfolio objective. By using a bundle order, an investor can summarize a complex trading strategy by a few orders without requiring further monitoring or communications with the exchange (Amihud and Mendelson, 1985).

The electronic bond market will implement a regular single asset auction mechanism as well as the bundle matching mechanism. Single bond orders will be routed and executed by the regular auction mechanism while bundle orders will be routed to the bundle auction mechanism. The bundle auction mechanism will activate only when there are bundle orders. The bundle matching mechanism will include bundle orders as well as all related single bond orders submitted for execution through the regular auction mechanism.

16.5 Demand for Bundles in Bond Markets

Depending on the investment objective, there are different bond portfolio management strategies. In this section, we present cases to show that in many real world situations investors have to acquire a bundle or a portfolio of bonds in order to fulfill a particular investment objective. The complementarity between the selected bonds makes the portfolio possess some special qualities that are desirable to investors.

Immunization

Many firms use a fixed-income portfolio to pay for a future cash outflow obligation. We learn from bond pricing theory (Luenberger, 1998) that the price change (dP) of a bond relates to its duration (D) when the interest rate (λ) changes:

$$\frac{dP}{d\lambda} = -D \cdot P$$

Duration of a bond is a weighted average of the times that future cash flows are made. The longer the duration, the larger the impact of interest rate changes. The immunization procedure in bond portfolio management is to structure a bond portfolio in a way to protect the portfolio value against interest rate changes. It is one of the most widely used bond portfolio management techniques employed by many pension funds, insurance companies, and other institutional investors.

Let us look at an example. Suppose a company has one cash outflow obligation of $1 million in five years. One solution is to purchase a set of zero-coupon bonds that have maturities and face values exactly matching the cash outflow. But many times, a perfect matching is impossible. The company may also want to look at non-Treasury bonds that have a higher yield. After selecting the fixed-income securities, the manager has to make sure the value of the investment equals the present value of the cash obligation. However, if the selected bond or bond portfolio has a duration other than five years, the value of the investment will be quite variable depending on the interest rate movement. The company will thus be exposed to high risks to meet its cash payment obligation. Immunization solves the problem by matching the duration of the promised cash outflow and the investment portfolio. The present value of the portfolio and the obligation payment will respond almost identically to the interest rate change. Suppose the company decides to invest in two bonds. Let (x_1, x_2) be the number of units of bond 1 and 2, respectively. Let (v_1, v_2) be the current price, and ($D1$, $D2$) be the duration for the two bonds. PV denotes the present value of the future cash outflow obligation. Then the number of units of the two bonds (x_1, x_2) can be calculated using the following formulas:

$$v_1 x_1 + v_2 x_2 = PV$$

$$\frac{v_1 x_1 D_1 + v_2 x_2 D_2}{PV} = D$$

The first equation means the present value of the portfolio equals the present value of the future cash obligation. The second equation states that the duration of the bond portfolio should equal that of the obligation. We can then calculate the exact units of the two bonds that form the portfolio. In its simplest form, immunization is based on the calculation of Macaulay duration, which assumes horizontal yield curve with parallel shifts. In reality, the simple immunization model has to be extended to a term structure framework. More complex approaches for bond portfolio immunization such as quasi-modified duration (Luenberger, 1998) and key-rate duration (Ho, 1992) can be applied.

Another problem with the use of immunization is the effect of time and interest rate changes. After an initial interest rate change or the simple passage of time, the durations of the portfolio and the cash outflow obligation change at different rates. The duration of the bond portfolio will not match that of the cash obligation. Thus, the portfolio will not be immunized against new interest rate changes. A portfolio manager is required to rebalance or re-immunize the portfolio from time to time. Re-immunization follows the same idea as immunization. It, again, requires the manager to trade a bundle of bonds in order to form the new immunized portfolio.

Cash Flow Matching

The immunization strategy described above is used to immunize a portfolio created for a single liability in the future against adverse interest rate movements. However, it is more common to have multiple future liabilities, e.g., the liability structure of pension funds and life insurance annuities. The approach taken by those companies is called cash flow matching. The investment objective is to construct a fixed-income portfolio that can be used to fund a schedule of liabilities from the portfolio return and asset value, with the portfolio's value diminishing to zero after payment of the last liability.

Let us represent the obligation as a stream $s' = (s_1, s_2, \ldots s_n)$, starting one period from now. If there are m bonds, we denote c_{ij} as the cash flow at time i generated by bond j. The $C_{n \times m}$ is the cash flow matrix for the m bonds in n periods. The vector v denotes the prices of the m bonds. The vector $x' = (x_1, x_2, \ldots, x_m)$ represents the amount of each bond to be acquired in the portfolio. The cash matching problem can be formulated as follows:

$$\min vx$$

Subject to:

$$Cx \geq s$$

$$x \geq 0$$

The objective function is to minimize the total cost of the portfolio, which is equal to the sum of the bonds prices times the amount purchased. The first set of constraints is the cash matching constraints, i.e. the total cash generated in period i from all m bonds must be at least equal to the obligation in period i. The last constraint means no short sales. The solution of the above problem will determine the value of vector x, which represents the security weights for the bond portfolio.

Swap

Bond swapping is an active bond management strategy, simultaneously selling one bond and buying another. Many institutional investors use bond swaps to maximize the yield. There are different swap strategies, one of which is known as "riding the yield curve". It is often used by fund managers who need to maintain a large pool of short-term bonds for liquidity purposes and want to increase the yield. For example, some money market funds invest solely in Treasury bills, which are safer than commercial paper but yield less. To get yields competitive with those investing in commercial paper, the fund managers will ride the yield curve by using bond swaps.

Suppose a fund manager only wants to invest in Treasury bills with a maturity of six months or less. Assume the current yield for the 6-month T-bills is 8.5%. Three months later the yield on these T-bills has fallen to 8.1%, primarily due to the movement along the yield curve. If the fund manager sells his 6-month T-bills after holding them for three months, he will realize a yield of about 8.7%, higher than the yield of 8.5% if he holds the 6-month T-bill to maturity. According to Stigum and Fabozzi (1987), large institutional investors who ride the yield curve normally swap T-bills purchased for newly issued securities every two weeks. This constant swapping keeps fund managers long the on-the-run Treasury issues, which are the most liquid in the bond market.

Portfolio Support System for Bond Trading

As we discussed earlier, the portfolio subsystem is an important component of the integrated fixed-income trading system. Based on current market information and the investor's portfolio positions, the portfolio support system computes the optimal portfolio that satisfies the investor's investment objective. The portfolio system can range from relatively simple spreadsheet models, to more advanced in-house applications and large commercial software packages such as the Barra Cosmos System and Capital Management Sciences' BondEdge. The analytic software tools should contain a large database of bond securities that are traded in the marketplace and be able to access live data feeds from the market. The analytical results of the portfolio support systems are simply the portfolio composition vector $(x_1,..., x_m)$, which represents the quantity of each of the m securities, and the reservation value of the portfolio. Using bundle trading, a trader can submit an order that captures complex portfolio objectives.

16.6 Market Matching Mechanism

We have designed an automated bundle matching mechanism in response to the needs of portfolio/bundle trading in the bond market. We introduce a market mechanism that will facilitate financial engineering by investors. We have witnessed that financial innovation has brought about revolutionary changes in our financial system in the past two decades. Financial engineering designs and develops innovative financial instruments to meet the specific financial problems of the customers. Generally, those highly customized financial products are sold through OTC markets and customers have to pay high commissions to the financial institutions that design these products. Examples of these innovative products include swaps and synthetic bonds. Instead of relying solely on the financial institutions to develop customized products, investors and fund managers can construct synthetic securities that meet their specific corporate or personal financial needs by using analytic tools. The bundle market facilitates such a process.

The bundle matching algorithm will match orders in bundles and provide a price discovery mechanism for bundles as well as the securities that form the bundle. The mechanism, however, allows but does not require traders to submit bundle orders. It can match single security orders as well. The following is the specification of the matching mechanism operated in a continuous market:

Problem **M**

$$\max vy \qquad \qquad (1)$$

Subject to:

$$By \leq 0 \qquad \qquad (2)$$
$$1 \cdot y \leq 1 \qquad \qquad (3)$$
$$y \geq 0 \qquad \qquad (4)$$

The vector v denotes the limit price for each bundle submitted by a trader. The vector y represents the proportion of the matched trade, and each element of y should be nonnegative (constraint (4)). The matrix $B = [b_1, b_2, \ldots, b_n]$ contains n column vectors. Each vector represents the composition of a particular bundle submitted for trade. For example, suppose we have two securities to trade. Then, $b_j' = [2, 1]$ implies that the bundle j contains 2 units of security 1, and one unit of security 2. A positive number in the bundle vector means buy and a negative number means sell. A bundle $b_j' = [-1, 1]$ implies a swap – selling security 1 and buying security 2. Constraint (2) means that for a bundle to be matched, each buy order in the bundle should be matched with a sell order of the same asset from another bundle or bundles. Constraint (3) standardizes the matched trade to be a number less or equal to 1.

The price discovery process is automated and the price for each asset is calculated by solving the dual of *Problem M*. The prices are shadow prices for the assets that make up the bundles. The transaction price of a matched bundle trade is calculated as follows:

$$t_j = \sum_{i=1}^{m} b_{ij} p_i \qquad (5)$$

where p_i is the dual price for asset i $(i=1, ..., m)$, and b_{ij} represents bundle j's composition.

Proposition 1: The transaction price t_j for the matched bundle j is at least as good as the submitted limit price v_j, i.e. $v_j \geq t_j$.

For proofs, see Fan et al. (1998b).

According to Proposition 1, when a trader submits a buy order, he expects to pay at most his limit price. For a sell order, he can expect the transaction price to be equal to or higher than his ask price.

Investors or fund managers wanting to acquire a bundle of securities as we discussed in the last section have the following order submission decision to make:

1. Using market orders or limit orders?
2. If limit orders are to be used, will investors choose single security limit orders or bundle limit orders? In an example of two securities, single security limit orders will be $\{x_1, v_1\}$ and $\{x_2, v_2\}$, while a bundle order will be $\{b, v, N\} = \{\{x_1, x_2\}, v, 1\}$.

Trading with market or limit orders is an important decision each investor has to face. Harris and Hasbrouck (1996) conducted a study on market vs. limit orders based on a sample of NYSE SuperDOT orders. Their studies show that limit orders placed at or better than the prevailing quote perform better than market orders, even after imputing a penalty for unexecuted orders and after taking into account market order price improvement. Specifically, in a $1/8 bid-ask market, at-the-quote limit orders achieve better performance than market orders while in a $1/4 bid-ask market, limit orders that better the quote by $1/8 perform well. In the case of acquiring a portfolio, using market orders may incur difficulties in controlling the cost of the portfolio if some securities are being traded at a high price temporarily. Monitoring the price movement of each security could also be costly to the investor or manager. In some cases, when the securities are not very liquid and there exists a large bid-ask spread, the market actually relies on the limit orders to discover the price for the underlying security. We assume a certain proportion of traders choose to trade using limit orders. Then, the question is whether a bundle trading strategy is better.

Let us define traders' utility function for selecting different trading strategies as

$$E(U) = \Delta \cdot \rho, \quad \rho \in [0,1] \tag{6}$$

where Δ is the gain from trading or the difference between reservation and the transaction price, and ρ is the probability that the order will be filled.

Proposition 2: Trading in limit bundle orders is a dominant strategy over trading in single security limit orders if an investor's trading utility function is defined as equation (6).

For proofs, see Fan et al. (1998b).

According to Proposition 2, if a trader desires a portfolio or bundle of bonds, it is advantageous to submit a bundle order rather than submitting multiple single asset limit orders. If bond prices move such that all single asset orders can be executed, the bundle order will certainly be executed. But when a bundle order can be executed, some individual orders could remain unexecuted. Therefore, a trader will be better off using the bundle trading mechanism if he wants to acquire a balanced portfolio. In addition, traders can submit fewer orders by using bundle orders.

We have to discuss the complexity of bundle trading mechanism for bond trading. Let us look at the immunization example. Assume the individual bond prices will fluctuate after the limit order has been submitted. The executed market prices (p_i) for the bonds that form the portfolio will be different from the limit prices (v_i). Theoretically, the shares of different bonds in the portfolio are functions of the bond prices. However, if there are no major new announcements such as changes in employment data or the consumer price index that will cause big price volatility when orders are placed, intra-day bond price volatility is largely caused by the temporary imbalance of the bid and ask orders. Therefore, price movements can be viewed as temporary and reversible. In this case, it is appropriate for us to use v_i as the estimate of the real market price. One strategy to determine v_i is to simply use the at-the-quote price, i.e., the current bid (ask) price for a buy (sell) order.

16.7 Web-Based Platform

From a computing point of view, an electronic market is a large-scale distributed computing system. For new electronic markets to function, we have to have a secure, scalable computing environment where people from virtually anywhere can conduct trading interactively and dynamically. We have implemented an experimental financial bundle trading system executing on IBM RS6000 workstations (Fan et al., 1998a, 1999). The system is based on distributed object technology and is highly scalable. We implemented the user trading interface application as a Java Applet, which supports dynamic communication between traders and the market. Traders can access the system from anywhere at anytime. The market application manages and coordinates the trading activities across heterogeneous computing platforms. It contains the following services or components: a Web server, a naming and directory server, a limit order book, an order routing and notification system, an automated matching program, and a database server. The main advantages of this architecture are scalability and transparency. As the number of users increases, more computers can be added to the system. Different services as represented by different objects can be distributed among different computers, balancing the workload and increasing the system performance. The distributed object architecture ensures that application programs do not have to change when the scale of the system increases, providing location and access transparency throughout the system. The trading application on the client side does not have to know exactly on which machine the limit order table is located. The naming and directory service will present a coherent marketplace to traders and hide the internal configuration of the system. Components located on different computers can call the methods from other objects consistently.

In our opinion, the computing platform for the future electronic market shall be based on the convergence of the Internet and distributed object technologies, including the WWW, Java, and CORBA. The next generation electronic market should be accessible to investors from anywhere at any time. The adoption of proprietary platforms and applications are inappropriate because it could prohibit people from accessing the market for technology reasons. The Web is the ideal platform for our electronic markets. It provides the ability to display multimedia documents with hypertext links, making itself the universal interface for different applications at different computer platforms. Earlier Web-based applications predominantly use a server centric model based heavily on CGI scripts, which greatly limits system performance. For example, communications between clients and Web server cannot be interactive. Traders have to continuously reload the Web page in order to get updates from the server, which is very cumbersome and error-prone. In contrast, Web-based applications developed in Java/CORBA are well suited for interactive and dynamic applications of electronic markets. First, Java source code can be compiled into a platform-independent format called byte code, which can run in a Java run time environment on any system. This guarantees that the bond trading applications can be deployed without additional effort in different platforms. Secondly, Java applets can be seamlessly integrated in a Web page. Traders can interact with the market maker using Java applets and Web browser universally. Thirdly, Java/CORBA provides a distributed computing framework that allows agents to interact with the market dynamically and interactively. Price and other market information can be pushed to the traders' screen display in real-time. Further, portfolio management and market analytic tools for managing fixed-income investment and trading, such as immunization and cash flow management, can be developed using Java and dynamically linked with trading applications on the Web. Traders can access these tools and get real-time decision support for trading.

Figure 1. FBTS Architecture

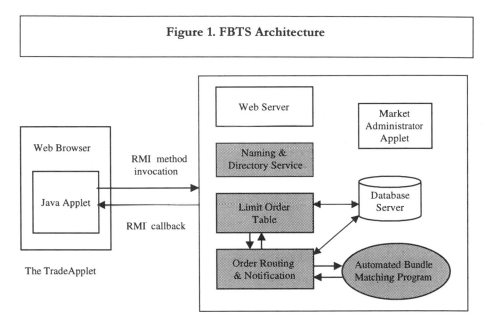

The Exchange

Two initial concerns of Web/Java technology, i.e., security and speed, are quickly being resolved as the technology advances. With the wide adoption of cryptographic technologies and secure communication and transaction protocols, Web-based commerce has been proved to be fairly secure. Java is the technology that has been perceived with problems in speed and reliability. However, the technology has made tremendous advances since its first release. Today, financial institutions such as the Arizona Stock Exchange, EASDAQ, and Union Bank of Switzerland are adopting Java technology. As it becomes more mature, a growing number of financial institutions and other mission critical operations will experiment with this technology because of its tremendous functionality for Web-based applications. In our experimental financial market, we use the Java technology to develop user interfaces that efficiently link traders with the market. But the market matching algorithm is still—for performance reasons—implemented using C++. In fact, strong interoperability with other languages is one of the major strengths of Web/Java technology.

16.8 Conclusion

We have discussed the present market structure and the advances in electronic trading for fixed-income securities. Computer and information technology, especially the Internet, will transform the overall bond market in the next few years. Computerized trading and clearing, and electronic dissemination of market information will make the market more efficient and transparent. We have proposed an auction market mechanism with the presence of dealers, combining the advantages of both an auction market and a dealer market. The market aggregates orders in a single marketplace and helps to enhance both pre-trade and post-trade market transparency. It also implements an automated bundle trading mechanism that can match bundle orders. The design of such a market mechanism is motivated by the demands of bundles or synthetic securities in the bond markets. Investors can submit bundle orders that capture a complex trading strategy without constantly monitoring the market. For future research, we will conduct a series experimental analysis based on the market institution design and investigate the overall market performance as well as traders' behavior in the marketplace.

References

1. Amihud, Y. and H. Mendelson. 1985. An integrated computerized trading system. In *Market Making and the Changing Structure of the Securities Industry.* Amihud, Y., T. Ho, and Schwartz (Eds.). Lexington Books, Lexington, MA.
2. Harris, L. and J. Hasbrouck. 1996. Market vs. limit orders: the SuperDOT evidence on order submission strategy. *Journal of Financial and Quantitative Analysis*, 31(2), 213-231.
3. Luenberger, D. 1998. *Investment Science*. Oxford University Press.
4. Fabozzi, F. and F. Modigliani. 1996. *Capital Markets: Institutions and Instruments*. Second Edition. Prentice Hall.
5. Fan, M., J. Stallaert and A. B. Whinston. 1998a. Creating electronic markets. *Dr. Dobb's Journal*, 291, 52-57.

6. Fan, M., J. Stallaert and A. B. Whinston. 1998b. Mechanism and process design for supply chain agent organization based on bundle markets. Working paper, Center for Research in Electronic Commerce, the University of Texas at Austin.

7. Fan, M., J. Stallaert and A. B. Whinston. 1999. Implementing a financial market using Java and web-based distributed computing. *IEEE Computer*, 32(4), 64-70.

8. Fleming, M. and E. Remolona. 1996. Price formation and liquidity in the U.S. Treasuries market: evidence from intra-day patterns around announcements. Federal Reserve Bank of New York Research Paper #9633.

9. Grossman, S. and M. Miller. 1988. Liquidity and market structure. *Journal of Finance* , 43, 617-633.

10. Ho, T. 1992. Key rate durations: measures of interest rate risks. *Journal of Fixed Income* , 2(2), 29-44.

11. O'Hara, M. 1995. *Market Microstructure Theory*. Blackwell Business.

12. Pagano, M. and A. Roell. 1992. Auction and dealership markets: what is the difference? *European Economic Review* , 36, 613-623.

13. Pagano, M. and A. Roell. 1996. Transparency and liquidity: a comparison of auction and dealer markets with informed trading. *Journal of Finance* , 51(2), 579-611.

14. Pensions and Investments. 1998. Electronics move bond side out of the shadows. June.

15. SEC 1998a. *Testimony of Chairman Arthur Levitt before the Congress Concerning Transparency in the United States Debt Market and Mutual Fund Fees and Expenses.*

16. SEC 1998b. *Report to the Congress: the Impact of Recent Technological Advances on the Securities Markets.*

17. Stigum, M. and F. Fabozzi. 1987. *The Dow Jones-Irwin Guide to Bond and Money Market Investments*. Dow Jones-Irwin.

18. The Bond Buyer. 1999. InterVest to subpoena brokerages. Nearly 20 targeted. March 3.

19. The Bond Market Association. 1997a. *Special Survey on the Future of Electronic Bond Trading Systems.*

20. The Bond Market Association. 1998a. *Bond Market Statistics.*

21. The Bond Market Association. 1998b. *The 1998 Review of Electronic Transaction System in the U.S. Fixed Income Securities Markets.*

22. Wall Street & Technology. 1996. Traders gain split-second advantage by going wireless. August.

23. Wall Street & Technology. 1997. Bond market waits for electronic trading champ. March.

24. Whinston, A. B., D. Stahl, and S. Choi. 1988. *The Economics of Electronic Commerce*. Macmillan Technical Publishing. Indianapolis, IN.

Chapter 17

Staffing Challenges in Financial Services

Richard C. Larson
Massachusetts Institute of Technology
Edieal J. Pinker
University of Rochester

17.1 Introduction

The people of a financial services firm comprise its most important asset. A customer's impression of the firm is influenced greatly by every interchange she/he has with a professional employed by the firm. These professionals create the perceptual realities of the firm to its customers. In more traditional retailing this has been recognized and acted upon by such industry leaders as Wal-Mart and Home Depot. But that which is an asset can also be a liability. By this we mean that professional staff members comprise a labor pool that - with paid benefits - may be the largest single cost category of the firm. So, managers of financial services firms are faced with the dual responsibilities of having to hire, train and keep very talented and motivated professionals and yet do this in a way that is cost conscience. The cost part of the equation can become quite complicated. Each worker comes with a unique skill set but can be trained to enlarge that skill set - usually at a cost of training and promotion. Customers of financial services firms have widely differing needs and expectations; and can show up requiring service at quite unpredictable times.

Employing some combination of the following strategies can control costs:

1. *Demand Reduction.* Off-loading customers to technology, away from those professionals who serve customers directly. Examples: ATM's, trading securities over the Internet; at home banking via computer.

2. *Minimization of Head Count.* By this we mean to do the best job possible in scheduling workers to meet hour of day and day of week and season of year demand variations so as to minimize excess personnel that may be present (and paid) at any given time.

3. *Be Efficient in use of Specialists.* Not unlike physicians, financial services professionals are available in a wide variety of skill categories, ranging from generalists (analogous to "general practitioners") to highly trained and highly paid specialists (analogous to brain surgeons). To keep costs under control, everything else being equal, one wants to use specialists only when one has to. Or, stated another way, apply only that skill level to a customer that the customer really needs. A brain surgeon should not perform routine medical exams any more than a merger and acquisition specialist should accept bank deposits at a teller window.

In this chapter we discuss some of the ways we have found to be useful in workforce management in financial services. Our experience is not limited to financial services, as one or both of us have also had experiences in a variety of other settings as well, including: the United States Postal Services (having over 700,000 professionals), logistics firms, police departments, airlines, and movie theaters.

17.2 Queues

In many cases the setting for workers in financial services is within a "queueing context." A queue is a waiting line, or - in Canada - a lineup. In financial services, as we shall discuss, queues can occur in brick and mortar facilities, on the phone, even over the Internet. In Figure 1 we depict a simple queueing system that might represent, for example, banking customers seeking service from a floor-located CSR (Customer Service Representative). Customers seeking service arrive at the queueing system (entering from the left, in the diagram). Usually but not always their arrival times and service requirements are uncertain ("probabilistic") quantities. If the CSR is busy handling another customer, the newly arrived customer joins the queue or line, usually at the back of the line. As one customer completes his service with the CSR, he leaves and the next waiting customer enters service with the CSR. Queues can fluctuate greatly in size over the course of the day due to uncertainties in arrival times and service times of customers and due to lack of proper scheduling of servers (CSR's in this instance). As we shall see, the balancing of service quality with personnel cost is a delicate act. A more complete introduction to queues and queueing theory is found in [15].

Financial services have traditionally cared a great deal about service quality as measured by queue delay. In the early 1990's Chemical Bank in New York offered a "547" program, meaning that the branch manager would give to any customer reporting that he had spent seven or more minutes waiting in a teller queue the following three things: a smile, a handshake and a crisp five dollar bill. The customer reporting was on the honor system. Our understanding is that the number of payouts per month per branch was usually a very small number, countable on the fingers of one hand. But the marketing statement demonstrated clearly to Chemical's customers that the bank cared about its customers and valued their time. Bank America in California offered a similar program, "545," meaning a delay limit equal to five minutes, not seven.

Figure 1: A Simple Queueing System

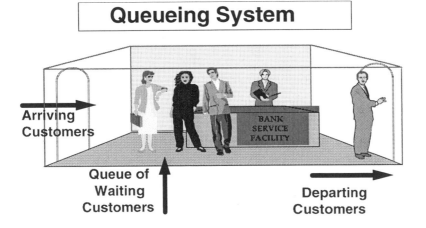

The Psychology of Queueing

Queueing is more than the mathematics of customer flows. It has a lot to do with perceptions and experiences - experiences transcending the ticking of a wristwatch. Let's start in a very familiar place: the lobby of a retail bank. We need to focus on both the customer and on the bank's staff. The customer has one or more transactions to carry out, we assume with a real person and not an ATM. Let's assume it's with a bank teller. Now things become complex. Multiple parallel queueing lines characterized Banks through the 1950's and '60's. The customer selected one and waited until "his" teller was available to serve him. The scene is still available today via videos of pre-1960's films of U.S. banks - with their granite facades and detailed iron grating about each teller window. Thanks to pioneering efforts by Chemical Bank (now merged with Chase) and by the original Chase Bank (and others as well), the multiple parallel lines configuration was replaced by the mid-1980's with the single serpentine line. This latter line configuration guarantees first come first served queueing to all customers, thereby assuring "social justice in queues." Customers generally prefer this type social justice. But this is not so simple. Consider supermarkets: customers generally do not mind if those with "12 items or less" join a special express service line, thereby violating first come first served. So a socially just queue is not always one that assures first come first served service. The reason is found in the field of "psychology of queueing." One of the findings of that field is the following:

A customer's tolerance for wait in queue is proportional to the complexity or quantity of service anticipated by that customer.

In a supermarket a customer with a week's worth of groceries overflowing a shopping cart expects to wait in line longer than someone stopping by to pick up a quart of milk does. In an airport a passenger tolerates a multi-hour delay in making a connection to an overseas flight while even a fraction of that wait for a New York to Washington Shuttle would not be tolerated. This principal in banking has yet to be moved on in any major way. Those with a simple one-check deposit are lumped together in the serpentine queue with businesspersons that are depositing yesterday's store revenues into twelve different accounts. This makes the simple one-transaction customer angry, frustrated and looking for options. Of course, the bank hopes that the option taken by the customer is his movement to an ATM, not to a competing bank -- but one can never be sure.

In fact, in typical U.S. banking today the situation is even worse than neglecting this mixing of high service time and low service time customers. With "preferred customers" now in demand, banks will routinely set up special queue channels for those with preferred accounts (usually defined to be customers whose total linked assets in accounts exceeds some threshold, such as $25,000). This policy has been commonplace in Latin America for many years but only recently has it become ubiquitous in the U.S. The policy is similar to that of airlines in airports, which now regularly offer special priority queue channels for first class and business class passengers. But "non-priority" bank customers do not yet perceive the complete analogy. In airlines the first class and business class customers pay more for their seats, so perhaps they deserve better treatment. This is not so apparent in a teller line when some "preferred" "Johnny-Come-Lately" walks in front of 20 or so Jane and John Doe's standing in the regular line to get service before them. Our belief is that some very focused research must be done quickly on this issue before banks start loosing customers to banks that do not have this policy. Banks might like to remember that even the most affluent preferred customer started life as a John or Jane Doe, not eligible for the preferred line. And customer loyalty plus inertia often keep a customer at the same bank until one or more bad service encounters creates the energy within the customer to switch. In a commodity business bad service encounters can cause brand switching usually meaning "lost for life" to the original service provider. That is why all aspects of the service encounter are so important.

We have just touched briefly on some aspects of the psychology of queueing. More can be found in references, such as [11], [12] and [13]. You may wonder what that has to do with workforce management in financial institutions. Well, to a large extent the way a customer feels in a queue is dependent on two things: the duration of the wait and the "total environment" around her. The duration of the wait depends critically on the physics of queueing, which is driven primarily by the staffing level at the service facility. More tellers mean shorter waits; fewer tellers mean longer waits. But more tellers also mean higher costs, so what to do to keep customers happy and yet cap the labor expense? Think of what Disney does in its theme parks: it surrounds its queue lines with entertainment and other diversions. The pivotal research finding in this area dates to the mid-1950's, in New York City. According to legend of operations researchers (and Professor Russell Ackoff in particular), complaints started to soar at that time as more and more people found themselves in high-rise buildings (hotels, office or apartment buildings), waiting, waiting, waiting for elevators. A consultant was hired to examine the problem. A "left brain approach" might have led to the "finding" that the building had been designed with too few elevators, leading to two options: dynamite the building and start over with additional elevator shafts, or simply tell people that they will have to endure the waits. But a right brain approach prevailed: the consultant stated that the problem was not the duration of the elevator delays; the problem was the number of complaints about the delays. The challenge was to reduce the number of complaints; not necessarily the durations of the delays themselves. The ingenious solution was to place floor-to-ceiling mirrors next to each elevator door. People waiting for the elevator found that they could comb their hair, adjust their tie, fix their makeup, and sometimes even coyly flirt through the mirror with someone standing next to them. The complaints about delay plummeted! Problem solved. *Moral: It's not the duration of the delay that matters; it's what you experience while you are waiting that matters.*

What can a financial services firm do to exploit this finding? For when exploited intelligently, one gets happy customers with lower labor costs. That is, customers are willing to trade longer queue delays for better queue experiences. In a study we did in 1990 at Bank of Boston (now BankBoston) we studied bank teller lines for three weeks, each week the line operating in a different mode. The three treatments were:

1. Status quo ("control")
2. "Silent Radio"
3. Digital queue wait advisory

Treatment 1 is self-explanatory. Treatment 2 involved the placement of a "Times Square" type scrolling alphanumeric readout with live news, sports, weather and even advertisements for bank services. A private vendor provided the service with the oxymoronic name, "Silent Radio." The name made sense: the content was not unlike one would get from a (sound) radio, but it was seen in scrolling letters running across a large screen - silently. Everyone standing in the teller line could easily see the readout of Silent Radio, if they choose to look at it; but its silent feature also assured no disruption to those who were not interested. Treatment 3 used a new technology to estimate the line wait if you were to enter now. At the queue entrance, on a poll attached to one of the queue stanchions marking the wait lane, the readout would say: "Current Wait = 8 minutes" (or some other value). This (expensive) device would estimate the value of estimated wait using electric eye "customer counters" at the queue lane entrance and exit, plus knowledge of the average service time for the tellers. The results of the study are published in *Sloan Management Review* [10]. Here, the main finding is that the customers loved the Silent Radio innovation, so much so that several regular customers complained to the bank manager the Monday following the removal of the display. The bank followed up by purchasing or leasing several of these systems for implementation not only at teller lines but also in front of busy congested ATM's as well. The queue wait estimation device was less well received. Knowledge of an estimate of the delay focused everyone's attention on just that -- the duration of the wait. Examination of videotapes of the line during this period showed a large number of customers repeatedly looking at their wristwatches, trying to play the game of "Beat the Clock." What one wants to do when employing principals of psychology of queueing is to get the customer's mind off the duration of the wait, onto something else more pleasant. The digital readout device did just the opposite.

In financial services there are myriad ways imaginative managers can exploit the principals of the psychology of queueing. In the 1980's the Savings Bank of New York employed not fancy technology but rather live piano recitals each day during the lunch hour. Visiting the bank was so appealing that - unbeknownst to the branch manager - an enterprising entrepreneur once sold tickets to sidewalk passersby just to get into the bank lobby! The bank had made something unpleasant - waiting in line for the teller -- into something not only pleasant but also apparently highly valued. This can be a double win for a bank - as part of the queue line diversion can be advertising for additional bank products and services - perhaps leading to cross selling. We helped a large bank in Toronto accomplish this goal - showing an eight minute looped videotape to its in-line customers. The psychology of queueing extends beyond the physical lobby or office of a financial institution: it extends to phone waits (using a combination of entertainment, news and advertising) and even Internet waits. But this field is exploding so rapidly that little systematic research is done and many of the successes are passed by 'word of mouth." Let's all keep our ears tuned....

So, assume now that we have utilized the concepts of psychology of queueing to create happy customers in the presence of tolerable queues. That policy assures maximum utilization of expensive human tellers and reduces the number of FTE's (Full Time Equivalent employees) as much as possible. How do we assure that the teller deployments are as efficient as possible? Now we bring in applied mathematics, using the physics of mathematical queueing theory and also the mathematics of personnel scheduling.

The Way in Which Customers Arrive: The Poisson Process

Let's start with principal number 1. With few exceptions, the way in which customers appear seeking transactions from a financial services firm is unscheduled and in most ways unpredictable. Customers going to a bank, a stockbroker, a call center, or an Internet web site usually do not schedule their arrival times as do patients going for a routine doctor's visit. This unscheduled customer arrival process has over the years been studied extensively. Usually one finds that the so-called "Poisson Process" is the probabilistic process that best describes the arrival patterns of customers. The Poisson Process needs only one numerically estimated parameter to fully describe it: the average rate at which customers arrive to the service facility. In Figure 2 we display the Poisson Probability Law for a Poisson Customer arrival process having average customer arrival rate equal to 32 customers per hour. In the figure we show the probabilities that any given number of customers will appear in any specified 15-minute window. Since 32 customers appear (on average) in one hour, we may expect an average of 8 customers appearing within any 15-minute window. But Figure 2 shows that the probability that exactly 8 customers appear in the 15 minute window is only about 14%. If one sums the appropriate probabilities one finds that there is about a one in five chance that the number of customers appearing will be 5 or fewer and also about a one in five chance that the number of customers appearing will be 11 or greater. So, simply by what we might call "nature's coin flips," the next 15 minutes of our operation may be light workload (5 or fewer customers) or heavy workload (11 or more customers). This natural variation in the number of arriving customers causes system managers headaches and confusion. But we must manage around these types of uncertainties - uncertainties almost guaranteed to be associated with unscheduled customer arrivals.

Important Properties of Multi-Server Queues

Mathematical queueing theory applied to the type of situation just described also yields the following findings:

- In scheduling personnel to serve the randomly (Poisson) arriving customers, one must deliberately schedule *server idleness* into the system.
- Creating larger server pools serving larger numbers of customers can reduce the percentage of time that a server is idle.

In our own professional practice we have seen alleged consultants measuring server capacity and then using the following reasoning. *"We have determined that the average time for a server to serve one customer is two minutes. Thus, for this call center facing a demand of 90 calls per hour, we need precisely three servers. This is justified because each server can handle one customer every two minutes, so she can handle 30 customers per hour. In that way, three servers are required to handle 90 customers per hour."*

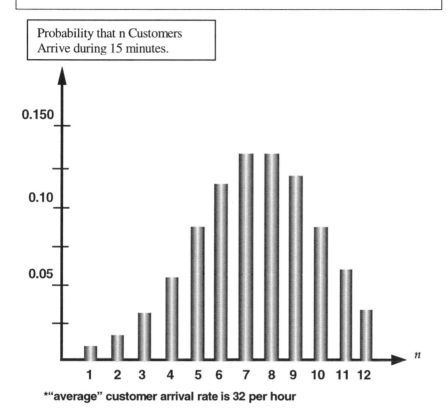

Figure 2: Poisson Probability Law

Probability that n Customers Arrive during 15 minutes.

*"average" customer arrival rate is 32 per hour

The logic just quoted is wrong. If the service facility is staffed in that manner, queueing delays will become exceedingly large, so large that a significant fraction of callers will abandon their calls in frustration. It is likely that the call center just described will require four or perhaps even five servers in order to keep average queueing delays below some target level, thereby assuring quality service to the customers. If say four servers are staffing the call center during the period just described, then there would be an average idleness for each server of $(120 - 90)/120 = .25 = 25\%$. That is, 25 percent of the time each server would not be serving customers. But that is the price one has to pay if service quality (as measured by average queue delay) is to be maintained.

The second feature of multi-server queues stated above says that if two identical call centers could be merged, thereby creating one larger center having a demand rate of 180 calls per hour, then the server idleness fraction can often be reduced. If we worked the numbers, perhaps four servers would be required in each of the centers if they continued to operate independently, but the same high level of service could be obtained by having only seven servers in the merged call center. The savings of one server out of eight represents a 12.5% reduction in personnel costs. This economy of scale in multi-server queueing systems is the reason why many financial services firms and other firms route all their calls nationally into one large call center. Such an aggregation of customer demand minimizes labor costs subject to a service quality constraint. Similar logic applies to merged bank branches, in which customers of both near-by branch offices would be vectored into one merged branch, now staffed with more personnel than before in one facility but with fewer personnel than had been deployed before in the two separate facilities.

17.3 Scheduling Servers

The Poisson nature of customer arrivals is good in one sense: over time, by collecting data, we can estimate to a remarkable level of accuracy the average customer arrival rate, by office or branch, hour of day, day of week, season of the year. This resulting set of estimated Poisson arrival rates gives us all we need to schedule servers efficiently and effectively. We illustrate this using a new technology that has recently been implemented at Chase Bank (in New York City and in nearby communities in New Jersey). The new technology is based on a research result that one of us (Larson) found about ten years ago. The result is called the "Queue Inference Engine," or simply the "QIE." (See Refs. [9], [14])

The QIE estimates the lengths of queues and delays in queue over the course of the day with no electronic eyes, no queue stanchions, no television cameras, in fact with virtually no hardware monitoring devices. By estimating queue performance the branch manager can monitor service quality (as represented by queue delays and queue lengths) to assure herself that servers are being scheduled appropriately to meet the desired service standard. The QIE uses as input data only the data describing start and stop times of every customer served. Imagine an ATM.[1] A customer places her ATM card into the machine at 2:12:34 PM, meaning 12 minutes and 34 seconds after 2:00 PM. The customer finishes the transaction and the card is ejected at 2:14:04 PM. The entire ATM transaction took 90 seconds. Suppose that the service start and stop times are saved on the

---

[1] While we are focusing on workforce management, ATM's play a role in that process - as ATM's in some ways provide substitutes for personnel, especially for simple banking transactions. For more on optimal planning of ATM's, including the science of their location, see [5] and [6].

computer. If the next customer commences service at 2:14:09 PM, then we can reasonably conclude that this second customer had been delayed in queue behind the first customer. If on the other hand the second customer had started his service at 2:23:19, then we can reasonably conclude that he had just arrived to the ATM and started service immediately, without any queue delay. By applying this logic throughout the day, to each and every customer served, we can partition the customers into those who have been delayed in queue and those who have not suffered that inconvenience. The QIE performs statistical operations on each contiguous set of queued customers.

For instance, if we have determined that exactly 14 customers in a row had been queued, starting at 2:12:34 PM, then the QIE operates on all 14 of those customers simultaneously to compute the queue statistics of those customers. The technical details are somewhat complex, but the result is easy to understand. If the server had been human tellers rather than an ATM, the same data can be recorded from teller keystrokes. This is what is done in Chase Bank in New York. Similar logic gets required data for the QIE from call centers and from the Internet. The QIE is thus a silent monitor of queue performance. It stands vigilant. It is unobtrusive yet accurate.

Armed with the QIE a service facility manager can then systematically and intelligently schedule personnel, i.e., "servers." We show how this is done by one available commercialization of the QIE, a software system called SwiftLine™. SwiftLine is a Windows GUI[2] type piece of software that sits on a branch manager's PC. It is fed data by the bank's computer system about teller keystrokes that in turn are used by SwiftLine to set up the required data for QIE calculations. SwiftLine also is fed data about all personnel who may be scheduled to be servers, "tellers" in our example here.

Figure 3 shows a SwiftLine transaction report, displaying by 30 minute segment of the day: number of service sessions; average duration of sessions during that 30 minute segment; largest session; total session minutes, average number of active tellers and teller utilization (in terms of fraction of time busy serving customers). This is one of several standard text oriented reports available from SwiftLine.

---

[2] GUI - Graphical User Interface.

Figure 3: SwiftLine Session Report

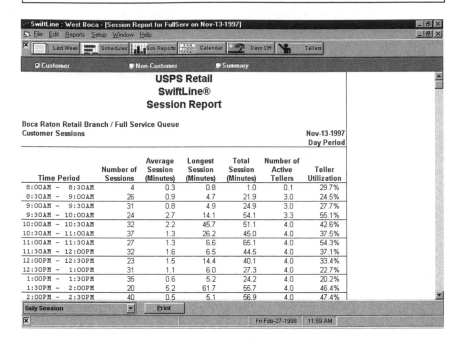

SwiftLine : West Boca - [Session Report for FullServ on Nov-13-1997]

File Edit Reports Setup Window Help

Last Week | Schedules | Sch Reports | Calendar | Days Off | Tellers

Customer   Non-Customer   Summary

USPS Retail
SwiftLine®
Session Report

Boca Raton Retail Branch / Full Service Queue
Customer Sessions   Nov-13-1997
                                                                      Day Period

Time Period	Number of Sessions	Average Session (Minutes)	Longest Session (Minutes)	Total Session (Minutes)	Number of Active Tellers	Teller Utilization
8:00AM – 8:30AM	4	0.3	0.8	1.0	0.1	29.7%
8:30AM – 9:00AM	26	0.9	4.7	21.9	3.0	24.5%
9:00AM – 9:30AM	31	0.8	4.9	24.9	3.0	27.7%
9:30AM – 10:00AM	24	2.7	14.1	54.1	3.3	55.1%
10:00AM – 10:30AM	32	2.2	45.7	51.1	4.0	42.6%
10:30AM – 11:00AM	37	1.3	26.2	45.0	4.0	37.5%
11:00AM – 11:30AM	27	1.3	6.6	65.1	4.0	54.3%
11:30AM – 12:00PM	32	1.6	6.5	44.5	4.0	37.1%
12:00PM – 12:30PM	23	1.5	14.4	40.1	4.0	33.4%
12:30PM – 1:00PM	31	1.1	6.0	27.3	4.0	22.7%
1:00PM – 1:30PM	35	0.6	5.2	24.2	4.0	20.2%
1:30PM – 2:00PM	20	5.2	61.7	55.7	4.0	46.4%
2:00PM – 2:30PM	40	0.5	5.1	56.9	4.0	47.4%

Daily Session   Print

                                        Fri Feb-27-1998   11:59 AM

Figures 4 and 5 show SwiftLine "Cigarette Charts." For each 30-minute segment of the working day, the charts show a vertical bar in up to three colors (blue at the bottom, red in the middle and yellow at the top, all shown here in grayscale). The height of each bar is proportional to the total number of customers served during that 30-minute segment. The amount of each bar that is colored blue (bottom) is equal to the number of customers who experienced no queue delay. For instance, all 20 customers served in Chart 1 from 8:00 AM to 8:30 AM on Wednesday March 4, 1998 experienced no queue delay. The amount colored red (middle) is equal to the number of customers who experienced a queue delay of less than five minutes. For example, again in Chart 1, for the time segment 12:00 noon to 12:30 PM, about 18 customers were delayed in the queue for between 0 and 5 minutes. Finally the amount colored yellow (top) is equal to the number of customers who were delayed in the queue for more than five minutes. We see one or two such customers during the time segment 1:30 PM to 2:00 PM in Chart 1. These charts are called cigarette charts because the red and yellow upper portions resemble ashes of a lit cigarette. The goal of the branch manager—by effectively scheduling personnel—is to "knock the ashes from the cigarette." That is, to reduce the yellow to almost zero and to keep the red to a reasonable amount.

Figure 4: SwiftLine "Cigarette Chart" 1

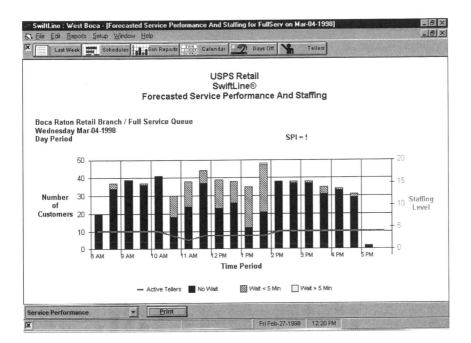

The branch manager can use SwiftLine to schedule each and every one of her people working in a branch. An illustration is shown in Figure 6. The idea is to "cover" all the obligations regarding required number of servers - as calculated by SwiftLine- and yet be responsive to available work hours of each employee and offer them required meal breaks and other amenities. This can be done "by hand," in a sense hand crafting a reasonable if not optimal solution, or automatically by the computer.

SwiftLine is representative of a growing family of commercially available software packages that allow managers of financial services industries to carefully and accurately deploy their personnel in an efficient and effective manner. These products are examples of how computer-acquired data can be "mined" to offer the manager "golden information" that will both improve service to customers and reduce costs.

Figure 5: SwiftLine "Cigarette Chart" 2

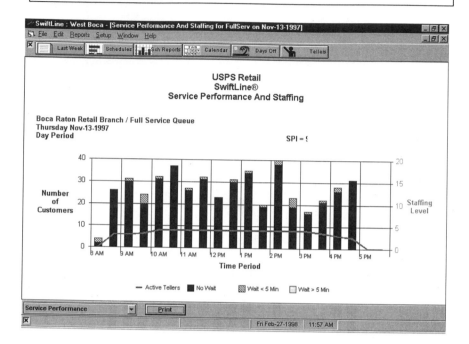

17.4 Call Center Staffing

In financial services, call centers have become the primary point of contact with the customer. Call centers have always been an access point for customers with questions or problems but they have increasingly become channels for providing differentiated levels of service and for the initiation of sales activity. Achieving these new goals requires a combination of new telecommunication and information technology and new staffing strategies.

Figure 6: SwiftLine Scheduling of Personnel

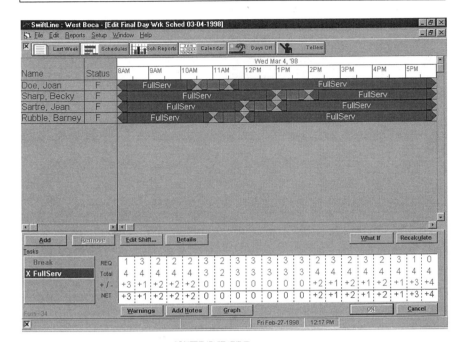

The concept of skills based routing forms the basis of the efforts in this area. In theory every customer that calls a call center has a set of needs and attributes that can be matched to the skills of the available phone agents so that the resulting interaction between agent and customer yields the best result to the firm. In practice it is not always clear what the needs and attributes of a caller are nor is it clear how to define the skills of an agent. Even if these properties are well defined it is a technical feat to match the customer with the correct agent. Finally it is not always obvious to a firm what the best matching of customers to agents is. Consider the following example:

A mutual fund company wants to increase the sales generated by its call center. Using a caller identification technology, the call management system knows that a particular caller has called twice before for information regarding a specific fund group and is 28 years old. The call management system (CMS) automatically sends the call to an agent that is registered and licensed to sell mutual funds over the phone and has a good record at closing sales with young investors. The CMS is programmed to route the call in this way to increase the probability of a sale to this customer.

To operate a system such as the one described in the example the firm needs a number of sophisticated technologies in place and needs a no less sophisticated approach to work force management.

Technologies

In the previous section we have described a technology for the collection of and analysis of real-time queuing data. To link the customer service function with effective marketing efforts the firm needs to also collect and analyze detailed data about its customers. Through a combination of customer input and caller id capabilities the firm should be able to identify a large number of incoming calls. This identification capability can be matched to a database of customer information that includes account histories, demographic information and previous interactions. The firm also needs to maintain a database of the skills of each phone agent. All of these kinds of data can be stored in *data warehouses*. Data warehouses are large centralized repositories of a firm's transactional data that are organized in a subject-oriented fashion [1]. The warehouses are integrated into the firm's transaction systems so that they are continuously updated with the latest data from the entire organization.

Data collection for the sake of data collection will quickly create what is known as a "data jailhouse". In the financial services the detailed data describing one's customers and operations can be a major competitive weapon if it is analyzed and put into action in the ways described above and as First Union Corp. has done [8]. This simple fact has been recognized in many industries and now the major makers of *enterprise resource planning (ERP)* software like SAP, Baan, and PeopleSoft are adding data warehousing and *data-mining* tools to their original enterprise wide transaction processing systems. Data mining is a new field growing around the need for tools for analyzing the terabytes of data firms, especially in the financial services, are sitting on.   For more information on data warehousing and data mining the interested reader is referred to references [1] and [7].

Finally the firm needs a CMS that can create virtual phone queues in front of groups of agents to be able to reorganize the workforce along different criteria.   These systems draw upon rules derived from the analysis of the historical transaction data to manage the call routing in real-time.   The technologies to do this call-center queue management have been developed to varying levels of sophistication and are in use in the marketplace. With a combination of the above technologies the firm is in a position to turn routine interactions with customers into part of a virtuous cycle involving data collection, analysis and marketing.   Customer call data can be mined for one-to-one marketing opportunities [17], which can be tested and refined over time.

Work force management

If a firm wants to provide its customers with differing services it must decide how to allocate human resources to these different services. This decision affects the amount of training the firm must provide and the quality and speed of service experienced by the different types of customers.   Training all phone agents to handle all types of customers creates an easy system to manage, that makes more efficient use of agent time (see Figure 7)[3], however it has several major drawbacks.   Training all agents is expensive, and can also involve purchasing registrations and licenses for some activities in the financial services.   Furthermore not everyone is suited to do every task and there is a benefit to having individuals focus on a smaller number of tasks so that they can learn from experience and improve their skills.   Breaking up a workforce into more specialized groups of workers may improve the quality service and reduce training costs but has its drawbacks as well.   Specialization results in a less efficient use of agent time and is much more complex to manage.   The CMS must decide which queue to send each call and how to adjust that routing when the system is more or less congested.

---

[3] As a representative example we plot the average customer waiting time as a function of traffic intensity for an M/M/1 queue with service rate 1 representing a specialist queue. We represent the generalist queue by an M/M/2 queue with service rate 1.

Figure 7: Comparison of Queues

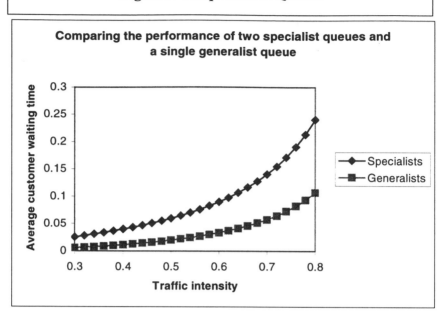

We have already discussed the management of queues and the scheduling of staff. Pinedo, Seshadri and Shanthikumar (chapter 18, this volume) describe the specific techniques used in call-center management. Beyond the challenges of scheduling of workers and routing of calls the definition of jobs by grouping tasks or skills involves the management of knowledge resources. As we have noted there is efficiency in cross-training call center staff to be more versatile, at the same time there is a quality gain when workers specialize. Defining call center job 1 as the group of all workers who can perform tasks a, b, c and d not only defines where the skills required to perform tasks a, b, c and d reside, but also the rate at which experience with these skills is acquired. A worker that divides her time between tasks a, b, c, and d will gain experience with the task c skill set at a different rate than a worker that only works on task c. The nature of the tradeoffs inherent in these decisions is only now being studied.

Preliminary research conducted by one of us (Pinker [19]) has found that the quality-efficiency tradeoff is strongly linked to the size of the call center[4] and the rate at which service quality increases with experience (depicted as low or high in Table 1 below). For an experimental system in which there are two skill groupings and the manager must decide how

---

[4] Where the size is determined by the sheer number servers involved

many specialists and generalists to employ, we have found that the quality-efficiency tradeoff can be described by Table 1.

Table 1: Quality-Efficiency Trade-off		
	Small system	**Large system**
Low	Favoring generalists important	Staff mix less important
High	Optimal mix important	Favoring specialists important

The results show when the quality benefits of specialization tend to outweigh the efficiency benefits of flexibility and when there is a significant benefit to using the model to find the optimal mix of specialists and generalists to have on staff.

17.5 Staffing backroom operations

Despite the growth of electronic commerce and spread of Internet based financial services, paper processing remains a large part of the operation of banks, mutual fund companies and insurance companies. Check processing, new account setups, insurance claims processing, statement printing, and error correction and research all take place in the back room operations of financial services firms. These operations can be likened to service factories. While they are organized very much like production facilities, they produce services that respond to a customer request. Since customers often require customized service such operations are also difficult to automate making them very labor intensive. Inefficient use of labor resources in such a setting can increase operating costs tremendously and increase capital costs by delaying the processing of incoming cash. In this section we describe an approach developed to improve the management of work and workers in these back room operations.

The service factory

Service factories come in many forms, from the blue-collar mail processing plant with large machines and forklifts moving material around to very sterile white-collar cubicles in which documents are transferred between workers electronically and each worker sits at a terminal with a headset for communicating with customers by telephone. While in some cases the processing of a customer request is done in a completely electronic fashion the inputs and outputs of these operations are typically in paper form[5]. For example, a customer may request that their IRA account be rolled-over into a fund of a different mutual fund company. The customer mails the appropriate forms to their current fund company and it may be scanned into a digital format. The digital document may then be routed to different employees via an automated work distribution (AWD) system.   An employee may find that information is missing or incorrect on the form and must contact the customer to proceed with the transaction. When the mutual fund company has successfully initiated the rollover it will send a confirmation letter to the customer, paper in – paper out.

Financial transactions may be very time sensitive to customers and therefore they expect minimal delay.   When these transactions involve deposits into bank accounts or fund accounts they represent revenue to the financial institution that is not realized until they are completely processed. Minimizing "float" brings firms a tangible benefit from efficient backroom operations.   Two phenomena complicate a firm's efforts to process transactions quickly without excessive labor costs, volume seasonality and volume uncertainty. Transaction requests arrive to a backroom operation through many channels. Multiple mail drops by the USPS, express mail, collections from different branches, internal transfers from different departments, some are voice initiated, and some Internet initiated. As a result these requests are arriving in differing quantities throughout the day although possibly in predictable patterns, i.e. time of day seasonal patterns. These patterns and the absolute volume each day might vary according to a day of week seasonal pattern as well.   In some cases there may be considerable uncertainty about the actual volume arriving each day. In this section we discuss staffing strategies for dealing with the volume seasonality and later in this chapter discuss the management of uncertainty in staffing requirements through the use of contingent workforces.

Staffing a backroom operation with seasonal work patterns

If work arrived to the backroom operation or processing system, at a constant rate, it would be easy to generate work schedules for the employees and determine the number of workers required to process all the transaction within a particular time frame. If processing of each type of transaction only involved a single possibly distinct step, each step could be staffed independently.   There is a large literature on the staffing of

---

[5] There are many reasons for this but the most important one is that it is easier to standardize technology within a firm than with all a firm's potential customers.

individual tasks given a schedule of workload. There are also a large number of software products available to manage the scheduling of workers in this setting. When work arrives in an uneven pattern to a system made up of networked workstations as depicted in Figure 8 the management of staffing is much more complex. The system consists of 5 processing tasks with the arrows denoting the flow of documents or work. Transaction requests arrive to tasks A and C and completed transactions leave the system from task E. Self-loops denote rework. For example, of the work processed at station A, some fraction is routed to task B, some fraction to job C and, some fraction is defective and must be reworked at A.

Figure 8: Configuration of Workstations

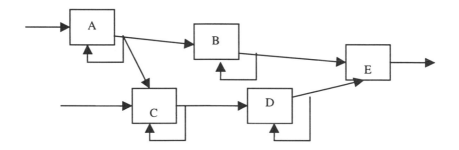

In a networked system staffing at one station determines the flow of work to downstream stations. This means that in addition to using part time work hours to better match staff levels to the work load a manager has two other methods for better managing the workforce.

1. Cross-trained workers can be shifted from upstream activities to downstream activities as work progresses through the system.
2. Managers can choose to intentionally delay the flow of work through the system by judicious buffering of unprocessed transactions at selected workstations.

Use of cross-trained workers reduces the amount of time workers are underutilized because they are staffing a task where volume has diminished before their shift is completed. Cross-trained workers can also work at different tasks on different days of the week if the mix of transaction types has daily seasonality. Buffering unprocessed transactions can enable a manager to smooth the flow of work to downstream work stations potentially allowing cross-trained workers to shift to a new work station or reducing the use of overtime.

Berman, Larson and Pinker have developed the first general mathematical model of the backroom operations staffing problem that schedules the workforce and workflow simultaneously [2]. Since then, a variation of that model tailored to check processing operations at Signet Bank of Richmond was implemented as a software tool with great success [20]. The use of the model to support the management of staff in a processing operation involving 75 machines is credited with saving the bank over $200,000 in annual float fees. By using the scheduling software to optimize staffing and inform re-engineering decisions an additional $300,000 of annual staffing expenses were cut.

Staffing a back room operation with uncertainty in work volume

In addition to strong seasonal patterns to their demand for labor, managers of financial services must also contend with uncertainty in their demand for labor. Consider the following two scenarios:

Scenario A: A bank announces the roll-out of a PC banking service to its customers with a flyer sent out with monthly account statements over a period of three months. Interested customers will have to call to request a special setup packet. In all likelihood many customers who try to use the system will have questions and will call for technical support. It is expected that wide acceptance of the PC banking option will eventually lead to reduced customer volume in branches and overall lower staff levels and labor costs. Until that auspicious time there will be an additional workload placed on the service staff and considerable uncertainty as to what that load will be. How should a manager staff the PC banking area?

Scenario B: The number of customer requests to open a new account that arrive to a mutual fund company each day is affected by many factors. Prevailing financial market conditions, new product offerings, marketing activities, and time of year all conspire to determine the physical number of envelopes with checks and application forms requiring processing that arrive each day. Accurate forecasting of these volumes has typically failed most firms. How should a manager staff such a new accounts processing area?

If we realize that, in financial services, new products and services are introduced all the time the two scenarios pose similar staffing challenges to the firm. In both cases there is uncertainty in the demand for a service. In Scenario A, it is over periods of months while in Scenario B it is a daily phenomenon. In both cases the firm would like to staff in a manner that would allow it to flexibly adjust its staff contingent upon demand. In the next section we discuss the main issues a firm must consider in designing a contingent workforce and the tools available to manage such a workforce.

17.6 The Design of Contingent Workforces

When designing a contingent workforce a firm has three options:
1. Staff such operations with regular full-time[6] employees and turn to temporary help agencies when demand exceeds supply in an ad hoc manner,
2. Create a pool of part time flexible workers that have hours that can be expanded or contracted to satisfy the demand as needed, or
3. Enter into a formal partnership with a temporary labor supply agency that will manage the staff in operations with uncertain demand.

Ad hoc use of temporary workers

There are a number of advantages to maintaining a predominantly full time workforce. Schedules are fixed so it is easier for managers to keep track of who is available at all times of day. Standard hours make tracking and payment of wages easier for HR staff. Full time workers also develop firm specific experience that may make them more flexible[7]. For example an employee that knows all the different account types available to customers may be more able to explain how a new PC banking service will improve an individual customer's banking experience.

The major disadvantage of relying on a full-time workforce with inflexible hours is that uncertain workloads can make this option very expensive. In Figure 9 we depict the monthly workload in full-time equivalent workers of a new accounts processing operation of a mutual fund company. We also plot the staff required to completely satisfy demand 76% and 88% of the months. One can see that achieving these moderate levels of service results

---

[6] We use the designation "full-time worker" broadly to include workers who have fixed schedules that are less than 40 hours per week and are inflexible about changes in their hours. For example parents with children in daycare for part of the day or not all days of the week want to have a very predictable work schedule that is less than full-time. Such workers may find overtime burdensome and view any cuts in hours due to rescheduling as significant lost opportunities for income.

[7] We are making the implicit assumption that full-time workers have lower turnover than other workers do. This added job tenure allows them to gain the experience necessary to develop more of the firm specific knowledge than temporary or part-time workers.

in frequent and significant over-staffing of the operation. During periods of reduced demand a firm with a large full-time workforce may feel pressure to layoff unnecessary workers. Frequent layoffs may reduce staff stability by increasing turnover, thereby negating one of the potential benefits of a full-time workforce.

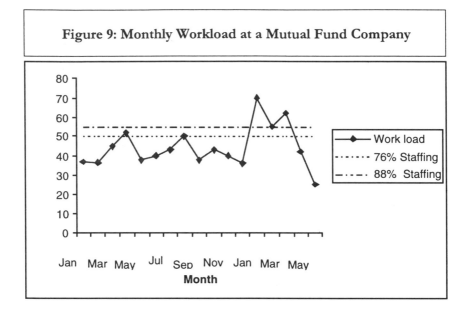

Figure 9: Monthly Workload at a Mutual Fund Company

If the firm is able to forecast or identify an upswing in demand soon enough it is possible to expand the work force by hiring temporary employees and maintain a smaller full-time workforce. The potential benefits of this strategy are that the full-time workers will be protected from fluctuations in workload and the firm will be able maintain the same capacity with lower labor costs. Achieving these benefits will depend heavily upon the type of training required.

The advantage temporary workers provide is maximized by waiting until one has the most information possible about the true workload before hiring them. However, if temporary workers require a lot of training before starting their jobs their advantages may not be achieved. It is useful to think about the skills required for a job as consisting of two components, firm specific and general components. Each component may require a different level of sophistication and knowledge. For example in the case of support for PC banking sign-up inquiries, very little extra training may be required of current workers since they are familiar with the work environment and other services provided to customers. Temporary workers may need significantly more training even if they have previous call center work experience, since very few workers in the temporary labor market would have the firm specific experience required. On the other hand the skills required for PC banking technical support might have a larger general component.   The firm may be able to train its current employees with little PC knowledge in a focused way that limits the technical skills required.   These two examples are depicted in Figure 10.

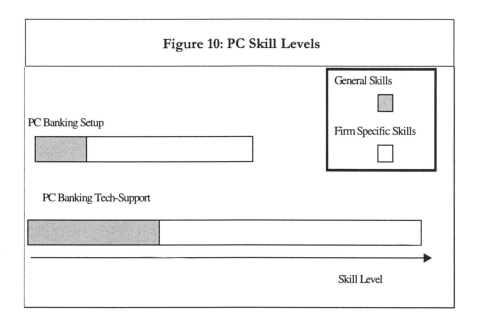

If considerable firm specific skills are required for the job temporary workers must be hired earlier and if the general skills required are significant it may be difficult to find temporary workers with the appropriate skill with short notice.   Both these effects may force any temporary worker hiring decisions to be made before all labor demand information is available and therefore reduce the flexibility benefits they provide. These limitations of a full time worker based staff with an ad hoc use of temporary labor can be avoided by choosing from the remaining two staffing strategies.

Internal pool of flexible workers

Firms have the option of forming internal pools[8] of flexible workers whose hours of work can be adjusted to better match demand as needed. There are a wide variety of such arrangements, including on-call, comp-time, and part-time work. The common element in all these flexible arrangements is that they involve schedules with some degree of flexibility in the times and number of hours worked.

The use of an internal pool of flexible workers has several advantages regarding the training of workers. First it enables the firm to create a pool of qualified workers without committing to providing them full employment. Second, the development of firm specific knowledge is facilitated by longer relationships with the workers. Finally, the firm is more likely to recover investments it makes in training over a longer relationship. These benefits are attainable if one assumes that there are people willing to take such jobs and if there are, that they will tend to develop employment relationships with the firm that are significantly longer than those of temporary agency workers. These assumptions are more likely to be satisfied the more consistent a worker's schedule and hours are, and if they are partly compensated for the uncertainty in their work hours. For example a hourly worker whose hours fluctuate between 20 and 30 hours a week but receives full health benefits can be viewed as being compensated for the uncertainty in their hours by receiving a total compensation per hour that may exceed that of a full-time worker.

Guaranteeing flexible workers a minimum number of hours of work per time period reduces uncertainty in work hours. Consider the situation shown in Figure 10. If the operation was staffed each month with 25 full-time workers and 30 flexible workers with guaranteed half-time work, it would have an effective staff of 40 workers per month that could be expanded up to 55 in any month. Such an arrangement provides the capacity of an 88% staffing level while using 175 fewer person months. Integrating flexible and full-time workers reduces uncertainty in work hours. All employees could be rotated through flexible positions on a regular basis. Despite these methods for reducing uncertainty it may be difficult for a firm to have sufficient flexibility from an internal pool of flexible workers. Providing consistent employment is an area where temporary help agencies have an advantage over a single firm.

---

[8] We do not preclude the existence of a full-time component to the workforce. We are only assuming that the flexible component of the workforce is drawn from an internal pool rather than a temporary labor supplier.

Partnership with labor supply agency

Temporary labor supply agencies have grown more sophisticated over the years. Among the key developments in this industry have been the increased levels of training these agencies provide their employees and the increased management responsibilities they have taken via partnering agreements with their client firms. The partnership agreements typically state that the temp agency will provide qualified labor to the firm with some level of service over some period while the firm promises to use the agency as its primary supplier.

Temp agencies have developed new training tools to expand their pool of workers (see [21]). They also have a greater ability than individual firms to keep their best employees occupied. A temp agency may have partnering agreements with several different firms each with similar worker skill set requirements and uncertain labor demand. By pooling the uncertainty of all the firms the agency can provide more consistent employment to their workers than any of the individual firms can.

An individual firm can be relieved of many of the challenges of directly managing a contingent workforce by outsourcing the responsibility to a temporary labor supply agency. This approach should provide a more reliable flexible workforce than the ad hoc use of temporary help but the commitment of the partnering agreement may add costs to the transaction. Furthermore the agency may not be effective at providing the firm specific knowledge required for the job.

Selecting a contingent labor strategy

Given the three strategies we have discussed and the numerous tradeoffs involved selecting an appropriate contingent labor strategy is a complex decision. This is a decision problem is an area of operations management and labor economics that could benefit from further research and the development of theoretical and empirical models. However, research [16] suggests that three environmental factors should guide a firm in selecting a staffing strategy: the volatility of demand, the availability of labor and the profit margin on a unit of labor. The greater the volatility in demand the greater the need for some form of contingent worker arrangement. As the profit margin on a unit of labor increases, firms should turn to external providers of contingent labor. As the availability of contingent workers decreases firms should establish formal partnerships with suppliers of contingent labor. These guidelines are depicted in Table 2.

Table 2: Value Added and Availability

		Low Availability High	
Value Added	High	Partnership	Ad hoc temp use
	Low	Internal Pool	Ad hoc temp use

By assessing the work environment being staffed in terms of these three parameters a manager can use the guidelines to select the appropriate contingent worker strategy.

Management of contingent workforces

Once a firm has designed its contingent workforce, by selecting one of the strategies we have discussed, it still must manage it on a daily or weekly basis. For example if a firm has guaranteed the workers in an internal contingent labor pool half-time work, managers must determine on a daily basis how many hours of work to give these workers. This decision is made by taking into account the work load on that day, the anticipated future work, absenteeism of regular workers, the cost overtime and the amount of work guaranteed that has yet been provided to the workers.

Computer based decision support tools have been developed to aid firms in the direct management of contingent workforces. A model for the management of a call-in workforce, in which daily decisions are made independently, and with full information about the workload that day, appears in [3] and [4]. We generalize this model to consider a variety of contingent labor contracts, allow for differing information available to the decision maker, and allow for the backlogging of unfinished work in [18].

Each work environment has its unique problems requiring tailor made decision support tools. However, our experience suggests, that we are not far from providing desktop-based management tools for contingent work forces.

17.7 Conclusion

Financial services companies must provide effective, efficient and reliable service or quickly lose customers to competitors. To avoid huge labor costs, financial services firms must develop innovative approaches to managing their workforces and their service delivery process. The people of a financial services firm comprise its most important asset. A customer's impression of the firm is influenced greatly by every interchange she/he has with a professional employed by the firm. These professionals create the perceptual realities of the firm to its customers. Integrating the effective management of human resources with the use of new data collection and analysis technologies is one of the most challenging tasks managers face. Drawing upon our experiences in financial services firms, the USPS, logistics firms, police departments, airlines, and movie theaters, we have outlined effective techniques for: managing part-time and flexible personnel in back room operations; bank teller scheduling and management; improving the psychology of customer queueing experiences; and the design and operation of call centers to take into account cross-training, learning and cross selling.

References

1. Barquin, R. and H. Edelstein. 1996. (Eds.) Planning and designing the data warehouse. Prentice Hall.
2. Berman, O., R. C. Larson and E. Pinker. Scheduling Workforce and Workflow in a High Volume Factory. *Management Science*, 43(2), 1997, pp. 158-172.
3. Berman, O., and R. C. Larson. Determining Optimal Pool Size of a Temporary Call-In Work Force. *European Journal of Operations Research*, 73, 1994, pp. 55-64.
4. Berman, O., and R. C. Larson. Optimal Workforce Configuration Incorporating Absenteeism and Daily Workload Variability. *Socio-Economic Planning Sciences*, 27(2), 1993, pp. 91-96.
5. Berman, O., N. Fouska, and R. C. Larson. Optimal Locations for Discretionary Service Facilities. *Transportation Science*, 26(3), 1992, pp. 201-211.
6. Berman, O., D. Bertsimas and R. C. Larson. Locating Discretionary Service Facilities II: Maximizing Market Size, Minimizing Inconvenience. *Operations Research*.
7. Berry, M. J., and G. Linoff. 1997. Data mining techniques, for marketing, sales and customer support. New York, John Wiley and Sons.

8.   Greising, D. Fast Eddie's Future Bank. *Business Week,* March 23, 1998, pp. 74-77.
9.   Jones, L. K. and R. C. Larson. Efficient Computation of Probabilities of Events Described by Order Statistics and Applications to Queue Inference. *ORSA Journal on Computation,* 7(1), 1995, pp. 89-100.
10. Katz, K. L., Larson, B. M., and Larson, R. C. Prescription for the Waiting-in-Line Blues: Entertain, Enlighten, and Engage. *Sloan Management Review,* 32(2), 1991, pp. 44-53.
11. Larson, R. C. Perspectives on Queues: Social Justice and The Psychology of Queueing. *Operations Research,* 35(6), 1987, pp. 895-905.
12. Larson, R. C. Operations Research and the Services Industries. In *Managing Innovation: Cases From the Services Industries,* B. R. Guiles and J. B. Quinn (Eds.). Washington, D.C.: National Academy Press, 1988, pp. 115-143.
13. Larson, R. C. There's More to a Line Than Its Wait. *Technology Review,* July 1988.
14. Larson, R. C. The Queue Inference Engine: Deducing Queue Statistics From Transactional Data. *Management Science,* 36(5), 1990, pp. 586-601.
15. Larson, R. C. Queues. *McGraw Hill Yearbook of Science and Technology,* McGraw Hill, Inc., 1992, pp. 377-379.
16. Milner, J. and Pinker E. Optimal Staffing Strategies: Use of Temporary Workers, Contract Workers and Internal Pools of Contingent. Working Paper CIS-97-7, 1997, Simon School, University of Rochester.
17. Pine, B. J., et al. Do you want to keep your customers forever? Harvard Business Review, March 1995, pp. 103-114.
18. Pinker, E. and Larson R. C. A Model of Contingent Labor when Demand is Uncertain. Working Paper CIS-97-8, 1997, Simon School, University of Rochester.
19. Pinker, E. and Shumsky, R.. The Efficiency-Quality Tradeoff of Crosstrained Workers. Working Paper OP-98-03, 1998, Simon School, University of Rochester.
20. Shah A, and A. P. Rimm-Kaufmann, Practice Abstracts, *Interfaces,* 1998.
21. Staffing Industry Analysts, Inc. Customer profile: Abbot Laboratories HQ partners with Manpower, Kelly, Volt, Butler, and others, help provide 1000+ daily temps. *Staffing Industry Report,* 7(19), 1997.

Chapter 18

Call Centers in Financial Services: Strategies, Technologies, and Operations

Michael Pinedo
Sridhar Seshadri
New York University
J. George Shanthikumar
University of California – Berkeley

18.1 Introduction

The importance of call centers in the economy has grown dramatically since 1878, when the Bell Telephone Company began using operators to connect calls. The National American Call Center Summit (NACCS) estimates that the percentage of the U.S. working population currently employed in call centers is around 3%. In other words, in the United States, more people work in call centers than in, for example, agriculture. The annual spending on call centers is currently estimated to be somewhere between $120 and $150 billion (Anupindi and Smythe 1997). Operations budgets for all call centers in the U.S. are estimated to grow from $7 billion in 1998 to $18 billion in 2002, i.e., at a projected annual growth rate of 21% (NACCS).

Call centers play an important role in many industries. Industries that have used call centers extensively in the past include:

    i.   The telecommunication industry (AT&T, MCI)
    ii.   The airline industry (United, Delta)
    iii.   The retail industry (L.L. Bean, Dell)

The telecommunications industry traditionally has used large call centers to provide a myriad of services to customers, such as information regarding phone numbers and addresses, operator assistance in establishing connections, and resolution of billing problems. The airlines have, through their call centers, taken business away from travel agents; as more and more customers book flights over the phone and obtain tickets either in the mail or electronically. Mail order houses send out catalogues, enabling consumers to shop at home by calling 800 numbers. Reflecting the consumer preference for remote shopping, call centers that support consumer products represent approximately 44% of all the call center operations in the U.S. (NACCS).

A call center can serve different purposes for a company, depending on the industry the firm is in and the overall strategy of the firm. It may be used to provide information (e.g., phone numbers and flight schedules), handle orders or reservations (e.g., mail order houses, airlines and car rental companies), or conduct more complex transactions such as providing medical advice or opening accounts (e.g., HMOs and banks). In some industries, call centers have to be tightly tuned into the marketing material that the company sends out; in other industries the call centers need to be more focused on the customer history. Consequently, the intensity of the customer interaction as well as the technological requirements varies from industry to industry.

There are several reasons for firms in the financial services industry to invest in call centers. The first one is to lower operating costs. Consolidation of operations and Information Technology (IT) typically decreases labor costs. For example, Ohio Casualty's short-term goal with its call center strategy was to decrease headcount. The firm replaced 39 regional offices with five call centers and obtained productivity gains of more than 100% over its previous regional office structure.

Another reason for investing in call centers is to improve customer service and provide access 24 hours a day, 7 days a week. Sanwa Bank's call center, for example, was set up to perform loan-related and basic account data retrieval functions. But, as PC banking emerged, and customers began relying on 24-hour banking, the center had to be reconfigured to handle more incoming calls and to provide more extensive data access (Baljko 1998).

Call centers and Information Technology (IT) investments typically take into consideration the potential for cross selling. Cross selling can be viewed as turning a service request into an opportunity to market additional products (Aksin and Harker, 1996). This improves customer service as well as transforms the call center into a revenue generating segment of the business: "banks created their own call centers primarily as a means to cut costs and route ordinary inquiries away from branches. By rerouting these commonplace calls, bankers theorized, their branches could develop into more sophisticated sales centers. Moreover, souped-up call center intelligence would support both inbound and outbound telemarketing opportunities" (Holliday, 1997). In July 1997, the Fleet Financial Group began using call center software that allows operators to see simultaneously information regarding customers and sales prompts with scripts. "That way, a customer, calling for information on a checking account, can also be told about the latest rate on a certificate of deposit, a low-interest credit card or another product that fits the customer's lifestyle and investment needs," (Hamblen, 1997). Schwartz (1998) observes that the Fleet Financial Group increased the number of customers converted to buyers from those calling for information by 30%. Revenue also increased because the new system permitted more effective cross selling of products (i.e., products that are related to those that customers inquire about). The USAA Group has long been admired by the insurance industry, since it consistently exceeds the industry benchmarks for implementations of call center, database and networking technologies fostering exceptional customer service with a full range of insurance, banking and investment products. USAA has implemented a system which, "automatically profiles callers, giving agents (operators) suggested scripts that correspond with products the system believes fit customers' profiles, such as flood insurance for customers living in high-risk areas," (Schwartz 1998).

A call center also increases the ability of the firm to reach customers outside the firm's traditional geographical market areas because of the easy access through an 800 number. Finally, a call center allows the firm to package its services and products and then target its customers with these packages. "(T)he customer data can be shared across the combined organization to provide new selling opportunities for both call centers and agents," (Tauhert, 1998).

The efficiency of a call center depends on the methods used to generate and retrieve data as well as the database and interface needs. For example, the following is a call center model developed by Meridien Research (Figure 1). It is a generic model of a financial services firm's call center, incorporating all the different options that can be considered in the design of such a center. Of course, not all call centers are this complex and some are much simpler than simplification of this model (Meridien Research).

Figure 1: Generic Model of a Call Center

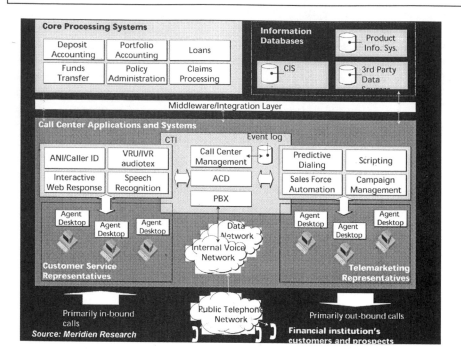

Source: Meridien Research

The operations management decisions in a call center can be categorized as follows: (i) those involving long term strategic planning including the design of the facility, (ii) those related to medium term aggregate planning of services, and (iii) those decisions that are made on a daily or weekly basis.

The strategic decisions involve the allocation of resources (e.g., equipment and communication systems) as well as the layout and location of the facilities. Included in this category of decisions are those regarding the routing of the calls, whether the caller should be switched from one customer service representative (CSR) to another or served by a single CSR, whether or not in-bound and out-bound calls are dealt with by the same pool of operators, whether to automate parts of the service, etc. These decisions depend on the anticipated variety and volume of services to be provided over a 2 or 3 year planning horizon. The selection of hardware and software depends on these decisions. Standard models for the design of such facilities are described in Buzacott and Shanthikumar (1993). In describing these decisions we implicitly assume that the strategic objectives of call center management are derived from an overall plan that specifies how different distribution channels are to be used for serving the corporate objectives. For example, the decision whether to sell related products is sometimes considered outside the scope of the call center strategic decision making process. Evenson, Harker and Frei (1998) recommend considering an integrative perspective that includes service delivery, IT, process design, and human resource management.

The medium term decisions involve the development of a semi-annual or annual manpower plan. The plan will have as inputs the anticipated demand for different skill sets over the planning horizon, the costs of training, and the time to train. Factors such as absenteeism, overtime, personnel turnover and attrition rates can be incorporated in such planning. Forecasts are usually made monthly and queueing models are used to determine the appropriate staffing levels on an aggregate basis. The models have to be sufficiently refined to determine the training requirements for the different skills. (A brief discussion of these models is provided in the section on modeling.) The queueing models used for aggregate planning can feed into the models that are used in the design stage.

Short and medium term management issues in a call center include:

i.   the forecast of call volume (monthly, weekly, hourly),

ii.   the determination of appropriate staffing levels (monthly, weekly),

iii.   the development of staffing schedules that meet the staffing needs (by shift),

iv.   the tracking of the performance of the staff as well as of the system and of the overall call center (monthly, weekly, hourly).

Managers must first forecast call volume and then determine staffing levels to handle that volume. After they have determined appropriate staffing levels they must determine an efficient workforce schedule. Then they have to track the performance against the plan; this is a feedback loop because this last step is taken after the management has completed the first three steps. According to the TCS Management Group, the first three steps are traditionally determined from historical and current data as well as from the predicted arrival rates of calls and the availability of each operator. Call center managers target an optimal utilization of their facility based on what they found has worked well in the past. The call center utilization is a product of the arrival rate of calls and the expected processing time of a call divided by the total time available.

The processing times of the different types of calls have different stochastic properties. More standard calls have a lower variability whereas less standard calls have a higher variability. As call centers become more common, we expect customers to measure the service according to several criteria, such as convenience and reliability, as well as according to the access to other services the firm provides.

Additionally, the fourth step serves as an indicator of overall customer service. Staffing levels may be optimal but customers may not be served according to their expectations. From this, managers can look into new IT investments to improve the service that the firm provides to its customers.

18.2 Technologies, Personnel Costs and Performance Measures

Nowadays, there are several technological tools that are commonplace in the industry and that make it possible for operators to provide a high level of service.

(i) Interactive Voice Response (IVR) is a menu system that a customer accesses when connecting to a call center. The IVR routes a call to the most appropriate person or desk. The structure of the menu system can be a simple list of two or three items, or a more elaborate decision tree. This tool enables the system and the operator to provide the service in minimum time. The technology is relatively inexpensive when compared to the time wasted in the transfers of customers via live operators. Large banks pay between $2.50 and $3.00 per in-branch staffed teller transaction; they spend $1.75 to $2.00 for an operator handled call center transaction and between $0.25 to $0.75 for an IVR transaction (NACCS). However, these costs are relatively low compared to the estimated $17.85 for an e-mail transaction which has an average response time of 16 hours (see Racine 1998). Today almost 90% of all call centers have a web page and e-mail contacts are predicted to grow by more than 250% over the next three years (NACCS). It appears that the Internet and e-mail will play a more and more important role in call centers. However, the costs of handling e-mails should come down.

(ii) Automated Call Distribution (ACD) is a service provided by telephone companies that makes physically dispersed operators appear to a caller as residing at one location. The phone company handles the necessary switching in order to make this happen. Some of the benefits are fairly obvious, such as lower network costs (phone bills) since the phone companies connect incoming calls to the regional representative that incurs the lowest long-distance charges.

(iii) Computer Telephone Integration (CTI) refers to the combination of computers and telephone systems. Roughly 15% of all call centers today use some form of CTI technology. However, Meridien Research has predicted that by 2002, 30% of all call centers will use CTI technology. Spending on CTI technology in the U.S. is expected to grow from $3.5 billion in 1997 to over $6.1 billion in the year 2000. Anupindi and Smythe describe some interesting applications of CTI technology in use today, such as Intelligent Call Routing, Screen Pops and

Whispers. Intelligent Call Routing is an application that reads the phone number of an incoming call, retrieves information concerning the caller from a database, and presents it to the operator when they take the call. Screen Pops and Whispers are pieces of information that either pop onto the operator's computer screen or into his or her headset. They provide information about the customer that the operator has on the line.

Predictive dialing is another application that is an efficient way of making an operator's day more productive, especially when the actual demand is lower than the forecasted level of inbound calls. The computer system keeps track of when an operator is talking to customers and when he or she is not. The computer system also compiles a list of customers that should be contacted (possibly because of recent calls or unresolved problems) and calls them for the operator whenever he or she is not busy. This implies that an operator receives inbound calls and makes outbound calls. Additional training is necessary to manage such a mix of tasks. Ultimately, predictive dialing utilizes operators more efficiently and has a large impact on operator scheduling and customer satisfaction. It has been estimated by some that this sort of outbound calling technique increases operator productivity by 200% to 300% (Anupindi and Smythe, 1997).

Conversely, it remains to be seen how effective call centers are in achieving their management's objectives. "Bank investments in call centers are not paying off as anticipated. Of 122 institutions surveyed, 47% stated that their call centers had helped increase market penetration-but 72% stated that they had expected it to do so. Similarly, Luhby's 1998 findings indicate 89% said the phone-based services had improved customer satisfaction-short of the 96% that they had thought it would."

Cross selling has not yet proven to be effective. A recent study of financial institutions reveals that, "bankers were intent on making call centers generate profits. But because call center personnel generally were not furnished with information that would let them sell new products effectively, relatively few banks have seen dramatic profit improvements from the phone operations. The sales shortcomings are not limited to the call center; banks also have had trouble creating sales cultures in branches. But, Luhby (1998) stated that, with an increasing number of customers using call centers as their primary point of contact with bank personnel, many view the phone as the most important sales channel of the future." Holliday's (1997) survey showed that 64% of the responding banks expected increased sales and cross sales, while only 48% saw an actual increase. Of the responding banks, 71% expected the call center to increase customer retention; however, only 53% said that it actually did. Evenson, Harker and Frei's (1998) study suggests that outbound sales efforts can shift attention from effective sales delivery.

Reynolds' findings indicate that close to 70% of the operating expenses of a call center are personnel related, with the remainder of the expenses spread out over network, overhead and equipment costs. It seems that call center managers in the future will focus primarily on lowering their personnel related expenses (because that has the biggest impact.) There are several ways in which managers can lower these costs. First they can try to reduce training and other recurring expenses (currently, the average cost of recruiting and training a representative is between $5,000 and $18,000, NACCS). They can do so by lowering their training costs (more web training sessions) or by reducing the need for operators through increased IVR usage. "Using a product called Automatic Coaching and Mentoring from Witness.com (Austin), USAA synchronizes voice and computer screen playback to augment training of representatives and agents" (Schwartz 1998).

Other areas for improvement will emerge with the development of virtual intelligence automated speech recognition software. This software can be used via the phone or in response to emails. Recently, Charles Schwab has implemented a voice-automated system that allows customers to buy and sell mutual funds over the phone. Markoff (1998) states that the system recognizes over 1,300 mutual fund names and can also respond to price quote inquiries for more than 13,000 publicly traded stocks.

The advance in technology and training methods will also increase the ability of operators to work from home. This will be advantageous for both the operator and the call center because it lowers overhead costs and increases employee satisfaction. Of course, it remains to be seen how effective operators are working from home and how effective training and other guidelines are with little or no supervision. Other means of supervision will have to be developed and, possibly, different methods of remuneration (e.g., by the number of customers handled.) However, the opportunities of call centers to reach a larger employee base because of improved flexibility will undoubtedly increase their efficiencies and performance.

Today it is difficult to measure the true performance of a call center because of the difficulty in establishing good measures of performance. The three common metrics of performance are the level of customer service, the operator's level of job satisfaction and the system's responsiveness. While these are the common drivers to a successful call center, they are difficult to quantify, measure and track. Consequently, the industry typically adheres to some commonly used indicators as proxies. The following table contains a list of those indicators as well as the common target values set by call centers.

Table 1: Common Indicators Used by Call Centers in the U.S.

Category	Indicators	Target Value
Customer Satisfaction	1. Speed of answer	15 seconds
	2. Abandoned Call Rate	Less than 2%
	3. Busy Rate	Less than 1%
	4. First Call Resolution	85%
	5. Availability	24 hrs by 7 days
	6. Busy Signal if queue exceeds target value	3 minutes
Operator Job Satisfaction	1. Applicants Interviewed per Hire	30
	2. Hire Time	6 to 8 weeks
	3. Attrition Rate	3 to 7% per year
	4. Training	90 to 150 hours per year per agent
	5. Agent Suggestions Implemented	Greater than 5 per agent per year
	6. Agent Suggestions Processed	Less than 72 hours
	7. Call Monitoring	5 to 10 per month per agent
System Responsiveness	1. System Reliability	99.999%
	2. Database Updates	At least one per 24 hour period
	3. Forecasts	12-18 months in advance

Source: (Anupindi and Smythe, 1997)

In the remaining sections of this chapter we will consider inbound call centers in financial services. The design and operation of an inbound call center is more complex than that of an outbound call center. Inbound call centers are more difficult to manage than outbound call centers, because of a lower level of control and more randomness. In what follows, we attempt to give an overview of the most important issues, the design parameters, and the modeling and solution approaches. We will not go into the technological issues; for those issues the reader is referred to Gable (1993).

18.3 Applications of Call Centers in Finance

There are many applications of call centers in the finance world. The four most important application areas are:

    i.   Retail Banking, (status of checking accounts, support of ATM networks)

    ii.   Retail brokerage and mutual fund institutions (transfer of funds),

    iii.   Credit Card operations (balance inquiries, disputes),

    iv.   Insurance (claim processing).

In retail banking, call centers are playing a more and more important role. Today it is estimated that there are approximately 1,300 call centers run by large banks (of an estimated 60,000 to 90,000 call centers in the U.S., NACCS). Redman (1998) predicted that IT spending for call centers in retail banking will increase by 10% annually over the next four years (in 1999 banks will spend roughly $1.31 billion on call centers), while spending on branch systems and check processing will increase by 2% and –2% respectively (or $1.42 billion and $1.03 billion in 1999 respectively.) Banks are looking at call centers as a way to cut operating expenses while providing better service to their customers. "A 1996 survey by the American Bankers Association and Lombard, IL-based FTR Inc. showed that 68% of U.S. bank survey respondents viewed their call centers as a place to reduce operating expenses and provide a 'necessary service' for bank customers. Only 9% said they perceived call centers as profit centers" (Holliday 1997).

Banks are forced to use call centers for several other reasons. First of all, if the bank has an ATM network, then typically every machine has a phone attached to it enabling a customer to call in case of a problem. Also, if the customer receives a (monthly) statement and has an inquiry, or if the customer wants to stop payment on a check, he or she has to contact a call center. Mortgage applications processing in retail banking are handled by call centers as well. Anupindi and Smythe (1997) state that approximately 90% of all banks use call centers for sales, delivery and product support. However, it is not yet clear whether PC banking and call centers are substitute channels or complementary channels.

Datamonitor has predicted that call centers within securities firms will grow at an annual rate of 12% over the next five years (NACCS). In retail brokerage and mutual fund institutions, a call center may have to handle calls that represent inquiries with regard to the value of the accounts (these calls typically can be handled by an IVR) or transfer funds from one mutual fund to another (which also can be handled by an IVR). However, a call with an order to buy .shares of a company is often still handled by a human, since the placement of such an order may involve a certain amount of information, detail and judgment that an IVR may not be able to provide.

Call centers for credit card operations handle a variety of standard inquiries involving account balance (issues that can be handled by IVRs), and account maintenance such as an address or phone number change. However, they also have to handle settlements of disputes, which are typically done by operators. The functionality of IVRs is increasing and the number of calls handled by IVRs is also increasing. It is interesting to note, however, that credit card companies are beginning to add account maintenance functionality to their web sites and they are beginning to see an increased usage of their web sites for these functions. It remains to be seen what type of long term effect this will have on the inbound call volume at the call centers. There has been a decrease in maintenance inquiries but an increase in the number of calls requesting help with navigating the web site and resolving problems encountered in using the web site.

In the insurance world call centers are used for the processing of claims, account maintenance, sales and so on. Travelers Property & Casualty Corporation believes that the overall cost structure of its call centers is lower than the cost structure of its sales force of agents in the field. "'One of our primary call center objectives is to provide an alternate sales channel at a minimum cost,' states Dean Collins, director of project management for direct response at Travelers P&C."

Schwartz (1998) estimated that there are approximately 60,000 call center agents in the insurance industry and that that number is expected to grow anywhere from 2% to 4% over the next three years.

A number of characteristics distinguish call centers in the finance world from those in other industries (such as airlines). Examples of such differences are:

i. The customer is very often, to a certain degree, captive.
ii. There are significant database requirements (data pertinent to the customer).
iii. Security and confidentiality issues.
iv. Fast (real time) execution (in contrast with order executions in mail order houses).
v. Less tolerance for errors.

In financial call centers the customer is moderately captive. The cost of switching from one financial institution to another is higher than the cost of using a different retailer or airline. The fact that the customer is somewhat captive allows the institution to let the customer wait slightly longer without running the immediate risk of losing him or her (the waiting time consideration, is of course much more important at a call center of an airline). The performance standards in call centers in the finance world are therefore different from the standards in other industries.

The database requirements in financial call centers are more extensive due to the nature of the relationships between the firms and their customers. The operator must have the entire profile of the customer at hand. For example, a customer may have several accounts with an insurance firm. The customer probably expects the operator to be aware of this aspect when answering his or her inquiries. It is not unusual for the profile of a customer to comprise several pages of information, which must be shown to the operator in a user-friendly way. The database requirements in the insurance industry may be different from those in other types of financial institutions; for example, the databases may have image bases containing photos.

If the customer wishes to make a transaction, (e.g., transferring funds at a retail bank or at a mutual funds institution from one account to another), then certain security requirements have to be met (e.g., in the form of a social security number or PIN number). It may have to be followed up with signed confirmations, etc. There are also regulatory issues that the financial services firms may have to face. A financial services firm may have one call center for all of its operations but it may offer different services and products in different states because of different state laws. A call center operator must know the products that the firm offers in different states and must also be familiar with the laws that are applicable in each state.

The probability of an error in a transaction or execution at a call center of a financial institution must be kept at lower levels than in other industries. Such a performance measure is often not an objective that has to be minimized but rather a constraint that may not be violated.

18.4 Design and Modeling

We first discuss the modeling assumptions. Any call center is subject to a number of different types (or classes) of calls. Each class has its own interarrival time distribution and processing time distribution and each type may have its own dependency on mailings or other periodic events (monthly statements, billings, advertisements, and so on). For example, at a mutual fund company a large number of calls come in between 3 and 4 p.m., right before the market closes, in order to complete a transaction, and a large number also come in between 4 and 5 p.m. to check the status of an account or outcome of a transaction. Certain classes of calls may be combinations of other classes.

A call center may also have different classes of employees with each class having a specific skill set and capable of handling a given set of call types. To prepare an operator to handle a particular call type requires specific training, which has a certain cost associated with it. Each type of operation has a learning curve and operators are subject to a specific turnover rate.

The call routing depends on the skill sets of the operators. This call routing is based on matching and assignment algorithms. The cross training of operators implies that one employee can handle requests of different types without having to transfer calls too different desks. But with cross training there are certain costs and trade-offs involved. Cross training allows for a higher utilization of the operators. From a queueing perspective the system behaves better and the delays are shorter. The routing hierarchy of a call center may be based on a tree structure. The customer has to be routed towards a particular leaf of the tree. Each level of the tree is associated with a queue and a given pool of operators (with specific training).

We make a distinction between two types of analyses of call centers.
- Phase I: The static design phase dealing with medium term aggregate planning.
- Phase II: The dynamic operational phase with short term staffing and control policies.

In Phase I, the number of operators is determined along with the hours of the shifts based on historical data, medium term, and long term forecasts. Other types of work may also be assigned to the operators in order to smooth out the workload. This work may be, for example, administrative tasks related to the calls received. The level of cross training has to be determined. An important part of the call center design focuses on the topology of the tree and the cross training of operators.

Phase II constitutes the dynamic operational issues. That is, given the number of operators and shifts, how should the operations be managed on an hour-by-hour and day-to-day basis? For example, what are the rules for the real-time scheduling of coffee breaks and lunch breaks?

Task Design

Gable (1993) recommends adopting three principles in the design of call centers: isolation, standardization, and simplification. Isolation refers to dedicating resources to the provision of a specific service. For example, requests for account openings have to be handled by a specific pool of operators. Prudential securities follows this design principle in dedicating groups of operators to deal with requests for account information based on the type of account. The rationale is that to answer queries concerning a particular type of account (or product) not only do operators require a special set of skills and training but also the privileges given to the account holder may be different depending on the type of account. While, at the surface, it appears to be easy to train operators to handle different types of products/accounts, there are several problems associated with implementing this concept (Rappaport 1996). Some of these problems include different software and hardware requirements for different products, the time required to train operators, and the cost-benefit trade-off of training and retaining operators. Standardization and simplification of tasks appear to be difficult to achieve in practice.

Call center managers have the following goals:

- the customer should be answered to his/her satisfaction within a single call without being put on hold during the call or forwarded from one operator to another;
- in answering the customer the operator should not have to waste time searching for data, or verifying the validity or time stamp of the data, or obtaining clearance for providing information to the customer;
- call statistics should be collected and be available for quality assurance and training purposes without having to waste time searching;
- after call data processing, either by the operator or by the group that processes the customer's request, should be zero or minimal (for example, re-entering the customer's address after the call on a box of new checks requested by the customer is a waste);
- key strokes for the processing of any request should be reduced to a minimum;
- procedures for eliciting information (scripts) should be available and easily accessible (on line) while the customer is on-line;
- audio and visual clues should be available to sensitize operators and managers to call congestion, security lapses, and equipment related emergencies;
- the working environment should be comfortable, professional, and lend itself to a flexible assignment of tasks.

Economic Optimization

As stated in the introduction, call centers usually consider the percentage of calls answered within a predetermined time interval an important performance measure. Andrews and Parsons (1993) describe an application at L.L. Bean that deviates from this tradition. In their approach, they use a linear combination of (i) the cost of lost orders, (ii) the cost of queueing time, and (iii) the loaded cost of direct labor. In view of their results, (the authors do not make the connection themselves) the gain is provided by exploiting a well-known phenomenon in queueing, namely that when the number of servers increases while the load is kept constant, the service improves. Thus, instead of attempting to maintain the same standards of performance regardless of the load offered, the design can be "improved" by changing the performance levels dependent on the load. It should be clear that an economic justification of such an approach has to be provided by formulating the problem as a multi-objective optimization problem.

18.5 Modeling the static Phase I problem

The research methodology for a Phase I analysis, i.e., the design and optimization of a call center (see Fig. 2), is based on various different fields of research, namely

- forecasting and data mining,
- non-stationary queueing theory,
- workforce scheduling.

Figure 2: The Static or Phase I Design Problem

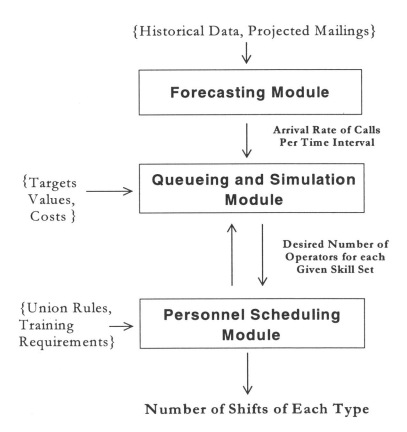

{Historical Data, Projected Mailings}

Forecasting Module

*Arrival Rate of Calls
Per Time Interval*

{Targets Values, Costs }

Queueing and Simulation Module

*Desired Number of
Operators for each
Given Skill Set*

{Union Rules, Training Requirements}

Personnel Scheduling Module

Number of Shifts of Each Type

An enormous amount of data is being gathered at call centers. These data include call frequencies as well as durations of calls. The data tend to be highly non-stationary, since the number of calls fluctuates heavily over the course of a day and over the course of a year. However, in practice only aggregate data tends to be used. The time interval used for data gathering is 15 minutes, with a day consisting of 96 time units. Even though the data allows for segmentation of calls, only a very limited analysis of the data has been done. Also, statistics of past years typically are not very indicative of the future.

Forecasting methods tend to be more sophisticated than just exponential smoothing methods; they typically include Box and Jenkins (ARIMA) techniques. Forecasts also need confidence intervals. Forecasts may require an enormous amount of data mining. There is also a strong dependency between the frequencies of the calls and the recent mailings or ad campaigns of the company. The forecast of a response to a mailing (either a billing or a catalogue) is hard to measure (unless a significant amount of past data is available).

Queueing analysis is often hard to perform due to the very significant non-stationarities in the system. The arrival process of the calls can be modeled as a non-homogeneous Poisson process, which would be a fairly accurate representation of reality. However, a queueing model subject to such an input process is often difficult to analyze. Actually, it is known that the non-homogeneity of the arrival process makes the process perform worse than a process subject to a homogenous Poisson process with the same number of arrivals over the long term, see Chang and Pinedo (1990) and Chang, Chao, Pinedo, and Shanthikumar (1991). One way of getting a feel for the queueing behavior is through simulation. However, because of the non-stationarities and the fact that the system is often congested, even simulation is hard.

The short-term workforce scheduling problem is usually tackled using an integer programming approach. Since this problem is NP-Hard, one has to resort to heuristics. These heuristics have to schedule lunch breaks and coffee breaks of various shifts and have to do so while abiding to union and other rules.

It is clear that the three sub-problems are intertwined. Forecasting tells us how the intensity of the call arrivals varies over the hours of the day. If the intensity is in an upswing, then this has to be anticipated by the workforce scheduling module. That is, a sufficient number of operators have to be ready just to be able to handle the incoming flux of calls and prevent a queue from building up. Because it takes a relatively long time for operators to wind down a queue, a build-up implies that a large number of customers will have a long waiting time. In what follows, we discuss some of the issues and models in detail.

Queueing Analysis

An intuitive approach for dealing with the non-stationarity of the arrival process of customers is to segment the day or shift into intervals, and to assume a fixed arrival rate within each time interval. Recently, research has focused on queueing models with non-stationary input processes. In the context of modeling the arrival process, Melamed (1993) proposed the TES system. TES, or Transform--Expand--Sample, is a versatile method for generating traces of traffic when the inter-arrival times are correlated. It is a tool for modeling *stationary* time series with a given marginal distribution and dependency structure. Positive autocorrelation of inter-arrival times can significantly degrade performance. Analytical solutions with TES are hard to compute with current technology, but for simulation TES is both accurate and very fast. The software package TEStool (Hill and Melamed, 1995) produces sample paths and can be used to "visualize" traffic.

Green and Kolesar (1991) describe how to use the Pointwise Stationary Approximation (PSA) to obtain queueing performance measures. The user is often interested in measures such as the probability of delay, the fraction of lost customers, the length of the queue, and the delay experienced by customers. In the PSA, as described by Green and Kolesar, the service times of customers are independent and identically distributed according to the exponential distribution, with mean service time equal to μ. The number of servers is assumed to be constant and equal to s. The arrival process is assumed to be a non-homogenous Poisson process with arrival rate $\lambda(t)$ at time t. They assume that the arrival rate is a periodic function, with the length of the period equal to T. Let $L_q(x)$, $W_q(x)$, $p_d(x)$, and $p_b(x)$ be the average queue length, the average time spent in queue, the probability of delay, and the probability that all servers are busy with arrival rate x. (These quantities can be computed using standard formulae.) Let L_q, W_q, p_d, and p_b be the same quantities when the arrival rate is the periodic function alluded to above. The PSA approximations yield:

$$L_q \approx \frac{1}{T}\int_0^T L_q(\lambda(t))dt ,$$

$$W_q \approx \frac{1}{\overline{\lambda}T}\int_0^T \lambda(t)W_q(\lambda(t))dt ,$$

$$p_d \approx \frac{1}{\overline{\lambda}T}\int_0^T \lambda(t)p_d(\lambda(t))dt ,$$

$$p_b \approx \frac{1}{T} \int_0^T p_b(\lambda(t)) dt \,.$$

In a recent article, Green and Kolesar (1998) describe the use of the normal approximation to the formula for the probability of delay in the design of a call center. (The normal approximation simplifies the use of the standard queueing formulae.) They suggest that this approximation can be used with non-stationary arrival patterns by segmenting the time, provided

- the service transactions are short relative to the duration of the busy period,
- the arrival rate function does not exhibit spikes, and
- the system is not heavily loaded.

Jennings, Mandelbaum, Massey, and Whitt (1996) suggest using instead an infinite server (IS) approximation to determine staffing levels. They consider an operator staffing problem in which

- any number of operators can be assigned as a function of time to projected loads,
- forecasting uncertainty is not a problem,
- server assignments can not be changed dynamically in response to actual loads, and
- the number of servers has to be determined as a function of time to achieve a target value of probability of delay.

The IS approximation was motivated by the fact that the PSA performs poorly when the arrival rate fluctuates rapidly. When this happens there is a carry forward of the backlog from periods with heavy loads to periods in which the load is relatively light. The PSA method performs poorly under these circumstances because it cannot anticipate such an eventuality (PSA assumes that time periods are independent and also that the queue assumes to achieve its stationary characteristics within each time period). The IS approximation was proposed to deal with this problem. It is based on the assumption that there are an infinite number of servers. Given this assumption the mean, $m(t)$, and variance, $v(t)$, of the number of busy servers at time t can be determined. It turns out that the mean number of servers can be determined using minimal assumptions about the arrival process (e.g., the arrival process need not be Poisson and the service times need not be exponentially distributed). Good approximations are available for determining the variance of the number of busy servers.

Once these two quantities have been obtained, the IS approximation sets the number of servers at time t equal to

$$s(t) = \left| m(t) + z_\alpha \sqrt{v(t)} \right|,$$

where α is the desired service level, i.e., the probability of experiencing delay, and z_α is the standardized normal deviation that gives this service level.

Other approaches are described in Abate and Whitt (1998), Falin (1990), Massey and Whitt (1996), and Massey and Whitt (1997). The work of Kelly (1991) and Ross (1995) also relate to the study of loss networks. While they do not deal with non-stationarity, the work of Kelly and Ross can be used as starting points towards extending the single stage models discussed above to networks of servers.

Research is also required in a number of areas with regard to the following issues:

- Workforce scheduling.
- The revision of staffing plans as a function of updates in forecasts based on observed call volumes as well as on external events.
- The economic optimization of staffing with time varying demand.

Workforce Scheduling Models

One can formulate an optimization model to obtain ballpark figures for various important decision variables. The input data for such an optimization problem includes personnel costs, costs of (cross) training, personnel turnover rate and goodwill costs (waiting costs). The decision variables are numbers of employees in the various shifts and levels of cross training. The objectives include operational costs and queueing (goodwill) costs.

The operational objectives include the utilization of the personnel as well as the potential cross training costs. The goodwill costs depend on the delays of the customers waiting in queue. Another aspect is the minimization of the percentage of calls that abandon. Trade-offs between cross training, number of operators, and waiting times have to be computed. (If the requests for a specific type of service have a high variability, then cross training as well as combining the particular workload with other work, which can be used as "filler", has advantages). The optimal level of cross training has to be determined.

Summarizing, the optimization problem involves the following decision variables:

- The number of operators of each type (in a more elaborate non-linear program the number of operators in each shift).
- The levels of cross training over the different skill sets.

The cost components of the objective include:

- Personnel costs (an increasing function of the number of people hired).
- Waiting costs (a decreasing function of the number of people hired and amount of cross training).
- Cross training costs (proportional to the level of cross training).

The constraints of the program include:

- The expected waiting time has to be less than a given value.
- The percentage of the calls abandoned has to be less than a given value.

Within this optimization problem there is a personnel scheduling problem (which itself is already NP-Hard). The time unit in personnel scheduling models for call centers is typically 15 minutes with a day consisting of 96 time units. Within a time unit the number of operators is assumed to be constant. After the desired number of operators for each time unit has been specified through the forecasting and queueing modules, the personnel scheduling module has to determine the number of operators that should be hired for each shift type.

A shift type is characterized by its starting time, ending time and also by the timing of its breaks. There are typically three breaks: one coffee break in the first half of the shift (a single 15 minute time interval), a lunch break (anywhere between two and four intervals) and another coffee break (again one 15 minute time interval). There may also be various union rules with regard to the timing of the breaks. The days of the week that a particular shift has to work typically have a cyclical pattern. Each shift type has a given cost structure.

The objective is to find the number of operators for each type of shift such that the total cost is minimized. This problem is typically unary NP-Hard. However, given the demand for operators and the shift types, this problem can be formulated as an integer program.

$$\textit{Minimize} \quad c_1 x_1 + c_2 x_2 + \cdots + c_n x_n$$

subject to

$$a_{11} x_1 + a_{12} x_2 + \cdots + a_{1n} x_n \geq b_1$$
$$a_{21} x_1 + a_{22} x_2 + \cdots + a_{2n} x_n \geq b_2$$
$$\vdots$$
$$a_{m1} x_1 + a_{m2} x_2 + \cdots + a_{mn} x_n \geq b_m$$
$$x_j \geq 0 \quad \textit{for} \quad j = 1, 2, \cdots, n$$

with $x_1, ..., x_n$ integer.

In matrix form this integer program is written as follows.

$$\textit{Minimize} \quad \overline{c} \overline{x}$$

subject to

$$\overline{A} \overline{x} \geq \overline{b}$$
$$\overline{x} \geq 0$$

The integer decision variable x_j represents the number of people hired for a shift of type j. Column j of the A matrix represents a shift of type j. A row in the A matrix represents a specific time interval i. The A matrix is a matrix of zeroes and ones. If an entry a_{ij} in the A matrix assumes the value 1 then an operator in shift j has to work during the time interval i. The entry b_i in the column vector $\overline{b}$ represents the minimum number of operators required during interval i. If a shift would not have any breaks, then the column may consist of some zeroes, followed by a contiguous set of ones, and then followed by another set of zeroes, e.g.,

$$
A = \begin{bmatrix}
1 & 0 & 0 & 1 & 0 \\
1 & 0 & 0 & 1 & 0 \\
1 & 0 & 1 & 1 & 0 \\
1 & 1 & 1 & 1 & 0 \\
1 & 1 & 1 & 1 & 0 \\
1 & 1 & 1 & 1 & 0 \\
1 & 1 & 1 & 0 & 1 \\
1 & 1 & 1 & 0 & 1 \\
0 & 1 & 0 & 0 & 1 \\
0 & 1 & 0 & 0 & 1 \\
0 & 1 & 0 & 0 & 1
\end{bmatrix}
$$

However, breaks in a shift cause the set of ones to be non-contiguous, e.g.,

$$A = \begin{bmatrix} 1 & 0 & 0 & 1 & 0 \\ 1 & 0 & 0 & 1 & 0 \\ 0 & 0 & 1 & 0 & 0 \\ 1 & 1 & 1 & 0 & 0 \\ 1 & 1 & 0 & 1 & 0 \\ 0 & 0 & 1 & 1 & 0 \\ 1 & 1 & 1 & 0 & 1 \\ 1 & 1 & 1 & 0 & 1 \\ 0 & 0 & 0 & 0 & 0 \\ 0 & 1 & 0 & 0 & 1 \\ 0 & 1 & 0 & 0 & 1 \end{bmatrix}$$

The flexibility in the break schedules imply that there may be many different columns in the matrix with the same start and end times but with different break periods. The fact that there is some freedom in the timing of the break periods makes the problem very hard. So, even though the problem can be formulated as an integer program, it may in practice not be solvable to optimality. One way of finding a workforce schedule is to solve first the problem without breaks (i.e., ignoring the coffee breaks and the lunch breaks) and then insert the break periods using a heuristic in a way that minimizes the total number of people to be hired. Developing good heuristics for this problem is an important research area, see Pinedo and Chao (1999).

Staffing and Training Models

The models discussed above can be combined to determine the mix of skills required in a call center. We provide a simple formulation below and discuss later the extensions that are possible. (A similar model can be found in Aksin and Harker (1996a); they model a call center to determine whether cross selling is profitable, and find that the profitability will depend on the call characteristics.) Assume that n products have to be serviced at the call center. A product can be either the sale of a financial product or the servicing of a certain type of account. We assume that K types of customer service representatives (CSR) can be trained. A CSR of type k can service a given set of products, S_k. We assume that the service time for product i is independent of the type of CSR and has mean $1/\mu_i$. Service times of type i customers are assumed to be independent and identically distributed. This assumption can be violated in three different ways. First, the CSRs may respond at different rates during busy periods, see, for example, Larson (1987) and Carmon, Shanthikumar, and Carmon (1996). Second, the CSRs may use a different script at different times of the day or at different levels of congestion, see for example the discussion below on dynamic control models. Third, due to shared resources such as computer and communication systems, all customers may experience similar delays when the system is congested (see Aksin and Harker, 1996b).

In what follows, we consider the static problem of determining the number of CSRs of each type. That is, the customers are not dynamically routed to the different types of CSRs. The arrival process of type i customers is Poisson with hourly rate equal to λ_i. The routing is fixed and a certain fraction f_{ik} of type i customers are routed to CSRs of type k. (The routing is external and there is no internal routing.) Customers that find all CSRs busy are lost. (Ideally we should include also the possibilities of customers reneging after waiting for some time and possibly retrying after reneging or balking.) The hourly wages of a CSR of type k is w_k and the cost associated with the loss of a customer of type i is l_i. It follows from the formulation that the average rate of work that presents itself to CSRs of type k, denoted as ρ_k, is given by

$$\rho_k = \sum_{i \in S_k} \frac{\lambda_i f_{ik}}{\mu_i}.$$

Let the fraction of customers lost in an Erlang loss system with c servers and work arrival rate equal to ρ be denoted by $G(c, \rho)$. Therefore, if m_k CSRs of type k are assigned to the call center, then the rate of customers of type i lost due to the unavailability of CSRs of type k, using the Erlang loss formula, is

$$\lambda_i f_{ik} G(m_k, \rho_k).$$

Define the set of CSR types to which a customer of type i is routed as R_i. It is now straightforward to formulate the following optimization problem:

$$\min \sum_{k=1}^{K} w_k m_k + \sum_{i=1}^{n} l_i \left(\sum_{k \in R_i} \lambda_i f_{ik} G(m_k, \rho_k) \right)$$

subject to

$$\sum_{k \in R_i} f_{ik} = 1 \qquad \forall i = 1, 2, \cdots, n.$$

$$f_{ik} \geq 0.$$

Research is required to modify this formulation and accommodate the following aspects:

- Non-stationary arrival processes (see, for example, Whitt, 1998).
- Determination of the sets Sk. It may be appropriate to initially consider only nested sets, i.e., $S_1 \subseteq S_2 \subseteq \cdots \subseteq S_K$.
- Consideration of not only the probability of loss but also of the waiting time of customers.
- Queue length dependent service rates.

- Reneging, balking, and retrials by customers.
- Server vacations (to cater to short breaks), absenteeism, and attrition.
- The effects of the use of shared resources and assessment of the criticality of various shared system components.
- Forecast errors and non-Poisson arrival processes.
- After call processing of work.

With some or all of these modifications, this model can then feed into the medium term planning problem and determine the training needs. It is important to keep in mind the rather different trade-offs in the medium term planning problem when compared to similar problems in manufacturing operations (known as aggregate planning problems). In the financial services sector, products and services change rapidly and become obsolete relatively quickly. With greater skills and wider availability of alternative employment, CSRs tend to stay with the same firm only for a relatively short time. Technological advances are rather rapid with the growth of Internet-based services and changes in computing and communication technology. Thus the financial services firms are faced with multiple risks that have to be traded-off against the flexibility of CSR skills. A detailed formulation of the resulting stochastic programming problem is beyond the scope of this survey. However, a simplified formulation is given below. Assume that there is only one type of CSR. The time to train a CSR is exponentially distributed with mean $1/\mu_T$. CSRs, once trained, remain with the firm for a random duration. This duration is also assumed to be exponentially distributed with mean equal to $1/\mu_L$. There is an unlimited supply of labor. The cost of training is proportional to the time spent and equals c_T. The wages of a CSR is c_W per unit time. The expected benefit of operating a call center with m trained CSRs is increasing concave in m (a result that can be obtained by analyzing an appropriate queueing model). The decision variable is the number of CSRs to train. It can be shown that under these assumptions it is optimal to have $f(m)$ CSRs in training when there are m trained CSRs in the call center, where $f(m)$ is a decreasing function of m. Extending this model to multiple types of CSRs and incorporating technological change as well as product introductions and changes in products and services offered is a complex problem.

18.6 Modeling the Dynamic Phase II Problem

The operations management of call centers can be modeled as a control problem. In the daily operations of a call center there are certain variables that can be controlled, see Figure 3. One of the variables that can be controlled is the long script versus the short script option. For example, a long script may include information about related products that is not contained in a corresponding short script. A second control variable is based on the flexibility in the scheduling of coffee breaks and lunch breaks. A third control variable determines a possible mobilization of supervisory personnel.

Figure 3: The Dynamic or Phase II Design Problem

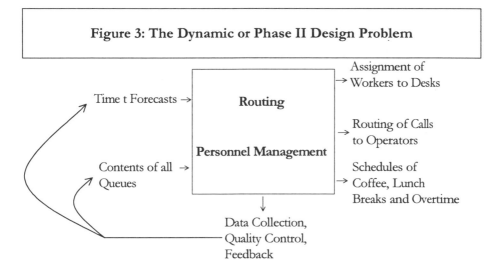

There are two important input parameters in this control process, namely
- the current queue lengths, and
- the time of day and the day of the week.

The most important input parameter in this control process is the queue length (the number of calls waiting). There may actually be various different queues and the content of each queue is an input parameter. The second input parameter is the time of day; the time of day is important because the rate of change in the intensity of the calls. A forecast of what is to be expected during the next hour may have an important effect on the management of the operators.

The actions to be taken based on these input parameters include:
- Operators may postpone any administrative work that has to be done with regard to calls just completed,
- going from a long script to a short script,
- the rescheduling of the (coffee and lunch) breaks, and
- the mobilization of additional personnel.

From results in the control theory literature we do expect that certain types of threshold rules will be a basis of the decision-making process. That is, if at a certain time of day, the queue length reaches a certain level, then the operators may be required to switch over to the short script. If the queue length reaches a higher level, then coffee breaks may be postponed. If the queue length reaches an even higher level, then additional personnel is mobilized. Any one of these actions involves a switchover cost. These switchover costs are, of course, hard to measure, but estimates do have to be made in order to be able to determine the trade-offs. These thresholds will also depend on the time of day. Threshold values that trigger a certain action will be lower when the intensity of the call arrivals is expected to increase rather than decrease. The research methodology for a Phase II analysis may be based on control theory. The outcome of the Phase I analysis is an input into Phase II. To determine appropriate threshold values at which certain actions should be taken, we can use optimal control theory or dynamic programming. There is an extensive body of literature on the control of queues. In a typical framework for controlling queues, the problem is formulated as a Markov Decision Process. Structural results can be obtained that indicate in which regions of the state space (values of the input parameters) the system operates in a particular mode (see Figure 4). Some control modeling issues and models are described below.

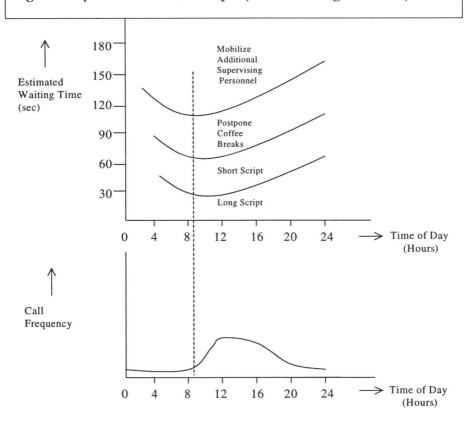

Figure 4: Dynamic Control of Scripts (Phase II Design Problem)

Dynamic Control Models

The dynamic control models are more complex than the ones described above. The models can be categorized as follows: models for dynamic routing, models for predicting workloads, and models with time varying service times due to changes in the script.

Dynamic routing models are used to determine where to route a caller. Such a model becomes advantageous when operators with different skill sets are available to take calls. Xu, Righter, and Shanthikumar (1992) have studied a model that captures this flavor. There are certain drawbacks in adopting dynamic routing. For example, faster operators may end up getting more work and customers may not be able to speak with their preferred CSR. The call routing software is sufficiently sophisticated to track the time spent by each CSR and route calls to level the workload, see Gable (1993). From a system point of level view such a strategy is not optimal, see for example Chen, Rotem, and Seshadri (1995). From an operator's perspective, phasing the workload depending on previous work history as well as on current physiological and psychological status is better. Evenson, Harker, and Frei (1998) state that the work environment is more critical than the compensation in matters of employee retention. Increasing the average retention period from 12 to 18 months represents a significant benefit. This can be achieved through different methods including charting career paths that show progress beyond the current job.

Prediction of workload can be useful in three ways. First, by predicting the overflow of current work into the future, immediate forecasts of operator requirements can be made. Thus some degree of dynamic staffing can be achieved. This aspect is addressed in Whitt (1998a) and Whitt (1999). In call centers, it is current practice to show to all operators in real time the workload in terms of operators that are busy, idle or not available, calls that are in progress as well as the number of customers waiting. Managers and supervisors take corrective action based on these statistics. One other feature that may not be that useful is the practice of tracking the average of statistics and reporting them at periodic intervals. For example, if the call center performance is assessed on the percentage of calls answered within 20 seconds, the performance may drift and then be brought under control by such tracking methods. The customers who rarely if ever view average performance of the call center may not be pleased with a varying degree of responsiveness. Research is required to determine if and whether such methods provide stable service to customers.

Second, a prediction of the workload can be given to customers, see Whitt (1999a). The effect of this would be that customers may hang up and try again later. Third, based on observed call volumes, the forecast of call volumes in the immediate future can be improved, allowing the manager to call in reserves or arrange for the overflow volume to go to another center that offers non-critical services.

Finally, as alluded to above, the service time can be changed depending on the current load or customers can be switched to a more specialized VRU during times of congestion. A 10% reduction in the length of the script can accommodate a 10% increase in the arrival rate of calls. Routing of longer calls (determined by a screening of the callers) to a different pool of operators can also improve service during peak times. Models that capture the effect of dynamically varying service times in response to time varying demand have not been fully developed in the literature (although they have been discussed in some of the papers cited in the section on Non-Stationarity).

18.7 Discussion

The call center issues discussed in this chapter are currently still evolving at a very rapid pace. Research and development is being done at a number of levels. In universities and research laboratories work is being done on non-stationary queues, workforce scheduling algorithms, and algorithms that route calls based on skill sets. At the same time software companies are embedding simplified versions of these algorithms into systems that are suitable for implementation.

A number of software companies have emerged in the last couple of years doing development work in these areas. Some of the better known companies in this field are IEX, TCS and Siebel systems. These companies have experienced extremely rapid growth over the last few years.

Some large financial services companies do all the software development needed for the management of their call centers themselves. An example of such a development is PruServ™, which is a system developed by Prudential Securities for its own use. A description of this system is given in the next chapter of this book.

One very important issue that is not clear yet is the following: How will call centers in the future function in conjunction with the Internet? Are these channels of communications between the firms and their customers complementary? How are the financial firms going to integrate these two channels of communication and take advantage of the synergies?

Acknowledgments

We gratefully acknowledge the research and writing support given by Jimmy Soujin Kow and Matthew Michaels of the Stern School of Business.

References

1. Abate, J. and Whitt, W. (1998). Calculating Transient Characteristics of the Erlang Loss Model by Numerical Transform Inversion, *Commun. Statist. -- Stochastic Models*, 14, 3, 663-680.
2. Aksin, O. Z., and Harker, P. T. (1996a). To Sell or Not to Sell: Determining the Tradeoffs between Service and Sales in Retail Banking Phone Centers, Financial Institutions Center working paper 96-02-B, The Wharton School, University of Pennsylvania.
3. Aksin, O. Z., and Harker, P. T. (1996b). Computing Performance Measures in a Multi-Class Multi-Resource Processor-Shared Loss System, Financial Institutions Center working paper 96-02-C, The Wharton School, University of Pennsylvania.
4. Aksin, O. Z. and Harker, P. T. (1997). Computing Performance Measures in a Multi-Channel Multi-resource Processor Shared Loss System, Working Paper, Fishman-Davidson Center, The Wharton School.
5. Andrews, B. and Parsons, H. (1989). L. L. Bean Chooses a Telephone Agent Scheduling System, *Interfaces*, 19, 6, 1-9.
6. Andrews, B. and Parsons, H. (1993). Establishing Telephone-Agent Staffing Levels through Economic Optimization, *Interfaces*, 23, 4, 14-20.
7. Andrews, B. and Cunningham, S. (1995). L.L. Bean Improves Call-Center Forecasting, *Interfaces*, 25, 6, 1-13.
8. Anupindi, R. and Smythe, B. T. (1997). Call Centers and Rapid Technological Change, Working Paper, *J.L. Kellogg Graduate School of Management, Northwestern University.*
9. Baljko, J. L. (1998). Sanwa Bank California Irons Out Wrinkles in Telephone Service, *Bank Systems + Technology*, 35, 4, 66.
10. Box, G. and Jenkins, G. (1970). *Time Series Analysis: Forecasting and Control*, Holden Day, San Francisco.
11. Burgess, W. J., and Busby, R. E. (1992). Personnel Scheduling, In *Handbook of Industrial Engineering* (G. Salvendy, Ed.), 2155-2169, John Wiley, New York.
12. Buzacott, J. A. and Shanthikumar. J. G. (1993). *Stochastic Models of Manufacturing Systems*. Prentice Hall, Engelwood Cliffs, NJ.
13. C. S. Chang, Chao, X., Pinedo, M., and Shanthikumar, J. G. (1991). Stochastic Convexity for Multi-Dimensional Processes and its Applications, *IEEE Transactions on Automatic Control*, Special Issue on Multi-Dimensional Queueing Systems, 1347-1356.

14. Carmon, Z., Shanthikumar, J. G., and Carmon, T. F. (1996). A psychological perspective on service segmentation models: The significance of accounting for consumers' perceptions of waiting and service, *Management Science*, 41, 11, 1806-1815.
15. Chang, C-S., and Pinedo, M. (1990). Bounds and Inequalities for Single Server Loss Systems, *Queueing Systems: Theory and Applications*, 425-436.
16. Chen, L. T., Rotem, D. and Seshadri, S. (1995). Declustering Databases on Heterogeneous Disk Systems, Proceedings, *21st VLDB Conference*, Zurich, Switzerland, 110-121.
17. Crabill, T. B. Gross, D. and Magazine, M. (1977). A Classified Bibliography of Research on Optimal Design and Control of Queues, *Operations Research*, 25, 2, 219-232.
18. Evenson, A., Harker, P. T., and Frei, F. X. (1998). Effective Call Center Management: Evidence from Financial Services, Financial Institutions Center working paper 98-25-B, The Wharton School, University of Pennsylvania.
19. Falin, G. (1990). A survey of retrial queues, *Queueing Systems*, 7, 127-167.
20. Frei, F. X. and Harker, P. T. (1996). Process Design and Efficiency: Evidence from Retail Banking, Working Paper 96-04, Wharton Financial Institutions Center.
21. Gable, R. A. (1993). *Inbound Call Centers: Design, Implementation and Management*, Artech House, Boston.
22. Green, L. and Kolesar, P. (1991). The Pointwise Stationary Approximation for Queues with Non-stationary Arrivals, *Management Science*, 37, 1, 84-97.
23. Hamblen, M. (1997), Bank Call Center System Pays Dividends, *Computerworld*, 31, 45, 55-56.
24. Hassler, K. W., Jones, C. C., Kohler, J. E. and Nalbone, R. D. (1995). Revolutionizing DEFINITY Call Centers in the 1990s, *AT&T Technical Journal*, July/August.
25. Hill, J. R. and Melamed, B. (1995). TEStool: A Visual Interactive Environment for Modeling Autocorrelated Time Series, *Performance Evaluation*, 24, 1&2, 3–22.
26. Holliday, K. K. (1997), Talking Heads or Talking Leads? *USBanker*, 107, 10, 61-64.
27. Jennings, O. B., Mandelbaum, A., Massey, W. A., and Whitt, W. (1996). Server Staffing to Meet Time-Varying Demand, *Management Science*, 42, 10, 1383-1394.
28. Kelly, F. P. (1991). Loss Networks, *Annals of Applied Probability*, 1, 319-378.
29. Kolesar, P. and Green, L. (1998). Insights on service system design from a normal approximation to Erlang's formula, *Production and Operations Management*, 7, 3, 282-293.
30. Larson, R. C. (1987). Perspectives on Queues - Social Justice and the Psychology of Queuing, *Operations Research*, 35, 6, 895-905.

31. Lippman, S. A. (1975). Applying a New Device in the Optimization of Exponential Queuing Systems, *Operations Research*, 23, 4, 687-710.
32. Livny, M., Melamed, B., and Tsiolis, A. K. (1993). The Impact of Autocorrelation on Queuing Systems, *Management Science*, 39, 3, 322-339.
33. Luhby, T. (1998), Call Centers Failing to Ring the Bell, Survey Finds, *American Banker*, 163, 1, 11.
34. Markoff, J. (June 21, 1998), Voice on Phone Is Not Human, But It's Helpful, *New York Time*.
35. Massey, W. A. and Whitt, W. (1996). Stationary-Process Approximations for the Nonstationary Erlang Loss Model, *Operations Research*, 44, 6, 976-983.
36. Massey, W. A. and Whitt, W. (1997). Peak Congestion in a multi-server service system with slowly varying arrival rates, *Queueing Systems*, 25, 157-172.
37. Melamed, B. (1993). An Overview of TES Processes and Modeling Methodology, *Performance Evaluation of Computer and Communications Systems*, L. Donatiallo and R. Nelson, Eds., Springer-Verlag Lecture Notes in Computer Science, 359-393.
38. Meridien Research, (1999) Strategic Information Technology Investments: Who's Spending What on IT for Competitive Advantage
39. Nanda, R. and Browne, J. (1992). Introduction to Employee Scheduling, Van Nostrand Reinhold, New York.
40. North American Call Center Summit (NACCS), Call Center Statistics, Call Center Summit on Strategic Outsourcing., http://www.callcenternews.com/resources/statistics.shtml.
41. Pinedo, M. and Chao, X. (1999). *Operations Scheduling with Applications in Manufacturing and Services*, Irwin/McGraw-Hill, Burr Ridge, IL.
42. Racine, J. (1998), Information Technology: Call Centers to the Rescue: Bridging the Physical, virtual Sales Worlds, *American Banker*, 1, 2, 9.
43. Rappaport, D. M. (1996). Key Role of Integration in Call Centers *Business Comm. Rev.*, July, 44-48.
44. Redman, R. (Apr 1998), Emerging Technologies to Lure More IT Dollars but Core Channels, Systems Remain the Focus, *Bank Systems + Technology*, 35, 4, 10-11.
45. Reynolds, P. (May 1994), Real-Time Adherence Monitoring in the Call Center, *Voice Processing*.
46. Ross, K. W. (1995). *Multiservice Loss Models for Broadband Communication Networks*, Springer, New York.
47. Schwartz, S. (Jun 1998), Preparing for Massive Growth, *Insurance & Technology*, 23, 6, 57-58
48. Stidham, S. Jr. (1985). Optimal Control of Admission to a Queueing System, *IEEE Trans. AC*, 30, 8, 705-713.
49. Tauhert, C. (Sep 1998), Merger of the Century, *Insurance & Technology*, 23, 9, 49-51.

50. TCS Management Group, Inc., Workforce Management Overview, Brentwood Tennessee.

51. Tien, J. M., and Kamiyama, A. (1982). On Manpower Scheduling Algorithms, *SIAM Review*, 24, 275-287.

52. Weber, R. R. and Stidham, S. (1987). Optimal Control of Service Rates in Networks of Queues, *Adv. Appl. Prob.*, 19, 202-218.

53. Whitt, W. (1998). Decomposition Approximations for Time-Dependent Markovian Queueing Networks, *forthcoming, Operations Research Letters*.

54. Whitt, W. (1998a). Predicting Queueing Delays, *forthcoming, Management Science*.

55. Whitt, W. (1999). Dynamic Staffing in a Telephone Call Center Aiming to Immediately Answer All Calls, *submitted to Operations Research Letters*.

56. Whitt, W. (1999). Improving Service by Informing Customers About Anticipated Delays, *Management Science*, 45, 1, 1-16.

57. Xu, S. H., Rhighter, R. and Shanthikumar, J. G. (1992). Optimal Dynamic Assignment of Customers to Heterogeneous Servers in Parallel, *Operations Research*, 40, 6, 1126-1138.

Chapter 19

PruServ™:
A Call Center
Support System

John Alouisa
William Anderson
Richard Castro
Raymond Ennis
Jeffrey Gevarter
Russell Pandolfo
Prudential Securities Incorporated

19.1 Introduction and Overview

Prudential Securities Incorporated, as a full service brokerage firm, operates a number of call centers with supporting service departments on a 24 x 7 basis. Among the most critical are the call centers and support areas dedicated to servicing clients who have established COMMAND[SM] and Advantage accounts with the firm. These "premium" level accounts offer clients complete cash management functionality well beyond a traditional securities account. COMMAND[SM] and Advantage clients receive an upgraded account statement, full checking and Visa® debit card transactional capability, and a host of other value-added services. The primary goal of these products is to make a client's investment relationship with Prudential as convenient and complete as possible.

Client research indicates that one of the most valued services available to COMMAND℠ and Advantage clients is the call center support. The call centers allow clients to make inquiries, and manage their accounts at their convenience – often outside of traditional banking or investing hours. Prudential needed a system that would allow Customer Service Representatives to respond to customers: inquiries and requests promptly and accurately. The system that was in use had the following problems:

- Outdated Legacy System
- Inefficient Call Tracking and Case Management Tools
- Unsatisfactory First Call Resolution
- High Error Rate
- Dissatisfied and Disempowered Users
- Extensive Training Time
- Multiple Logons

Since Prudential is a service oriented business, its success and competitive advantage lies in the ability to give its customers the highest quality of service possible, "wherever and whenever" they want it. Without the proper tools to do the job, service quality was diminished. The need for a powerful call center application was critical to the enterprise.

PruServ™ effectively solved the business problem by providing users with a robust and exciting application that resulted in:

- Fully Automated Call Tracking and Case Management
- First Call Resolution Increased from 80% to 91%
- Reduction in Number of Steps to Complete a Task
- All Request/Inquiries Processed from a Single Desktop Environment
- Reduction of Call Time from 3.2 to 2.1 minutes
- Data Entry and Processing Errors Eliminated
- Quicker Inquiry and Transaction Processing
- Users Becoming More Productive in their New Point and Click Environment
- Minimal Training Required
- Viewing Simplified by Using a Single Window

The information provided by the call tracking and case management component has been integral to Prudential's efforts to provide "World Class" customer service. Management is now able to review the data returned from the system and combine it with the input of "front line" employees. This allows Prudential to meet the ever-changing needs of its customers on a day-to-day basis. This translated to the firm capturing an increased percentage of clients' assets and generating incremental revenues.

PruServ™ went from concept to production in less than two years. Development began on July 1, 1997 for the COMMAND℠ call center. With a target date of September 28, 1998, PruServ™ was delivered to the desktop on September 1, 1998, 28 days ahead of schedule. It was estimated that the net cost to build the application would be $2 Million. At the time it was deployed, PruServ™ had cost Prudential only $1.2 Million.

19.2 The Development Process

PruServ™'s development cycle was split into three parts: Design, Coding and Testing. The design phase began with a three-month analysis of the business problem. Various business and IS groups were visited to begin gathering the required information. Specification documents were drawn up, presented to management and placed under change control for the duration of the project. Diagrams were constructed to outline the object model and mock-ups were done to design the Graphical User Interface (GUI). "Business use cases" were used to evaluate the overall object model, validating the intended system architecture. Finally all documents were approved and coding began.

Due to the object-oriented design of the application, the team was split up into subgroups so components could be built independently. The first pieces to be built were the common services of PruServ™. Once this was completed and tested, the team was ready to begin building the first snap-ins for PruServ™. The team was again split up as these documents were built. With the common services in place, development of these snap-ins proved to be even faster than expected. Testing was done by the Business Support & Development team. These testers knew the business process and were able to ensure that PruServ™ and the initial snap-ins were built according to specifications and bug free.

PruServ™ made its public debut on February 27, 1998 in a demonstration for upper management. The results were so impressive that the scope of the project quickly shifted from being an application to be deployed in a single call center to the new gateway to Prudential's Digital Nervous System. The top executives of the company saw how powerful PruServ™ was and realized that it could substantially reduce operating costs and improve the quality of customer service.

The PruServ™ framework is distributed via Internet download – users simply navigate to a secured internal website where they answer a simple questionnaire before the installation process begins. A user profile is then automatically built with default security settings based on the information. Using CAB file technology, the supporting components are version checked and installed. The snap-ins are automatically installed and updated when a user navigates to them, keeping the user's machine clear of unnecessary programs.

When PruServ™ was deployed, it went beyond the needs of the COMMAND^SM call center; it was ready to serve the enterprise. The project was extremely successful, finishing ahead of schedule and within budget. Across the enterprise there are more than 18 different departments, nine of which are in production, developing snap-ins for PruServ™, constantly saving Prudential valuable resources with each new snap-in.

19.3 The Technical Aspects of PruServ™

PruServ™ is an n-tier, object-oriented Windows based application built using Microsoft Visual Basic 5.0 Enterprise Edition. It is a scalable COM framework for building and deploying applications, referred to as snap-ins, which leverage its generic functionality. PruServ™ has become the central gateway to Prudential's Digital Nervous System.

Visual Basic ActiveX Documents have been the preferred tool for developing snap-ins for the following reasons:

- Executed in a Container
- Looks and Behaves Like a Standard Visual Basic Form
- Centrally Deployed from a Web Server
- Automatically Downloaded and Version Control by Internet Explorer
- Visual Basic Developers Can Begin Developing Snap-Ins without any Additional Training

Snap-ins are preferably built as ActiveX documents but they can be developed in a variety of programming languages such as Java, HTML, and C++. It is the flexible architecture of PruServ™ itself that has the most impact on the speed and efficiency with which snap-ins can be built. PruServ™'s architecture can be broken down into User, Business and Data Services.

User Services

PruServ™ offers generic User Services to developers to accomplish common tasks. This makes similar actions simpler by providing the same interface for each snap-in. Some of the User Services found in PruServ™ are:

- Online Reporting
- Internet/Intranet Access
- Email/Faxing Functionality
- Document Workflow Imaging
- Online Scripting

PruServ™ takes full advantage of Internet Explorer's object model, using its browsing ability and leveraging its powerful download and version management capabilities. Its streamlined look and feel makes it completely intuitive to the end user. PruServ™ also offers to developers multiple methods to inform the end user and manipulate its interface. It has a "Tip of the Day" as well as multimedia tutorials, wizards, online help, and video to the desktop.

Business Services

A number of Business services can be found in PruServ™. By placing the business process and entities in a central component, the application can scale as the company grows and develops without affecting the individual snap-ins. Below are a few of the Business services provided:

- Individual User Profiles
- Security Model
- Call Tracking/Case Management Model
- Client Account Object Model

A partial diagram of the object model has been provided below in Figure 1.

PruServ™ can handle individual user profiles, allowing security to be set on a field-by-field basis for each user. Developers writing snap-ins are offered a variety of security options through PruServ™'s robust security model for building secure snap-ins. End users log on once and instantly have access to all of the snap-ins that they have rights to.

Going "hand-in-hand" with the security model, PruServ™ offers a rich global tracking mechanism. As a business rule, all transactions must be tracked from start to finish. Developers can access this functionality by instantiating a single case management object.

When coding for PruServ™, developers need not worry about data format or structures since PruServ™ provides a full set of data consumer objects which mirror the business entities. Development is simplified since programmers are able to think abstractly about their information and in terms of real life situations. In addition, teams from different business groups are able to collaborate and work effectively since all of the code is uniform.

Figure 1: Object Model

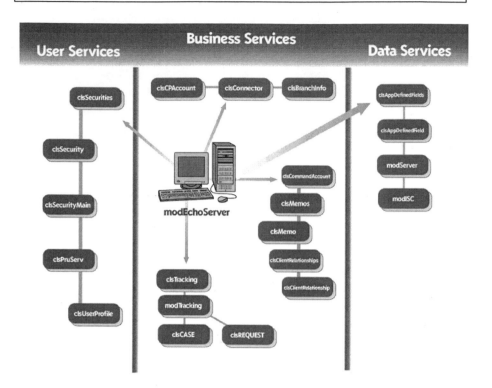

Data Services

Perhaps the most important functions provided by PruServ™ are its Data Services. Developed as a COM enabled executable with several supporting ActiveX/COM objects, PruServ™ is referenced by each snap-in that requires access to the corporate data warehouse. It communicates using an internally built component called Enterprise Middleware which parses XML data passed across TCP/IP using the HTTP protocol. PruServ™ "exposes" the Enterprise Middleware, standardizing how developers will "talk" to the data store, allowing applications to be developed rapidly.

While database connectivity is primarily achieved using Enterprise Middleware, a number of other methods are used. PruServ™ also uses Microsoft SNA server, IBM MQ Series and ODBC, depending on the system being accessed.

Keeping true to its flexible architecture, PruServ™ manages all connections, returning the data through its Business Services allowing the connectivity method to be changed without recompiling and redistributing each snap-in.

Leveraging the capabilities of Microsoft Windows and Internet Explorer, PruServ™ provides an architecture with unlimited scalability and the capability to tap into the Digital Nervous System of one of world's largest financial and insurance institutions, the Prudential enterprise.

19.4 Technical Challenges

PruServ™ faced a number of technical challenges during its evolution. Some of the challenges encountered were:
- Designing for the User and the Developer
- Scalability
- Deployment and Version Control

Perhaps the greatest challenge was to design an application that was both end user and developer friendly. It was almost like building an application within an application. This challenge was met by carefully building and testing the object model and interface "from both sides of the fence".

19.5 User Interface Issues

PruServ™ was originally designed as a standard MDI Visual Basic EXE for the COMMAND^SM call center. Upon analysis it became evident that this would not scale properly as the center's needs grew. The result was a re-evaluation and a decision to build PruServ™ as a COM enabled framework building upon the capabilities of the Windows Operating System, Internet Explorer and ActiveX. This new design has allowed over 100 developers to work asynchronously, developing each component and snap-in independently. This capability has expanded PruServ™'s user base to so many different departments.

Another big challenge was a centralized deployment and version control mechanism. PruServ™'s architecture relies on snap-ins, most of which have been developed as ActiveX Documents. Installing the snap-ins and version maintenance is handled automatically by Internet Explorer; the snap-ins are also updated automatically.

Throughout the initial phase, users actively participated in design sessions. A number of issues were considered when designing the user interface for PruServ™ such as:

- Usability
- Consistency
- Robustness
- Feedback
- Aesthetics
- Simplicity

Windows based applications built at Prudential traditionally sported a "Gray Screen" user interface. Throughout the multitude of business groups, standardization of controls and GUI design was difficult to maintain. This was neither easy to use nor exciting to the user. PruServ™ now brings a highly intuitive graphical and interactive user interface with exposed functionality to the developer and end user. Standardization of user controls and GUI design are strictly enforced to maintain a consistent "look and feel" throughout the multitude of snap-ins that have been built.

PruServ™ features an intelligent graphical navigation bar that allows the user to navigate through its many snap-ins. It is dynamically built on startup based on the individual user profiles. Additionally, this navigation bar allows developers to add their own buttons to the navigation bar through the PruServ™ framework. Developers also have complete access to PruServ™'s Wizard menu, allowing a programmer to add a wizard to the button.

PruServ™ also features a status bar and an informational marquee as well as a "Tip Of the Day" to provide information to the user. Like the navigation bar and wizard menu, developers can easily provide feedback to the user using these tools. The status marquee is linked to INOVA's LightLink server that displays call center statistics.

Additionally, PruServ™ offers video to the desktop with a variety of media options. It can be streamed from a web server or loaded locally. This capability combined with multimedia tutorials gives PruServ™'s users a richer experience when using the application.

Online scripting is another valuable feature of PruServ™'s GUI. It is a highly visible location for error messages and other information. In the COMMAND℠ service center, it is utilized to provide the same quality of service to each caller.

Now developers can design robust business applications that the end user can easily incorporate in their daily tasks. The standardization of interfaces and intuitiveness of PruServ™ makes the user feel more comfortable as they are empowered with more productivity tools, all with the same style interface.

Some screen shots of the system are shown on the next page. Figure 2 shows the main screen of the application. Figure 3 displays a screen that shows the client information available to the agent when speaking to a customer. Notice that the agent has information about all accounts held by the customer plus a variety of information about the customer, a script, and the status of the call center performance at the top of the screen. Figure 4 contains a transaction screen that can be pulled up to deal with customer inquiries. Notice the script, the system status about the customers being served or waiting and the ability of the agent to connect to other systems such as the Main Frame. Figure 5 shows a stop payment transaction that utilizes information from local as well as remote systems. A key feature is the wizard that guides the agent through the possible actions as well as the comprehensive screen that can be used to input all the information within a single screen to complete the transaction.

Figure 2: Main Screen

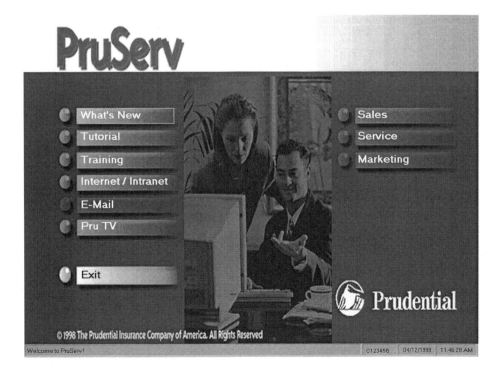

Figure 3: Account Information Screen

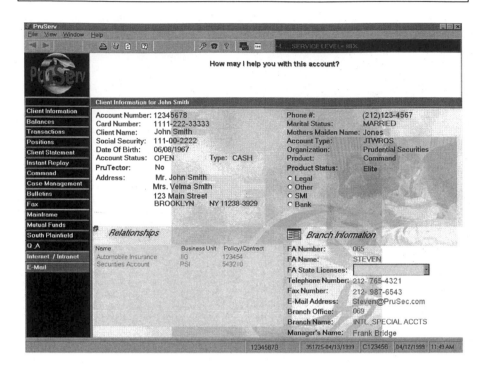

19.6 Benefits of the System for Prudential

PruServ™ was developed and introduced to the call center environment at an estimated cost of $1.2 million. Several third party solutions were considered by the company at an average cost of $43 million. Due to this tremendous cost it was decided to build an "in-house" solution. Significant savings have been realized in both call center and back office operations.

Since its inception, PruServ™ has been deployed in the call center and service departments at the following locations: Minneapolis, Atlanta, New York and New Jersey. PruServ™ has also been deployed on the laptops of many mobile users. More importantly, PruServ™ has become the "model" by which future Prudential back-office systems will be implemented. Also, since PruServ™ provides a standardized user interface, there are valuable collaboration benefits throughout the enterprise. An employee in one business group who is familiar with PruServ™ can easily work with other groups because of the common business and messaging services that are provided.

Figure 4: Transaction Screen

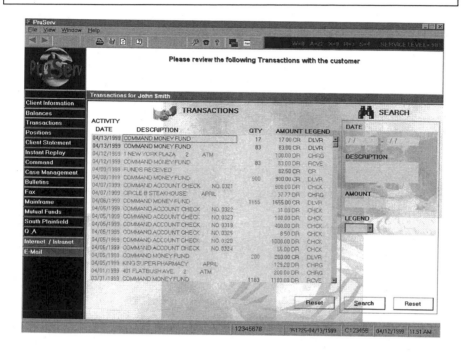

Another tremendous benefit lies in the fact that PruServ™ has refined business workflows by automating many of the tasks. A customer can now call a representative, order one or multiple products or request one or more services, and receive it within hours where previously it may have taken several days. This is possible because PruServ™ automates the many steps that were previously processed by different groups. The representative now has the power to complete the transaction at the point of contact increasing both employee efficiency and customer satisfaction.

With its flexible application deployment features, adaptable graphical user interface and its "plug and play" structure, PruServ™ is laying the groundwork for future systems development within the Prudential enterprise.

PruServ™ has become the central gateway to the Prudential enterprise's Digital Nervous System. By bringing all of the systems in the enterprise to a common interface, it enables users to make "well informed" decisions at the point of contact. Before the existence of PruServ™, information did not flow freely from system to system. Customer service representatives were required to access multiple systems in order to get the information needed to help the customer. The information gathered was not complete because of the broad gaps between business groups. This wasted valuable time and resources. Information gathered by one business entity can now be viewed across the enterprise from one desktop to the next, regardless of location or point of entry, making Prudential one continuous entity.

Figure 5: Stop Payment Screen

Interoperability between business groups has eliminated many steps of the processes through automation. For example one business function, placing a stop payment on a check, was reduced from 112 steps to 1. Many tasks were processed manually with a potential for human error. It would even require the involvement of many departments just to complete one transaction. Like the human nervous system, stimuli or user input triggers automatic response, streamlining the business as a whole. With the emergence of PruServ™, workers spend less time doing manual tasks and more time concentrating on the customer and "World Class" service.

19.7 Discussion

PruServ™ was originally intended to support only the COMMAND^SM and Advantage products. As the development cycle progressed it became evident that PruServ™ was much more. Since then it has become the framework for nearly all back office and call center development. Several of the departments that have leveraged PruServ™ are:

- Automated Custom Account Transfer System (ACATS)
- Insurance Retention Product
- Retirements
- Mutual Funds
- Credit
- Hybrid Life Insurance and Mutual Fund Product
- Cashiers ("Cage")
- LockBox
- COMMAND^SM
- Advantage

PruServ™ has broken free of the traditional software development philosophy at Prudential. Grasping the most cutting edge technology such as ActiveX and Internet download technologies, PruServ™ has taken Windows-based programming to the next level. The power of the Web has been leveraged to build applications that are more robust and scalable than ever before. As the first Rapid Application Development (RAD) framework built for the enterprise, there are currently over 100 programmers writing code to PruServ™.

Business applications that may have taken 6 months or more to develop can now be built in a little over 10 weeks. For example, where it may have taken a month to develop security for an application, it can now be done in less than one week due to PruServ's security model. PruServ™ provides a solid framework to develop Windows applications within Prudential. It exposes all of the tools a developer could need to develop "World Class" business applications.

Acknowledgements

The editors gratefully acknowledge the editorial help of Julia Herbert, First Vice President, Prudential Securities Incorporated, and thank her for bringing to our attention this state of the art call center support system.

SECTION IV:

CUSTOMER VALUE FOCUSED
MEASURES OF SUCCESS

Chapter 20

Process Improvement in Financial Services: A Focused Approach[1]

Paresh D. Patel
Corporate Executive Board Company

20.1   Faltering After a Fast Start

According to various sources, the number of formal service quality programs among the top 300 U.S. commercial banks grew from only 28 in 1985 to 232 in 1994[2]. The reasons for their implementation range from worthy service quality concerns to simple "follow-the-leader" strategies. The benefits garnered from such programs, however, were not as widespread as their implementation: a majority of institutions surveyed in the U.S. and U.K. remain hard-pressed to find any tangible financial benefits from their quality initiatives (see Figure 1).[3]

That is not to say that these programs had no effect. TQM proponents validly argue that the number of defections stemming from poor service quality (as opposed to poor product quality) fell drastically from 1986 to 1994 (see Figure 2)[4]. Although the data here are neither comprehensive nor necessarily causal, it

---

[1] The conclusions in this chapter are based on over 250 interviews with senior financial services executives in the U.S., Canada, Europe and Australia. The research was conducted in 1995 for the Operations Council of The Corporate Executive Board Company and was published in *Breath of Life: Infusing Quality Initiatives with Market Discipline.*

[2] Federal Reserve Board; Bank Administration Institute

[3] McCabe, Knights and Wilkinson, 1994.

[4] The Forum Group; University of Tennessee Financial Institutions Center

appears that across these eight years, consumers began to defect more because of concerns with the products they were buying rather than the service they were receiving.

Figure 1: Benefits from Quality Programs

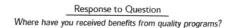

Response to Question
Where have you received benefits from quality programs?

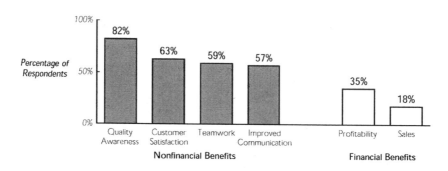

Figure 2: Root Causes of Controllable Defections, 1986-1994

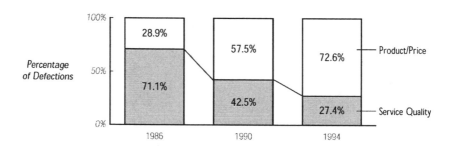

By 1992, in the U.S., the vast majority of institutions were able to meet their own, internal service quality standards for process efficiency (see Figure 3).[5] Attaining these standards, however, did not translate into greater returns for two reasons. First, because these gains were so broadly achieved, consumers could not perceive discernible quality differences between providers (see Figure 4).[6] Second, the industry had improved service performance in "lock-step", simply raising baseline service levels across the board. Empirical evidence supports this conclusion: even though service levels were continuously improving (see Figure 5)[7], customer satisfaction leveled off (see Figure 6)[8] and customer retention remained virtually unchanged (see Figure 7).[9]

Figure 3: Areas Where Bankers Have Met Service Quality Goals in the Past Five Years

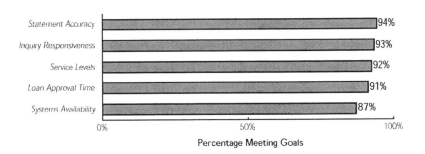

Figure 4: Service A Differentiating Attribute?

Percentage of Customers That Consider Customer Service
to Be Differentiating Attribute of Their Financial Service Institution

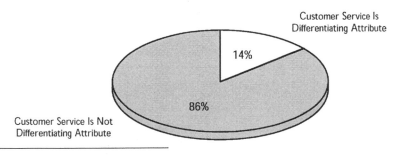

---

[5] Roth, A. & van der Velde, M. 1992.
[6] *ibid.*
[7] Operations Council, 1995.
[8] American Banker, 1995.
[9] Council on Financial Competition, 1994.

Figure 5: Back-Office Process Efficiency Statistics

Check Processing MICR Error Rates, 1985–1995

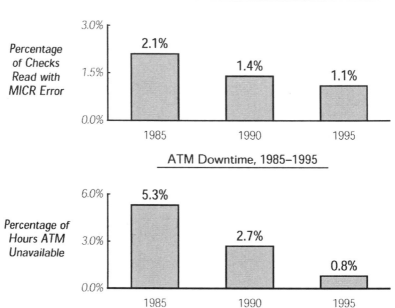

ATM Downtime, 1985–1995

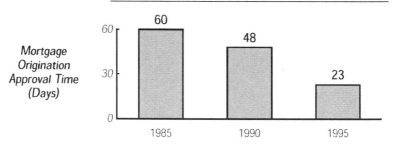

Mortgage Origination Approval Time, 1985–1995

Figure 6: Percentage of Customers Very Satisfied with Primary Financial Institution

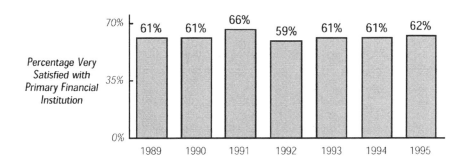

Figure 7: Average Retention Rates, 1991-1994

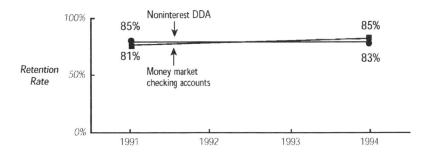

By 1992-1994, it appeared that TQM programs reached the point of diminishing returns. Quality had improved so drastically across the industry that service levels were well into the customer's "zone of indifference." In other words, consumers could not perceive or did not value the difference in incremental changes in service levels. Anecdotal evidence suggests that by 1994 senior executives, recognizing that their investments in service quality had already paid off or were not conclusively value-added, cancelled quality programs.[10] In fact, in a 1994 survey of senior retail banking executives, institutions revealed how low "differentiating by service levels" was on their list of strategic priorities (see Figure 8).[11]

---

[10] Although no firm figures for the exact number are available, interviews with senior executives and heads of quality estimate that two-thirds of all quality programs were cancelled or not renewed between 1993-1995.
[11] American Banker, The Tower Group, Andersen Consulting. 1994.

Figure 8: Top Retail Business Objectives

Top Retail Business Objectives, 1994

	1994 Ranking
1	Grow by acquisition
2	Grow fee income
3	Cross-sell existing customers
4	Acquire new customers
5	Reengineer the distribution system
6	Standardize product/service offerings
7	Improve customer retention
8	Enhance/introduce new products
9	Better manage credit risk
10	Reengineer the back office
11	Create new distribution channels
12	Improve product/relationship profitability
13	Differentiate by service levels

Service Quality

20.2 Problems with Implementation

This chapter posits that this decision to abandon or downsize quality programs was premature. Indeed, many institutions mistook diminishing returns from TQM investments as an inherent flaw with the model rather than as shortcomings with how service quality programs were implemented. While TQM's implementation problems include organizational structure, incentive and leadership issues, this chapter will focus on the problems with service quality stemming from poor measurement systems.

As currently constructed, traditional measurement programs have three major flaws:

1. *Lack of Focus* – Measurement systems tend to "focus on everything", dissipating resources on improving all processes continuously rather than those with the greatest potential impact on perceived quality and customer purchase behavior
2. *Disconnect from financial outcomes* – Measurement systems rely heavily on intermediate metrics (process efficiency, customer satisfaction) that

3. lack explicit linkages to financial outcomes and, ultimately, remain unhelpful in resource allocation decisions
3. *Internal View* – More often than not quality measures benchmark progress temporally rather than cross-sectionally, often ignoring perceived quality relative to competitors.

Lack of Focus

The average financial institution tracks 61 different process efficiency metrics in their IT back-office, 63 in transaction processing, 26 in loan operations and 29 in account systems (see Figure 9).[12] These activities comprise only a small portion of the total operations in a financial institution. Yet, efforts and resources to improve quality are often dispersed across all these functions, regardless of their impact on internal or external customers. In addition, approximately 71% of institutions raise the minimum acceptable service standards on an annual basis on the majority of the metrics they use[13].

Figure 9: Number of Metrics Tracked in Back Office

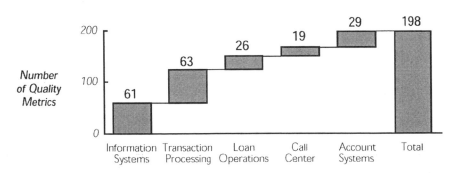

Five Sample Functions, Average Bank

This lack of focus is problematic because neither do all processes affect internal or external customers equally nor do all process improvements provide increasing or constant returns. Indeed, consumer perceptions of service quality are not linear. Within every process, there are broad bands of indifference within which customers can either perceive little difference in performance or are unwilling to change behavior given the difference. Successful quality measurement systems should recognize that indifference levels exist and should focus on those changes that can be perceived or are valued by customers.

---

[12] Operations Council, 1995.
[13] *ibid.*

Disconnect from Financial Outcomes

Another shortcoming of traditional process efficiency metrics is their disconnect from financial outcomes. Traditional quality metrics such as process efficiency and customer satisfaction are intermediate in nature and are difficult to correlate with customer purchase behavior. As a result, when institutions allocate resources across potential process improvement programs, it is often unclear which projects will generate the greatest returns and thus deserve the greatest share of investment. Problems with linking quality improvements to financial returns is not particular to service industries. 71% of quality practitioners in manufacturing companies report difficulty in relating the benefits of quality programs to accounting returns.[14]

Internal View

The third problem with current measurement systems is the tendency to benchmark internally across time as opposed to externally across institutions. In 1992, only 37% of financial institutions benchmarked performance against competitors (see Figure 10).[15] Since consumers' evaluations of service quality and total experience with an institution are made relative to other options in the marketplace, an internal focus can often lead to high internal efficiency on variables that provide little differentiation in the marketplace.

Figure 10: Percentage Of Banks Benchmarking Performance Against Competitors

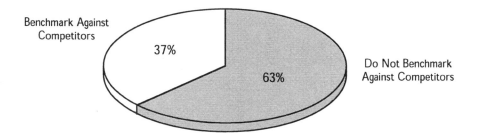

---

[14] Ittner, C.D. & Larcker, D.F., 1996.
[15] American Quality Foundation & Ernst & Young, 1992.

20.3   Four New Methods for Measuring Process Performance

Recognizing these limitations with traditional metrics, pioneering institutions have shown an increased interest in improving the diagnostic and predictive value of their quality measures. To do so, institutions need to understand how changes in underlying processes or absolute service levels affect consumer perceptions of the service provided (or the institution) and, ultimately, consumer purchase behavior.

New statistical techniques allow institutions to better understand the linkages between process measures, customer satisfaction and financial results. These tools were first developed in the telecommunications industry in the early 1990s and were transferred to financial services in the mid-1990s. At the most basic level, these new techniques attempt to measure the statistical relationships between individual process performance, customer satisfaction and customer purchase behavior. For example, if an institution decided to reduce call center wait time by two minutes, these techniques would estimate the impact on customer satisfaction and the subsequent impact on purchase behavior (see Figure 11)[16]. There are four established methods for estimating these linkages.

Figure 11: Linkages Between Prophecies and Outcomes

Method 1

The first method (Fornell, Johnson, Anderson, Cha & Bryant, 1996) statistically links subprocess satisfaction with process satisfaction, process satisfaction with process perceived quality, process perceived quality with overall perceived quality, overall perceived quality with overall satisfaction, and finally overall satisfaction with loyalty and repurchase intent (see Figure 12)[17]. The differentiating features of this approach include the use of perceived quality as a diagnostic variable and the associated inclusion of price in determining perceived value.

---

[16] Operations Council, 1995.
[17] *ibid*, 75.

A major European universal bank incorporated this analysis in its private banking division to evaluate the service and proficiency of its advisor force. The firm surveyed its client base on 21 broad attributes, with each attribute comprised of 4-5 subcomponents (see Figure 13)[18]. The results were mapped across multiple client groups (see Figure 14)[19] as well as multiple branch locations (see Figure 15)[20] to determine potential problem areas. The statistical relationships were ultimately used to prioritize service enhancements within the private banking group.

Figure 12: Method #1

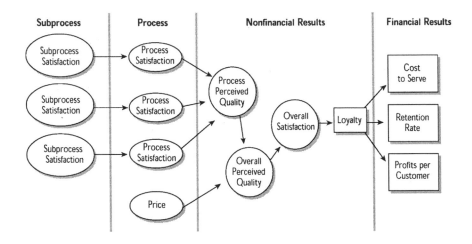

---

[18] *ibid*, 68.
[19] *ibid*, 76.
[20] *ibid*, 77.

Figure 13: Customer Preference Data

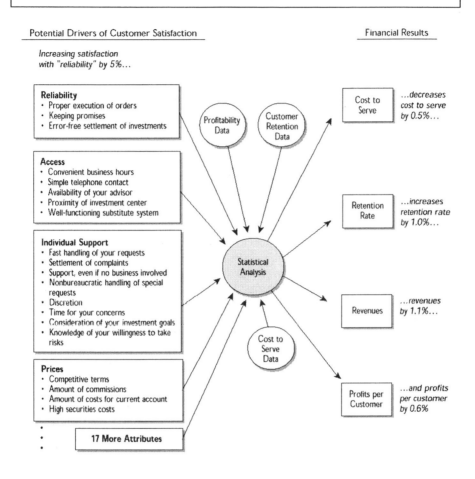

Potential Drivers of Customer Satisfaction

Financial Results

Increasing satisfaction with "reliability" by 5%...

Reliability
- Proper execution of orders
- Keeping promises
- Error-free settlement of investments

Access
- Convenient business hours
- Simple telephone contact
- Availability of your advisor
- Proximity of investment center
- Well-functioning substitute system

Individual Support
- Fast handling of your requests
- Settlement of complaints
- Support, even if no business involved
- Nonbureaucratic handling of special requests
- Discretion
- Time for your concerns
- Consideration of your investment goals
- Knowledge of your willingness to take risks

Prices
- Competitive terms
- Amount of commissions
- Amount of costs for current account
- High securities costs

-
- **17 More Attributes**
-

Profitability Data

Customer Retention Data

Statistical Analysis

Cost to Serve Data

Cost to Serve — *...decreases cost to serve by 0.5%...*

Retention Rate — *...increases retention rate by 1.0%...*

Revenues — *...revenues by 1.1%...*

Profits per Customer — *...and profits per customer by 0.6%*

Figure 14: Importance of Satisfaction Variables on Revenues and Retention by Customer Segment

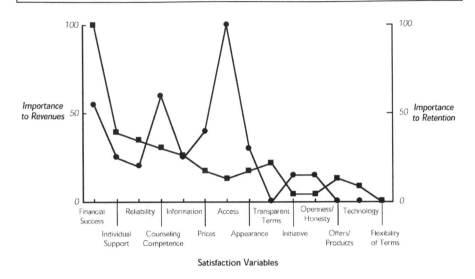

Method 2

The second method uses a similar methodology with two variations (see Figure 16)[21]. First, this process excludes a price variable and, as such, does not attempt to estimate perceived value (Rust, Zahorik & Keiningham, 1994, 1995). Instead linkages are estimated between process satisfaction and overall satisfaction directly. Second, overall satisfaction is linked to repurchase intent (not to loyalty), which is then linked to retention rates[22]. Repurchase intention is based on self-reported customer expectations of their future behavior rather than actual retention/repurchase data. Consequently, this analysis predicts behavior based on customer expectations of their own future preferences or needs rather than on historical purchase and repurchase patterns.

---

[21] *ibid*, 75.

[22] Where a customer has several products with an institution, linking to actual retention data can generate inaccurate results. If consumers are freely switching across substitute products (between savings assets and money market assets or credit card balances and home equity line of credit balances), product-level retention may be low, but customer-level retention would remain constant. Institutions should carefully screen all retention data before undertaking any of the four statistical models.

Figure 15: French Market Quality Profile

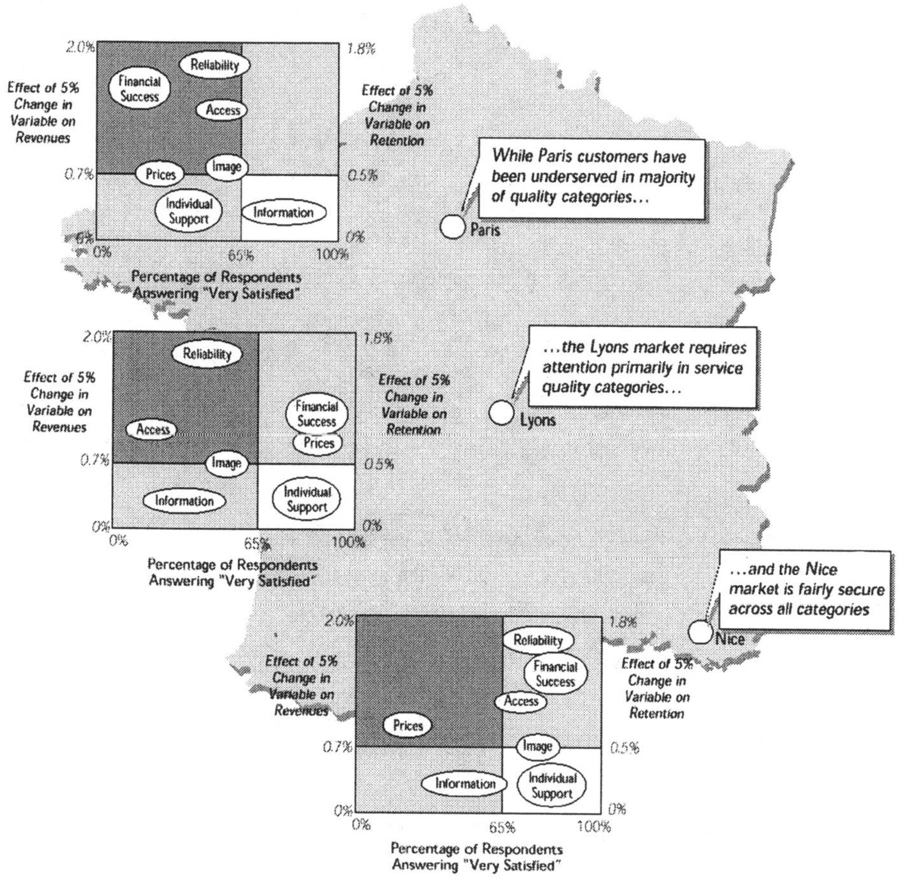

Paris chart

Effect of 5% Change in Variable on Revenues — 2.0%, 0.7%, 0%
Effect of 5% Change in Variable on Retention — 1.8%, 0.5%, 0%
Percentage of Respondents Answering "Very Satisfied" — 0%, 65%, 100%

Categories: Reliability, Financial Success, Access, Prices, Image, Individual Support, Information

While Paris customers have been underserved in majority of quality categories... Paris

Lyons chart

Effect of 5% Change in Variable on Revenues — 2.0%, 0.7%, 0%
Effect of 5% Change in Variable on Retention — 1.8%, 0.5%, 0%
Percentage of Respondents Answering "Very Satisfied" — 0%, 65%, 100%

Categories: Reliability, Access, Financial Success, Prices, Image, Information, Individual Support

...the Lyons market requires attention primarily in service quality categories... Lyons

Nice chart

Effect of 5% Change in Variable on Revenues — 2.0%, 0.7%, 0%
Effect of 5% Change in Variable on Retention — 1.8%, 0.5%, 0%
Percentage of Respondents Answering "Very Satisfied" — 0%, 65%, 100%

Categories: Reliability, Financial Success, Access, Prices, Image, Information, Individual Support

...and the Nice market is fairly secure across all categories Nice

Figure 16: Method #2

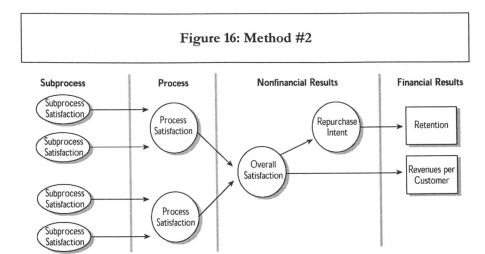

Several U.S. money center and regional banking institutions have implemented this approach. The analyses in these instances have been segmented according to dissatisfied, satisfied and delighted customers (see Figure 17)[23]. This extra layer of precision allows the institution to understand the threshold levels within which increasing service would increase customer perceived value. This analysis, however, is not linked directly back to actual service levels (individual customer record numbers are not kept during the survey process). Hence, institutions using this method still need to rely on their own judgement when designing and planning process changes.

Figure 17: Repurchase Intention by Degree of Satisfaction

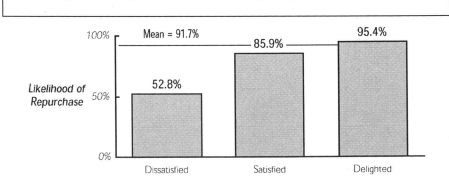

---

[23] *ibid*, 78.

Method 3

The third method (Bolton & Drew, 1991a, 1991b) measures the relationship between process-specific service events and service levels with customer satisfaction, customer satisfaction with historical purchase behavior and historical purchase behavior with customer repurchase intention (see Figure 18)[24]. This methodology has three variations from the first model. First, this approach uses actual service levels rather than satisfaction with different processes. Second, this approach includes actual service events (e.g. customer complaint calls) in addition to service levels. Third, satisfaction data is linked to historical purchase behavior rather than self-reported expected behavior.

Figure 18: Method #3

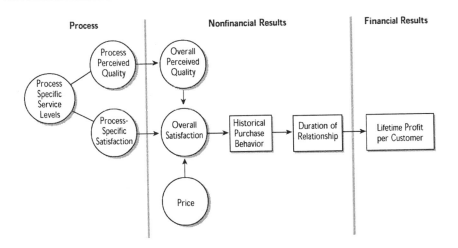

---

[24] *ibid*, 74.

This variant is advantageous where data collection at the customer level is possible. An analysis that starts with actual service levels or events rather than satisfaction with a process can be more informative when evaluating where to alter or improve processes. Not all service levels for all processes, however, can be reasonably linked to customer satisfaction. For example, with processes such as check processing, customers typically do not have meaningful opinions about their level of satisfaction.

This methodology was first used by GTE to assess potential responses to high customer churn in its cellular services unit. The analysis helped GTE evaluate two proposals for reducing churn: first, improve service when customers call to complain, and second, mitigate complaints by improving customers' product knowledge (see Figure 19)[25]. Recognizing that delighting customers at the point of service recovery was unreasonable (see Figure 20)[26], GTE ultimately decided to focus on educating users at point of sale.

Figure 19: Analysis for GTE Cellular Services

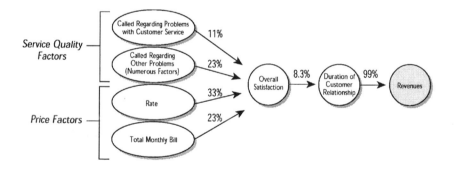

---

[25] *ibid*, 84.
[26] *ibid*.

Figure 20: Performance Required by CSRs after Service Failure to Offset Penalty of Poor Service

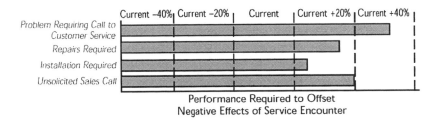

The three methodologies discussed above analyze consumer behavior in a single-firm context. The single-firm context, however, is problematic because satisfaction with a firm and repurchase intention often are not correlated (see Figure 21)[27] due to consumer perception of greater value in the marketplace (see Figure 22)[28].

Figure 21: Repurchase Intention of Customers rating Service to be "Good" or "Excellent"

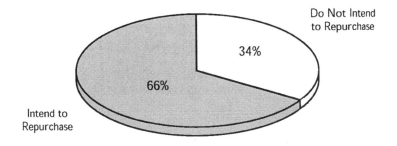

---

27 Gale and Wood, 1994.
28 *ibid.*

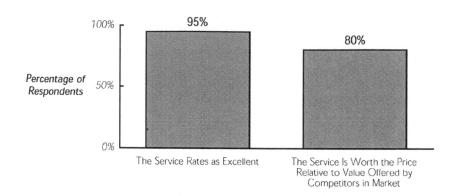

Figure 22: Comparison of Customer Value and Satisfaction

Method 4

To address this problem, the fourth method (Gale & Wood, 1994) measures the linkages between perceived value[29] (defined as perceived service quality, price and product quality) and customer purchase behavior. Measuring perceived value involves consumer surveying and statistical modeling techniques (see Figure 23)[30] similar to the prior three methods, with two key exceptions. First, the data describes relationships between firms rather than for one institution on a stand-alone basis. Second, the survey process includes interviews with both customers and non-customers.

This analysis is replicated for all competitors in the marketplace and are plotted on "value maps" to understand an institution's position relative to the competition (see Figure 24)[31]. These value maps were first used at AT&T and New Zealand Telecom and have been used since by a number of large U.S. and Canadian financial institutions. Ideally an institution would locate one's position on the map and alter underlying service, product or price attributes to gain a better value position relative to competitors.

---

[29] Although the first and fourth approaches appear to be similar, they are different. While the first approach estimates a perceived value using a price variable, the fourth approach estimates relative perceived value using a price variable and competitor preference data.

[30] Council on Financial Competition, 1996.

[31] *ibid.*

Figure 23: Perceived Value Map

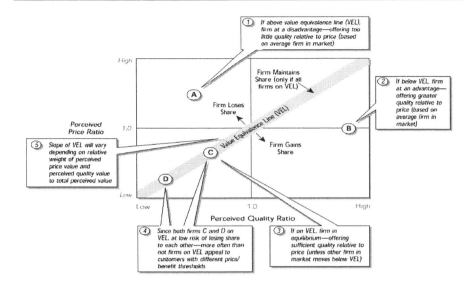

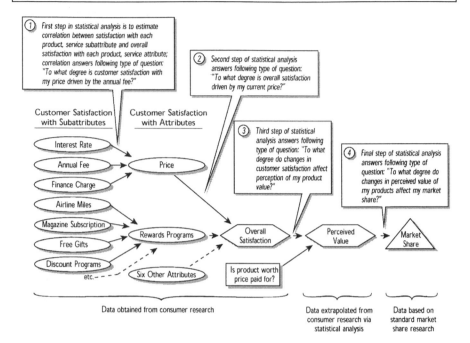

Figure 24: Statistical Analysis for Credit Card Product

This chapter presents four statistical models to estimate the linkages between service processes and consumer behavior. For the average financial institution, finding the most accurate model is less important than understanding how to interpret the data. Because these models cannot include all possible antecedents of purchase behavior and still provide very specific data on the financial impact of different process improvements, institutions should be cautious when interpreting the results. As with most statistical techniques, these methods are meant to guide, rather than to instruct, the user to potential remedies.

20.4 From Incremental Improvements to Wholesale Process Change

While all four methodologies have distinct advantages over traditional measurement programs, because they rely on improving current processes, they foster incremental process changes. Yet, given the maturity of the financial services industry, incremental changes in service standards often are too small to be discernible to customers or are too small to impact costs appreciably. In such an environment, programs based upon continuous improvement and market benchmarks are less effective than wholesale process redesign.

Indeed, oftentimes the highest returns from quality investments accrue to those who look beyond internal operations and attempt to reset market standards for service quality. Fidelity Investments and Countrywide Mortgage are prime examples of institutions that reestablished industry norms for service via drastic service enhancements. In the 1980s while the banking industry was focused on extending branch hours during the workweek, Fidelity radically redesigned service delivery with the 24/7 call center, bringing service previously reserved for the affluent market to the middle market. In the early 1990s, Countrywide reduced mortgage origination time from 45 days to 28 days and ultimately from 28 days to less than one hour (the industry still averaged between 30-40 days). Such drastic improvements, enabled by vendor and internally developed technology, lay the stage for rapid growth in production volume over the same time period.

The common element behind both service improvements is that market differentiation was created by radically redesigning internal process flow and recalibrating service standards beyond customer expectations. Indeed, continuous and incremental improvement programs did not play a role in either case.

20.5 Conclusion

The first step for institutions looking to improve process quality is to upgrade internal measurement systems, moving away from intermediate metrics towards more actionable measures of performance. These measures should help the institution identify those variables with the greatest impact on customer purchase behavior and should identify performance relative to the competition. In the long run, however, traditional incremental improvements will not create sustainable differentiation in the marketplace. Indeed, the greatest rewards will accrue to those institutions that reset service norms (and expectations) via wholesale process change.

References

1. American Banker, The Tower Group & Andersen Consulting. 1994. *Information Technology in Banking Survey.* Washington DC: American Banker Inc.
2. American Banker. 1995. *American Banker Consumer Survey.* American Banker, Inc.
3. American Quality Foundation & Ernst & Young. 1992. *International Quality Study (IQS) Best Practices Report: Banking Industry.* Cleveland: Ernst & Young.
4. Bolton, R. & Drew, J. 1991a. A Longitudinal Analysis of the Impact of Service Changes on Customer Attitudes. *Journal of Marketing*, 55 (Jan), 1-9.
5. Bolton, R. & Drew, J. 1991b. A Multistage Model of Customers' Assessment of Service Quality and Value. *Journal of Consumer Research*, 17 (Mar), 375-384.
6. Council on Financial Competition. 1994. *Council on Financial Competition Retention Database.* Washington, DC: Corporate Executive Board Company.
7. Council on Financial Competition. 1996. *Beyond Commodity Status: Responding to the New Mandate for Growth.* Washington, DC: Corporate Executive Board Company.
8. Fornell, C., Johnson, M. D., Anderson, E. W., Cha, J. & Bryant, B. E. 1996. The American Customer Satisfaction Index: Nature, purpose, and findings. *Journal of Marketing*, 60 (4), 7-18.
9. Gale, B. T. & Wood, R. C. 1994. *Managing Customer Value: Creating Quality and Service that Customers Can See.* New York: Free Press.
10. Ittner, C. D. & Larcker, D. F. 1996. Measuring the Impact of Quality Initiatives on Firm Financial Performance. In S. Ghosh & D. Fedor (Eds.) *Advances in the Management of Organizational Quality, Vol. 1*: 1-37. Greenwich, CT: JAI Press.
11. McCabe, Knights and Wilkinson. 1994. *Quality Initiatives in the Financial Services.* Manchester, England: Financial Services Research Center, UMIST.
12. Operations Council. 1995. *Breath of Life: Infusing Quality Initiatives with Market Discipline.* Washington, DC: The Corporate Executive Board Company.
13. Operations Council. 1995. *Operations Council Benchmarking Database,* Washington, DC: The Corporate Executive Board Company.
14. Roth, A. & van der Velde, M. 1992. *World Class Banking: Benchmarking the Strategies of Retail Banking Leaders.* Washington, DC: Bank Administration Institute.
15. Rust, R. T., Zahorik, A. J. & Keiningham, T. L. 1994. *Return on Quality: Measuring the Financial Impact of Your Company's Quest for Quality.* Chicago, Ill: Probus Pub. Co.
16. Rust, R. T, Zahorik, A. J. & Keiningham, T. L. 1995. Return on quality (ROQ): Making service quality financially accountable. *Journal of Marketing.* 59 (2), 58-80.

Chapter 21

How Do Financial Services Stack Up? Findings from a Benchmarking Study of the US Financial Service Sector

Richard B. Chase
University of Southern California
Aleda V. Roth
University of North Carolina-Chapel Hill
Chris Voss
London Business School

21.1 Introduction

Since the early 1980s, numerous universities and institutes have conducted competitiveness benchmarking studies comparing practices and performance of firms in various industries worldwide (see, for example, Roth, Gray, Singhal, and Singhal, 1997). The goal of such studies is to develop an understanding of what works and what does not work in manufacturing, what are best practices, and as the name implies, benchmarking one's own company and industry against others as a starting point for improving operational performance. One would expect that similar benefits would accrue to financial services, yet there are few systematic benchmarking studies reported in the literature. (An exception being the series of benchmarking studies of world class strategies and performance in retail banking conducted by researchers at University of North Carolina under the aegis of the Bank Administration Institute from 1987 to 1993 (Roth and Van der Velde, 1991 and 1992; Roth, 1993; Roth and Jackson, 1995).)

There are several reasons why benchmarking of the financial sector is important. One is that with the eventual emergence of the trillion dollar bank (Greising et al., 1998), the ability to provide one-stop, full-service banking is becoming a competitive necessity as customers seemingly desire "everything" from their financial service providers (Milligan, 1997). Another is to gauge organizational learning and subsequent adaptation to an increasingly turbulent environment. Indeed, globalization, sweeping industry consolidations, hyper-competition, and continuous product innovation through technological advancement will continue to characterize the US financial sector in the next decade (White, 1998; Crane and Bodie, 1996). But beyond these trends in the macro environment of the sector, financial services are faced with even more basic service problems that need to be addressed. Consider the declining levels of customer satisfaction with banks as measured by *Fortune Magazine's* American Customer Satisfaction Index (ACSI). In 1996, the ACSI score for commercial banks was "74," and one year later, dropped to "72". This drop is not surprising as seen, for example, in a study of Phoenix bank customers conducted by O'Neil Associates (Vandeveire, 1997). When asked, a sample of 459 bank customers showed little loyalty for their institutions. About 41 percent indicated they "would shop for a new bank and switch if it matched their needs. Eight percent said they didn't know." This survey, and other surveys like it, simply tell financial service providers that they will have to work hard to keep customers. Their study, however, stopped short of providing guidance on where and how this should be done-- this calls for benchmarking with industries outside the financial services sector. Making such benchmarking comparisons is the purpose of this chapter.

Specifically, we compare the practices and performance of a sample of firms in financial services with world class hotels that were found to be exemplars of service practices and performance. Beyond just being at the top of the list in our study, hotels have some major issues in common with financial services, which make them particularly attractive for benchmarking. They are among the most competitive of services; they are represented by some of the largest private service organizations in the world; and they need to do an effective job in managing the service encounter. The chapter also draws international comparisons of US and UK financial services practices and performance, and touches on the UK hotel sector, which was also found to be the exemplar in Britain. (In this benchmarking study, we define *practices* as the established processes that an organization has in place to design, deliver, and measure its service. *Performance* is defined as the ways an organization's impacts and influences are measured, including both financial and non-financial outcomes.)

21.2 The Database

The results in this chapter are based on the benchmarking data collected in a research project called *The International Service Study (ISS)*, an international study conducted by the Center for Service Excellence, Marshall School of Business, University of Southern California, the Kenan-Flagler Business School at the University of North Carolina -Chapel Hill, and London Business School. (See Roth, Chase, and Voss 1997 for a detailed description of the study.)

The research model is predicated on the hypothesis that the adoption of best practices has a direct link with the attainment of high service performance which, in turn, leads to superior business performance and competitiveness (Voss et al, 1997). It also draws on established models of practice and performance in service organizations. These include: 1) the "service profit chain" (Heskett et al, 1994, Loveman, 1998), which posits that there are strong links between customer satisfaction and loyalty, and business performance with employee satisfaction and loyalty, productivity, and service value; 2) Chase and Hayes (1995) four stage model of service competitiveness; 3) SERVQUAL (Parasuraman et al, 1985) a well-known instrument for measuring service quality; 4) Roth's Service Capabilities Indexes which link service capabilities, strategy, and performance (C-S-P) (Roth 1993 and Roth and Jackson 1995); and 5) several national quality awards, such as the US Department of Commerce's Malcolm Baldrige National Quality Award (NIST, 1997) and the European/British Quality Award (EFQM, 1997) frameworks.

The ISS survey instrument consists of a set of 80 questions that examine each of 12 practice drivers and six performance outcome areas specified in the model. Each of the questions was scored on five-point interval scale, with "1" representing the poorest level and "5" the outstanding practice or performance. Each question was anchored by descriptors denoting how the values 1, 3 and 5 should be interpreted, and thus, enabled interviewees and interviewers to consistently rate responses on a psychometric continuum.

The data collection was performed by research teams from the cooperating universities, who conducted personal interviews with senior executive teams from a broad sample of service firms. Each of the research teams applied the ISS questionnaire, as described above, and identical data collection methods to ensure the comparability of the results. Cross-training among the researchers was performed to ensure interviewer reliability. The interviews, which ranged between two and four hours, were typically conducted face-to-face with executive teams from the company. Interviewers were instructed to obtain the organization's actual practices and performance at the time of the interview. Interviewees were instructed to state the current situation at their firm, not what was planned or anticipated to be the circumstance in the future.

To assure comparability between organizations, the final scores were assigned by interviewers who would challenge managers to substantiate their responses where appropriate. Secondary documents that helped to confirm the results were frequently collected. This approach was adopted to mitigate the tendency of executives to promote themselves and their company's image rather than basing their answers on fact (Roth 1993). To lessen any internal pressure to provide inflated responses, each interviewee was assured that all data – including identities - was strictly confidential.

A total of 182 firms in the US participated in the survey, with 32 in the financial sector and 15 in the hotel sector. Company sizes varied from more than 500 to less than 50 employees; very small companies were excluded on the basis that firms such as family run hotels would be unable to relate their practices to those described in the survey instrument. The breakdown of US firms in the financial sector was as follows: 17 banks, 9 insurance companies, three credit card issuers, two credit unions, and one financial services firm. The multi-attribute scales derived from the 80 survey questions were used to evaluate each practice driver and performance outcome (Roth, Chase, and Voss 1997). Each scale was computed by averaging the defining items. The definitions are summarized below:

Practice Driver Scales:

1) *Using a balanced scorecard:* Includes measures for managing service practice using a variety of metrics such as quality data, complaints, managing client loyalty, as well as cost based performance measures. (7 questions).
2) *Quality Leadership:* Defines CEO leadership, shared quality vision and goals, etc. (10 questions).
3) *Empowerment:* Indicates employee empowerment, work force flexibility, handling of failures, complaint handling procedures (4 questions).
4) *Kaizen:* Continuous improvement, quality education and training, quality procedures (3 questions).
5) *New Service Development:* Covers the design and development process, organizational structure for new services, and customer input (3 questions).

6) *Moments of Truth:* Defines the interactions (or encounters) between the service firm and the customer, include service recovery, service guarantees, employee loyalty, mapping service processes (4 questions).

7) *Cycle of Virtue:* Designates a positively reinforcing personnel practice cycle that come from hiring the best workers, training them well, and rewarding them well; often contrasted with the "cycle of failure", where the opposite polices are used, and includes items related to job training, recognition, employee involvement (3 questions).

8) *Value Orientation:* Highlights how value is created, including providing value for money, elimination of non-value adding activities, recognizing the role of the back office in creating value (3 questions).

9) *Business Process Reengineering (BPR):* Covers the radical redesign of processes including the use of information technology and extent of business process implementation (2 questions).

10) *Service Representations:* Pertains to the service tangibles (or sensory features of the service) and access to the service (2 questions).

11) *Market Acuity:* Deals with sensors to outside the firm, such as benchmarking, competitive positioning, listening to the customer, understanding value drivers, etc. (9 questions).

12) *Service Standards:* Designates service standards, challenging standards, and visibility of service targets (5 questions).

Performance Outcome Scales:

1) *Service Quality:* Covers performance in the "three Ts" of service encounters: the task to be done, the treatment accorded the customer, and the tangible features of the service system; distinctive service, employee satisfaction, etc. (11 questions).

2) *Customer Growth:* Measures customer base, innovation performance, development speed, customer retention (4 questions).

3) *Altruism:* Shows impact on society, employee loyalty (2 questions).

4) *Organizational Productivity:* Reflects productivity gains, productivity and efficiency, market share change (3 questions).

5) *Business Performance:* Indicates cash flow, margins, return on assets (3 questions)

6) *Cost/Price:* Describes relative prices, production costs (2 questions).

21.3 Results and Analysis

A general model of service competitiveness

A major output of the ISS research project was an hypothesized theoretical model which groups the practice drivers into four "value constellations" which must operate in a synergistic fashion to achieve maximum results for the service organization. (See Roth, Chase, and Voss, 1997.)   This model is depicted in Figure 1, and will be discussed as it pertains to financial services later.

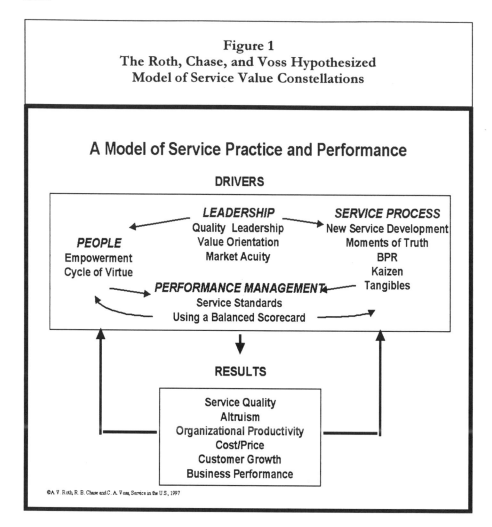

Figure 1
The Roth, Chase, and Voss Hypothesized
Model of Service Value Constellations

A Model of Service Practice and Performance

DRIVERS

LEADERSHIP
Quality Leadership
Value Orientation
Market Acuity

PEOPLE
Empowerment
Cycle of Virtue

SERVICE PROCESS
New Service Development
Moments of Truth
BPR
Kaizen
Tangibles

PERFORMANCE MANAGEMENT
Service Standards
Using a Balanced Scorecard

RESULTS

Service Quality
Altruism
Organizational Productivity
Cost/Price
Customer Growth
Business Performance

©A. V. Roth, R. B. Chase and C. A. Voss, Service in the U.S., 1997

Sector comparisons

Service sectors as a whole differ vastly in their overall practices and performance. The practice-performance map in Figure 2 highlights the relative competitive positioning for US service sectors. As can be seen from the figure, financial services are slightly above the average in service performance, and rates about average in terms of their efforts toward world class service practices.

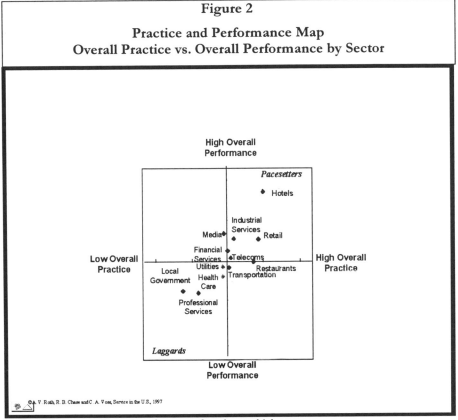

Figure 2

**Practice and Performance Map
Overall Practice vs. Overall Performance by Sector**

©A. V. Roth, R. B. Chase and C. A. Voss, Service in the U.S., 1997

Scale: Relative practice and performance from low to high.

As is apparent in Figure 2, the financial services sector fares better than about half of the other sectors studied. The "laggards" tended to fall into the more 'regulated' and not-for-profit sectors, with the exception of the professional services group.) Professional services are characterized by a "special projects" type work that creates a great deal of subjectivity in conducting practice and evaluating performance. The profession, as opposed to the market, generally sets standards for practice and performance. It is also apparent that the hotel sector is the clear pacesetter in service practices and performance, and as such, provides a key benchmark for financial services. We believe benchmarks outside the financial services industry are critically important, as financial services are increasingly becoming deregulated and subjected to competitive market forces and new forms of competition. For this reason, we hypothesize:

H1:   In the long run, financial services will need superior practices to achieve superior performance.

We contrast the practice drivers and performance for financial services and hotels in Table 1 to test our hypothesis. A negative gap indicates those areas where the average practices (performance) of hotels exceeds that of the financial sector and the p-value is the level of statistical significance of the group mean differences.

Table 1. How Do Financial Institutions Stack Up Against Hotels?

1a. Practice Driver Means and t-tests by Size of Gaps

Sector Comparisons PRACTICE DRIVERS	Sector Means (1 –5 scale)*			
	US Financial (n = 32)	US Hotel (n = 15)	"Gap"	t-statistic (p-value)
Moments of Truth	2.67	3.53	-.86	-3.78 (p < .00)
Service Representations	3.88	4.57	-.69	-3.14 (p < .00)
Empowerment	3.34	3.98	-.64	-3.01 (p < .00)
Balanced Scorecard	3.32	3.87	-.55	-1.89 (p < .07)
Service Standards	3.43	3.93	-.50	-2.23 (p < .03)
Quality Leadership	3.54	4.01	-.47	-2.18 (p < .04)
Value Orientation	3.39	3.67	-.28	-1.08 (p < .28)
Market Acuity	3.52	3.75	-.23	-0.99 (p < .33)
Kaizen	2.99	3.16	-.17	-0.52 (p < .61)
Cycle of Virtue	3.48	3.62	-.14	-0.58 (p < .57)
BPR	3.61	3.06	+.55	+2.31 (p < .03)
New Service Development	3.30	3.18	+.12	+0.40 (p < .69)

*1=little/no emphasis; 3=average; 5= "state-of-the-art practice"

1b. Performance Outcome Means and t-tests by Size of Gaps

Sector Comparisons PRACTICE DRIVERS	Sector Means (1 –5 scale)**			
	US Financial (n = 32)	US Hotel (n = 15)	"Gap"	t-statistic (p-value)
Service Quality	3.59	4.24	-.65	-3.28 (p < .00)
Customer Growth	3.21	3.78	-.57	-2.28 (p <.03)
Organizational Productivity	3.62	4.16	-.54	-2.51 (p < .02)
Business Performance	3.95	4.20	-.25	-1.07 (p < .29)
Cost/Price	3.16	3.20	-.04	-0.11 (p <.92)
Altruism	4.00	3.90	+.10	+0.36 (p < .71)

**1=poor performance; 3=average; 5= world class/outstanding performance achieved

To briefly summarize these data, the top three practices on the strategic operations agendas of financial institutions are (in order of highest emphasis):

1. Service Representations
2. Business Process Reengineering (BPR)
3. Quality Leadership

Even so, as indicated in table 1a, world class hotels placed a significantly higher emphasis on service representations and quality leadership, whereas the financial sector was more likely to emphasize business process reengineering. In contrast, practices deemed least important to managers of financial institutions were:

10. New Service Development
11. Kaizen
12. Moments of Truth

Managing moments of truth was significantly more important for hotels. The relatively low emphasis on Kaizen techniques suggests that financial institutions are not systematically applying quality tools, on average. This signals a lack of discipline in their approach to delivering consistent quality. Regarding the relatively low ratings for new service development, combined with the high emphasis on BPR, suggests that financial institutions are working on the "expense" side of the ledger, and not as likely to target new ways of using processes to create a steady stream of differentiable, value-added products.

For financial services, the overall pattern of performance outcomes lag those of hotels, in all but *Altruism*, but the mean differences are not significant. Of the model's six performance outcome areas, the hotel sector reported scores significantly higher than the financial service sector in three areas: *Service Quality, Customer Growth* and *Organizational Productivity*. This finding coincides with the service profit chain model (Heskett, et al, 1994) that quality leads to growth. Interestingly, there was no statistically significant difference in *Business Performance*. This is because, as stated in our full report:

"Financial institutions are getting good performance without, apparently, being brilliant strategists. Many may be riding a wave of low interest rates and a favorable economy" (Roth et al., 1997, p 8).

Examination of the financial institutions' practices in more detail partially supports our assertion. To summarize, of the Roth, Chase and Voss model's 12 practice drivers, the hotel sector had significantly higher scores in five categories—1) *Moments of Truth*, 2) *Service Representations*, 3) *Empowerment*, 4) *Service Standards*, and 5) *Quality Leadership*. Hotels were also more apt to use *Balanced Scorecards* than financial services, although the statistical significance was weaker. The need to relate to customers literally as paying guests rather than as retail account holders, gives rise to a broader range and more explicit *Service Standards* for hotels. The relatively high mean score of *Quality Leadership* in hotels (4.01) suggests the importance of leadership in driving hotel service performance. Not surprisingly, financial services scored noticeably higher than hotels in only one area, *BPR*. Financial services are among the most prominent advocates of reengineering in the US. Over the past decade this sector has been investing in the redesign of systems and expanding its use of information and communications technology to become lean and mean competitors. Yet investing in technology itself is neither a safe nor a complete strategy. Roth and Jackson (1995), for example, showed that technology might lead to deterioration in service quality. Haywood-Farmer and Nollet (1991, p. 188) álso report: "Managing the implementation of new technology always poses problems."

US - UK Country Comparisons

Customer expectations are shaped by many factors, including past experience, word-of-mouth, and formal communications. Mounting evidence suggests that international travel and the globalization of businesses strongly influence customer expectations. Globalization comes from the spread of service firms internationally, and the transfer of management practices from one country to another. Increasingly, the success of a world class service hinges on its ability to compete on a global scale, and financial services are among the leaders in globalization. Take Citibank, for example, which has aggressively expanded in Europe; and in the reverse direction, Deutsche Bank, which has recently acquired Banker's Trust of New York.

To the extent that financial services must meet global standards, benchmarks between countries will help our understanding of the diffusion processes of best practices. To learn more about cross-cultural practices, we contrasted the US financial services with those of their ISS counterparts sampled in the UK. Mounting evidence of an ever-expanding globalization of customer expectations of financial services led to the following hypotheses:

H2:   There will be no differences between the practices of UK and US financial services.

To test our hypothesis, we employed the UK sample of 23 financial service companies from the ISS (Voss et al., 1997). In the UK group, eight are banks, six are building societies (credit unions), five are insurance firms, two are retail, one is general administration, and one is classified as other. As hypothesized, management practices have diffused cross-culturally, with no significant differences in any of the 12 drivers (See Table 2). However, the US had better performance outcomes on *Service Quality* and *Altruism*.

Table 2. Are U.S. and U.K. Financial Services Similar?

2a. Practice Driver Means and t-tests by Size of Gaps

Country Comparisons PRACTICE DRIVERS	Country Means (1 –5 scale)*			t-statistic (p-value)
	U.S. (n = 32)	U.K. (n = 23)	"Gap"	
Moments of Truth	2.67	2.93	-0.26	-1.44 (p < .16)
Service Representations	3.88	3.50	+0.38	+1.59 (p < .12)
Empowerment	3.34	3.22	+0.12	+0.68 (p < .50)
Balanced Scorecard	3.32	3.18	+0.14	+0.55 (p < .58)
Service Standards	3.43	3.24	+0.19	+0.99 (p < .33)
Quality Leadership	3.54	3.31	+0.23	+1.27 (p < .21)
Value Orientation	3.39	3.30	+0.09	+0.36 (p < .72)
Market Acuity	3.52	3.24	+0.29	+1.42 (p < .16)
Kaizen	2.99	3.05	-0.06	-0.23 (p < .82)
Cycle of Virtue	3.48	3.28	+0.20	+0.95 (p < .35)
BPR	3.61	3.57	+0.04	+0.23 (p < .82)
New Service Development	3.30	3.33	-0.03	-0.15 (p < .80)

*1=little/no emphasis; 3=average; 5= "state-of-the-art practice"

2b. Performance Outcome Means and t-tests by Size of Gaps

Country Comparisons PRACTICE DRIVERS	Country Means (1 –5 scale)**			t-statistic (p-value)
	U.S. (n = 32)	U. K. (n = 23)	"Gap"	
Service Quality	3.59	3.20	+0.39	+2.64 (p < .01)
Customer Growth	3.21	3.17	+0.04	+0.21 (p < 84)
Organizational Productivity	3.62	3.35	+0.27	+1.10 (p < .28)
Business Performance	3.95	3.60	+0.35	+1.61 (p < .11)
Cost/Price	3.16	3.10	+0.06	+0.24 (p < .81)
Altruism	4.00	3.52	+0.48	+2.61 (p < .01)

**1=poor performance; 3=average; 5= world class/outstanding performance achieved

What is the explanation for this? Further inspection of our data revealed that the financial service sector ranked last in results among the UK service sectors. Hotels were also the leading sector in the UK, as in the US. Like the US, the UK financial service sector has invested heavily in BPR (as well as information technology). And, as in the case of the US, the magnitude of these efforts may be diverting management focus away from both customer service and human resource management, resulting in poor performance. Notwithstanding low employee morale, the US financial firms appear to have managed these changes more effectively than their UK counterparts. The better US performance in customer satisfaction and service quality measures, including hours of operation, reliability, and service reputation is evidence of this. One underlying reason for the disparity may be the time lag between implementation of BPR and information technology in each sector. In general terms, since the US financial sector began its transformation earlier than UK firms, it may have begun to reap the benefits sooner. In the UK, performance may have fallen to its nadir just before realizing the benefits of BPR and IT. The challenge for the UK financial sector is to manage successfully the changes being implemented and maintaining focus on both customer satisfaction and HR management. Returning to hypothesis 2, despite aforementioned timing issues, these findings provide tentative support for the basic similarity of UK and US financial services.

21.4 Discussion

The critical role of Moments of Truth in achieving Service Quality

A 1991 benchmarking study by Roth and van der Velde indicated that leading banks – those that are "market driven" – target perceived quality as their number one priority. Roth and Jackson (1995) empirically found that service quality was linked to overall business performance in retail banks.   It is axiomatic in the service literature that such quality is judged at the point of delivery, i.e., during the service encounter, or what Jan Carlzon former President of SAS Airlines, coined as "Moments of Truth" (Albrecht and Zemke, 1985).   A service encounter by our definition refers to the direct interaction between the customer and the service organization in the creation of the product (Chase, 1978, Solomon, et. al, 1983). The encounter can be viewed as consisting of Three Ts: task, treatment, and tangible features (Chase and Stewart, 1994). Task refers to whether the service was performed properly and in a timely fashion. Treatment refers to the attitude of the service provider. And, tangible features (or service representations) refers to aspects such as the service provider's appearance, cleanliness of the facility, or paperwork produced as a by-product of the service process. The key element of the encounter is the first line worker. Thus, effective management of moments of truth obviously requires that service employees are selected for their people handling skills and are well-trained in the transactions they must perform.

This is only part of the story, however. The real test for a service employee is his or her ability to handle the variability in service tasks that arise from customer induced uncertainty (Chase and Tansik, 1983, Tansik and Chase, 1988), and system induced complexity that arise from rules and procedures "built in" to the job itself. There is a growing body of research that suggests that coping with these uncertainties and complexities necessitates that employees be empowered with the flexibility to take non-programmed actions and make judgment calls regarding policies on behalf of the customer (see, for example, Bowen and Lawler, 1991). As the survey shows, empowerment is a significant relative weakness of financial services.

Another piece of evidence supporting the importance of Moments of Truth and Empowerment as drivers of service quality is seen by the hotel sector's extraordinary emphasis on Quality Leadership. This is supported in the companies that were identified as "Top Industry Icons" by survey respondents (See Roth, Chase, and Voss, 1997, p. 17). As shown in Table 3, three financial service companies were listed as top industry icons by 20 percent or more of their peers: USAA (35.3 % of industry respondents), AT&T Universal Card (23.5%) and Wachovia Bank (23.5%). Each of these firms is widely regarded for its personnel management that stresses these HR practices. (Note that respondents could not list their own companies as a "service exemplar".)

Table 3. Top Industry Icons
USAA **AT&T Universal Card** **Wachovia Bank** **American Express** **Mellon Bank**

It is difficult to draw implications from the significant differences in service representations between financial services and hotels as they relate to Moments of Truth, especially since both sectors rated them at the top of their service agendas. Certainly, the nature of the business demands that hotels excel on this dimension, since service representations are part and parcel of the service offering. Nevertheless, the physical appearance of the bank and its ease of accessibility to the customer can affect perceptions of the entire service encounter. Indeed, while banks may be neat and clean, the cattle chute look of some branch waiting lines, the lack of pens to use to fill out deposit slips, or out-of-stock deposit envelopes at ATMs act as annoyances to the bank branch customer. Defining accessibility in terms of the "business day", hotels must accommodate customers' requirements for 24 hour access, while most financial institutions still follow "bankers' hours" to reach a live person. These physical and temporal factors spill over into how customers evaluate the Moments of Truth.

Why do financial services have problems with the Moment of Truth?

Retail banks, the dominant financial services category in the study, will now be examined in more detail. We posit six major causes for retail banks' difficulty in excelling in the management of Moments of Truth. We believe that these pertain to other "laggard" services as well.

1. *Lack of a service culture.* Banks have not changed their *order-taker* mentality identified nearly a decade ago in a landmark benchmarking study by Roth and van Velde (1991). While there are exceptions such as Wachovia Bank which emphasizes the "Wachovia way" of treating customers, and University National Bank in Palo Alto, California with its home spun management approach, banks are rarely a place people associate with a strong service culture. The reasons for this stem from the nature of the business as a fiduciary service, where protecting customers' assets comes before all else, and where the legal system focuses attention on policies and rules, and not the customer. Deregulation permitting megabanks to exist, downsizing, and the de-skilling of service workers also discourage a strong service culture.

2. *Lack of focus on customer's service needs.* There is a rich literature on the gaps between what customers want and what bank management believes they want in customer service. An oft-replicated finding is that customers want the basics done right. (See, for example, Berry and Parasuraman, 1994.) Unfortunately, this is still honored in the breach, despite the fact that a number of banks have tried service guarantees to focus on such elemental measures as waiting time for service and errors in statements. Among the possible reasons such service guarantees are not totally successful is that financial services only deal with the "task" part of the encounter, not the "treatment" part, and that steps to invoke guarantees are poorly designed. For example, Bank of America's ill-fated satisfaction guarantee required customers to leave the bank in order to collect. (Hart, 1988). In fairness to banks, making any type of process-driven, customer focused program work requires rewiring linkages between the back- and the front-office.

3. *Conflicting task requirements facing front-line workers and supervisors.* Frequently this boils down to making a real time trade-off between production efficiency and sales opportunity (Chase 1981, 1984; Frei, et al. 1997; Heute and Roth, 1987.) That is, do we maximize customer contact time to increase sales opportunity, or minimize contact time to maximize customer throughput? Of more recent vintage is the need to integrate new products into the bank, such as brokerage services. Thus, this cross-selling dilemma is complicated by the need to make additional products available at the bank platform, if not the teller line, and usually by "de-skilled" front-line workers. Much anecdotal evidence suggests that most front-line workers have no real idea about how to "cross-sell," and retain their legacy order-taking mentality.

4. *Poor process design practices.* Despite its appearance in service training courses and operations management textbooks, and the fact that it was developed

by an executive at Bankers Trust, *service blueprinting* (Shostack, 1984), is still not common in bank process design. A blueprint, as opposed to a workflow diagram, not only tells the functions that must be included in a transaction, but of particular relevance to Moments of Truth, also indicates where and when the customer is involved. In on-site banking, it shows whom the customer interacts with, and for processes that take place across time and space tell all bank employees their role in customer encounters, particularly phone interactions. Ironically, despite the significant leadership investments in BPR, the industry still falls short in good designs for delivering service excellence. For example, Bank of America recently advertised a new upscale investment product. When the second author went to a branch of the bank, she found a special product kiosk with a direct phone line to the corporate broker located in a public area of the branch, offering no privacy for clients. Adding injury to insult, the branch staff could provide no assistance about the corporate product and the kiosk was placed adjacent to a children's play area.

5. *Frequent changes in rules regarding charges for using in-branch services.* Customers are often confused as to whether they will face a penalty for going to the bank or receive a reward. "Do you want me here, or not?" Such flip-flopping creates problems for branch personnel planning and for supervisors who must enforce the flavor of the month in bank pricing strategy. Much of this confusion probably arises as banks attempt to retreat from the mass markets toward the more lucrative, fee-paying customers — middle, upscale and professional. In assessing this 1990's trend, Roth and van der Velde (1992, p. 21) reported, "Many executives believe that they will receive top returns from the upper echelons, where loans are typically in the $300,000 to $6 million range." Bankers now talk about "firing" unprofitable customers. The recent rash of charging fees to use a teller illustrates this point.

6. *Personnel policies that discourage worker initiative.* The typical bank seems to be in the "cost trap" – a vicious circle generated by an inordinate focus on cost control. Roth and van der Velde (1990, p. 13) hypothesized this "Excessive attention to the expense side of the ledger can hamper workers' ability to perform their jobs, creating an unstable condition. This activity reduces the sales potential of the bank and places a greater burden on cost control. The cost trap poses a significant barrier to success." In fact, these authors' observations suggest that banks are creating the "cycle of failure" in personnel practices identified by Schlesinger and Heskett (1991). That is, the trend towards task narrowing and cost cutting provides less opportunity for new hires, and less training to broaden their skills. This, in turn, reduces the attractiveness of banks for beginning workers, and at the same time, reduces the loyalty of bank employees who have mastered a broader range of skills.

What can financial services learn from the best hotels?

First and foremost, financial services, and especially banks, must recognize that they are in the service business. Nothing is more passive than a room to sleep in, yet a person's stay at a hotel is greatly enhanced by pleasant contacts (or degraded by unpleasant ones) with the hotel experience and its personnel. At the bank of the first author, the teller who was cutting a set of traveler's checks was asked if the $3 fee could be waived for having a check which could also be signed by his wife (who was present as well). The author had an average deposit level and the appropriate card classification to permit free traveler's checks. This "special" request apparently had to be cleared with the branch manager, who came to the teller's station, scowled, and then signed something, and moved on. It was approved, but the manager missed a golden opportunity to say that it wasn't really part of my deal, but she "... was happy to do it for a valued customer;" or to simply smile and say, "Hello." While the manager may have been overworked due to anything from staff reductions from downsizing efforts or simply heavy volume at that time of day, smart hotels understand the importance of such touches. For example, the second author recently checked into a Wyndham Hotel and noted an advertisement for airline upgrades that had recently expired. When she inquired about it, the "empowered" front-line worker checked it out and graciously said he would "take care of it."

Second, financial services must train staff members in professional behavior. We have yet to check into a major hotel chain within the last ten years where the registration desk clerk was chewing gum, or called us by our first names. This situation happened last week where one of the authors banks. These etiquette breaches have been trained out long ago, even in the less than world class hotels.

The trend towards reducing skill requirements in banks perhaps leaves the door open to emphasize hiring based upon attitude. An exemplar hotel, the Ritz Carlton select employees who fit their motto of "Ladies and gentlemen serving ladies and gentlemen;" and an exemplar from the airline industry, Southwest Airlines, was cited by Behling (1998) as a company that seeks employees with the right mindset, rather than with the right experience. Roth and van der Velde (1990, p. 58) inferred that service excellence means financial services "cannot recruit merely to fill positions; they must recruit to develop the competitive capabilities of the organization. Recruiting the right people from the outset is the least painful and least costly, as well as the most beneficial course of action."

Third, develop systems for handling variation that do not make customers go through hoops to deal with it. When something goes wrong in the best run hotels, a hotel staff members takes ownership of the problem, and attempts to mitigate the guest's involvement in the resolution process. In banking, solving problems at the level beyond the branch manager often involves the customer in long waits on the phone, and hand-offs around the organization to get the problem solved.

Fourth, financial services should take an active role in benchmarking exemplars in other service sectors, like hotels, and across global regions. This involves a pro-active approach to learning and effective change management. We found that changing culture is the biggest barrier to achieving service excellence, yet other service companies have managed this process better. Managers of financial services must be realistic about competitiveness and not be blind-sided by the "regulatory" aspects of their businesses, to the detriment of things such as teamwork and recognition. We anticipate that customer expectations will only increase, and the most competitive financial service providers will establish more positive worker attitudes and service cultures.

Finally, and this goes for all of the above suggestions, don't let technology drive customer service. Often this means not letting technology get in the way of doing things the easy way for the customer. The second author wanted to buy stocks and was told by her personal banker that it was easy: "Just sign up through on line services." Alas, it took a week to get on line, and once she got to the bank's home page, she found it was simply a one-page application that she had to print out, fill out, and mail to the bank. All the banker had to do was resort to another technology, a fax machine and send the form immediately. After 10 years with this bank, she then quit out of frustration.

21.5 Conclusions

Financial services are in the midst of massive changes due to technological advancement and industry deregulation. Despite these upheavals, to be competitive in the long run, financial institutions must adhere to the basic 'laws of service.' As long as financial organizations have branches staffed by people, the need to perform well in face-to-face interactions will remain. This will be true even when many of the branches are simply kiosks staffed by bank employees who are on video screens, rather than on site. We recently tried out a phone kiosk of a regional bank, Union Bank, situated in a mall. Our videoconference via TV screen and hand-held phone was conducted expertly by the bank associate on the other end of the line. This is clearly a good blending of technology and people, and represents a good start in making banking much more user friendly. The challenge is to enable such positive encounters across the entire range of the bank's portfolio of services, no matter how or when they are accessed by their customers.

Acknowledgments

The authors wish to acknowledge the financial support for the ISS provided by Severn Trent Plc and the UK Government's Departments of Trade and Industry and National Heritage. We are also grateful for the work of Dr. Robert Johnston of the University of Warwick in the design of the original questionnaire and the collection of the UK data, along with Ian Jones and, and Beth Rose (now at the University of Auckland) in the collection of the data in the US. Finally, we also wish to acknowledge the work of the research teams at each university—Larry Menor, Craig Froehle, and Wayne Johansson—as well as the significant research support received from the respective business schools.

References

1. Albrecht, K. and Zemke, R. 1985. *Service America!* Homewood IL, Dow Jones-Irwin.
2. Behling, O. 1998. Employee selection: Will intelligence and conscientiousness do the job? *Academy of Management Executive*, 12(1): 77-86.
3. Berry, L. L. and Parasuraman, A. 1994. Lessons from a ten-year study of service quality in America. In E. Scheuing, C. Little, B. Edvardsson, and S. Brown (Eds.), Quality In Service Conference Proceedings: 153-162, St. Johns University, Jamaica NY.
4. Bowen, D. and Lawler, E. 1991. Empowering service employees. *Sloan Management Review*, 31 (3): 73-84.
5. Chase, R. B. 1978. Where does the customer fit in a service operation? *Harvard Business Review*, 56 (4): 137-42.
6. Chase, R. B. and Hayes, R. H. 1991. Beefing up operations in service firms, *Sloan Management Review*, 31(4): 15-26.
7. Chase, R. B. and D. Stewart 1994. Make your service failsafe. *Sloan Management Review*, 35(3): 35-44.
8. Chase, R. B. and Tansik, D. A. 1983. The customer contact approach to organizational design. *Management Science*, 29 (9): 1037-1050.
9. Crane, D. B. and Z. Bodie. 1996. Form follows function: The transformation of banking. *Harvard Business Review*, 74 (5) 109-117.
10. European Foundation for Quality Management. 1997. *The European Quality Award.*
11. Frei, F. X., Harker, P. T. and Hunter, L. W. 1997. Inside the black box: what makes a bank efficient? Wharton Financial Institutions Working Paper 97-20.

12. Hart, C. W. L. 1988. The power of unconditional service guarantees. *Harvard Business Review*, 66 (4): 54-62.
13. Haywood-Farmer, J. and Nollet, J. 1991. *Service Plus*. G. Morin Publishers, Quebec Canada.
14. Heskett, J. L., Jones, T. O., Loveman, G. E., Sasser, W. E. and Schlesinger, L. A. 1994. Putting the service profit chain to work. *Harvard Business Review*, 72 (2): 164-174.
15. Huete, L. and Roth, A. V. 1987. The industrialization and the span of banks service delivery system. *International Journal of Production and Operations Management*, 8 (3): 46-66.
16. Grant, L. 1998. Now are you satisfied? - The 1998 American customer satisfaction index. *Fortune Magazine*. February 16: 161-166.
17. Greising, D., Galuszka, P., Morris, K., Osterland, A. and G. Smith. 1998. $1,000,000,000,000 Banks. *Business Week*. April 27: 32-39.
18. Loveman, G. W. 1998. Employee satisfaction, customer loyalty, and financial performance. *Journal of Service Research*, 1 (1): 18-31
19. Milligan, J. W. 1997. What do customers want from you? Everything! *US Banker*. December: 27-33.
20. National Institute of Standards and Technology (NIST). 1997. *Malcolm Baldrige National Quality Award - 1997 Award Criteria*, Gaithersburg, Maryland.
21. Parasuraman, A., Zeithaml, V. A. and Berry, L. A. 1988. SERVQUAL: A multiple-item scale for measuring consumer perceptions of service quality. *Journal of Retailing*, (64) 1, 12-40.
22. Roth, A. V. 1993. Performance dimensions in services: An empirical investigation of strategic performance. In T. Swartz, D. Bowen, and S. Brown, (Eds.). *Services Marketing and Management*, 2, 1-47. JAI Press, Greenwich, CT.
23. Roth, A. V., Chase, R. B. and Voss, C. A., 1997. *Service in the US: Progress Towards Global Leadership*. Severn Trent Plc, London.
24. Roth, A. V., Gray, A. E., Singhal, J. and Singhal, K., 1997. International technology operations management: Resource toolkit for research and teaching. *Journal of the Production and Operations Management Society*, 6 (1): 167-187.
25. Roth, A. V. and Jackson, W. E. 1995. Strategic determinants of service quality and performance: Evidence from the banking industry. *Management Science*, 41 (11): 1720-1733.
26. Roth, A. V. and van der Velde, M. 1990. *Retail Banking Strategies: Opportunities for the 1990s*. Bank Administration Institute, Chicago IL.
27. Roth, A. V. and van der Velde, M. 1991. Operations as marketing: A competitive service strategy. *Journal of Operations Management*, 10 (3): 303-328.
28. Roth A. V. and van der Velde, M. 1992. *World Class Banking: Benchmarking the Strategies of the Retail Banking Leaders*. Bank Administration Institute, Chicago IL.

29. Shostack, G. L. 1984. Designing services that deliver. *Harvard Business Review*, 62(1), 133-139.
30. Solomon, M. R., Surprenant, C., Czepiel, J. A., and Gutman, E. G. 1985. A role theory perspective on dyadic interactions: the service encounter. *Journal of Marketing*, 49 (4), 99- 111.
31. Tansik D. A. and Chase, R. B. 1988.The effects of customer induced uncertainty on the design of service systems. *Proceedings of the 1988 Academy of Management Meetings*. Anaheim, CA.: 200-204.
32. Vandeveire, M. 1997. Survey: Major banks lack customer loyalty. *The Business Journal*, Dec 26, 18 (9), 1-2.
33. Voss, C. A., Blackmon, K., Chase, R. B., Rose, E., Roth, A. V. 1997. Service competitiveness – an Anglo-US study. *Business Strategy Review*, 8 (1): 7-22.
34. Voss, C. A. and Johnston, R., 1995. *Service in Britain: How Do We Measure Up?* London Business School.
35. White, L. J., 1998. Financial services in the United States: the next decade. *Business Economics*, October: 25-27.

Chapter 22

Value Creation
and Process Management:
Evidence from Retail Banking

Frances X. Frei
Harvard Business School
Patrick T. Harker
University of Pennsylvania

22.1 Introduction

The design and implementation of service delivery processes plays a key role in the overall competitiveness of modern organizations. For example, Roth and Jackson (1995) provide clear evidence that process capability and execution are major drivers of performance due to their impact on customer satisfaction and service quality in banking. Thus, any study of the efficiency of service organizations *must* focus on the role of process design and performance.

The development of quality management, reengineering and other process management methodologies have led organizations to focus on the design and management of production processes. In services, and in particular in banking, this process orientation deals most directly with customer interactions with the organization. This focus raises two important questions: (a) does such a process-orientation matter to the overall efficiency of the organization, and (b) what are the characteristics of effective process management in financial services?

There is a rich history of literature demonstrating the importance of processes in analyzing firm performance (Chase, 1981; Chase and Tansik, 1983; Levitt, 1972; Roth and van der Velde, 1991; Roth and Jackson, 1995, Shostack, 1987). In addition, there has been a stream of literature on strategic frameworks to help conceptualize performance specifically in retail banking (Chase, Northcraft, and Wolf, 1984; Huete and Roth, 1988; Sherman and Gold, 1985, Haag and Jaska, 1995, Roth and van der Velde, 1989). The framework presented in Roth and Jackson (1995) describes how both process capabilities and people impact business performance.

Banks are getting much better at optimizing the customer service delivery processes for a single channel but they are still coming up short when these processes involve the interaction of more than one channel. This chapter will rely on three channel-specific studies of the retail banking industry to talk about optimizing individual channel performance through process management, which includes work design, human resource policies, and information technology capabilities. To date these service channels have largely been considered as discrete and independent entities. Subsequently, their optimization has been diagnosed and enacted at a micro level, and with the primary goal of decreasing the overall cost structure. However, when firms consider optimizing a particular channel, they tend to underestimate the impact of customer interactions with other channels.

In this chapter, we present what we have learned from studying the branch, call center, and PC distribution channels both at the individual channel level as well as, and perhaps more importantly, at their aggregate level. It is our belief that when firms design their service delivery channels from the perspective of customer interactions, they are better able to anticipate the changes in customer behavior that will (eventually) affect their cost structure throughout all of their channels. We end this chapter with a set of recommendation to managers of financial service organizations that delineate the most effective approaches for designing and managing their key service delivery processes.

22.2 Channel-Specific Analyses

We begin our discussion of process management in the retail banking industry by considering the management of each individual distribution channel.

The Branch

There is a growing body of literature that has demonstrated that customer-service delivery processes at the branch level affect firm performance, as measured by financial measures and customer satisfaction. Frei, Kalakota, Leone, and Marx (1999) studied the effect of a group of branch-based customer service delivery processes on a retail bank's financial performance, as measured by return on assets (ROA). Their study analyzed eleven of the most common customer-service delivery processes within a branch across five products: checking, CD, home equity loan, small business loan, and mutual funds. The types of processes they analyzed were opening of accounts, basic transactions, and problem resolution within the account. The process analysis looked at the inputs and outputs of each process and determined the relative performance of each bank for each process. The inputs and outputs consisted of measures of convenience (the amount of time a customer is involved in the process), labor, technology, and duration (the time from beginning to end from the customer's perspective). Their study, which analyzed branches in 121 retail banks in 1994, demonstrated that both the aggregate performance as well as the variation of performance across these eleven processes was closely associated with firm financial performance. In addition, they found that the variation in process performance, what they called process variation, was the stronger of the two predictors of overall financial performance for the firm.

In Frei, and Harker (1999), this work on process variation was extended to demonstrate that process variation was not only a strong predictor of financial performance, but that it was also strongly correlated with customer satisfaction. The customer satisfaction measures used in their paper were the result of detailed phone interviews with customers. A bank's average customer satisfaction score was used as the firm's performance measure. In addition, their research found that banks with more consistent process performance also had more consistent human resource policies and more consistent deployment of technology[1].

In both of the above-mentioned papers, the major theme was how process consistency affects firm performance. That is, when attempting to improve firm performance through the branch, it is important to consider the collection of processes performed in the branch, rather than optimizing individual

---

[1] The human resource policy score used in Frei, and Harker (1999) relied on five different human resource measures. These measures covered training, individual performance incentives, group performance incentives, non-monetary incentives, and cross training. Banks received a score of one if they were above average in each of these fields and a score of zero otherwise. The five scores were then summed to determine a human resource policy score for the bank. Banks with scores of five were considered to have high empowerment workplaces, whereas banks with scores of one were considered to have low empowerment workplaces. In addition, banks were classified as consistent along the human resource policy dimension if they had either high or low empowerment scores, and inconsistent if they were somewhere in-between. Similarly, the technology measures used in their paper relied on five different technology measures. Each measure represented the level of technology functionality deployed in a bank branch's customer service delivery process in the account opening procedure across the five products mentioned above. Banks received a technology functionality score for each product based on their ability to perform product-related tasks online. The technology variation measure was determined by taking the standard deviation of these five product-based technology scores.

processes. This point is further illustrated by the example presented in Frei, and Harker (1999). In the customer satisfaction interviews conducted for this paper, customers were asked to consider their most recent experience in which they had a problem with their retail bank. They were then asked whom they blamed for the problem. Next, the customer's were asked to consider their most recent experience in which they had a pleasurable experience with their retail bank. They were then asked whom they praised for this experience. In 80% of the cases, when customers had a problem they blamed their financial institution; however in 100% of the cases, when customers had a pleasurable experience they credited a specific person.

Thus, institutions get the blame when things go wrong, but when things go particularly well, they get little credit, at least at the individual experience level. This is further evidence of the need for retail banks to have consistency in their processes since they seem to get most of the down-side blame, yet little of the upside credit. Thus, when attempting to improve firm performance through the branch, it is important to consider the collection of processes performed in the branch, rather than optimizing individual processes.

The Call Center

Call centers are undergoing a dramatic change in focus in the retail banking industry. What began as a way to handle routine customer transactions in a lower-cost environment has become an enormous resource-consuming channel, necessitating call centers to generate revenue in order to justify their costs. This shift from the call center as a pure service channel to a sales and service channel is not without tremendous difficulties. Increasingly, banks have gotten quite good at optimizing their call centers across service measures such as average speed of answer, queue length, time since last balk, and other easily quantified measures. However, many have struggled with the shift from a cost center to a profit center for call centers that the new banking climate has necessitated. In this section, we describe a few of the common situations that occur with this shift.

In their study of effective call center management, Evenson, Harker and Frei (1998) found that call centers that shifted resources from service to sales commonly experienced an unanticipated *decrease* in sales. The cause of this decrease was explained in part by the degradation of service levels resulting from a shift of resources away from this function in order to fulfill the new sales function. With the decrease in service levels, customer retention suffered, which then prompted increased efforts on sales to make up for the exiting customers. However, customer acquisition is typically more expensive than selling to existing customers, requiring even more resources (and, thus, shifting resources away from service efforts, continuing the downward spiral of service versus sales). When the new customers arrive, the decreasing service levels provide an obstacle for making them long-term and high-value customers. Firms that did not have this problem tended to have separate functions for sales and service, often with outbound sales outsourced to completely separate the two functions[2].

The study of effective call center management also demonstrated another potential hazard in optimizing call center performance. Most firms, in response to the escalating costs of the call center, are attempting to have more calls handled by the automated voice response system (VRU) instead of by people. The intention is to decrease the call volume that reaches the call center representatives (CSR) by increasing the functionality of the VRU. After increasing the functionality in the VRU, a significant number of firms had just the opposite effect; that is, firms that spent the resources to increase the VRU functionality in an attempt to decrease CSR call volume actually ended up increasing CSR call volumes. The cause of this increase in CSR call volume was explained in part by the customer's frustration with what they perceived to be a more cumbersome VRU. The increase in functionality of the VRU resulted in fewer customers using the VRU to complete their calls because the customers found the VRU's complexity too difficult to navigate. However, not all firms had this unfortunate consequence. Through conversations with the firms, we found that those who spent more time on the VRU design from the customer's perspective (e.g., analyzing the number of levels and touch-tones various requests required) had a higher proportion of calls answered by the VRU (and, thereby, successfully decreased the CSR call volume). When firms did not consider the VRU as a customer service delivery process, necessitating customer-oriented design, their efforts to increase the VRU functionality and decrease the calls reaching the CSRs tended to result in the opposite, undesired behavior.

PC Banking

The newest and lower marginal cost channel in this industry is PC or home computer-based banking. To date, this channel has had the same effect of each previous lower cost channel – it has resulted in an increase in the overall channel cost structure and an inability to generate the originally anticipated cost savings. A precursor to this example is the advent of ATMs. When banks introduced ATMs in the late 1970s, they did so with the expectation of decreasing their distribution system cost structure by providing customers with a lower cost channel to perform their transactions. The anticipated decrease in branch and teller use was not realized; instead, customer behavior changed,

---

[2] An analytical model that explains the tension caused by sales versus service mixing in call center operations can be found in Aksin and Harker (1996).

increasing the distribution cost structure. Cost savings were not realized until banks decided to charge usage fees over a decade after ATMs were introduced. Similarly, when call centers were introduced in financial services, it was again anticipated that they would decrease the distribution system cost structure. Due to a change in customer behavior in the channels (i.e., an increase in the number of transactions customers performed with the addition of each new channel) as well as an inability to realize the cost savings through branch closings, call centers also resulted in a net increase in costs. PC banking has proved to be no different.

In a study of seven North American retail banks, Hitt and Frei (1999) found that PC banking customers are unusually valuable when compared to regular customers with similar demographics. In fact, PC banking customers consistently carry higher product balances, use more products and are as much as 200% more profitable than a regular banking customer (i.e., non-PC banking users). However, it appears that most of these differences are due to pre-existing characteristics of the customers that choose PC banking -- there is little evidence that the use of PC banking made existing customers more valuable. Moreover, only about 20% of all PC banking customers are new to the bank when they adopt the PC channel; these customers do not appear to be unusually profitable. Overall, this suggests that the primary value of PC banking is in identifying and retaining a small group of highly profitable customers; cost savings, customer acquisition, cross-sell or customer profitability improvement appear to contribute little incremental value.

The implication of these findings for PC banking is that banks need to narrow the scope of anticipated benefits generated from the PC channel and design the processes of the PC banking service channel to accommodate their strategic goals. For example, if the real value is in *retaining* a good customer group rather than attracting new customers, then banks should seriously consider not investing in state-of-the-art PC banking functionality. That is, the capital might be more effectively invested in building better product options that further enhance the value of the bank to the customer and the value of the customer relationship to the bank.

22.3 Interaction Between Channels

The previous section discussed the management of each individual delivery channel as if they are separate and distinct. In reality, customers are rarely channel-specific; rather, they use a wide variety of distribution channels when interacting with the bank. In their analysis of the 1995 Survey of Consumer Finances conducted by the U.S. Federal Reserve Bank, Kennickell and Kwast (1997) point out that only 15.1% of households used only one distribution channel (branch, phone, electronic transfers, ATM cards, electronic payments, etc.), whereas 24.2% used two channels, 25.0% used three channels, and 35.7% used four or more methods to interact with their bank (see Figure 1).

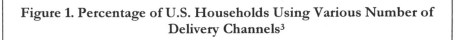

Figure 1. Percentage of U.S. Households Using Various Number of Delivery Channels[3]

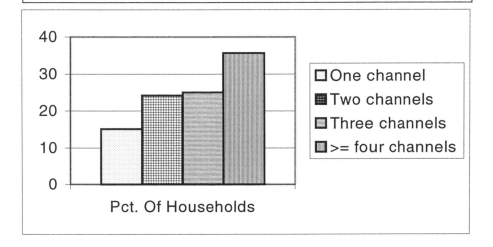

Thus, it is imperative for banks to manage the interactions between distribution channels just as rigorously as they manage each channel in isolation. We now switch from independent consideration of the three service channels to consideration of their interactions. Our underlying theory is that the points of interactions between service channels and processes have generally been overlooked, and that processes dedicated to these interaction are of critical importance, often more so than the independent service channel processes themselves. It is in the unanticipated consequences of how changes in one channel effect another that is at the heart of this issue. Below we will provide examples of when this occurred and describe how having the appropriate processes in place can avoid these difficulties in the future.

The Branch and Call Center

When optimizing the branch, banks need to also understand the capabilities of the call center and have in place adequate processes for customers to use one or both channels. When customers interact with more than one channel, special care needs to be given to the customer service delivery processes that facilitate

---

[3] From Table 2 in Kennickell and Kwast (1997).

this interaction. Within the firm, different organizational units may manage this interaction. To the customer, these channels are perceived as part of a single institution.

Frei, Harker, and Hunter (1999a) describe a case study of a large North American commercial bank where the implementation of a major redesign of the retail delivery system was tracked (called National Bank as a pseudonym). The bank under investigation was confronted by an increasingly competitive environment and wanted to improve the cost-efficiency of its far-flung retail delivery system, comprising hundreds of branches, while simultaneously transforming these branches and other channels into retail stores focused more directly on the sale of financial products and services.

The redesign at National Bank was initially focused around very basic business process reengineering in the branches. Over a period of decades, a large number of administrative functions had accumulated in the branch systems, so that branch managers and service representatives spent a considerable amount of time on these activities rather than in contact with customers. Further, most of the time spent with customers was centered on simple, transaction-oriented activities and basic servicing of accounts rather than on activities that were thought to be likely to lead to sales opportunities. The initial goal of the redesign was to streamline branch processes and shift the routine servicing of accounts to the call center in order to free up the branch employees for sales. To take one simple example, incoming telephone calls from customers were to be re-routed so that the phones in the branch did not ring. Rather, customers calling National and dialing the same number they always had used to contact the branch would now find their calls routed to a central call center.

The innovation required a redesign of the physical layout of the branches, encouraging more customers to use automatic teller machines and telephones for routine transactions. Customers entering the redesigned branch, therefore, were to be greeted by an ATM, an available telephone, and a dedicated bank employee ready to instruct them in the use of these technologies. Customers would be directed toward a teller or a service representative only when they persisted or when a bank employee deemed such personal attention clearly necessary (e.g., when a customer needs to access a safe deposit box or to meet with a sales representative about the purchase of a product or service).

These technological innovations, along with the redirection of customers to alternative delivery channels, were intended to realize efficiencies. As an example of the expected efficiencies, early projections, which were quickly revealed to be overly optimistic, envisioned a 65% decrease in the number of tellers required in the branch system. Over time, it was hoped that many customers would cease to rely on the branch and its employees for routine transactions and services. The reengineering was also expected to transform service employees into sales personnel, by allowing them to concentrate their efforts on activities that had potentially higher added value such as customized transactions and the provision of financial advice coupled with sales efforts.

A clear requirement for effective innovation at National Bank, then, was the participation of the customers in the new service processes. In its design, National Bank elected not to pursue some of the more notorious routes favored by other banks (such as charging fees to see tellers), but to lead customers somewhat more gently, by making customer relations a key feature of the redesigned retail bank. The redesign created a customer relations manager in each branch, and it was to be the responsibility of this employee to ensure that each retail customer that entered the branch was guided to a service employee, or alternatively, a technological interface, in order to receive the appropriate level of service.

The redesign also required a large degree of innovation in two further areas: the information system and the telephone call center. The information system was to enable the relocation and standardization of a large number of routine types of account transactions (address changes, for example). Further, information systems were to be improved to give National Bank employees a fuller picture of each customer's financial position and potential. This more complete picture of the customer's portfolio was thought to enhance sales efforts, enabling service representatives to suggest an optimal fit between customers and services, and to refer the customers to areas in the bank with particular expertise in a product as that became necessary.

The centrality of the telephone call center in this redesign raised a new set of challenges. In the sophistication of its telephone banking system, National Bank had lagged behind a number of its competitors. Yet through the redesign, it hoped to make telephone banking, and, eventually, PC or home-banking, cornerstones of its delivery system. Implicitly, branch redesign, therefore, also required the construction of new call centers, staffing them as the customers began to be directed toward them, and developing an organizational structure that went beyond the scope of traditional call center and could manage the relationship between the call centers and the branches.

With this redesign, the National Bank call center pilot was implemented in two small local markets. Most of the literally hundreds of administrative and servicing processes were removed from the branch. Telephones no longer rang in the branches. The financial specialists were freed to concentrate on sales activities, and found themselves with time available to pursue sales opportunities prospectively rather than simply reacting to walk-in traffic. Most customers responded to the innovation positively, quickly migrating to the new technologies with few problems. The active roles played by the customer-relations managers, many of whom were former branch managers, helped this migration along. However, while most customers migrated quickly, and the new processes that were accompanied by supportive technology worked effectively, turning the retail bank branch into a sales-focused financial store proved more difficult. Branch employees found it difficult to move from the idea of reacting to the sales opportunities that routine servicing occasionally provided, to the more pro-active sales role that the redesign called for. Further, some of the streamlining designed to supplement or improve employee-customer interaction replaced these interactions; this resulted in missed sales opportunities and fewer chances for bank representatives to assess and attempt to meet customers' needs.

When attempting to migrate a subset of customer transactions from one channel to another it is imperative to understand in detail how customers interact with the bank for each class of transactions. For example, National Bank took great care to understand how customers interacted with the bank for routine service transactions and thus successfully built processes that facilitated the switch from one channel (the branch) to another (ATM and call center). However, they understood in less detail the way in which customers interacted with the bank for sales transactions and thus experienced a noticeable drop in sales as a result of their migration strategy.

PC Banking and the Call Center

Just as the relationship between the branch and call center was implicated in the bank's attempt to optimize the branch, optimizing the PC channel implicates the capabilities of the call center. Banks need to understand the interactions between these two channels and adequate processes for customer to use one or both channels have to be in place. Virtually all of the service aspects of the PC channel are handled by the call center, including answering requests that are made electronically, by phone, or far less likely, by mail. However as we demonstrate below, the particular service requirements for the PC channel seem to be at odds with how the call center has traditionally been optimized.

For example, when a customer sends an email to the bank, this email is typically handled by the call center. What would have taken a couple of minutes as a verbal transaction on the phone, however, now requires several times as much labor. This new mode of customer interaction requires the email to be directed to the appropriate person (all too often by printing out the email and putting it in the inbox of an employee), the response carefully crafted and forwarded to a manager to check for regulatory implications, and then sent to the customer. Thus, the strength of the phone center at handling routine questions and service requests does not translate seamlessly to supporting a new channel: the processes by which these channels need to be as carefully planned as the existing call center service processes.

In addition, when introducing the PC channel, banks now face a similar set of service issues that the software industry faces: they have to decide how to deal with hardware related questions about customer's PCs and modems. On the one hand, it is very expensive to train and retain technically-savvy CSR's, but on the other hand, the bank is trying to encourage use of this lower cost channel and thus, wants to make it as easy for the customer to use as possible. The same service-delivery issues hold when thinking about interactions between PC banking and the branch. If a PC banking customer goes into the branch to ask a question about PC banking, it is an expensive proposition on the bank's side to make sure that the appropriate training and technology to meet these customer needs is in place in every single branch. To provide PC banking support at the branch level would further increase the costs associated with the branch. However, to not provide PC banking support at *every* customer contact point could potentially discourage customer migration.

In the end, banks do not really have the option of not providing the PC banking channel at this point due to its inherent competitive necessity. Given this, and the large up-front costs associated with PC banking, planning and implementation of this new channel has to be considered most carefully, down to the precise objectives and detailed descriptions of how the customer will interact with the channel.

22.4 Recommendations to Managers of Financial Service Organizations

Based on the summary of the various distribution channels in banking, the following issues must be addressed if the industry is to continue to prosper in the future:

- Process consistency within and across service channels is paramount in customer service delivery processes. Resist the temptation to make investments to be best in class in a single type of process and rather make investments that will improve a set of processes to a consistent level. Also, process consistency is significantly affected by human resource policies and technology functionality that are complementary and that are aligned with the overall goals of the organization.
- Research shows that focusing on sales at the expense of service can actually reduce sales. When shifting from a pure-service to a sales-and-service culture, it is important not to place too much emphasis on sales at the expense of service, as this can result in a reduction in sales indirectly and

retention of new customers over time, through a lack of attention to service.

- The Voice Response Unit (VRU) must be seen as a customer service delivery process. It needs to be treated as such, replete with consideration of customer interface and careful design of the appropriate steps and functionality to enhance this interface so that the VRU can offset the call volume directed to customer service representatives.

- The PC is a channel with a value proposition of retention and cross-sell, rather than acquisition and cost savings. It is important to design those service processes PC banking delivers to take advantage of this.

- The lessons of PC banking and the need to integrate the new channels seamlessly into the existing methods of interacting with the customer become even more important in the movement toward Internet banking. As all of the previous changes in the industry have demonstrated, the Internet will not replace the other channels of interaction with the customer, just like VCRs did not replace the experience of going to the movies. Rather, the Internet will enable entirely new services to be offered, as well as increasing the sheer volume of interaction with the customer, if done right. The need to take a holistic approach to channel/process management will only increase as we move toward electronic banking.

The deeper issue for banks lies in the question of who is responsible for ensuring process consistency. Most banks are organized along lines of business (retail, credit card, mortgage, etc.). However, customers cut across all of these business units. Who makes sure that the customer experience is seamless?

Frei, Harker and Hunter (1999b), in summarizing their various analyses of retail banking efficiency, paint a picture of what makes an effective bank. The good news (or bad news, depending on your perspective), is that is there is simply no "silver bullet", no one set of management practices, capital investments and strategies that lead to success. Rather, it appears that the "Devil" is truly in the details. The alignment of technology, human resource management, and capital investments with appropriate delivery processes appears to be the key to efficiency in this industry.

To achieve this alignment, banks need to invest in a cadre of "organizational architects" that are capable of integrating these varied pieces together to form a coherent structure. In fact, several leading financial services firms have realized the need for such talents and are investing heavily in senior managers from outside the industry (most notably, from manufacturing enterprises) to drive this alignment of technology, human resource management, and strategy. The challenge, therefore, is not to undertake any one set of practices but rather, to develop senior management talent that is capable of this alignment of practices.

References

1. Aksin, Z. and Harker, P. T. 1996. To sell or not to sell: determining the tradeoffs between service and sales in retail banking phone centers. Working Paper 96-07, Wharton Financial Institutions Center, The Wharton School, University of Pennsylvania (Philadelphia, PA).

2. Chase, R. B. 1981. The Customer Contact Approach to Services: Theoretical Bases and Practical Extensions. *Operations Research, 29*, 698-706.

3. Chase, R. B. Northcraft, G. B. and Wolf, G. 1984. Designing High Contact Service Systems: Applications to Branches of a Savings and Loan. *Decision Sciences, 15*, 542-556.

4. Chase, R. B. and Tansik, D. A. 1983. The Customer Contact Approach to Organization Design. *Management Science, 29*, 1037-1050.

5. Evenson, A., Harker, P. T. and Frei F. 1998. Effective Call Center Management: Evidence from Financial Services. Working Paper 98-25, Wharton Financial Institutions Center, The Wharton School, University of Pennsylvania (Philadelphia, PA).

6. Frei, F. X., and Harker, P. T. 1999. Process Performance and Customer Satisfaction: Evidence from the Retail Banking Study. Working Paper, Wharton Financial Institutions Center, The Wharton School, University of Pennsylvania (Philadelphia, PA).

7. Frei, F. X., R. Kalakota, A. Leone, and L. Marx. 1999. Process Variation as a Determinant of Service Quality and Bank Performance: Evidence from the Retail Banking Study. *Management Science, 45*, (9).

8. Frei, F. X., Harker, P. T., and Hunter, L. 1999a. Retail Banking. In Mowery, D. (ed.) U. S. Industry in 2000: Studies in Competitive Performance, National Academy Press, Washington, DC.

9. Frei, F. X., Harker, P. T., and Hunter, L. 1999b. Inside the Black Box: What Makes a Bank Efficient. In Harker, P. T. and Zenios, S. Financial Institutions: Efficiency, Innovation, Regulation. Cambridge University Press, New York.

10. Haag, S. and Jaska, P. 1995. Interpreting Inefficiency Ratings: An Application of Bank Branch Operating Efficiencies. *Managerial and Decision Economics, 16*, 7-14.

11. Hitt, L. and Frei, F. X. 1999. Do Better Customers Utilize Electronic Distribution Channels? The Case of PC Banking. Working Paper, Wharton Financial Institutions Center, The Wharton School, University of Pennsylvania (Philadelphia, PA).

12. Huete, L. M. and Roth, A. V. 1988. The Industrialization and Span of Retail Banks' Delivery Systems. *International Journal of Operations & Production Management, 8*, 46-66.

13. Kennickell, A. B. and M. L. Kwast. 1997. Who Uses Electronic Banking?

Results from the 1995 Survey of Consumer Finances. *Proceedings of the 33rd Annual Conference on Bank Structure and Competition* (Federal Reserve Bank of Chicago, May), 56-75.

14. Levitt, T. 1972. Production Line Approach to Service. *Harvard Business Review, 50*, 41-52.

15. Roth, A. V. and Jackson, W. E. 1995. Strategic Determinants of Service Quality and Performance: Evidence from the Banking Industry. *Management Science, 41*, 1720-1733.

16. Roth, A. V. and van der Velde, M. 1989. Investing in Retail Delivery Systems Technology. *Journal of Retail Banking, 11*, 23-34.

17. Roth, A. V. and van der Velde, M. 1991 Operations as Marketing: A Competitive Service Strategy. *Journal of Operations Management, 10*, 303-328.

18. Sherman, H. and Gold, F. 1985. Bank Branch Operating Efficiency. *Journal of Banking and Finance, 9*, 297-315.

19. Shostack, G. L. 1987. Service Positioning Through Structural Change. *Journal of Marketing, 51*, 34-43.

Chapter 23

Bank Productivity: Promises Unrealized

Wayne I. Cutler

First Manhattan Consulting Group

23.1 The Productivity Promises

During the past decade, banks have been undertaking a variety of programs to improve productivity. This includes a combination of "reengineering" efforts (a.k.a. process redesign, change management, strategic sourcing, OVA, etc.) and wholesale acquisitions to achieve greater scale. In fact, the number of bank mergers has increased eight-fold since 1987 (from 44 to 369). The reengineering and merger initiatives have resulted in banks making three major promises with regard to improving productivity. First, that new technologies will significantly reduce labor-intensive activities leading to lower servicing and processing costs. Second, that closing branches and migrating customers to alternative distribution channels will reduce customer service costs. And third, that by improving productivity, banks will be able to focus more of their energies on providing true value-added services resulting in greater customer satisfaction. Unfortunately our analysis indicates that, for the most part, banks have failed to consistently deliver these promises. This chapter explains why we believe this is the case and highlights some best practices for managing bank productivity going forward.

23.2 Impact On The Efficiency Ratio (ER)

Against a number of traditional measures, banks appear to have improved productivity. Yet some careful analysis proves these improvements are illusory or transitory.

A first look at the primary measure of bank productivity – the cost to income ratio – indicates that productivity for the top 120 institutions has only improved marginally since 1994 (see figure 1). Costs include typical bank operating expenses such as staff wages, technology, premises, supplies, and administrative. Income includes net interest margin (interest revenue less interest expenses) plus fee income.

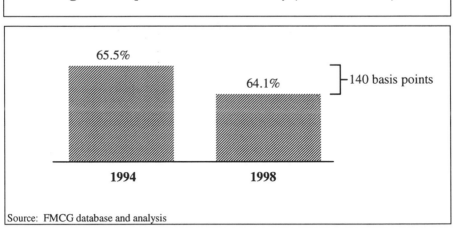

Figure 1: Reported Bank Productivity (Cost to Income)

65.5%

64.1%

140 basis points

1994   1998

Source: FMCG database and analysis

However, adjusting for mergers, non-recurring items, such as restructuring costs and one-time gains, and differences in bank balance sheets reveals a fundamentally different story. This First Manhattan Consulting Group (FMCG) normalization analysis shows that bank productivity has actually improved significantly by 340 basis points (see figure 2). It is interesting to note that during this period non-recurring expenses rose almost twice as fast as non-recurring income (45% vs. 27%) and as most bank executives know, one-time expenses can tend to be "stickier" (i.e., less easy to get rid of) than reported.

Figure 2: Normalized Bank Efficiency Ratio (Cost to Income)

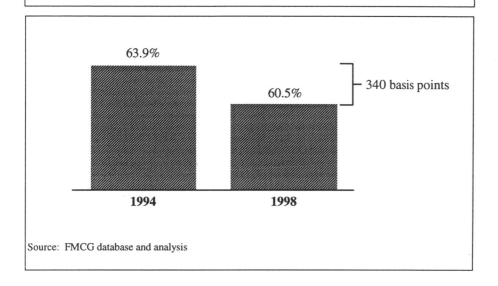

Source: FMCG database and analysis

Examining the efficiency ratio of the top 40 banks does not reveal any insights regarding the correlation of size and productivity; in fact, the larger banks actually appear to have lower productivity than several of their smaller counterparts (see figure 3).

A major shortcoming of the cost to income ratio is that it is heavily influenced by changes in bank margins and business mix, which have little to do with productivity. An alternative measure is the cost to asset ratio, which measures how much it costs a bank to manage each dollar of assets. Looking at the movement in this ratio versus the income to asset ratio is very revealing. It appears that the majority, if not all, of the benefits have been derived from increased income (net interest income and fee income). In fact, it appears that expense management actually worsened during the past 5 years (see figure 4).

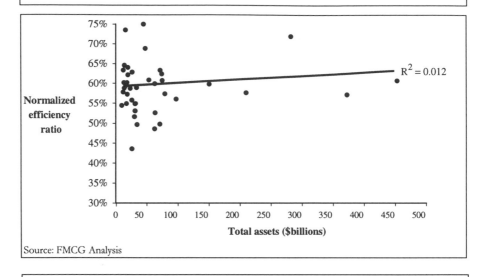

Figure 3: Correlation of Size and Productivity

Source: FMCG Analysis

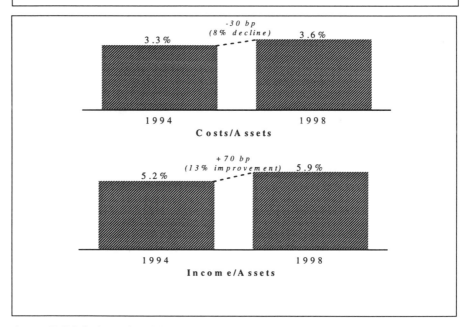

Figure 4: Ratio of Costs and Income to Assets

Source: FMCG database; adjusted for non-recurrences; top 120 banks by assets

23.3 Another Measure of Bank Productivity

The story is not all that bleak. Taking another measure, "labor productivity" as measured by the Bureau of Labor Statistics (BLS), shows that bank productivity has improved by 2.1% CAGR since 1987. The BLS statistic is determined by analyzing "the relationship between output and the employee hours expended in producing that output." The output measure is comprised of transactions processed for deposits, lending and trust businesses with appropriate unit weights assigned to each. Employee hours are calculated by taking the average hours worked per week times the number of non-supervisory workers in the above functions. While this is a somewhat "industrialized" measure, it does show that banks have been beating the average gains for some traditional service industries while lagging behind other high growth service industries such as electronic/computer stores and catalog and mail-order houses (see figure 5).

Figure 5: Bank Labor Productivity

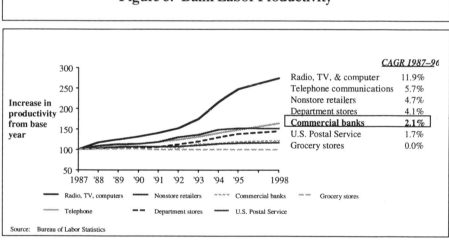

Source: Bureau of Labor Statistics

23.4 What's Really Going On?

Turning our attention back to the three promises – technology investments, distribution reconfiguration, and service level improvement – how can banks invest in all of these improvement programs and not raise productivity? First, banks have been increasing their spending on technology quite significantly. Since 1987, banks have doubled the amount of money they spend on technology (from $10.7 billion to $21.0 billion – $14.7 billion in constant 1987 dollars). This is not necessarily bad as long as capital is being substituted for labor and service levels are improving. Unfortunately, capital has not been effectively replacing the labor component of bank expenses. While the number of commercial bank employees has declined by about 3% since 1987, banks are now spending 16% more on technology and labor combined (see figure 6).

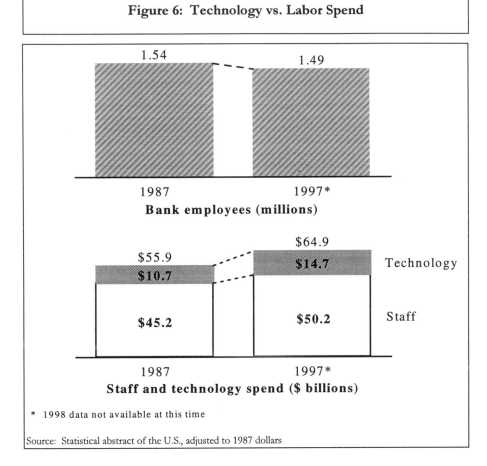

Figure 6: Technology vs. Labor Spend

How about the brick and mortar issue – did closing branches and migrating customers to lower cost distribution improve productivity? Over the past ten years, while the number of banks declined by almost 5,000, or 33%, the number of branches actually *increased!* Even taking into account the substitution of smaller supermarket-type branches for full-service branches, there are 33% more bank branches today than there were in 1987 (see figure 7).

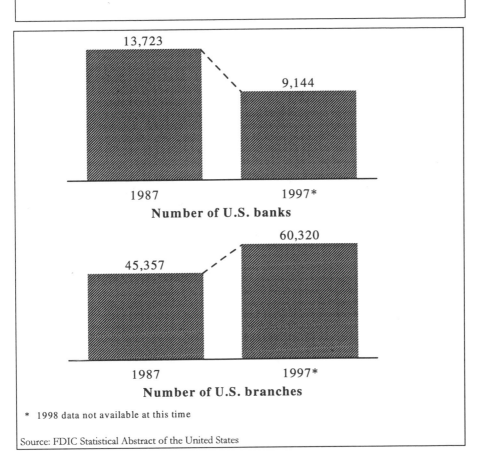

Figure 7: Change in Banks and Branches

13,723

9,144

1987   1997*

Number of U.S. banks

60,320

45,357

1987   1997*

Number of U.S. branches

* 1998 data not available at this time

Source: FDIC Statistical Abstract of the United States

Even with the growth in the U.S. population, the branch geographic densities (as measured by population per branch) has softened from 5,300 people per branch to 4,400 people per branch (see figure 8).

This means that for branches to maintain or improve their performance, they have to be extracting greater net income from each customer. Some of this softening could be due to the adoption of supermarket branches/kiosks (i.e., lower average square feet per branch) and the more complex coverage requirements due to the urbanization of the U.S. population.

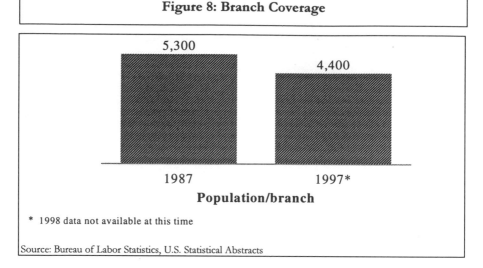

Figure 8: Branch Coverage

5,300

4,400

1987   1997*

Population/branch

* 1998 data not available at this time

Source: Bureau of Labor Statistics, U.S. Statistical Abstracts

Finally, we examined the impact that alternative channels such as ATMs and other electronic avenues may be having on bank productivity. Clearly the growth of these channels has been extraordinary, especially over the last ten years (see figure 9).

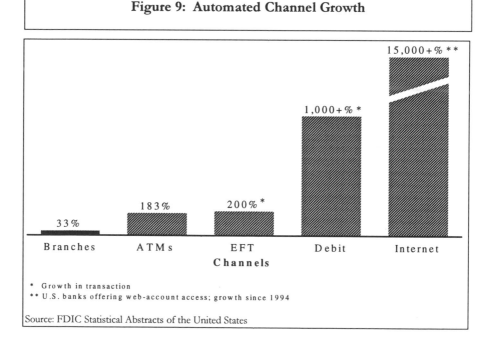

Figure 9: Automated Channel Growth

15,000+%**

1,000+%*

183%   200%*

33%

Branches   ATMs   EFT   Debit   Internet

Channels

*   Growth in transaction
** U.S. banks offering web-account access; growth since 1994

Source: FDIC Statistical Abstracts of the United States

Some would say that these channels have fundamentally shifted the convenience factor in selecting banks. While these channels are much cheaper on a transaction-by-transaction basis, when compared to the frequency of use, it appears that the overall cost to banks on an account basis has actually increased by more than 15%. This is not surprising since there has been an emergence of what is termed in the industry as financial "optimizers." These are bank customers who look for ways to maximize their earning assets while minimizing their bank fees. They accomplish this by transacting abnormally high levels of inquiries through all of the new channels banks have been expanding into – ATMs, telephone banking, Internet, etc. These unprofitable optimizers constitute nearly 50% of retail customers, which is costing U.S. banks anywhere from $10 billion to $15 billion per year (see figure 10).

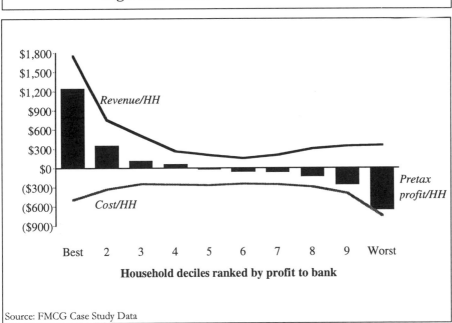

Figure 10: Customer Profit Distribution

Source: FMCG Case Study Data

Interestingly, traditional methods of determining who are the "optimizers" (e.g., age and income) are proving to be quite erroneous measures. In fact, optimizers come in all shapes and sizes. Recent research at various FMCG clients reveals that both higher income households (e.g., those with more than $75,000 in income) as well as lower income households (e.g., those with less than $15,000 in income) are "churning" transactions at a rapid rate as more and more convenient channels are added.

What about service levels? Unfortunately these appear to have declined, at least over the past few years. This could be a result of other factors such as customer expectations, price gouging by banks, and other intermediaries becoming better alternatives (see figure 11).

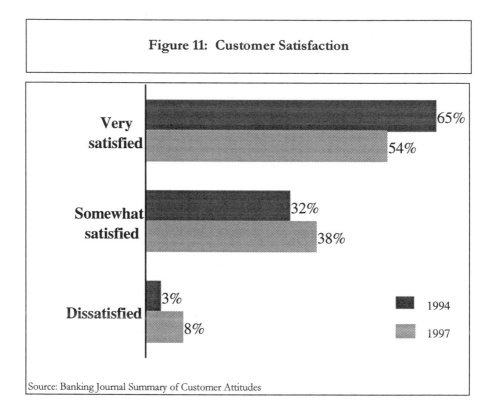

Figure 11: Customer Satisfaction

Source: Banking Journal Summary of Customer Attitudes

23.5 Winning Plays

Surely there must be some winning banks over the last 10 years. In fact, some banks have been using existing productivity improvement strategies and tools quite successfully. Take Marine Midland for instance. Marine's cost to income ratio improved from 71% to 49% since 1987. The bank accomplished this through aggressive centralization of staff and branch back-office functions along with disciplined technology spending. Wachovia also performed reasonably well, reducing its efficiency ratio from 64% to 55% by closing approximately 10% of their branches, achieving scale economies through acquisitions, and better customizing services and products to customer needs.

Five major themes seem to repeat themselves in productive banks:

- A keen understanding of their customer base and associated cost levers

- Tight discipline of capital/employee substitution

- Keeping cost management a top management agenda

- A concerted effort to modify customer channel preferences

- Operations recognized and treated as a core competency.

23.6 Breaking The 50% Cost To Income Ratio

While these five disciplines should position most banks well, they will not allow banks to break the 50% cost to income barrier. In fact, if you look on a worldwide basis, the banks that have been able to break the barrier have done so by leveraging off of government policies and local oligopolies rather than superior productivity management. For example, the Hong Kong banking market is controlled by a cartel of banks that jointly manage interest rates. In addition, the banks in Hong Kong benefit from disproportionately low wage rates. Does this mean we should view the 50% barrier as unbeatable? We think not. Banks that are able to institutionalize the "perennial" disciplines listed above while seriously exploring less conventional approaches can potentially break this barrier. Several of the less conventional approaches are discussed below.

A. Collapsing The Value Chain

Historically banks have viewed and organized their organizations around front, middle, and back-offices. Each department was managed separately. This "hand-off" approach often resulted in delays, errors and customer dissatisfaction. In the future, a new paradigm will emerge whereby the former front, middle, and back-office structures will collapse along channel distribution lines. Specifically, there will be face-to-face, remote and electronic channels, each comprised of front, middle, and back-office operations. This alignment allows for more seamless transaction processing and a better design around the affordability of the customer's touch points (see figure 12).

B. Aggressive Channel Migration

While we touched on this as part of the operational perennials, here we take it a big step forward. The ultimate objective is to gently encourage the customer to do the processing. This can be accomplished in a variety of ways, including pricing, real-time education, promotion, and continued reduction of other convenient high cost channels. Clearly with the advent of other timesaving channels like the Internet, the winners will be the banks that can create superior designs, a.k.a. "killer applications", and handhold the customers to ensure they are comfortable with the new technology.

Figure 12: New Value Chain Model

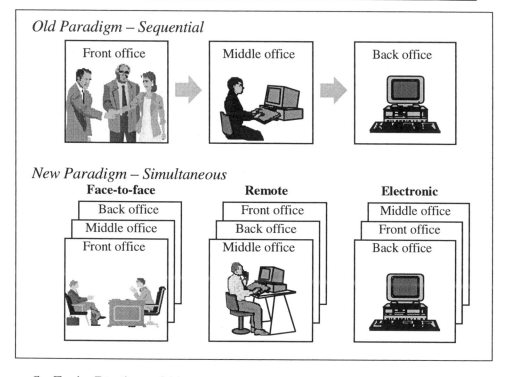

Old Paradigm – Sequential

New Paradigm – Simultaneous

C. Further Distribution Of Operations Beyond The Boundaries Of The Bank

Banks must lock up alternative real estate quickly in order to reduce facility costs and support the required touch points customers need. This is already happening in supermarkets, but again to date this strategy has only added costs to a bank's infrastructure. More creative alliances, and ways to be more than just a transaction point are required. In addition, banks should not ignore telecommuting. Since 1990, the telecommuting workforce has increased almost three-fold. As telecommunication fees come down and line speeds go up, banks will be able to leverage off of a huge and flexible workforce base that can be managed and operated on a virtual transnational and even global basis.

D. Further Leverage Fixed Infrastructure

Banks will need to become more creative with their remaining bank premises. For example, a typical branch is open five and half days a week which, if converted to a "premises seepage" equation (hours not open for the week/(24 hours x 7 days)), would reveal that, on average, 77% of the time branch space is underutilized. At an average branch rental cost of $10,000 per year, this equates to approximately $500 million per year for the U.S. banking industry. Exploring other uses such as off-hours telemarketing, collections processing, or off-hour office rentals would enable banks to better leverage fixed costs while providing greater staffing flexibility. Of course these alternatives would require changes to the current branch layouts for security purposes as well as an understanding of how to manage a widely distributed workforce.

23.7 Conclusion

In conclusion, our research has revealed some alarming insights into the true productivity trends of the major banks in the U.S. Notwithstanding this, there are some institutions that are achieving superior productivity by focusing on instilling disciplined operations and customer segment management capabilities.

Breaking the 50% cost to income barrier will require banks to move to a fundamentally new level of operations and customer management capabilities which few in the industry have begun to develop.

Figure 13: Bank Operational Best Practices		
Perennial practices		**Visionary practices**
• A keen understanding of their customer base and associated cost levers • Tight discipline of capital/employee substitution • Keeping cost management a top management agenda • A concerted effort to modify customer channel preferences • Operations recognized and treated as a core competency	+	• Collapsing the value chain • Aggressive channel migration • Further distribution of operations beyond the boundaries of the bank • Further leverage fixed infrastructure

References

1. Measuring Output and Labor Productivity of Commercial banks (SIC 602): A Transaction-Based Approach, Office of Productivity and Technology, Bureau of Labor Statistics, 11/98
2. American Bankers Association Technology Report, Ernst & Young
3. Statistical Abstract of the United States, Bureau of Labor Statistics, FDIC
4. Robert Muth, Chief Administrative Officer, Marine Midland Bank
5. Summary of Customer Attitudes, *Banking Journal*
6. Wachovia Corporation Investor Relations
7. Call Reports, FDIC
8. Y-9, Federal Reserve
9. Nielson Reports

Acknowledgements

Special thanks to two people — Jack Thompson and Chris Nolte, who spent hours putting together a lot of the supporting analyses and conducting painstaking reviews of the manuscript

Chapter 24

Productivity in Service Industries: Implications of the Boskin Commission Report

Robert M. Solow
Massachusetts Institute of Technology

24.1 Estimation of the Consumer Price Index

The topic I chose for this occasion is the Boskin Commission report on the Consumer Price Index (CPI) and its implications for your business or the business of this country. I am not going to try to tell you your business; I am going to try to tell you something about the way this broad issue relates to your business.

I don't know how well you keep up with this, but about two years ago (in 1995) the Senate Finance Committee created and appointed a sort of blue ribbon commission of five well-known economists to prepare a report on this question: "Does the Consumer Price Index, as it is produced monthly by the Bureau of Labor Statistics (BLS), fairly and accurately measure the rate of price inflation of consumer goods and services in the U.S.?" The Boskin Commission produced its report in December. Their conclusion was that the CPI overstates the true rate of inflation of consumer prices in the U.S. by something between 8/10th of 1% a year and 1.6% a year. In other words, the reported rate of inflation that you will read in the New York Times, or the Wall Street Journal every month, when the latest CPI is announced by the Commissioner of Labor Statistics, exceeds the true rate of inflation by something between 3/4 of 1% and 1 1/2 % a year. The Commission put its best estimate of the degree of overstatement at 1.1% a year. You should realize that the belief that the CPI overstates the true rate of inflation is not a new idea at all inside the economics profession. It has been talked about for a long time, at least since 1960.

This is after all not any old statistic. The fiscal implications of revision of the consumer price index are very great. There are two fiscally very important uses of the CPI. First, it is used to index Social Security benefits. I am a Social Security beneficiary. I get a check every month. And, once a year, I get a little form from the Social Security Administration that says: beginning in January your monthly check will be $5 or $6 higher, or whatever it is, because it is being escalated to cancel out the effect of last year's inflation. The second important role of the CPI is that it is used to index the brackets in the personal income tax. The income at which a higher marginal tax rate kicks in rises every year, so that you will not be pushed into a higher tax bracket just because inflation has increased your dollar income. If the inflation rate were revised down, more people would slip into the higher bracket, and tax revenues would be higher.

The numbers are such that this is a big deal. Suppose it were announced that beginning July 1, 1997, Social Security benefits and tax brackets will be indexed by the CPI inflation rate minus 1.1%. Probably half of what is needed to balance the budget by the magic year 2002 would automatically be taken care of. We are talking of a very substantial sum of money after 5 or 6 years. Obviously, the Boskin Commission report is of great importance to the Congress, because indexing by the CPI minus 1.1% would be equivalent to lowering social security benefits and raising tax rates as compared with legitimate expectations but it would be done with as close to perfect cover as you can imagine. "Getting the number right" is just correcting an error, not reducing benefits or raising taxes.

Now, the largest part, about 6/10th of 1% of the 1.1% of the Boskin Commission's estimate, is attributed by them to unmeasured quality improvement. The BLS compiles the consumer price index each month by actually sampling prices charged in retail outlets. Suppose a BLS enumerator records that the price of a shirt has risen by $1; that will go down as a price increase. But if it were known that the new shirt was of higher quality than last month or last year's shirt by approximately that amount, there would be no price increase to report. The Boskin Commission estimated that roughly 6/10th of 1% per year of overstatement of inflation occurs because some quality improvement goes unmeasured. Keep in mind that the BLS, currently and for the past decade or two, has had a major program trying to improve its ability to capture correctly quality improvements in consumer goods and services. They report currently that if they were not making the corrections that they have learned to make in the past few years the rate of CPI inflation would be something like 2 or 2 1/2% a year faster than now recorded. So when the CPI tells you that prices in January 1997 were 3% higher than in January 1996, they would have recorded 5-5 1/2%, if they had not made the improvements that they have undertaken. The Boskin Commission presumably means that despite these improvements, the BLS is still 6/10th of 1% per year behind reality.

It has to be said that the Boskin Commission did essentially no research of its own, nor could it have been expected to do much research. The report itself contains a couple of Gee-Whiz exercises pointing at cases where the CPI obviously fails to capture quality improvement. But its own numbers are all subjective judgment. There are observers of the process, in and out of BLS, who think that the Boskin Commission estimate is wrong and, in fact, there isn't any remaining failure to account for quality improvement in the CPI. It is easy to see how the Boskin Commission might have misled itself. Imagine you are intelligent people who have to write this report in less than a year and you want to say something about unaccounted-for quality improvement. Which examples will you pick to think about? You will pick out the dramatic cases, and that's what they do and that's what they talk about in the report. They would not claim to have done serious research. In fact, I would guess that at least 85% of all serious research on consumer price measurement in the U.S. today goes on inside the BLS. A statement as important as the one that the Boskin Commission has made and that is fraught with significance for budgetary matters cannot afford to be casual.

24.2 How to Deal with an overstatement of the CPI

There are three alternatives that seem to have arisen as possible next steps. The first alternative is the one that I mentioned earlier. Congress and the President could decree by statute that from now on income tax brackets and Social Security benefits and any other relevant things shall be indexed not by the CPI, but by the CPI minus x%. The statute would have to specify x: it could be 1.1%, as Commission estimates, or it could be 1.0% as a recognition that the second significant digit is hot air, or it could be a much smaller number like say a half of 1%, on the grounds that we don't yet have any verification of this figure, so let's take something small enough that we will be unlikely to regret as new information comes in. The CPI minus x% solution has been advocated by Martin Feldstein, a well-known economist, in a column in the WSJ, and it has been sort of talked about by Senator Roth and Senator

Moynihan who are the leaders of both sides of the Senate Finance Committee. I don't think that either of them has ever said in so many words that they are in favor of adopting the Boskin Commission conclusion straight away.

So far the second proposal for dealing with this has been made by Alan Greenspan, the Chairman of the Federal Reserve, and by Senator Lott of Mississippi, the Senate majority leader. They propose that there be another commission appointed; Senator Lott mentioned four "graybeards" (people with nothing to lose, is what I think he had in mind). This commission would recommend a value of x or perhaps actually determine x. This new commission of experts would presumably look at the rate at which the BLS improves its measurement procedures and look at other research, of which there will be more, now that this issue has come up on center stage. Eventually, this new group will extinguish itself when they can say that BLS has now got the CPI right, and is measuring the true rate of inflation. The third possibility, which is what I would advocate, is to say that the measurement of the inflation rate is an empirical matter; it's not something that Congress or any appointed commission should be guessing about. We should enlarge the budget of BLS and tell them to get on as quickly as they can with improving the way they measure the rate of inflation.

Now, you should keep in mind that an overstatement of the rate of inflation is by definition exactly the same thing as an understatement of the rate of productivity increase. The way you measure productivity in any sector of the economy is to agree on a measure of *real* output, and then divide it by the amount of labor input, or by some measure of aggregate inputs into that sector. Next, how do you get a measure of real output? In almost all cases you start with the one thing that there is a prayer of measuring directly, namely the *value* at current market prices of the output you are trying to measure. And then you deflate it; you divide it by a price index. So if you read that real consumption expenditures in the U.S. increased by 2 1/2% last year, what it means is that nominal dollar consumer spending in the U.S. increased by 6%, say, and the relevant price index (which is not quite the CPI but very close to it) rose by 3 1/2%. Therefore the ratio of nominal consumer spending to the appropriate index went up by 2 1/2%.

If it had turned out instead that nominal consumer spending rose by 6% but the price index had gone up only by 2%, then that's exactly the same thing as saying that real consumer spending went up by 4%. Essentially the same is true of all output measures. The point is that any overstatement of the rate of inflation amounts in practice to an equal corresponding understatement of the rate of productivity increase. Thus, if consumer prices had really been rising more slowly than we thought for the past 25 years, productivity has been rising faster than we knew for 25 years, and probably for 25 years before that as well, since there is absolutely nothing in the Boskin Commission report, and nothing that anybody else knows, to suggest that the overstatement of inflation of the CPI is greater since 1975 than it was earlier.

Now, go back to the proposition that the main reason why inflation may be overstated is that quality improvement is understated.   There is a common belief (and as with many common beliefs, there is very little evidence one way or another) that quality improvement is harder to measure properly in the service sector of the economy than in the goods-producing sector. If you ask why, people give answers like this: the production of services depends so much more on participation of the consumer that it's just intrinsically hard to know where output begins and ends. But it seems to me that if you replaced "audit services" by "automobile" in that sector it will be equally approximately true. In any case, I don't want to argue that question, because deep down I share the common feeling that we may be measuring the real output of the service producing sector of the economy badly and possibly understating quality improvement.

24.3 Measuring Productivity: The Service Industries

I should also say that the financial-services segment of the service sector is often singled out as a case where the measurement of real output and productivity fails, often because it is not even clear how to define the real output of financial services, let alone measure it. Suppose you wanted to know the real output of the life insurance and casualty insurance business or for that matter the real output of a mortgage vendor?   Would we want to say that the real output of the mortgage vendor has gone up if the real value of the mortgage written has gone up? If you write a $10,000 mortgage, are you producing more than a $20,000 mortgage?   Not if we just count the number of pieces of paper. But it is very dangerous just counting the number of pieces of paper, because there isn't anyone in this room who could not multiply the number of pieces of paper he or she produces by a large factor very easily.

So there is an argument that in financial services and in other services, as well -- health care is an obvious and perhaps more important example -- the definition and measurement of real output is particularly uncertain. But this is just another way of saying that the change in price of financial services is very badly measured and perhaps very badly overstated.

I don't really know how to give you a grasp of the magnitude we are talking about, but maybe it will help to mention one simple comparison. I am going to refer to the deflator for personal consumption expenditures in GDP. It is conceptually a bit different from the CPI, though it uses many of the raw data that go into the CPI. If you look at the personal consumption deflator between 1988 and 1996, here are the cumulative price increases for three categories of consumer spending: (i) The prices of durable goods rose by 10% between 1988 and end of 1996, that is by just a hair more than 1% a year. (ii) The prices of nondurable goods rose by 28% during that same 8-year period. (iii) The price index for services rose by 39%. Now, is it true that service prices rose 4 times as fast over that period as durable goods prices, or do the figures overstate the rise in service prices by more than the other categories? I don't know, and nobody knows really, and that's why I think this is worthwhile bringing to your attention. The question is not whether those three numbers that I gave you, 10%, 28%, and 39%, are accurate themselves, but whether the relation between them is accurate. Is the degree of overstatement, understatement or whatever different as between durable goods and nondurable goods and services?

This is especially interesting because of what is sometimes called the computer paradox. Many of the developments discussed at this NYU conference rest on the explosion of information technology in the U.S. What is more, an extraordinarily large share of business purchases of equipment these days is in computer or information technology. I didn't bother to look up the exact figures because the details are not so relevant. But if you just look at all business purchases of machinery, i.e., business fixed investment except for structures, a large fraction has been in hardware related to information technology. I suspect that is *especially* so in the service sector. The service sector of the economy is a much bigger purchaser of computers than its bulk in GDP would suggest. Well then, if there is so much buying of computers, so much installation of information technology, why has there been no visible acceleration of productivity growth in the economy? Where is the productivity increase that all this gee whiz about computers would lead you to expect? In actual fact, the age of information technology in the U.S. and elsewhere coincides with a period of slower productivity growth, not with a period of faster growth.

It is terribly tempting to suggest that this paradox is all due to overstatement of the rate of price increase. I don't know if that is true. I don't have the impression that the service industry sector itself has responded to this situation by offering concrete suggestions for the accurate measurement of real output, productivity and price. If the rest of us have a hard time defining a good measure of the real output of an insurance company, what do insurance companies think about it? I have not heard any useful statements about this from insiders, even in relatively simple cases like retailing and consumer banking. It would be helpful if the industries themselves would think through in a reasonably detached way, what would be a reasonable measure of their real output. It would be especially useful right now, as the Boskin Commission report gets debated, if the people who are most familiar with products and processes, either on their own, or through the instrumentality of collaboration with people in business schools, were to produce some guidelines for measuring real output and prices in their own sectors.

24.4 Other Related Issues

Finally, there is a deeper question lurking behind all this that is not involved in your day-to-day business activities, but is interesting and does concern you in a way. Let me illustrate what I would like to talk about now in the following way. The economist's general definition of the cost of living index, the index that should be used for making adjustments in benefits goes like this: the price index for this year against last year is defined by asking how much money I would need this year in order to achieve the same standard of living that I had last year. If I knew that amount of money, and divided it by the amount of money that I had last year, I would have a ratio of this year's cost of living to last year's. I could just as well do it the other way: I could see how much money it would have taken at last year's prices to achieve the standard of living that I reached this year; then I can divide that into the amount of money that I spent this year, and that ratio would be another index of last year's cost of living relative to this year's. Keep it in mind that the price index is determined by the amount of money you need to achieve the same level of well being as you had last year.

Now suppose between last year and this year the crime rate falls because New York's finest are finer still, or because of some other reason. People feel better off; they feel better off because they are better off living in an atmosphere with a lower crime rate. If we factor that into the standard of living, then that would tend to push the cost of living down; you need less money this year, in a crime-free environment, to achieve the standard of living that you achieved last year in a crime-ridden environment. Should you include that in the cost-of-living index? If you factor that kind of consideration into a price index and use it to index social security benefits, you would be saying that beneficiaries of social security are not entitled to share in the broad gain that everyone else feels. You will be giving them only the benefits that they need to achieve the level of well being that they achieved last year when you could not walk safely in the streets. That seems intuitively wrong. We do not mean that us old folks should not share in the general improvement in living standards that comes from the fall in the crime rate. That does not quite catch what we mean by the cost of living. But exactly the same thing could be said of other "environmental" variables, referring not only to the natural environment or the physical environment, but to the general social behavioral environment as well.

Obviously, you could say the same about air quality as I said about the crime rate. We don't actually mean that the elderly should not share in the sense of well being that comes from having cleaner air. The harder question is: are there improvements in service quality that should be treated like improvements in environmental quality or in the quality of the social environment and, therefore, be indexed away, not included in the measurement of true price index? I think that's quite possibly the case in health care. If there is a general improvement in the standard of health that can be achieved because of the advance of medical knowledge or because of an improvement in hospital organization, would you want to cut social security benefits so that those advantages should not be shared by people who last worked seven or eight years ago and are not now employed? Are there improvements in quality in goods, and, more likely, in services that represent changes in the standard of living that we in the inclusive sense think we should share? What is the meaning of the standard of living that should be fixed for pensioners? The other extreme would be to index social security benefits by wages, so then you would be saying that social security pensioners are entitled to share in the normal increase in productivity that goes on in the economy from year to year and therefore pushes wages up. I don't think anyone would want to go that far.

24.5 Conclusion

The idea that, in the course of debating how to give effect to the Boskin Commission's view of consumer prices, you might also have a debate on the definition of standard of living is a bit fanciful. What is not fanciful, I think, is the contribution that could be made by the industry itself to instructions for measuring real output in the financial services industry, and other related industries. This useful work could be done in collaboration with business schools or other interested research organizations.

Q: One place we might begin is to ask educational institutions how they would respond to your suggestion?

A. Educational institutions could easily take the lead here. My own institution, the Massachusetts Institute of Technology, is right now engaged in what it explicitly calls a reengineering process. It is after all an engineering school. It has not, so far as I know, undertaken this larger job of measuring the real output of the higher education sector. Is it the number of Bachelor's degrees weighted by 1, Master's degrees weighted by 1.7, Ph.D. degrees weighted by 2.5? Are we to suppose that if there is more chemical engineering to be taught that amounts to an increase in the real output of the chemical engineering department? That's a good question. Right now, I guess that the National Income and Product Accounts treat the output of some non-profits the way they treat general government: by measuring input instead of output. That can't be right.

Q: I want to ask you just about the quality improvement correction process. Suppose, for example, I want a car without ABS brakes. But all cars are made with ABS brakes; there is no market for me to buy a car without ABS brakes. Inflation is forced upon me; I have to buy a more expensive car but my utility function is that I don't want one. How would that be included?

A. Inevitably, in making this kind of calculation, we have to take market price as the basic criterion. If the market will accept a car equipped with ABS and pay 4% more for it than a precisely equivalent car without ABS, then we have to count ABS as 4% of real value of the car. There really is no alternative. You are undoubtedly not alone. For instance, I am a very late convert to using a computer even for word-processing. If I could conveniently buy and use a typewriter, I might still be doing it. All we can do on the scale of the national economy is accept market prices where they exist.

Q: Do some environmental variables find their way indirectly into the GDP?

A: I don't think you will ever know if they do so fully, or how much. Take the crime rate example. If I had pursued it all the way through, it has very distant ripples. There will be an effect on business costs, just as with air quality, in the efficiency of the distribution system for example. Furthermore, if the drop in the crime rate had been brought about by an addition to the size of the police force, then the work of those policemen would be included in the GDP. This line of reasoning shows one reason why you might want to allow a drop in the crime rate to reduce social security benefits, on the grounds that part of the benefit appears in lower market prices because of cheaper distribution cost.

Q: Aren't some of those environmental factors merely perceptual?

A: Well, you are getting into issues that verge on the philosophical here. Do you honestly think that the difference between one brand of toothpaste and another is not merely perceptual or that the difference between a new and improved shampoo and the old and unimproved one is not perceptual? From the point of view of the economist, all of consumption is perceptual. If a consumer is willing to pay the price, we have no grounds for second-guessing. If we try to eliminate all of the perceptual elements from the standard of living, we will be left only with very basic needs.

Q: If information technology creates a new product or a new service, a new financial instrument that did not exist last year or a new service that I can access through the internet, how does that get figured into the computation this year?

A: In principle, the way the BLS would like to do it is this. If we think of a wholly new product, something that no one has ever dreamed of before, it is very hard to see what you would do. But if you can imagine that any new product is in some way a substitute, even a partial substitute for an old product, even if the old product is so good a substitute that it's bound to disappear, there will be a period of overlap. You can ask how much more have consumers been willing to pay for the new product than for the old product. If the answer is 20% more, then the new product is worth 20% more than the old one. A problem is created here in practice, because it takes some time before a real new product actually gets into the CPI at all. The horrible example that everyone cites is that the cellular telephone is still not priced by the Bureau of Labor Statistics. If you ask the BLS how come, they would say of course, if you will increase our budget, we will get around to such things more quickly. By the way, that's what should happen, because a higher budget for BLS would be a drop in the bucket The Boskin Commission did not pay much attention to consumer services. In some consumer services, there are complaints that quality has deteriorated over the years. I am thinking of the amount of time you spend in line buying, or checking in at an airport, or any of the things that people complain about now. People complaining are not quite the same thing as measuring. It is possible, however, that adequate attention to the cases of quality deterioration in services as felt by the consumer would certainly reduce the Boskin Commission estimate of overstatement, though surely not to zero.

One of the things that need to be done is to look carefully at the consumer service sector. If I thought that human contact with a teller were an important part of the retail banking experience, then the ATM would involve a certain quality deterioration in the service that I am receiving. Actually, that's not the case, I am just as happy with the ATM as passing the time of day with the teller. This is an example of how difficult it might be to refine the price index and why I think it's a very bad idea to rush to judgment on this range of issues.

Editor's Note: *This chapter is based on a keynote address delivered by Robert M. Solow at Leonard N. Stern School of Business, New York University in 1997, during the first conference on "Creating Value in Financial Services."*